Praise for Candice Millard's

RIVER OF THE GODS

"Millard's research and very readable storytelling are admirable.... Ultimately, the identity of the person who first discovered the source of the White Nile may be a trivial matter. Millard conscientiously investigates the issue, of course, but *River of the Gods* is compelling because she does justice to the psyches and behavior of Burton and Speke—keenly flawed but enthralling, sometimes marvelous people."

—*The Wall Street Journal*

"Millard recounts all of these travails with a fluid grace that wears its learning lightly."   —*The Washington Post*

"When it comes to narrative nonfiction, [Millard's] the best... I love her books. She has this way of finding a really fresh way of telling an old story."

—Erik Larson, *New York Times* bestselling author of
The Splendid and the Vile

"Millard exhibits admirable skill in crafting narratives of uncommon drama and detail.... A first-rate tale of nineteenth-century exploration that rivals the best of the polar exploits."

—Air Mail

"Millard is an outstanding narrative historian, with the gift of breathing new life into long-forgotten stories, but what she does best is communicate to the reader the horrid details of suffering."
—Bookreporter

"Millard's lushly detailed adventure story keeps a steady eye on the racial power dynamics involved in this imperialist endeavor and brilliantly illuminates the characters of Burton, Speke, and Bombay. Readers will be riveted."
—*Publishers Weekly* (starred review)

"It's been nearly six years since popular Millard published *Hero of the Empire*, and eager fans and armchair travelers will gladly sign up for this enthralling and heartbreaking adventure."
—*Library Journal* (starred review)

"Bestselling author Millard, a former writer and editor for *National Geographic*, offers a tense, vibrant history of several dramatic expeditions across East Africa that finally resulted in a successful discovery.... An engrossing, sharply drawn adventure tale."
—*Kirkus Reviews* (starred review)

Candice Millard

RIVER OF THE GODS

Candice Millard is the author of the *New York Times* bestsellers *The River of Doubt*, *Destiny of the Republic*, and *Hero of the Empire*. She lives in Kansas City, with her husband and three children.

candicemillard.com

Also by Candice Millard

Hero of the Empire
Destiny of the Republic
The River of Doubt

RIVER OF THE GODS

River
of the
Gods

---◆---

GENIUS, COURAGE, AND BETRAYAL
IN THE SEARCH
FOR THE SOURCE OF THE NILE

---◆---

Candice Millard

ANCHOR BOOKS
A DIVISION OF PENGUIN RANDOM HOUSE LLC
NEW YORK

The Library of Congress has cataloged the Doubleday edition as follows:
Names: Millard, Candice, author.
Title: River of the gods : Genius, courage, and betrayal in the search
for the source of the Nile / Candice Millard.
Description: First edition. | New York : Doubleday, 2022. |
Includes bibliographical references and index.
Identifiers: LCCN 2021044497
Subjects: LCSH: Burton, Richard Francis, Sir, 1821–1890—Travel—Nile
River. | Speke, John Hanning, 1827–1864—Travel—Nile River. |
Bombay, Sidi Mubarak—Travel—Nile River. | Explorers—Nile River—
History—19th century. | Nile River—Discovery and exploration. |
Nile River Valley—Discovery and exploration.
Classification: LCC DT117 .M55 2022 | DDC 916.2043—dc23
LC record available at https://lccn.loc.gov/2021044497

Anchor Books Trade Paperback ISBN: 978-0-525-43564-8
eBook ISBN: 978-0-385-54311-8

Map designed by Jeffrey L. Ward
Author photograph © Laura Fitzgibbons
Book design by Maria Carella

anchorbooks.com

Printed in the United States of America
10 9 8 7 6 5 4 3 2 1

FOR MY CHILDREN

The lake rippled from one end of the world to the other.
Wide as a sea cradled in a giant's palm.

—"Sidi Mubarak Bombay" by Ranjit Hoskote

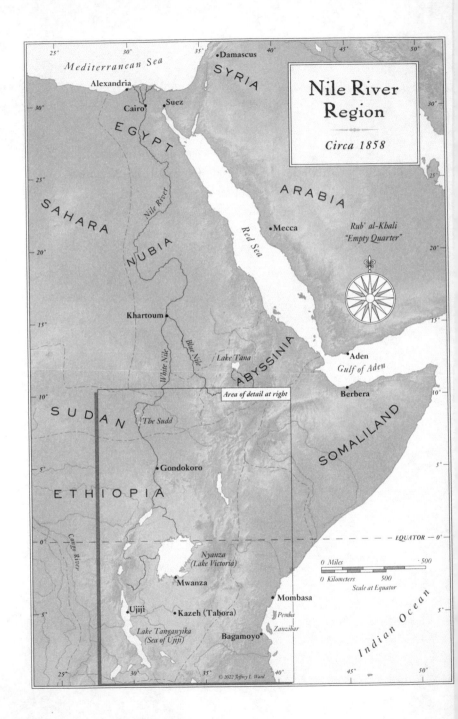

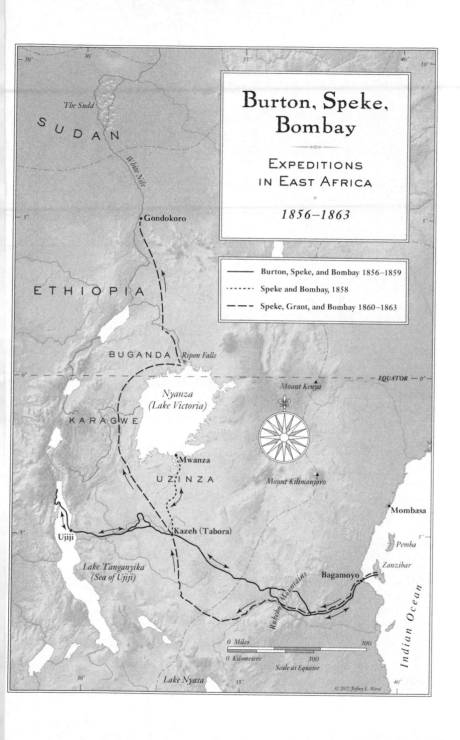

CONTENTS

Prologue: Obsession   I

Part One
Some Gallant Heart

CHAPTER ONE: A Blaze of Light   II
CHAPTER TWO: Shadows   27
CHAPTER THREE: Bond for Our Blood   36
CHAPTER FOUR: The Abban   48
CHAPTER FIVE: The Enemy Is Upon Us   57

Part Two
What Might Have Been, What Would Have Been

CHAPTER SIX: Into the Mouth of Hell   73
CHAPTER SEVEN: What a Curse Is a Heart   85
CHAPTER EIGHT: *Horror Vacui*   98
CHAPTER NINE: Bombay   115
CHAPTER TEN: Death Was Written   126
CHAPTER ELEVEN: An Old Enemy   139
CHAPTER TWELVE: Tanganyika   162
CHAPTER THIRTEEN: To the End of the World   182

Part Three
Fury

CHAPTER FOURTEEN: The Knives Are Sheathed   197
CHAPTER FIFTEEN: 'Twas Me He Shot   210
CHAPTER SIXTEEN: An Exile's Dream   228
CHAPTER SEVENTEEN: Hard as Bricks   237

Part Four
The Malignant Tongues of Friends

CHAPTER EIGHTEEN: The Prince   249
CHAPTER NINETEEN: Damn Their Souls   268
CHAPTER TWENTY: Neston Park   281
CHAPTER TWENTY-ONE: The Weary Heart Grows Cold 298
Epilogue: Ashes   315

Acknowledgments   329
Notes   337
Select Bibliography   381
Index   389

RIVER OF THE GODS

Prologue

OBSESSION

As he walked through the storied gates of Alexandria in the fall of 1801, a young British officer named William Richard Hamilton found himself in the middle of a stunning tableau—abject misery set against the lost grandeur of the Pharaohs. Once the ancient world's greatest center of learning, the city of Alexandria was now a burning ruin, caught in the grip of a European war played out on African land. In the wake of Britain's crushing victory over Napoleonic France, injured soldiers lay dying in the scorching sun; prisoners freed from dungeons dragged their battered bodies through the streets; starving families fought over the last of the armies' dead horses. To Hamilton, however, the moment was the opportunity of a lifetime. On his own, the twenty-four-year-old Cambridge-educated classicist had been sent to Egypt with a single mission: to find the Rosetta Stone.

Largely ignored for centuries by European elites schooled in the glory and languages of Greece and Rome, Egyptian culture had only recently begun to receive recognition for its astonishing achievements and even greater antiquity, making it a new and especially coveted prize for European powers obsessed by military and cultural supremacy. Three years earlier, in the summer of 1798, Napoleon Bonaparte had landed on the Egyptian coast, hoping to weaken Britain by blocking its land route to India. That conventional military objective, however, also forced open the door for a far more audacious scientific and cultural conquest. Behind his invading troops, Napoleon brought another, highly trained army—of scholars. These ambitious men from France, known as "savants," were charged with appropriating everything they could unearth from the tombs or pry from the ground, attempting to assert French sovereignty over Egypt's ancient culture. They measured the head of the Great Sphinx, mapped Cairo, surveyed towns, and painted everything that could not be rolled up and carried away. These men, botanists and engineers, artists and geologists, were living, as one of them excitedly wrote home, "at the center of a flaming core of reason," and they believed that there was no greater symbol of their military and intellectual power than their seizing of the Rosetta Stone.

Although its neatly carved hieroglyphs were as yet undeciphered, the stone offered access to the spectacular mysteries that European scholars now realized were waiting for them along Egypt's Nile River—mysteries that predated anything they understood, and that promised to rewrite everything they knew about history. The French had unearthed the forty-five-inch-tall stone two years earlier, in the summer of 1799, when Napoleon's soldiers were trying to reinforce a crumbling, ancient fort on the west bank of the Nile, in the port of Rosetta. His officers immediately recognized that the dark gray slab was an object of extraordinary value, what scholars spent lifetimes hoping to find. On its face was etched a two-thousand-year-old decree written in three different languages: two unknown—Demotic, once the everyday language of the Egyptian people, and hieroglyphs, the tantalizingly mysterious language of its priests—and one known: ancient Greek, which had the power to unlock the other two. News of the find had spread quickly, and scholars and scientists throughout Europe began speaking in hushed tones of the Rosetta Stone.

That Napoleon should possess such a treasure map to ancient wisdom was intolerable to France's imperial rival, Britain. Emerging victorious from the bloody siege of Alexandria, the British now demanded their rights as conquerors: every sarcophagus, every sculpture, every gleaming golden scarab, and, most of all, the Rosetta Stone. In defeat, hiding the stone had been France's only remaining option, so despite its massive size—estimated at some three quarters of a ton—Napoleon's soldiers had already moved it several times, from the fort where it was found, then to Cairo, and, finally, to Alexandria. Now it was in a warehouse, concealed in a pile of ordinary baggage and covered with mats. For the benefit of the British, the French let a rumor circulate that the stone was already gone, slipped aboard a ship leaving for Europe in the middle of the night, just as Bonaparte himself had done as soon as defeat had appeared imminent.

William Richard Hamilton, however, refused to accept such evasions. Working his way through the rubble of Alexandria, he would not believe that the Rosetta Stone had left Egypt and demanded to know where it was hidden. The commanding French general, who had personally supervised much of the cultural plunder, raged at the irritatingly determined young man, accusing the British of extorting him with "a cannon in each of my ears, and another in my mouth" and uttering a phrase that would live on as a timeless caricature of imperial double standards. *"Jamais on n'a pillé le monde!"* he railed scornfully—"the world had never been so pillaged!" As he knew he would, Hamilton eventually discovered the stone's hiding place, and five months later, carried aboard the captured French frigate HMS *Égyptienne,* it finally reached London, where it immediately became the greatest treasure in the British Museum.

Far from quenching Europe's interest in the mysteries of the Nile, the arrival of the Rosetta Stone fueled a decades-long obsession with Egypt, Middle Eastern cultures, and "orientalism." By the time the stone's hieroglyphs were finally deciphered twenty-three years later by a French scholar named Jean-François Champollion, Europe's fascination with Egyptian history and the Nile Valley had grown into a full-scale frenzy. Once the cryptic secrets of the Pharaohs' forgotten language were unlocked, they opened a floodgate of interest and scholarship, which in turn cascaded through popular culture. From archaeology to art, poetry to fashion, the allure of a vast, gleaming civilization lost in time proved irresistible to the public. Generations of aristocrats would devote their money and time competing to unearth new dimensions of this ancient world, and to reconcile it with the classical Greek and Roman texts and history they had been steeped in from their first days in school. Among the most beguiling of the stories they had read were the wide-ranging theories about the source of the Nile, from speculations by the Greek historian Herodotus to the failed expeditions of Roman emperor Nero's elite Praetorian Guard.

Having vaulted his country to the forefront of this new trend, Hamilton, like the rest of the world, only grew more captivated by the secrets of the Nile. As his youthful features became creased with lines and his patrician chin softened with age, he intensified his study, publishing his own translation of the Greek portion of the Rosetta Stone. Adding yet another controversial cultural icon to his record, he helped retrieve the Parthenon Sculptures after one of the ships carrying them sank to the bottom of the sea. In 1830, he then helped enshrine Britain's national preoccupation in institutional form by becoming an original member and later president of the Royal Geographical Society, even giving it its Latin motto: *Ob terras reclusas*—"For the discovery of lands."

Putting its greatest minds and vast imperial fortunes behind the task of exploring humanity's ancient roots, Britain rapidly took a leading role in the new fields that were opened up by that quest, with the Royal Geographical Society as its principal organizer and advocate. Even as it filled the British Museum with artifacts appropriated by imperial force, however, the Society's ambitions in pursuing ancient Egypt to the headwaters of the Nile were frustrated by the sheer scale of the majestic river, the longest in the world, which defeated countless attempts to reach its origins. Standing in the way of any attempted exploration were vast uncharted territories, defended by local peoples and countless physical hardships, that were presumed to conceal the secret heritage of the entire modern world.

Rather than fighting their way upriver, which would also entail discerning which of the bewildering number of tributaries would qualify as the principal source of the Nile, explorers shifted their attention to a bold alternative plan: landing on the eastern coast of Africa, well below the equator, and proceeding inland in hopes of finding the watershed where a stream began to course northward on the four-thousand-mile journey to Egypt. This epic end-around tactic was supported by rumors of a giant lake region that was said to exist in the central part of the continent. This strategy also took advantage of Britain's burgeoning military and naval strength, allowing the explorers to transport their supplies and equipment by sea to key ports and staging areas such as Aden and the island of Zanzibar, which lay protected by twenty miles of sea just off the coast where an expedition would need to land and start its journey inland.

By bringing British explorers into direct contact with the interior of Africa this undertaking would effectively reconnect, as DNA analysis would later prove, a culture from a more recent site of development to some of the most ancient lands where human migration first began. It thus set the stage for the "discovery" of regions that had in fact been occupied continuously by human beings for hundreds of thousands of years longer than London or Paris. As similar encounters from Hispaniola to Peru had amply proved, however, the disparity of power and resources between the two sides in such meetings was fraught with the potential for tragedy and exploitation. The consequences of that dangerous asymmetry had been demonstrated in Africa over the preceding centuries, as European, North American, and Arab traders who moved between two worlds capitalized on their power by enslaving African peoples and selling them for profit. For explorers, that wrenching injustice was as much a reality of the region as geography or climate, shaping everything from the location of ports and availability of food to the paths they would follow. In fact, their own efforts would doubtless lead to the plunder of the very land they wished to explore. As the British writer Samuel Johnson had written less than a century earlier, after the Arctic expedition of Captain Constantine Phipps, "I do not wish well to discoveries for I am always afraid they will end in conquest and robbery."

Still, with all of Britain's growing knowledge and imperial might, the task of searching such an unfamiliar region for the source of a faraway river was so difficult and forbidding that it remained all but impossible. By the 1850s, with Britain's national pride engaged and the prestige of transformative scientific discovery and the plans for imperial expansion at stake, the Royal Geographical Society resolved to mount one of the most complex and demanding expeditions ever attempted. Although among its members were scientific luminaries that ranged from Charles Darwin to David Livingstone, the Society knew that this undertaking would require experience and insight that were beyond the reach of anything it had accomplished in the past. It would need the help of skilled African guides and porters, a heavy debt that was rarely acknowledged, but it would also need more than just an explorer. It would need a scientist and scholar, an artist and linguist, an extraordinarily skilled writer and an ambitious, obsessive researcher—an army of savants in a single man.

Part One

———◆◆◆———

Some
Gallant Heart

CHAPTER ONE

A Blaze of Light

Sitting on a thin carpet in his tiny, rented room in Suez, Egypt, in 1854, Richard Francis Burton calmly watched as five men cast critical eyes over his meager belongings. The men, whom he had just met on the Hajj, the annual Islamic pilgrimage to Mecca, "looked at my clothes, overhauled my medicine chest, and criticised my pistols," Burton wrote. "They sneered at my copper-cased watch." He knew that if they discovered the truth, that he was not Shaykh Abdullah, an Afghan-born Indian doctor and devout, lifelong Muslim but a thirty-two-year-old lieutenant in the army of the British East India Company, not only would his elaborately planned expedition be in grave danger, but so would his life. Burton, however, was not worried. Even when his new friends found his sextant, the most indispensable, and obviously Western, scientific instrument in his possession, he did not think that he had anything to fear. "This," he later wrote, "was a mistake."

Burton's goal was to do something that no other Englishman had ever done, and that few had either the ability or audacity to do: enter Mecca disguised as a Muslim. It was an undertaking that simultaneously acknowledged what was most sacred to the Muslim faith and dismissed the right to protect it, making it irresistible to Burton, who studied every religion and respected none. The birthplace of the prophet Muhammad, Mecca is the holiest site in Islam and, as such, forbidden to non-Muslims. Burton knew that "to pass through the Moslem's Holy Land, you must either be a born believer, or have become one," but he had never even considered performing the Hajj as a convert. "Men do not willingly give information to a 'new Moslem,' especially a Frank [European]: they suspect his conversion to be feigned or forced, look upon him as a spy, and let him see as little of life as possible," he wrote. "I would have given up the dear project rather than purchase a doubtful and partial success at such a price." An Oxford dropout, self-taught scholar, compulsive explorer, and extraordinarily skilled polyglot, Burton wanted unfettered access to every holy site he reached, the trust of every man he met, and the answer to every ancient mystery he encountered—nothing less, he wrote, than to see and understand "Moslem inner life." He also wanted to return to England alive.

By disguising himself as a Muslim, Burton was risking the righteous wrath of those for whom the Hajj was the most sacred of religious rites. Although "neither the Koran nor the Sultan enjoins the killing of Hebrew or Christian intruders," he knew, "in the event of a pilgrim declaring himself to be an infidel, the authorities would be powerless to protect him." A single error could cost him his life. "A blunder, a hasty action, a misjudged word, a prayer or bow, not strictly the right shibboleth," he wrote, "and my bones would have whitened the desert sand."

Burton's plan, moreover, required crossing the Rub' al-Khali—"Empty Quarter"—the world's largest continuous desert and, in his words, a "huge white blot" on nineteenth-century maps. So ambitious was the expedition that it had captured the attention of the president of the Royal Geographical Society, Sir Roderick Impey Murchison. For Murchison, who had helped to found the Society nearly a quarter of a century earlier, this was exactly the kind of exploration that the Society had been created to encourage. He "honored me," Burton wrote, "by warmly supporting . . . my application for three years' leave of absence on special duty." The East India Company, a 250-year-old private corporation with armies of its own, had argued that the journey was too dangerous and that Burton, who had made more enemies than friends during his years in the military, should be given no more than a one-year furlough. The Royal Geographical Society stood by its promise to help finance the expedition. For a challenge of this magnitude, Murchison believed, Burton was "singularly well-qualified."

·

Although the members of the Royal Geographical Society were impressed by Burton's achievements, most had reservations about this unusual young man who seemed to be British in name only. Burton had been born in Devon, on the English Channel, but he had spent far less time in his homeland than he had roaming the rest of the world. It was a pattern that had begun early in life, when his father, Joseph Netterville Burton, a retired lieutenant colonel in the British Army, moved his family to France before Richard's first birthday. Over the next eighteen years, he moved thirteen more times, briefly settling in towns from Blois to Lyons, Marseilles to Pau, Pisa to Siena, Florence, Rome, and Naples. By the time he was an adult, Burton, along with his younger siblings, Maria and Edward, felt less like a citizen of the world than a man without a country. "In consequence of being brought up abroad, we never thoroughly understood English society," he wrote, "nor did society understand us."

Not only did Burton not feel British, he had often been told, and never in an admiring way, that neither did he look particularly British. No one who met him ever forgot his face. Bram Stoker, who would go on to write *Dracula*, was shaken by his first encounter with Burton. "The man riveted my attention," Stoker later wrote. "He was dark, and forceful, and masterful, and ruthless.... I never saw anyone like him. He is steel! He would go through you like a sword!" Burton's friend, the poet Algernon Charles Swinburne, wrote that he had "the jaw of a devil and the brow of a god," and described his eyes as having "a look of unspeakable horror." Burton's black eyes, which he had inherited from his English-Irish father, seemed to mesmerize everyone he met. Friends, enemies, and acquaintances described them variously as magnetic, imperious, aggressive, burning, even terrible, and compared them to every dangerous wild animal they could think of, from a panther to a "stinging serpent." Equally striking were his thick, black hair, his deep, resonant voice, and even his teeth, which may have inspired literature's most iconic vampire. Stoker would never forget watching, enthralled, as Burton spoke, his upper lip rising menacingly. "His canine tooth showed its full length," he wrote, "like the gleam of a dagger."

Burton had grown up fighting, from street brawls to school skirmishes to violent encounters with enraged tutors. Although his father had dragged his children from one European town to another, he wanted for them a British education, which began at a grim boarding school in Richmond. All that Burton remembered learning at the school, which he described as "the 'Blacking-shop' of Charles Dickens," was "a certain facility in using our fists, and a general development of ruffianism. I was in one perpetual scene of fights; at one time I had thirty-two affairs of honor to settle." When he and Edward were finally sent back to Boulogne, after an attack of measles killed several boys and shut down the school, they scandalized everyone on their ship by joyously celebrating the fact that they were leaving England at last. "We shrieked, we whooped, we danced for joy. We shook our fists at the white cliffs, and loudly hoped we should never see them again," he wrote. "We hurrah'd for France, and hooted for England; 'The Land on which the Sun ne'er sets—nor rises.'"

Burton's father taught him chess, but most of what he learned came from a succession of alternately terrifying and terrified tutors. No matter the subject, the tutors were given permission to beat their pupils, until the pupils were old enough to beat them back. In later years, Burton would express his sorrow for the incalculable harm done by "that unwise saying of the wise man, 'Spare the rod and spoil the child.'" As a teenager, he fought back. The poor, nervous musician Burton's parents hired to teach him violin—"nerves without flesh, hung on wires," as Burton would later contemptuously describe him, "all hair and no brain"—finally quit after his student broke a violin over his head.

The only childhood teacher Burton respected was his fencing master, a former soldier who had only one thumb, having lost the other in battle. Richard and his brother threw themselves into fencing with such wild enthusiasm that their studies nearly ended in tragedy. "We soon learned not to neglect the mask," Richard wrote. "I passed my foil down Edward's throat, and nearly destroyed his uvula, which caused me a good deal of sorrow." The lessons, however, not only paid off but eventually produced one of the most skilled swordsmen in Europe. Burton earned the coveted French title *Maître d'Armes;* perfected two sword strokes, the *une-deux* and the *manchette*—an upward slashing movement that disabled an opponent, often sparing his life; and wrote both *The Book of the Sword* and *A Complete System of Bayonet Exercise,* which the British Army published the same year he left for Mecca. Fencing, he would later say, "was the great solace of my life."

As Burton grew into a young man, he also developed another all-consuming, lifelong interest, one that would make him even less welcome in polite society: sex. What began as love affairs with beautiful women from Italy to India quickly transformed into something more enquiring and erotic, and far less acceptable in Victorian England. As a young officer in Sindh, now a province in southeastern Pakistan, he famously investigated the homosexual brothels, writing a report for his commander that he claimed later hindered his career. His ethnological writings, which in the end would range from Asia to Africa to North America, focused not only on the dress, religion, and familial structures of his subjects, but on their sexual practices. His readers would be shocked by open and detailed discussions of polygamy and polyandry, pederasty and prostitution. Burton, however, had little time for British priggishness and no interest in what he referred to as "innocence of the word not of the thought; morality of the tongue and not of the heart."

•

Although Burton's nomadic childhood and scandalous interests left him feeling cut off from his country and distrusted by his countrymen, he did learn one striking thing about himself along the way: He was, in the words of one of his flabbergasted tutors, "a man who could learn a language running." In the end, he would speak more than twenty-five different languages, along with at least another dozen dialects. To some extent, his gift for languages was a product of natural ability and early training. "I was intended for that wretched being, the infant phenomenon," he explained, "and so began Latin at three and Greek at four." It was his fascination with other cultures, however, and his methodical mind that made him one of the world's most gifted linguists. He had worked out a system early on that allowed him to learn most languages in two months, and he never seemed to understand why others found it so hard. "I never worked more than a quarter of an hour at a time, for after that the brain lost its freshness," he wrote. "After learning some three hundred words, easily done in a week, I stumbled through some easy book-work (one of the Gospels is the most come-atable), and underlined every word that I wished to recollect, in order to read over my pencillings at least once a day.... The neck of the language was now broken and progress was rapid."

After engineering his own expulsion from Oxford, where he had been ridiculed, ignored, and bored, Burton had joined the 18th Regiment of Bombay Native Infantry, a regiment within the East India Company. Realizing that one of the fastest ways to rise through the ranks was to become an interpreter, he learned twelve languages in seven years. He had begun studying Hindustani immediately upon arriving in India and six months later easily passed first among the many gifted linguists taking the exam. Over the following years, one after another, he steadily added languages to his long list: Gujarati, Marathi, Armenian, Persian, Sindhi, Punjabi, Pashto, Sanskrit, Arabic, Telugu, and Turkish, rarely placing second to even his most talented rivals.

So caught up did Burton become in his passion for languages, that he often forgot that not everyone shared his outsized enthusiasm. In his book *Falconry in the Valley of the Indus*—one of five books he wrote between 1851 and 1853—he used so many different Indian dialects that he was openly mocked in a British review. "Were it not that the author is so proud of his knowledge of oriental tongues that he thinks it desirable to display the said knowledge by a constant admixture of *Indianee* words with his narrative, this would be a most agreeable addition both to the Zoology and Falconry of the East," the reviewer admonished him. "We find his affectation all but insufferable, and devoutly wish that he were confined to the use of plain English for the remaining term of his natural life." Burton, however, was not to be shamed or dissuaded from his obsession. "For many years I have been employed in studying the Scindian literature and language," he wrote in reply. "You will...find it is the language of a country as large as England." He even wrote a letter to *The Bombay Times* openly criticizing the language examination process within the East India Company and claiming that, for a serious student, it was not particularly challenging. "The task may appear a formidable one: we can assure him that the appearance is much more tremendous than the reality," he wrote. "Any man of moderate abilities can, with careful, though not hard, study, qualify himself to pass the examination we have described in one year."

Such shrugging dismissal of the notoriously difficult and competitive exams was maddening for Burton's fellow officers, who struggled for years to learn the languages. One man in particular bristled at such casual arrogance, and would come to justify Burton's assertion that "linguists are a dangerous race." Christopher Palmer Rigby was considered one of the most distinguished linguists in the East India Company. At twenty years of age he had passed the language exams for both Hindustani and Marathi, adding Canarese, Persian, and Arabic before his thirtieth birthday. In 1840, while in Aden, he not only learned Somali but wrote *An Outline of the Somali Language and Vocabulary*, which Burton admired and used extensively when studying the language himself. When Rigby sat for his examination in Gujarati, he had been widely expected to receive the highest score. To everyone's shock, however, not least of all Rigby's, he had lost that honor to Richard Burton.

Many years later, Rigby would find himself in a position to prove to Burton that linguists were not only dangerous, they had long memories. Burton would not sit for the exam in Arabic, a language that he knew so well he referred to it as "my native tongue," until 1855. Soon after taking the test, he would leave the country, assuming that he had easily passed. "It may be said without immodesty," he wrote, "that I have forgotten as much as many Arabists have learned." As he would find out much later, however, he had in fact failed the exam, the Bombay Examination Committee refusing to pass him because, it argued, his examination had been informal. Seventeen years after Burton had taken the test, the Arabic scholar George Percy Badger would write to him explaining that he had remarked "upon the absurdity of the Bombay Committee being made the judge of your proficiency inasmuch as I did not believe that any of them possessed a tithe of the knowledge of Arabic which you did." The president of the committee at the time of the decision was Christopher Palmer Rigby.

•

Burton knew that even if he spoke Arabic like a local it would not be enough to preserve his disguise in Mecca, so he had spent months meticulously planning his journey. While still in England, he had quietly assumed the character of Shaykh Abdullah, shaving his head, growing a beard, donning loose robes, and using walnut juice to deepen the color of his skin. He had even undergone circumcision, ensuring that it was done according to the Arabic rite rather than the Jewish. Once in Cairo, despite already speaking Persian, Hindustani, and Arabic—the three languages he thought he needed to know in order to "pass muster"—and having such a detailed knowledge of Islam that he was able to recite a quarter of the Koran by heart, he had hired a former *khatib*, or Islamic preacher, to sharpen his grammar and expand his theology. Finally, like any pilgrim, he had carefully divided his money, sewing part of it into a leather belt and packing the rest in boxes, in expectation of being robbed by the men who haunted the Hajj's most heavily trafficked routes. "If they find a certain amount of ready money in his baggage, they do not search his person," Burton advised his readers. "If they find nothing they proceed to a bodily inspection, and if his waist-belt be empty they are rather disposed to rip open his stomach, in the belief that he must have some peculiarly ingenious way of secreting valuables."

Even the most serious study and painstaking planning, however, can be undone by a single mistake. In the weeks since Burton had first met the men who now sat in his room, examining his bags, he had carefully cultivated their friendship, offering them loans for their pilgrimages, engaging them in long, rambling conversations, and impressing them with his vast knowledge of Islamic theology and literature. By the time they were warily eyeing his sextant, they had not only willingly but eagerly embraced him as a fellow pilgrim.

There had been nothing else among Burton's belongings that had given these men a moment's pause. He didn't have much beyond a few items of clothing, a pistol and dagger, his Koran, three water skins, a seemingly indestructible pea-green medicine chest covered in red and yellow flowers, and a "housewife," a gift from his cousin, which consisted of "a roll of canvas, carefully soiled, and garnished with needles and thread, cobblers' wax, buttons." Anything that might have raised suspicion, and which he could possibly do without, he had left behind. He had sorely needed the sextant to measure distances when he reached Mecca, so he had done his best to disguise it by replacing its gold case with a facing that he had stained and covered in Arabic numerals. The moment the men laid eyes on it, however, Burton saw the look on their faces suddenly change, the easy camaraderie turn to simmering suspicion.

Nothing was said until he left the room, but as soon as Burton disappeared from view, his only servant, a short, stout, beardless Egyptian teenager named Mohammed al-Basyúni, turned on him with a vengeance. Although he was no more than eighteen years old, Mohammed was exceedingly clever—well traveled, a skilled bargainer, and able to adapt quickly to any circumstance. "Eloquent in abuse," Burton wrote of him, and "profound at Prayer." All Burton had wanted in a servant was "good health and a readiness to travel anywhere, a little skill in cooking, sewing and washing, willingness to fight, and a habit of regular prayers." What he had gotten was a quick-witted young man who kept a wary eye on him at all times. There had, moreover, been a thousand opportunities for Mohammed to catch him in a misstep. The way he held his prayer beads, sat in a chair, even lifted his glass to take a drink of water, all were riddled with complications and potential pitfalls. To be able to do what he had come to do—not just to see Mecca but to study, measure, sketch, and describe it in minute detail—Burton had been forced to resort to any subterfuge he could think of, even connecting a guide wire to his pen at night so that he could take notes in the dark, after Mohammed had fallen asleep.

Mohammed, Burton would later admit, had "suspected me from the first." Now, seeing his opportunity to finally expose the apparently pious Shaykh Abdullah, Mohammed seized it. Turning to the men staring at the sextant, he did not hesitate to express his most damning suspicion. "The would-be Haji," he declared, is "one of the Infidels." To Mohammed's surprise, instead of agreeing with him, the men leapt to their friend's defense. One swore that the "light of Al-Islam was upon my countenance," Burton later learned. Another, who just that morning had seen a letter Burton had written to a Muslim friend concerning matters of high theology, "felt himself justified in declaring, *ex cathedra,* the boy Mohammed's position perfectly untenable." After that, the verbal blows rained down on the stunned young man. He was called "a pauper, a 'fakir,' an owl, a cut-off one, a stranger . . . for daring to impugn the faith of a brother believer."

Burton had been saved. The knowledge he had spent years acquiring had made it impossible for his friends to believe that he was anything other than what he professed to be—a devout Indian Muslim. He knew, however, that his reprieve would not be complete without sacrifice. He would not be able to keep his sextant, the one tool that would have been most useful to him in the days to come. "Determining with a sigh to leave it behind," he wrote, "I prayed five times a day for nearly a week."

•

Mohammed must have continued to suspect the truth about Burton, but he did not abandon him on the Hajj. Instead, he led him not just to Mecca but to the heart of Islam: the Kaaba, a shrine at the center of the al-Masjid al-Haram, the world's most visited mosque. Although throughout his life Burton would be accused of blasphemy by outraged, puritanical Britons, he had always been fascinated by religion as a subject of study. He applied the same deep curiosity and steady, systematic approach to understanding the world's religions that he did to languages and cultures, and he contemptuously dismissed the Western idea that Christianity was the only religion to be taken seriously. "What nation, either in the West or in the East, has been able to cast out from its ceremonies every suspicion of its old idolatry? What are the mistletoe, the Irish wake, the Pardon of Brittany, the Carnival?" he asked. "Better far to consider the Meccan pilgrimage rites in the light of Evil-worship turned into lessons of Good than to philosophize about their strangeness, and to blunder in asserting them to be insignificant." Although he had devoted most of his study to Islam, Burton was fascinated by it all, from Catholicism to Judaism, Hinduism, Sufism, Sikhism, Spiritualism, even Satanism. In fact, he briefly considered writing a biography of Satan, who, to his mind, was "the true hero of Paradise Lost and by his side God and man are very ordinary." Nothing for Burton was out of bounds or impure, and he never feared heavenly and certainly not earthly condemnation. The only aspect of religion that he scorned was the idea that there existed any true believers. "The more I study religion," he wrote, "the more I am convinced that man never worshiped anyone but himself."

Although a spy and an infidel and an agnostic, Burton could not resist the power of this, one of the world's most profound religious experiences. Joining the thousands of men who filled the mosque's courtyard, he circled the Kaaba seven times counterclockwise, touching the Kiswah, an enormous black silk cloth draped over the top of the shrine. After years of study, he knew exactly what to say and do now that he was in the presence of the Kaaba, but the overwhelming emotions he felt swelling his heart were born not of religious zeal but personal triumph. "I may truly say that, of all the worshippers who clung weeping to the curtain, or who pressed their beating hearts to the stone, none felt for the moment a deeper emotion than did the Haji from the far-north," he wrote. "But, to confess humbling truth, theirs was the high feeling of religious enthusiasm, mine was the ecstasy of gratified pride."

Even while he let himself be swept up in the fervor surrounding him, Burton never for a moment forgot why he was there. He took in his surroundings with a searching eye, desperately trying to remember every detail so he could write them down as soon as he was alone. His powers of concentration, however, were put to the test as he stood in the courtyard, the September sun beating down on his bare head and arms, and was suddenly told that he had been sent for. "I thought, 'Now something is going to happen to me,' he later wrote, 'now I am suspected.'" Then, hearing men shouting, "Open a path for the Haji who would enter the House," he felt himself being lifted to the entrance of the Kaaba by three men, four arms pushing him from below and two pulling him from above, up the Kaaba's eastern wall. Although this privilege had been engineered by Mohammed and was the culmination of all of Burton's study and subterfuge, he knew that "nothing could preserve him from the ready knives of enraged fanatics if detected in the House."

Once inside the Kaaba, the cold fear that Burton had successfully staved off until that moment finally set in. "I will not deny that, looking at the windowless walls, the officials at the door," he wrote, "my feelings were of the trapped-rat description." After being interviewed by a guard, successfully answering his questions in Arabic, he focused his thoughts, studying the heavy pillars, the marble floor, the walls engraved with inscriptions, and the ceiling covered in a red damask, "flowered over with gold." Finally, as he pretended to pray, he reached down, slowly pulled out a pencil, and on the white sheeting of his ihram sketched a rough plan of the inside of Islam's holiest shrine.

•

Soon after he was lowered from the Kaaba, relieved to have left with his disguise and his life intact, Burton "began to long to leave Mecca." He was, he wrote, "worn out with fatigue, and the fatal fiery heat," and he felt that it was time to begin his long journey back. While the men he had traveled with believed themselves to be free from the sins they had carried to Mecca, Burton felt his burdens not lightened but multiplied. Although proud that he had joined the Hajj, he was skeptical of religious rebirths, believing that they rarely lasted long. It was true not just of Muslims but of the followers of any religion, he argued, "equally observed in the Calvinist, after a Sunday of prayer, sinning through Monday with a zest, and the Romanist falling back with new fervor upon the causes of his confession and penance." Those who had worshipped next to him at the foot of the Kaaba were "'whitewashed'—the book of their sins was a *tabula rasa*," he wrote, but "too many of them lost no time in…opening a fresh account."

Burton knew that, although he had entered the Kaaba, he was not a true believer and his demons had not been banished, even temporarily. He had no real home, moreover, to which he could return. His success in Mecca would bring him fame in England, admiration from the Royal Geographical Society, and opportunities in his homeland that he had not had before, but none of that would change the fact that he would always be an outsider. He did not expect a hero's welcome, but neither was he willing to let his countrymen stare at him with curiosity and then turn their backs. "It is a great thing to be welcomed home by some little corner of the Great World, which takes a pride in your exploits, because they reflect honour upon itself," he wrote. "In the contrary condition you are a waif, a stray; you are a blaze of light, without a focus. Nobody outside your own fireside cares."

When Burton finally set sail, still disguised as Shaykh Abdullah, it was not for the accolades awaiting him in England but for the ancient arms of Egypt. Crossing the narrow Red Sea, he traveled west and then north to Cairo, where the Nile River crept by on its winding journey from its still mysterious source thousands of miles away. Burton looked forward to rest and solitude while he wrote the story of his own journey and planned his next expedition, wherever and whatever that might be.

CHAPTER TWO

Shadows

Richard Burton was still in Cairo when he heard that the German missionary and explorer Johann Krapf had arrived in Egypt with tales of the Mountains of the Moon and the source of the Nile. Burton was holed up in the Shepheard Hotel, a thick, stone-walled building that "presented more the aspect of a grim old barrack," an American consul general wrote, "than that of a hostelry." Growing in grandeur over the years, it would one day welcome everyone from T. E. Lawrence to Theodore Roosevelt, Winston Churchill, the Aga Khan, and the Maharaja of Jodhpur. A hundred years later, it would have to be rebuilt after burning down during pre-revolutionary unrest, but in the fall of 1853 the Shepheard Hotel still sat in serene, leafy beauty on the same parkland where Napoleon had stationed his army during his invasion of Egypt. From its balconied windows, Burton could see a long bend of the Nile as it wound its way through the city.

Burton no longer needed the clothes he had worn on the Hajj, but he continued to wear them. Months after entering Mecca, he refused to cast off his disguise, speaking in Arabic and signing letters to his friends and even to the Royal Geographical Society as Shaykh Abdullah. One night, he repeatedly strode past a group of British officers who were lounging outside the hotel. With each pass he neared closer and closer to the men, several of whom he knew, finally sweeping his robes so that they brushed against one of them. Cursing what he considered to be impudence from an Arab, the man cried, "If he does that again I'll kick him." Hearing this, Burton stopped mid-stride, spun around to face the group, and, to their shock, said, "Well, damn it, Hawkins, that's a nice way to welcome a fellow after two years' absence."

The majority of Burton's time in Egypt was spent not with old friends but alone with his own thoughts, most of them regrets, and his exultation quickly collapsed into dejection. Despite his success in Mecca, he could focus only on the fact that he had not crossed the Arabian Peninsula as he had originally planned to do. Confiding in a letter to Norton Shaw, the secretary of the Royal Geographical Society, that he had suffered from dysentery since his return to Cairo, he wrote, "I won't say it was aggravated by my disgust at my failure in crossing the Peninsulas, but joking apart the 'physic' of a successful man differs wildly from that of the poor devil who has failed."

It was Burton's triumph, however, much more than his failure that had left him despondent. He expected and did not care that his accomplishments would be questioned and criticized by his suspicious countrymen and jealous rivals. What haunted him was knowing that he now had nothing left to set his mind and talents to. "How melancholy a thing is success," he would later write. "Whilst failure inspires a man, attainment reads the sad prosy lesson that all our glories 'are shadows, not substantial things.'" He needed another challenge, an escape from this persistent, haunting gloom, and Johann Krapf had just supplied it.

•

Krapf had spent the past seventeen years in East Africa. Like Burton, he was fascinated with languages, studying ancient Ge'ez, Amharic, and Swahili. After the deaths, one after another, of his two infant daughters and his wife, whose disease-stricken body he had burned in a pyre near Mombasa, he had established a station at New Rabai, about fifteen miles up the coast. Two years later, another missionary, Johannes Rebmann, had arrived from Germany, and together the two men had explored the region, becoming the first Europeans to see the two highest mountains in Africa—Kenya and Kilimanjaro.

Although Burton had little time for European missionaries, whose work he considered to be at best worthless and at worst cruel, he was very interested in the exploratory work Krapf had done, especially his travels with Rebmann and another young German missionary named Jakob Erhardt. Erhardt had joined Krapf and Rebmann at New Rabai four years earlier, and together the three men had made the most detailed exploration yet by Europeans of the East African coast. They had also brought back stories from ivory and slave traders, who had told them about not just snowcapped mountains but immense inland lakes. Burton himself had heard similar stories from Arabic traders while on the Hajj, scribbling everything they told him onto small strips of paper before hiding them in the hem of his robes. Now writing to the Royal Geographical Society from the Shepheard Hotel, he admitted that, although Krapf's stories "remind one of a de Lunatico," he was determined to track the missionary down in an effort to find out exactly what he, Rebmann, and Erhardt had accomplished. "I have not seen him but don't intend to miss the spectacle," he wrote, "especially to pump what really has been done & what remains to be done."

●

In the nineteenth century, explorers were scattered across the globe, clutching their compasses and sextants as they sought to fill in maps and solve geographical mysteries from Africa to Australia, Asia to Antarctica. Despite the fact that there was still much to be learned about nearly every corner of the world, however, there was little debate about what constituted the Holy Grail of exploration. It was a question that had frustrated astronomers, philosophers, historians, and explorers for the past two thousand years: Where did the Nile begin?

Fascination with the Nile had grown not only because it is the longest river in the world, with a basin that spans more than a million square miles, one tenth of the African continent, but because it has made possible one of the oldest and richest continuous civilizations on earth. The fertile green swath of the Nile floodplain covers less than 5 percent of Egypt but is home to more than 96 percent of its population. The rest of the land is desert. So vital are the river's annual floods that ancient Egyptians based their calendars on them, starting each new year with the first day of the floods.

Although the floods' timing is reassuringly predictable, the volume of its waters is not. If the river was too low, there would be a shortage of both water and the nutrients it carried, which made possible the valley's rich soil and abundant produce. If it was too high, it breached its banks, tearing away vast swaths of farmland and entire villages as it swept its way to the sea.

It was a fundamentally important question that had absorbed the best minds for centuries. "An average rise [of the Nile] is one of sixteen cubits [twenty-seven feet]," the Roman scholar Pliny the Elder had written in the first century. If the river rose only twelve cubits, he warned, the result was famine. Two more cubits, on the other hand, meant "cheerfulness, fifteen complete confidence and sixteen delight." Seventeen, Pliny warned, could spell disaster.

Fears about the Nile's floods and efforts to understand them had led to questions about its source. Early theories varied widely, from the ancient Greek historian Herodotus, who had been told by Egyptian priests that the river welled up out of a bottomless cavern, to Virgil and Alexander the Great, both of whom, three hundred years apart, briefly speculated that the river had its origins in India. The most famous early conjecturer about the source of the Nile was the legendary Egyptian mathematician, astronomer, and geographer Ptolemy. Relying largely on reports from a Greek trader named Diogenes, who had traveled twenty-five days inland from the eastern coast of Africa, Ptolemy placed the source of the Nile in two large lakes that flowed out of a snow-topped mountain range Diogenes had named the Mountains of the Moon. Although Ptolemy's second-century maps and writings were largely ignored by Europeans between the fifth and fourteenth centuries, there had been a resurgence of interest in him during the Renaissance. By the eighteenth century his work was among the principal sources for modern-day explorers.

It had long been known that the Nile was made up of two primary branches: the Blue and the White. The longest branch, the White Nile, named for the light gray silt that gives its waters a milky hue, joins the darker Blue Nile near Khartoum, in Sudan, before continuing its combined course to the Mediterranean Sea. In 1770, Scotsman James Bruce had claimed to be the first European to discover the source of the Blue Nile when he reached Lake Tana in northern Ethiopia. When told that he had actually been beaten to it by the Spanish Jesuit Pedro Páez, who had traced the river to its headwaters 150 years earlier, he had refused to relinquish the honor. More than two hundred years after Páez, however, and nearly a hundred years after Bruce, the source of the White Nile remained a mystery.

As anyone who sought to understand it quickly learned, the White Nile protected its secrets. When confronted with an impossibility, the Roman saying was *Facilius sit Nili caput invenire*—It would be easier to find the source of the Nile. Attempts to explore the river's length from north to south had been thwarted by a vast inland swamp known as the Sudd. Taken from *sadd,* the Arabic word for "barrier," the flat expanse of bogs and swamps stretches for hundreds of miles through modern-day South Sudan, choked with tall grasses, papyrus, weeds, and water hyacinth that make it impossible to navigate by boat. An expeditionary force sent by Roman emperor Caesar Augustus gave up before reaching the equator. More than fifty years later, Nero's Roman centurions were stopped by the same marshland, which they reported was so massive even the people who lived in the region had no idea how big it was. Not until the nineteenth century, when the Turkish officer Selim Bimbashi sent three expeditions up the Nile between 1839 and 1842, were explorers able to penetrate the Sudd. Two of Bimbashi's crews made it hundreds of miles south of the swamp, but still impossibly far from the river's source.

By the mid-1800s, explorers had begun to realize that if they were to have any hope of reaching the Nile's headwaters the best route was not an ascent from the north but an overland journey from the south. From their base at New Rabai on the eastern coast, the German missionaries Krapf, Rebmann, and Erhardt had been doing just that. Krapf, who had long been struggling with illness, was stopping off in Egypt on his way back to Europe after being told that if he stayed in Africa he would die. Erhardt and Rebmann were still in East Africa, at least for the time being. Erhardt, whose health was not much better than Krapf's, would also leave for Germany the following year, but he would bring with him a map that he and Rebmann had drawn together. Following a conversation about the long-standing questions surrounding the source of the Nile, they had had what Erhardt believed to be a sudden and shared spark of inspiration. "At one and the same moment, the problem flashed on both of us," he would later write, "solved by the simple supposition that where geographical hypothesis had hitherto supposed an enormous mountain-land, we must now look for an enormous valley and an inland sea."

·

A year earlier, the president of the Royal Geographical Society, Roderick Murchison, had declared that whoever found "the true sources of the White Nile" would be "justly considered among the greatest benefactors of this age to geographical science." In the Society's famed publication, *The Journal of the Royal Geographical Society of London,* the British naturalist Colonel William Sykes had predicted that it would take "some gallant heart to attempt the solution of geographical problems which have baffled inquiries for so many ages past." Burton, finally awakened from the heavy spell that his success in Mecca and lonely days in Cairo had cast over him, could think of no heart more gallant than his own. "I hear that the Geographical has been speaking about an expedition to Zanzibar," he wrote to Norton Shaw. "I shall strain every nerve to command it."

Burton had been on the Nile for the first time when he was on his way to Mecca, and, despite its exalted history, he had not been impressed. The surrounding landscape had reminded him of his years in India, in the hot and dusty province of Sindh. "To me there was a double dullness in the scenery," he had written. "Morning mist and noon-tide glare; the same hot wind and heat clouds, and fiery sunsets, and evening glow; the same pillars of dust and 'devils' of sand sweeping like giants over the plain; the same turbid water." The idea of finding the river's source, however, solving the greatest geographical mystery of his age, inspired in him precisely the opposite emotions, filling him with an almost overwhelming sense of adventure and the possibility of great achievement.

Although he had yet to recover from the dysentery that had plagued him since returning from Mecca, and he would soon have to sail to Bombay as his leave of absence from the East India Company was running out, Burton was not about to let any obstacle, physical or professional, prevent him from setting out in search of the source of the White Nile. It was not just a once-in-a-lifetime opportunity. It was a chance that few men in the history of exploration had ever been given. It was, he wrote, "the possibility of bringing my compass to bear upon...those 'Mountains of the Moon,' whose very existence have not, until lately, been proved by the geographers of 2,000 years—a range white with eternal snows even in the blaze of the African summer, supposed to be the father of the mysterious Nile, briefly a tract invested with all the romance of wild fable and hoar antiquity, and to this day the [most] worthwhile subject to which human energy and enterprise could be devoted."

Burton already had a plan. All he needed was "a few good men to accompany me (one to survey, another for physics and botany)," he wrote to Shaw. "I doubt not of our grand success." He still wanted to find Krapf, admitting that he "must be au courant of his discoveries," but while he respected the missionary and wanted his advice, he did not fear him as a competitor. Krapf may have been the first to bring news of the inland lakes to Europe, but Burton was confident that he would be the first European to actually find the lakes, and thus the source. Johann Krapf, he told Shaw, was "only my John the Baptist."

———◈◈◈———

CHAPTER THREE

Bond for Our Blood

When the Court of Directors of the East India Company finally agreed to let Burton search for the source of the Nile in the summer of 1854, it was under two conditions, one concerning the promise of trade and the other the threat of death. First, he would start his journey in Aden, a British-held port on the southern tip of the Arabian Peninsula, before crossing the Gulf of Aden to what was then known as Somaliland, from where he would enter the African interior. Perched on the Horn of Africa, Somaliland was of interest to Britain both because it was strategically positioned along the Bombay-to-Suez trade route and because it was largely unexplored. It was also believed to be extremely dangerous, which led to the second condition: The company bore no responsibility for keeping Burton alive while he was there. He would be supplied with "all the instruments required, afford[ed] a passage going and returning, and pa[id] the actual expenses of the journey," but beyond financial aid and professional leave, he was on his own. Despite the fact that he was still an officer in the East India Company, "he goes as a private traveller," the agreement warned, "the government giving no more protection to him than they would to an individual totally unconnected with the service."

Not only was Burton unconcerned about setting off on a dangerous expedition without a safety net, he preferred it that way. Even having to deal with James Outram, the newly appointed political resident and commandant in Aden, was more governmental interference than he wanted. Outram, moreover, had made it clear that he was there not to help Burton but to stand in his way. After being shuttled around India, and fighting in the First Afghan and Anglo-Persian Wars, Outram was ill and tired, and would soon request sick leave. In the meantime, he was determined to keep Burton from crossing the Gulf to Somaliland. "The countries opposite to Aden were so dangerous for any foreigners to travel in," he argued, that it was his "duty as a Christian to prevent, as far as he was able, anybody from hazarding his life there."

A largely pastoral people scattered throughout the lowlands of the eastern Horn of Africa, the Somalis had long ago developed a vigorous trade network with the towns along the Indian Ocean and Red Sea coast. With the rise of the Industrial Revolution, these networks had stretched even deeper into the interior and grew increasingly complex as Somali traders worked to meet European and North American demand for everything from goat and cow hides for leather to vegetable dyes for textiles and vegetable oils for cooking and soap, while still offering a wide variety of more traditional trade goods such as ivory, livestock, incense, ostrich feathers, and leopard skins. After the British seized Aden in 1839, the enclave there had quickly come to rely on the Somalis, who supplied them with fresh meat, and by the 1850s Somalis made up roughly 15 percent of Aden's total population.

Men like Outram, however, continued to fear the Somalis, remembering in particular two incidents that had shaken their confidence in the region. In 1825 a group of Somalis had seized the English brig *Mary Ann,* plundering the ship and killing most of its crew. Twenty years later, south of Somaliland, about sixty miles into the East African interior, a twenty-eight-year-old French explorer named Eugène Maizan had been tortured, emasculated, and murdered after becoming what may have been the first European to make it that far past the coast. The Royal Geographical Society had tried again five years later, in 1850, deciding to send Dr. Henry Carter, an assistant surgeon in the East India Company, to the region. As the planning had progressed, however, it had become increasingly clear that Carter's idea of what the expedition would entail was very different from the Society's. Burton suspected that Carter, having learned of Maizan's fate, did "not relish the chance of losing his cod." He wanted only to sail along the coast in a government-owned ship that would carry his provisions and safely and comfortably "convey him from place to place." Finally, the Society had given up, abandoning the expedition and dismissing Carter, whose timid plans did not "fulfil the primary and great object of the London Geographical Society, which was, and still is, to have the interior explored."

Despite the potential dangers, Burton doubted that Outram was trying to prevent him from sailing to Somaliland out of concern for his safety. The resident, Burton believed, was motivated by nothing more elevated than envy. "In his younger days, thirsting for distinction, Outram was ambitious to explore the Somali country," Burton complained, "but when I prepared to do so, he openly opposed me." In Outram's defense, a friend of his would later argue that he was "basing his views on the oldest and most experienced residents on the spot...and the tragedy that in some shape or other was certain to follow the wild adventure of a set of reckless young men." Burton, by then thirty-three years old, was neither particularly young nor terribly reckless. He was, however, very determined.

Eager to get out from under Outram's thumb, Burton finally offered to delay his expedition until the end of the Berbera Fair. A well-known annual trade bazaar that began in October and lasted until April, the Berbera Fair brought thousands of people to this Somali coastal town every year. If he waited until the massive caravans began their return to the interior in the spring, Burton could travel under their protection. In the meantime, he would fine-tune his plans, continue to learn the Somali language, which, he wrote, "abound[s] in poetry and eloquence," and wait for the final member of his expedition to arrive.

•

Among the first decisions Burton had made when planning his trip to East Africa was to invite three fellow officers, each of whom he not only knew well but trusted and admired, to join his expedition. One of the men had sailed with him to Aden from Bombay. Lieutenant G. E. Herne, who was in the 1st Bombay European Regiment of Fusiliers, was, Burton wrote, "accustomed to daguerreotype," the newly invented process of photography, "and to take astronomical observations, and well-known for his ingenuity in mathematics." Herne would assist William Stroyan, a geologist as well as a highly skilled and experienced surveyor.

A member of the Indian navy, Stroyan had already surveyed both the coast of western India and the Punjab Rivers. It had taken Burton three months to convince the Bombay government to let Stroyan join him. "It was not without difficulty," he wrote, "that such valuable services were spared for the deadly purpose of penetrating into Eastern Africa."

In Aden, Burton still anxiously awaited the arrival of the third member of his expedition: Assistant Surgeon John Ellerton Stocks, who had been delayed in England. Stocks was planning to join the expedition as its botanist and, when necessary, resident medic. Burton had met him in Sindh, where he had been a member of the medical staff, in charge of vaccinations and the inspection of medicine. Stocks was best known, however, for his encyclopedic knowledge of plants, especially those native to India. He had been named Conservator of Forests by the Bombay government and had spent the past winter in England at the Royal Botanic Gardens at Kew, where he was cataloging the extensive collection he had brought back from Sindh and working on a detailed description of the "geography, natural history, arts, and manufactures" of the region.

Like Burton, Stocks had also devoted himself to the serious study of other cultures. He approached his work with a humility, however, that Burton had never had. "So great was his knowledge of the native character and such was the confidence he inspired in those around him, that he was enabled to penetrate further into Baluchistan than any previous traveller had done since our armies quitted Afghanistan," a fellow Briton would write of Stocks. "His singleness of purpose and remarkable tact [had] disarm[ed] suspicion even amongst the most jealous of the native princes." Despite all that he had achieved, Stocks had also remained strikingly unpretentious, beloved for his "amiable, cheerful, and engaging disposition." Burton knew that Stocks would not only be a valuable member of the expedition but was someone who could keep the other men happy and united even in times of danger or deprivation. "The fellow writes well but is modest—shameful defect!" he had written affectionately of Stocks in a letter to Norton Shaw before leaving Cairo. "Above all things he's an excellent chap."

When the ship from England finally arrived in Aden, however, it carried not Burton's good-natured and talented friend, smiling as he walked toward him carrying his medical kit and botanical equipment, but the stunning news of his death. The announcement had been printed in the September 19 edition of *Allen's Indian Mail,* a "register of intelligence for British and Foreign India, China, and all parts of the East" that included everything from casualty reports to marriage announcements. Near the end of a long, somber column of death notices was a single, easily missed line: "Stocks, J. Ellerton, Bombay medical service, at Dottingham, near Hull, Aug. 30."

Although he was a medic, Stocks had not understood the dangers posed by the "neuralgic pains in the head and neck" that he had suffered while working at Kew. Thinking that they were related to a fever that he had been fighting off and on for some time and hoping that a change of scenery and a respite from his work would help, he had left London for the English countryside. While staying with friends in Cottingham, the town where he had been born, he had been "seized with an apoplectic stroke," and, ten days later in the wake of a second attack, had died at the age of thirty-two. Shocked by the news, Burton was left not only to mourn the loss of his friend but to accept that, at this late date, with months of planning behind him, supplies piled around him, and East Africa just a boat ride away, it would be nearly impossible to replace any member of his expedition, especially Stocks.

•

A few weeks before news of Stocks's death reached Burton, a P&O ship bound for England had docked in Aden. Built by the famed Peninsular and Oriental Steam Navigation Company, which had been founded just seventeen years earlier, the ship had begun its journey in Bombay. Among the few passengers who had disembarked was a young British officer named John Hanning Speke. A lieutenant in the 46th Regiment of the Bengal Native Infantry, Speke was an experienced traveler, a skilled surveyor, and an excellent shot. It was his passion for hunting, in fact, that had brought him to Aden, from where, like Burton, he hoped to sail to Somaliland. Speke was there not to try to unravel East Africa's geographical mysteries but to kill and carry home to his family estate as many of its rarest animals as he could find.

At twenty-seven years of age, Speke was not only six years Burton's junior, he was his opposite in almost every way. Thin and fine-boned, blond and blue-eyed, he had been born into British aristocracy and raised in a Georgian mansion in Somerset, built on land that his family had owned for centuries. Puritanical and prim, he prided himself on his discipline, saving his money and his leave so that he could go on hunting trips while harshly judging his fellow officers for, in his mind, squandering theirs. "My mess-mates wondered how it was I succeeded in getting so much leave, but the reason was simply this, and I tell it that others may profit by it," he boasted. "The Commander-in-Chief...observing to what good account I always turned my leave, instead of idling my time away, or running into debt, took great pleasure in encouraging my hobby; and his Staff were even heard to say it would be a pity if I did not get leave, as so much good resulted from it."

While Burton buried himself in books, Speke had devoted as much of his spare time as possible to what was known in India as *shikar*, big game hunting. He hoped to one day open a natural history museum in his ancestral home, Jordans, and had eagerly gathered specimens while traveling through India, Tibet, and the Himalayan Mountains. "Every year... I obtained leave of absence, and every year I marched across the Himalayas, and penetrated into some unknown portions of Tibet," he wrote, "shooting, collecting and mapping the country wherever I went." So passionate was Speke about hunting and collecting that he even went out of his way to kill pregnant animals so that he could study and at times even eat their fetuses. "He had acquired a curious taste for the youngest of meat," Burton would later write, "preferring it even when unborn." He also dismissed as ridiculous any complaint against the practice. "While on the subject of superstition," Speke wrote, "it may be worth mentioning what long ago struck me as a singular instance of the effect of supernatural impression on the uncultivated mind.... On once shooting a pregnant Kudu doe, I directed my native huntsman, a married man, to dissect her womb and expose the embryo; but he shrank from the work with horror, fearing lest the sight of the kid, striking his mind, should have an influence on his wife's future bearing, by metamorphosing her progeny to the likeness of a fawn."

For Speke, however, hunting was more than killing and collecting. It was a way to relieve stress, to lose himself in something he loved. It was also a way to prove his manliness. "A sedentary life," he insisted, "made him ill." He prided himself in walking farther, hiking higher, sleeping less, and enduring more than other men, and he had little sympathy or patience for those who fell either sick or behind. To Speke, hunting and traveling were tests of endurance, physical and mental, and he was determined to be master of both. "In shooting," he had explained in a letter to a friend before leaving Bombay, "you must have a thorough confidence in yourself & instrument or you will never excel."

After completing his tenth year of service in the infantry, and thus earning a three-year furlough, Speke had planned to travel with his friend and frequent hunting companion Edmund Smyth. An ensign with the 13th Bengal Native Infantry and an accomplished mountaineer, Smyth had spent many of his leaves traveling with Speke, even crossing over into western Tibet, where both men had swum in Lake Manasarovar, which is considered by both Buddhists and Hindus a sacred body of water. Despite Smyth's reputation for strength and fortitude and Speke's personal knowledge of his ability as an explorer, however, Speke had begun to doubt his value as a traveling companion. Finally he decided that, instead of continuing to England, where he was supposed to meet Smyth and begin their travels, he would make his own way to Somaliland, where he would travel alone.

•

Wasting no time after reaching Aden, Speke quickly presented himself at Outram's office, where he was confident that he would receive the letters of introduction and logistical help that he needed for his solo expedition. Having always found his way paved by older military officials who admired his discipline and approved of his aristocratic background, he expected this time to be no different. To his shock, however, the political resident was as obstinately opposed to his plans to enter Somaliland as he had been to Burton's. "To my utter astonishment and discomfiture,"

Speke wrote, "he at once said he would not only withhold his influence, but would prohibit my going there at all."

Unwilling to give up, Speke repeatedly asked Outram to reconsider, or, failing that, to find another way for him to enter East Africa. Perseverance, his fellow officers had learned, was one of Speke's most distinctive traits. "He eminently possessed the power of asking," Burton would soon learn, "no prospect of a refusal, however harsh, deterred him." Finally either taking pity on the young man or tiring of his supplications, Outram told him that, although he believed "the scheme to be quite unfeasible," there was one possibility. A British lieutenant who had successfully "made the pilgrimage of Mecca" had been able to persuade the government to let him explore what Outram, in a simultaneously fearful and denigrating description of Africa typical of the time, referred to as "this even darker land." If Speke could convince Burton to let him take Stocks's place in his expedition to Somaliland, Outram, although still convinced of the danger, would allow him to go.

Although this was not the journey he had envisioned, Speke now realized that it was his only hope of reaching East Africa. Approaching Burton, he offered his services as a surveyor. Burton, having had a great deal of experience over the years sizing people up, quickly assessed the young man standing before him. He was, in many ways, typically English, but his hunting expeditions had left him fit and well accustomed to long marches and short, uncomfortable nights. "A man of lithe, spare form," Burton would later describe Speke, "about six feet tall, blue-eyed, tawny-maned; the old Scandinavian type...with long, wiry, but not muscular limbs, that could cover the ground at a swinging pace." He had, Burton noticed with some concern, "a highly nervous temperament," but also a "strong nerve and clear head." It was immediately apparent that Speke brought no skills to the expedition that together Burton, Herne, and Stroyan did not already have, and in far greater measure. More than that, however, Burton was struck by what seemed to him to be Speke's general ignorance of the region and apparent disinterest in the people living there. "He had no qualifications for the excursion that he proposed to himself, except that of being a good sportsman," he would later write. "He was ignorant of the native races in Africa.... He did not know any of the manners and customs of the East; he did not know any language except a little Anglo-Hindustani; he did not even know the names of the Coast Towns."

Despite Burton's unpromising assessment of Speke's abilities as an explorer and his concern about his naïveté, he agreed to let him join the expedition. Speke was welcome to share with him "the hardships of African exploration." Speke was thrilled, not only because he could now travel to Somaliland, but because he could do it without having to use his furlough. "Since I have managed to square myself with the party going on Gov't account," he wrote to a friend, I "am now instead of being on 'Furlo' appointed Asst Surveyor and Collector of Zoological Specimens and draw my full pay." Outram, however, after hearing the news, went out of his way to make sure that Burton understood exactly the position he was putting himself in. By taking Speke onto his expedition, he was, Burton wrote, "assuming the fullest responsibility and giving a written bond for our blood."

Years later, filled with bitter regret, Burton would wonder what had moved him that day to make such a hasty decision. He had brought onto his long-planned and hard-won expedition a man who seemed to have little to contribute and whom he knew very little about. Speke was smart and skilled, but he was certainly no Stocks, either in ability or in temperament. The wrong personality thrown into the mix, Burton knew, could not only shatter an expedition's fragile equilibrium but endanger the lives of everyone on it. He could only guess that he had been moved by pity, unable to turn away a fellow traveler asking for help, a young man who perhaps reminded him of his own brother, Edward, who throughout their tumultuous childhood had always followed so closely in his footsteps. "I saw that he was going to lose his money and his 'leave' and his life," Burton would later write of Speke, marveling at his own disastrous decision. "Why should I have cared? I do not know."

CHAPTER FOUR

The Abban

Although Burton had promised Outram that he would not sail to Somaliland until the end of the Berbera Fair, he had never intended to spend that time waiting around in Aden. He believed not only that the port was a "hot-bed of scurry and ulcer" but that there was little to explore there. Restless and bored, he decided to use the six months that stretched before him to try to become the first European to enter the Ethiopian city of Harar. Nestled among the Ahmar Mountains, Harar was not only "the ancient metropolis of a once mighty race, the only permanent settlement in Eastern Africa, the reported seat of Moslem learning," but was, like Mecca, a holy city.

While Burton was in Ethiopia, disguised as an Arab merchant, Herne and Stroyan would be waiting for him in Berbera, where they would gather information about the region and buy pack animals for the journey into the interior. Forgotten in the rush to leave Aden, Speke suddenly realized that he was the only member of the expedition who had nothing to do, a situation that he found intolerable. "Thus everybody had a duty to perform during this interregnum but myself," he complained. "Dreading the monotony of a station life, I now volunteered to travel in any direction my commandant might think proper to direct, and to any length of time he might consider it advisable for me to be away."

Burton agreed to give Speke an assignment, but, keeping in mind Outram's warning that he alone was now responsible for the young man's life, he chose a destination that, he believed, held very little danger. Speke would travel, Burton told him, to the Wady Nogal, known within the Royal Geographical Society as the "Happy Valley." A trade route through northeastern Somaliland, the Wady Nogal was popular with traders because the landscape was conducive to travel and the people known to be peaceful. While there, Speke was to study the region's watershed, map his route, take note of the weather patterns, gather samples of the red dirt, which was rumored to contain gold dust, and purchase camels and ponies for the upcoming expedition. Burton knew that Speke would be eager to collect "specimens of natural history in all its branches," but he emphasized the importance of keeping "*copious* notes." Herne even helped him build a camera obscura with which he could take crude photographs.

To Speke's surprise, Burton then suggested that he travel in disguise. Burton, who felt more comfortable in Arab dress than European, looked forward to once again wearing the robes of his alter ego, El Haj Abdullah, and it made sense, he argued, that Speke and Herne should appear to be his disciples. Herne had already bought the necessary clothing for himself, but Speke, worried about dressing like an Arab, sought advice from Outram. Not only did Outram tell him that traveling in disguise would not be helpful, and, considering the fact that Speke was pale and blond, unlikely to fool anyone, he argued that it would undermine his authority. Speke would be much more likely to impress those he met, Outram insisted, if he were dressed in his British uniform rather than the robes of an Arab. "Lowering ourselves in this manner," he told Speke, "would operate against me in the estimation of the natives." In the end, Speke reluctantly donned the disguise, but he complained bitterly about it. "It was anything but pleasant to the feel," he wrote.

After overseeing the outfitting of Speke's expedition, Burton hired two men to travel with him: an interpreter and an Abban, or protector. "The Abban acts at once as broker, escort, agent, and interpreter," he explained, "and the institution may be considered the earliest form of transit dues." As well as food and lodging, Abbans were given a percentage of any sales conducted during the expedition and small gifts of beads, clothing, and other luxuries along the way. In return, they were expected to negotiate with locals on the expedition's behalf, find accommodations, guides, and camels, and, if necessary, fight in any battles that might arise, even against their own countrymen. Although abbanship, which had a long, useful, and respected history in East Africa, had been good for the local economy as well as for the trading and exploring expeditions it served, the system was ripe for exploitation on both sides.

Both of the men Burton chose for Speke's expedition were not just Somalis but members of the same sub clan, the Warsangali. The Warsangli had formed a powerful kingdom in the early thirteenth century that included vast stretches of the northwestern Horn of Africa and which would last for some six hundred years. Well known and respected as a peaceful and politically independent people, the Warsangali's name in Somali means "bringer of good news." Ahmed, the man who would be Speke's interpreter, spoke Hindustani, a language that Speke had some knowledge of after his years in India. His Abban was a man named Sumunter, who, Speke noted with some satisfaction, "ranked highly in his country," as did all Abbans.

Although this was his first time in East Africa, Speke understood the importance of choosing the right Abban. "It rests entirely on the Abban's honesty whether his client can succeed in doing anything in the country he takes him through," he wrote. "Arabs, when traveling under their protection, have to ask his permission for anything they may wish to do, and cannot even make a march, or purchase anything, without his sanction being first obtained." With little knowledge of the people, languages, or geography of the land through which he would be traveling, and with a face and physique that instantly betrayed his youth and naïveté, Speke knew that he was entirely at the mercy of his Abban. Sumunter knew it too.

·

As soon as Speke and his small entourage left Aden on October 18, he began to suspect that he was "being trifled with" and that the real danger to the expedition was the man who had been hired to protect it. Not only did Sumunter immediately take control of the porters, gaining their respect when Speke could not, but he then quickly left, informing Speke that he was going to return to Bunder Gori, the harbor where they had arrived. Taking 20 rupees from the expedition's reserve fund, which he said would be used to buy donkeys for the journey, he assured Speke that he would not be gone long, promising to catch up with the expedition. As soon as Sumunter left, the porters, realizing that they were now solely under the command of the young Englishman, refused to continue marching. "I strove with every effort in my power to induce the men to go a little further forward," Speke wrote, "but without the slightest effect."

While he waited impatiently for the return of his Abban, Speke began hearing rumors that Sumunter had returned to Bunder Gori not to buy pack animals but to pay off his own debts. "The Abban was detained...by a creditor to whom he had contracted debts in Aden," Speke learned. "Now, in part liquidation of them, he had given away all my salt, the twenty rupees he took for hiring donkeys, several pieces of cloth, and he had changed my good rice for bad." When Sumunter finally returned, he refused to admit any guilt. More galling for Speke, after staging a trial for the Abban in Speke's tent, the Warsangali sultan informed him that "he could see no harm in what had been done." In fact, he said, as the expedition's Abban, Sumunter was "at liberty to do whatever he pleased either with or to my property."

Although he was sickened by his failure to reach the Wady Nogal, Speke realized that he now had little choice but to abandon his expedition. At one point, he and Sumunter had even had a standoff in front of their men. Although Speke was enraged, he was also exhausted after months of fruitless struggle and desperate to end the showdown so that he could leave Somaliland. His nerves were so frayed and his pride so wounded that he was ready to do nearly anything to regain his dignity. "A wicked feeling was almost coming over me, which made me shudder again when I reflected more calmly on what my mind was now dilating," he later admitted. Sumunter "seemed to me only as an animal in satanical disguise; to have shot him would have given me great relief, for I fairly despaired of ever producing any good effect upon his mind."

•

By the time the expedition finally made it back to Aden on February 15, Speke was so relieved that his "three and a half months' persecution" was over that, as soon as he heard the blessed words, "let go the anchor," he dove into the sea and swam to shore. Burton was waiting for him, having returned a week earlier from his journey to Harar, which had been as successful as Speke's had been disastrous. He had already written to Norton Shaw at the Royal Geographical Society, briefly describing his journey to the forbidden city and making clear his plans to now search for the source of the White Nile. "My success at Harrar has emboldened me & I have applied for a 2d years leave," he wrote. "The Court of Directors will not I think refuse it, especially if it be at all backed up by the Roy. Geog. Soc. My plans (public) are now to march southward to the Webbe Shebayli and Ganana. Privately & entre nous I want to settle the question of Krapf's 'eternal snows.' There is little doubt of the White Nile being thereabouts."

Despite his success in Ethiopia, however, tragic news had awaited Burton in Aden. While he was gone, his mother, he learned, had died suddenly. Burton felt that his family, which had always been somewhat loosely held together, was now falling apart. Five years earlier, following the death of his aunt, he had written to his cousin Sarah, "All we can do is resign ourselves to calamities, and I confess to you that judging from the number of losses that our family has sustained during the last six years I fear that when able to return home I shall find no place capable of bearing that name." Heart disease had ended his mother's life on December 10, soon after moving to Bath. After entering her new house for the first time, she was said to have proclaimed, "I smell death here," a foreboding that did not surprise her superstitious son. Alone in Aden, Burton was left with only the present that he had bought for her in Mecca, a round, red cushion pierced with turquoise rings, a symbol of motherhood.

Now, hearing Speke describe repeated humiliations and threats at the hands of Sumunter, a man he had personally chosen to protect the expedition, Burton was outraged on the young man's behalf and determined to seek justice. "Speke has been plundered, threatened, detained & impeded from entering the country which he was directed to explore," he wrote in an official complaint. "If such conduct be allowed to pass unnoticed, or rather I should say if it be not visited with severe chastisement, I apprehend that it will be most prejudicial to future proceedings of the expedition." Speke, mortified and angry, wanted to put the whole episode behind him, but Burton insisted on prosecuting the Abban. "Against my inclination," Speke lamented, "I was appointed to be Sumunter's prosecutor, and with my servants as witnesses." A trial was quickly held and Sumunter instantly found guilty. His punishment, moreover, was surprisingly harsh. As well as being fined 200 rupees and given a two-month prison sentence, with hard labor and an additional six months if he could not pay the fine, he and his family were banished from Aden—"for ever," Speke wrote.

Burton, however, was still not satisfied. Declaring that not only was Sumunter corrupt, but so, fundamentally, was the institution of abbanship, he argued that, as Somalis were given free access to Aden, so Englishmen should be able to travel through Somaliland without paying an Abban. Already irritated that Burton's insistence on a trial had publicly exposed the fact that he had been unable to control his own men, Speke now worried that his commander's zeal for vengeance would endanger the entire expedition. "This perhaps was scarcely the right time," he pointed out, "to dictate a policy which would be distasteful as well as injurious (in a monetary sense) to the people among whom we were about to travel and with whom it was highly essential to our interest to be on the most friendly terms."

As Speke had feared, the Somalis instantly made clear their outrage. Shocked by Sumunter's banishment and enraged by Burton's open threat to a system that they not only relied on but took pride in, they vowed revenge. Dismissing their threats, Burton insisted that he saw "no grounds of apprehension." He was not about, moreover, to further delay an expedition that he had been waiting for months to begin. "During thirty years, not an Englishman of the many that had visited it had been molested at Berberah," he argued. "There was as little to fear in it as within the fortifications of Aden."

•

With nothing left to do in Aden but revise the notes he had taken on the grammar and vocabulary of the Harari language, Burton eagerly returned his attention to the central subject of his journey to Africa: his search for the source of the White Nile. Despite the anger and suspicion he had already aroused in the Somalis, Berbera still seemed the best place to begin. It was, he argued, "the true key of the Red Sea, the centre of East African traffic, and the only safe place for shipping upon the western Erythroean shore." From there, following in the path of a caravan, the expedition would travel south through Somaliland until finally reaching the coast directly across from Zanzibar.

Despite his confidence that everything had been smoothed over with the Somalis in the wake of Sumunter's trial, Burton thought it best to hire a few guards from the Aden police force to travel with them. Speke, still shaken from his own disastrous experience, argued that "by this means alone should we have men on whom we could depend." The police force, however, informed the expedition that it had no men to spare, forcing them to hire whoever happened to be available. In the end, they pieced together a diverse group of a dozen guards, from Egyptians to Arabs, Nubians to Sidis, and armed them with sabers and flint muskets. "They were all raw recruits, and unaccustomed to warfare," Speke admitted. "Still we could get no others."

When the expedition finally left Aden, it departed in shifts, stretching from late March to early April. The first to go was a group consisting of seven of their newly hired guards and eight camels, which Speke had somehow managed to buy in Bunder Gori. Speke set out for Berbera a few days later with a small contingent, and, on April 5, Burton brought up the rear.

Although eager to be on his way, Burton felt a growing uneasiness about the newest addition to his expedition. Not only had Speke floundered on what Burton had thought would be an easy journey to the Happy Valley, but, to his shock, before leaving for Berbera the young man had shared disturbing thoughts with his commander. He had "openly declared," Burton later wrote, "that being tired of life he had come to be killed in Africa." It was not what the leader of an expedition wanted to hear from one of his officers just as they were about to travel through a part of the world believed to be dangerous to Europeans. Although Burton himself had often struggled with self-doubt and depression, often in the wake of his greatest triumphs, he "aspired to something better," he wrote, "than the crown of martyrdom."

CHAPTER FIVE

The Enemy Is Upon Us

On April 7, 1855, Burton stepped off the schooner that had carried him to Berbera—its "guns roar[ing] forth a parting salute"—to find a town in chaos. Three thousand merchants from all over East Africa had descended on the coast to attend the famed fair, along with thousands of cattle and five hundred people in chains, destined for the slave markets. The dirt streets were lined with temporary framed huts covered in mats. Merchants shouted from their stalls, selling everything from coffee to frankincense and myrrh, ghee, gold, saffron, feathers, and livestock. The harbor was swarming with ships, and as many as six thousand camels might arrive in a single day, carrying goods from the interior. "During the height of the fair, Berbera is a perfect Babel, in confusion as in languages," a British lieutenant had written after witnessing the spectacle seven years earlier. "No chief is acknowledged, and the customs of bygone days are the laws of the place. Disputes between the inland tribes daily arise, and are settled by the spear and dagger."

The expedition, which now included forty-two men, set up its camp on a rocky rise of land about three quarters of a mile from the town. From the ridge, Burton could see both the harbor where he had landed and the final days of the fair. The four officers shared three tents, which they set up in a straight line: Speke's on the left, closest to the sea; Stroyan's on the right; and between them a small tent, or rowtie, supported by one transverse and two upright poles, that Burton and Herne would share. About a dozen yards separated each tent, with their baggage, grain, and saddles piled in between and the most coveted items—boxes of dates and valuable cloths—hidden beneath Speke's tent.

While waiting for Burton and Speke to arrive, Herne had been able to buy the additional animals they would need for their journey. The roughly fifty camels were kept on a sandy slope of land just beneath the ridge, and the half a dozen ponies and mules were tethered behind the tents. A sentry kept guard over the animals at night, and a group of soldiers, including Somali archers, accompanied them as they grazed during the day. They were all safe, they believed, as long as they stayed near the sea. "The Somali would never be so imprudent as to attack us in such a vital place to them as Berbera," Speke wrote, "where their whole interests of life were centered, and where, by the simple process of blockading, we could so easily take retribution in any way we liked."

The men themselves would have only two sentries, one posted in the front and one in the rear, keeping watch over them as they slept. It was more important, Burton reasoned, to have the sentries guard the animals during the day, and to conserve their energy for the long march ahead of them, than to watch over the expedition at night. Most nights, Burton, Herne, Stroyan, and Speke took turns patrolling the camp. If any threat occurred, they agreed, they would meet in the center tent, where Burton and Herne were sleeping. Speke stored his guns and sword there as well, while keeping his revolver and his dirk, a long military dagger meant for hand-to-hand combat, in his belt during the day and under his pillow at night.

·

At 8:00 on the night of April 9, two days after Burton had arrived in Berbera, a thunderstorm descended on the coast, hailing the beginning of Somaliland's annual monsoon. The season for trade, which lasted from November to April, when the winds blew in a single, steady direction, had come to an end. As Burton and his men watched lightning strike the surrounding hills and rain blanket the town, turning everything dark and dripping, the merchants raced to pack up and prepared to head back to the sea or into the interior.

Among those leaving the fair that night was the Ogaden caravan, under whose protection Burton had promised Outram his expedition would travel. Burton, however, wanted to stay in Berbera to watch the final days of the fair. He was also waiting for a ship from Aden that was carrying mail and surveying instruments from England that they had been expecting for weeks. The men watched from their ridge as thousands of people began streaming out of the coastal town in massive, clanging caravans. The Ogaden caravan, they knew, would soon join the mass exodus. At first, Speke would later write, they "were undecided what to do—whether to go with them without our things from

England, or wait and rely upon our strength in travelling alone." Finally deciding to stay, "we saw our wonted protector depart upon its journey."

By the 15th, Berbera was as empty and silent as it had been roaring with life when Burton had arrived just eight days earlier. Beyond heaps of camel and sheep bones and the splintering framework of huts that had been dismantled and left in piles on the beach for next year's fair, little was left to show that some twenty thousand people had so recently filled the streets. Quickly reclaiming the region, ostriches and lions stepped out of the shadows to once again silently tread the beach, leaving clawed prints in the sand. "We were now alone, and nobody came near us," Speke wrote. "In this isolated position we felt no alarm for our safety." So confident, in fact, were Burton and his officers that there was no danger of attack that they no longer thought it necessary to patrol the camp themselves at night.

•

On the night of April 18, three days after the Ogaden caravan had left Berbera, a small ship entered the deserted harbor. On board were an Arab captain named Yusuf, his crew, and roughly a dozen Somalis, who were trying to get home. Finding that they had missed the caravans and knowing that it was too dangerous to travel from the coast in such small numbers, the Somalis approached Burton's campsite, asking to accompany his expedition. "It was hard to refuse these poor creatures," Speke admitted, "but fearing our supply of dates and rice would not hold out with so many additional mouths to eat it, we reluctantly refused the men." There were, however, four women among the Somalis, and, as they were in greater danger, Burton agreed to let them join the expedition, hiring them to do odd jobs from bringing water to taking care of the camels. He also invited the captain and his crew to have dinner with them that night.

Later, soon after the sun had set, as Burton and the other Englishmen were relaxing on an improvised sofa in front of their tents, drinking coffee and entertaining each other with stories, they suddenly heard the sound of muskets being fired behind them. Leaping to his feet, Speke ran to find out what had happened. Rounding the tents, he saw three men walking toward the camp, leading their horses by the reins while the expedition's guards continued to shoot bullets over their heads. "My anger knew no bounds," Speke wrote, having repeatedly warned them that, "in case of any opposition to a challenge, they should fire into, and not over, their object."

Suspecting that the men were spies, Speke led both them and the expedition's own guards to the front of the tents, where Burton was waiting. After reprimanding the guards, Burton began to interrogate the strangers, assuming that they had been sent to scout out the camp before an attack. The men, however, insisted that they posed no danger to the expedition. "Our visitors swore by the divorce-oath,—the most solemn which the religious know,—that a vessel entering the creek at such an unusual season, they had been sent to ascertain whether it had been freighted with materials for building," Burton wrote, "and concluded by laughingly asking if we feared danger from the tribe of our own protectors." Burton, accepting the explanation, invited the Somalis to share a meal of dates with his men and to leave on their own accord when they had finished.

Soon after, everyone in the expedition lay down to sleep, leaving only two men to keep watch. Burton had been asleep for a few hours, when, around 2:00 a.m., he was suddenly wrenched awake by the sound of his caravan commander crying out, "The enemy [i]s upon us." "Hearing a rush of men like a storm wind,"

Burton later wrote, "I sprang up, [and] called for my sabre." Herne, who had been asleep in the same tent, pulled himself to his feet and seized his revolver, running first to the back of the tent, where the attack seemed to have started, and then to the front, where he arrived just in time to find the expedition's men struggling to fend off the enemy. Firing twice, he fell back into the tent where, getting tangled in the ropes, he found himself looking into the face of a man bearing down on him with a club. Herne was able to shoot his attacker before the man ran off, wounded but alive.

In his own tent, Speke woke up to Burton's voice shouting to Stroyan, "Get up, old fellow!" Confused, he lay listening to the sound of guns being fired in rapid succession behind his tent. Thinking that it must be the guards trying to scare someone off, he stayed where he was. Moments later, however, it became undeniably clear that they were under attack. "There suddenly arose a furious noise, as though the world were coming to end," he wrote. "There was a terrible rush and hurry, then came sticks and stones, flying as thick as hail, followed by a rapid discharge of firearms, and my tent shook as if it would come down." Jumping up and racing into Burton's tent, he shouted, is there "any shooting?" Burton, cursing the fact that he had only his saber with which to fight, wryly replied, "I should *rather* think that there is."

They were under attack, Burton would later learn, by some 350 Somalis. "The enemy swarmed like hornets," he wrote, "with shouts and screams intending to terrify, and proving that overwhelming odds were against us." Herne, Speke, and Burton stood next to each other in the center tent, Speke guarding the entrance and Herne kneeling next to Burton with his revolver. No one knew where Stroyan was, but there was no time to search for him. The blows were coming from all sides, fast and without respite, clubs pounding on the canvas walls, javelins and daggers thrust through and under the tent, aiming for their legs, heads, and hearts.

So fiercely were their assailants pummeling the tent that, fearing that it would come crashing down around them, trapping them in its folds and rendering them helpless, Burton finally decided they had no other option but to step out into the dark and the midst of their attackers. Turning to Speke he said, "Be sharp, and arm to defend the camp." Immediately stepping out of the tent, Speke found himself surrounded by chaos. As he stood trying to orient himself, he was suddenly hit by a rock that smashed into his knee, nearly knocking him down. Returning to the tent, as he later explained, to get a better view of the battle, he was stunned to hear Burton snap at him, "Don't step back, or they will think we are retiring." Bristling at what he took to be a rebuke and, worse, an accusation of cowardice, Speke immediately launched himself back into the melee, firing "at close quarters into the first man before me."

•

While Speke went out the front of the tent, Herne, out of ammunition, ran to the back, searching for his gunpowder or, failing that, the spears that they had tied to their tent pole. Leaving the tent before it collapsed around him, Burton peered through the darkness, seeing about twenty men crouching around the entrance. In the distance he could see others, among them the expedition's own men, throwing rocks, firing guns, slashing at their attackers with swords and spears. Glancing down, Burton saw what he thought was a body lying on the sand and, worried that it was one of his own men, began to fight his way toward it, dodging daggers and swinging clubs. Before he could get close enough to the body to find out who it was, however, the commander of his caravan, who had been fighting valiantly at his side, trying his best to protect Burton, suddenly stepped in front of him. Thinking he was one of the enemy, Burton turned, raised his saber, and was about to bring it down on his own man when he heard him cry out. "The well-known voice caused an instant's hesitation," Burton wrote, "at that moment a spearman stepped forward, and left his javelin in my mouth."

Although the man quickly disappeared, his javelin remained lodged in Burton's face, impaling him from cheek to cheek. His jaws were locked tight around the weapon, his palate shattered, and four of his back teeth knocked out. For the rest of his life, Burton would live with an indelible reminder of this one, terrifying night: a jagged, vertical scar that ran the length of his cheek. It would be the first thing that anyone who met him noticed, leaving them both startled and transfixed and only adding to his reputation as a dangerous man. Now, however, the javelin itself still protruded from both sides of his face, and Burton, unable to either push it through or pull it out, staggered under the pain and the heady loss of blood.

Reappearing at Burton's side, his caravan commander began to lead him to where he thought they might find Speke, Herne, and Stroyan. Before following him, Burton ordered one of his men to run to the harbor to find the Arab ship whose crew had had dinner with them only hours ago, to warn them of the attack and to ask for their help. Soon after the man set out for the harbor, Burton lost sight of his caravan commander in the darkness and was forced to struggle on by himself, the javelin still transecting his jaw. "I spent the interval before dawn wandering in search of my comrades, and lying down when overpowered with faintness and pain," he wrote. "As the day broke, with my remaining strength I reached the head of the creek, [and] was carried into the vessel."

The men aboard the ship were finally able to remove the javelin from Burton's face, and soon after he was relieved to see Herne climb aboard, bruised and battered but largely unharmed. Known for his photographic skills and mathematical mind, Herne had fought as hard as any man that night. Unable to find his powder horn in the tent, he had used the butt end of his revolver to strike out at the men in his path. He had then found refuge in an empty hut in the town and sent a messenger to the ship, stopping the crew just as they were about to set sail. Hearing Herne's story, Burton realized that their lives had "hung upon a thread. Had the vessel departed, as she intended ... nothing could have saved us from destruction."

Speke, however, was still fighting for his life. After lunging back out of the tent, seared by the thought that Burton had questioned his courage, he had immediately fired his revolver at three men in quick succession. Although unsure if he had hit any of them, he had at least frightened them away. Fumbling in the dark, he suddenly found himself at the edge of the ridge on which they were camped, surrounded by men on every other side. Pressing his revolver against the chest of the man directly in front of him, he pulled the trigger, but nothing happened. The trigger guard, he later guessed, must have jammed one of the cylinder caps, preventing it from rotating. With no time to think, he raised the revolver to strike the man in the face, when a powerful blow by a shillelagh, or wooden cudgel, to his chest caused his legs to suddenly give out from under him and he felt himself falling.

Several men quickly pinned Speke to the ground, wrenching his arms behind him. To his horror, after snatching the revolver from his hand, the man he had been about to shoot then thrust his hands between Speke's legs. "The way the scoundrel handled me sent a creeping shudder all over me. I felt as if my hair stood on end," Speke later wrote. "Not knowing who my opponents were, I feared that they belonged to a tribe called Eesa, who are notorious, not only for their ferocity in fighting, but for the unmanly mutilations they delight in." Finally realizing with a flood of relief that the man was only searching for concealed weapons, Speke lay helpless, his clothing now torn to shreds, staring at the men surrounding him while they shouted at him in Arabic and tied his hands behind his back with a rope.

The man Speke had tried to kill, who seemed to be in charge of the others, then took the end of the rope and pulled him to the back of the camp. Everywhere he looked, men lunged at him with their spears but seemed unwilling to harm him in front of his captor. "I was now becoming very weak and faint, and almost unable to breathe," he wrote. "A swelling had set in, which, with the tightness of the skin drawn over the chest, by my hands being tied behind, nearly prevented respiration." Using gestures and a few words of Arabic and Somali that he had picked up, Speke asked for his hands to be tied in front of him to make it easier to breathe, and for water and a place to lie down. His captor supplied everything he asked for, but continued to hold on to the rope.

Out of the jeering crowd, one man stepped forward and began speaking to Speke in Hindustani. Why, he wanted to know, was Speke in his country, where was he going, and, most important, was he Muslim. "Were I a good Mohammedan like themselves," Speke later recalled, "they would not touch me, but being a Christian I should be killed." Explaining that he wanted to see the country and was heading toward Zanzibar, Speke then said that he "was a Christian, and invited them, if it must be so, to dispatch their work at once." His inquisitor then turned to the other men standing near and translated for them what Speke had said. Bursting into laughter, they turned and left, intending to take what they could from the campsite.

Speke, left lying on the ground, his hands tied in front of him, could hear the sounds of the men around him. Some carried over their wounded comrades, who lay near Speke, tossing and turning, moaning in pain and calling for water. They were cared for attentively, their friends massaging their arms and legs, cleaning their wounds with water, and dropping dates into their curling palms, a Somali tradition for finding out how injured someone was. If they were too sick to eat even that delicacy, it was assumed that they did not have long to live. Others bent over the expedition's supplies, breaking boxes and tearing into bales of cloth. As the sun began to rise, Speke could see the damage that had been done. He also watched as the man who had been both his captor and his protector throughout the night now handed the rope tying his hands together to another man, telling him that he was going to oversee the distribution of property. This new man, who, to Speke's eyes, had "a very mean aspect," was to guard but also continue to protect the prisoner.

Not long after his original guard walked away, joining in the Somali victory song, three men walked up and stood over Speke, holding the spears that the expedition had left behind. One of the men raised his spear and brought it crashing down just a few inches to the side of Speke's body. Speke stared up at him, not moving or making a sound, as he repeated the threatening gesture, again and again. Finally, they left, Speke assuming that, had he cried out or showed fear of any kind, they would have killed him.

The man who had been left holding the rope, however, now stood over Speke in their place. Raising his own spear, he leaned down and, without hesitating, stabbed Speke. Shocked and arching his body in the only defense he could manage, Speke watched as the man stabbed him again, this time in the shoulder, dangerously close to his jugular. "I rose again as he poised his spear, and caught the next prod, which was intended for my heart, on the back of one of my shackled hands," Speke wrote. "This gouged the flesh up to the bone. The cruel villain now stepped back a pace or two, to get me off my guard, and dashed his spear down to the bone of my left thigh." Grabbing the spear with both hands, Speke held on to it as tightly as he could until the man finally picked up a club and smashed it into his arm, which collapsed as the spear dropped to the ground. Letting go of the rope attached to Speke's hands, the man now stepped back a dozen yards and, "rushing on me with savage fury," Speke wrote, "plunged his spear through the thick part of my right thigh into the ground, passing it between the thigh bone and large sinew below."

Speke suddenly realized that this man meant not just to torture him but to kill him. "With the action of lightning," he wrote, "seeing that death was inevitable if I remained lying there a moment longer, I sprang upon my legs, and gave the miscreant such a sharp back-hander in the face with my double-bound fists that he lost his presence of mind." Startled, the man gave Speke the only opportunity he needed, and, barefoot, nearly naked, bleeding and broken, he ran as fast as he could on his weak and gashed legs. The man threw his javelin, as did dozens of other men, who, looking up from their search of the campsite, tried to stop the escaping prisoner. Somehow, Speke was able to dodge men and spears as he raced toward the sea. Finally, seeing the last man give up the chase, he dared to rest on a mound of sand and, "fast fainting from loss of blood," used his teeth to tear open the knots that bound his hands.

Speke had, by some miracle, managed to escape with his life, but he had no idea what to do next, had nowhere to turn for help, and was too injured to run any farther or even to hide away and rest. "What a gloomy prospect was now before me," he wrote. "I was growing weaker every minute; my limbs were beginning to stiffen and the muscles to contract.... I must perish miserably by slow degrees, from starvation and exhaustion, in the dreary desert; far better, thought I, had the spear done its worst, and no lingering would have followed." At that moment, he looked up and saw four women standing not far away, beckoning to him. Although he could hardly walk, his right leg "nearly crooked up double," he managed to hobble over to where they stood watching him. To his astonishment and profound relief, they were the four Somali women the expedition had offered to hire so that they would not have to travel into the interior alone. In the next moment, several of the expedition's porters rushed up to join them and, holding Speke between them, carried him to the ship where Burton and Herne anxiously waited.

•

For those on board the only ship in Berbera's once crowded harbor, the new day brought both immense relief and stunning heartbreak. Soon after Speke was carried onto the ship, so torn and traumatized that he was close to unconsciousness, the captain, Yusuf, and his men returned from the camp, where they had gone at Burton's request, armed and ready to fight. Instead of a battle, however, they had found a deserted campsite, tents torn to the ground; animals stolen, dead, or dying; supplies ravaged, anything of value taken, from cloth and beads to travel and cooking supplies. The only items left behind were books and scientific instruments, for which Burton was deeply grateful. On the ground near his tent, however, where Burton had seen a dark and still shape in the midst of the fighting, the men had found William Stroyan.

They brought Stroyan's body back to the ship, where his friends waited in anguished silence. "Our lamented comrade was already stark and cold," Burton would later write. "A spear had traversed his heart, another had pierced his abdomen, and a frightful gash, apparently of a sword, had opened the upper part of his forehead: the body had been bruised with war-clubs, and the thighs showed marks of violence after death." Burton found it hard to reconcile Stroyan as he had seen him last, laughing and full of life as they sat in front of the tents telling stories after dinner, with the pale, stiffening corpse now lying before them. "We were overwhelmed with grief," he wrote. "We had lived like brothers."

Burton knew that his expedition was over before it had even begun. He was sickened by the magnitude of the loss—expensive supplies, nearly a year of his life, and an exceedingly rare opportunity to find one of the most sought after prizes in geographical history. Stroyan's death, however, eclipsed it all. "This was," he wrote, "the severest affliction that befell us." Although they left Berbera that night hoping to dig a grave in Aden befitting their brave friend, so quickly did his body begin to decompose that they had no choice but to bury him at sea. With the Somali coast disappearing in the distance, Stroyan's mutilated body slipped below the surface as Herne read a simple service, the second time in only a matter of months that both he and Burton had lost a friend. To Burton's mind, however, the fundamental difference between Stocks's death and Stroyan's was not the way in which they had died but the fact that, this time, he was to blame.

Part Two

———◆◆◆———

What Might Have Been, What Would Have Been

CHAPTER SIX

Into the Mouth of Hell

After the attack on his expedition in Somaliland, Burton returned home to a country at war. Begun nearly two years earlier, in the fall of 1853, the Crimean War pitted the Russians against an alliance of the British, French, and Ottoman Turkish, along with the Sardinia-Piedmont army, all fighting over access to holy sites in the Ottoman Empire and control over the Middle East. By the end, it would claim the lives of some three-quarters of a million people, most of whom would die not from battle wounds but from a stunning logistical incompetence that abandoned hundreds of thousands of men to disease, starvation, and merciless cold. Burton called the war "an unmitigated evil," but he knew that, as soon as he was well enough, he would find a way to join the fight. It seemed to him, he wrote, the only "opportunity of recovering my spirits."

Still struggling with the loss of his expedition and Stroyan's

brutal murder, Burton had been met in England not with congratulations for his success at Harar or even sympathy for the
attack in Berbera but with a rush of condemnation. Dr. George
Buist, famed journalist and editor of *The Bombay Times,* wrote a
scathing editorial attacking not just the failure of the expedition
but the very fact of its existence, which, he wrote, "did not promise any chance of success." Then he turned his sights directly on
its commander. After dismissing Burton as "a clever man, a good
writer, and a pleasant companion," he argued that he was "not a
philosopher.... Let him abjure science—it is not in his line," and
claimed that his failure to prevent the attack had endangered
not only the lives of his own men but the future of all British
endeavors in the region. "We have now," Buist claimed, "saddled
ourselves with a blood-feud of half a century's duration at least
with the most blood-thirsty set of cut-throats the world con-
tains."

Although William Coghlan, Outram's replacement as the
political resident in Aden, had been in tears at the foot of Speke's
sickbed, he now lashed out at all of the expedition's officers in
his official report. "It may seem harsh to criticize the conduct of
these officers who, to the grief of their wounds and the loss of
their property, must add the total failure of their long-cherished
scheme," he wrote, "but I cannot refrain from observing that
their whole proceeding is marked by a want of that caution and
vigilance, which the character of the people among whom they
dwell, ought to have suggested." He refused, moreover, to accept
Burton's explanation for the attack. "Although Lieut. Burton is
persuaded that the only object of this attack was the hope of
plunder and that blood was only shed in consequence of resistance," he wrote, "I am by no means satisfied that such was the
case." The tragedy could have been prevented, he insisted, with
"common prudence and forethought."

The men who had actually been at the camp in Berbera that night, however, the expedition's three surviving officers, all agreed that little could have been done to either avert the attack or to save the life of the man who had been lost. "The attack which occurred was an accident, not to be avoided by any of the ordinary methods of prudence," Herne wrote. "Under such overpowering numbers we had no chance." Their attackers had outnumbered them roughly eight to one. Even if every man in the expedition had been on watch throughout the night, they argued, the expedition would have been overwhelmed. "If all the guards had been on sentry that night and, if we had all been awake," Speke wrote, "I am certain that we could not have resisted the attack."

What Burton did not know was that, while Speke publicly defended the expedition, privately his thoughts had begun to turn against his commander. It was not a shortage of guards that had led to the attack that night, he would later claim, but "Burton's own confessed unpreparedness." Speke's pride, moreover, made it difficult for him to bear not only Burton's fame but his complete confidence in his own ability and his easy assumption of the role of leader, a position that Speke himself craved. "Burton's defying danger and bragging," Speke complained to Robert Playfair, Outram's assistant in Aden, "I regard as only so much clap-trap and not deserving of any notice."

Speke had also begun to rewrite the expedition in his own mind, making himself not simply a late addition to the group but its true commander. In his account of the attack, he would repeatedly refer to orders that he claimed to have given, decisions that he had made on behalf of the entire expedition, and feats of courage that he alone had performed. "He said that *he* was the Head of the Expedition," an outraged friend of Burton's would later write. "*He* had given the order for the night, it was before *him* the spies were brought, *he* was the first to turn out, and no one but *he* had the courage to defend himself. It is hardly worth while to contradict." Still nursing a grudge against Burton for insinuating that he had stepped back into the tent out of fear, Speke claimed that, on the contrary, out of the four officers only he had faced down their attackers. "Burton and Herne had run away with [Stroyan]," he claimed, "immediately after I left the central tent to fight."

Burton, moreover, had a maddening tendency to disregard what Speke considered to be not just his own contributions to the expedition but his own property. Believing that, as the leader of the expedition, it was his duty to put to public use anything that he and his men gathered during a government-funded expedition, Burton had assumed control of both Speke's journal and the natural history specimens he had collected during his aborted journey to the Wady Nogal. Burton had sent the entire collection to a British zoologist working in Calcutta named Edward Blyth, who had identified all of the species, including thirty-six birds, twenty mammals, three reptiles, a fish, and a scorpion. Publishing his findings in the *Journal of the Royal Asiatic Society of Bengal,* Blyth had added insult to injury by using only a handful of Speke's observations in his sixteen-page paper. To Burton, this public, scientific approach was the best use of the collection. To Speke, who had planned to add the specimens to the private natural history museum that he dreamed of building at Jordans, it was an outrage.

What Speke did not yet know, and would not learn until Burton's book about the expedition, *First Footsteps in East Africa,* was released two years later, was what Burton had done with his diary. Like other expedition leaders who had published their subordinates' journals in their own books, Burton had added Speke's to his appendices. What shocked and wounded Speke, however, was not the fact that Burton had published the diary but the heavy hand he had taken when editing it, casually cutting it nearly in half, from 24,000 words to 13,000, changing it from first person to third, and giving it a title that seemed calculated to further humiliate him: *Diary and Observations made by Lieutenant Speke, when Attempting to Reach the Wady Nogal.* More galling even than Burton pointing out that he had failed to complete his expedition was the commentary he had added at the end. "I venture to submit a few remarks upon the subject of the preceding diary," Burton wrote. "It is evident from the perusal of these pages that though the traveller... was delayed, persecuted by his 'protector,' and threatened with war, danger, and destruction, his life was never in real peril." Speke's failure, Burton believed, had been caused not by the situation in which he had found himself but by his own shortcomings as an explorer. Speke was "ignorant of the Moslem faith," Burton pointed out, and could not speak "either the Arabic or the Somali tongue." When he was finally given a copy of Burton's book, these words would fill Speke with impotent fury and a thirst for retribution. "Nothing," he wrote, "vexes the mind so much as feeling one's self injured in a way that cannot be prevented or avenged."

•

Whatever Speke lacked in languages and geographical knowledge he made up for in abundant youth and health, two things that Burton was steadily losing. Although Speke admitted that, in the days following the attack, he had been "a miserable-looking cripple, dreadfully emaciated from loss of blood, and with my arms and legs contracted into indescribable positions," he had already begun walking again before he left Aden just three weeks later. "A touching lesson how difficult it is to kill a man in sound health," Burton had written admiringly. The eleven stab wounds that Speke had sustained at the hands of his attackers had healed astonishingly fast, which he credited not only to his strong young body but to his long-vaunted discipline. "They literally closed as wounds do in an India-rubber ball after pricking with a penknife," he boasted. "It would be difficult to account for the rapidity with which my wounds closed, knowing, as everybody who has lived in Aden must do, that that is the worst place in the world for effecting cures, had I not, in addition to a strong constitution which I fortunately possess, been living for many months previously in a very abstemious manner...on dates, rice, and sour curds."

Only a few weeks after returning to England, Speke, to everyone's surprise but his own, was well enough to leave for the Crimean War. Finding the "summons for war...irresistible," he traveled to Marseilles, where he boarded a steamer bound for Constantinople. Despite his initial enthusiasm and the fact that he had been promoted to the rank of captain, Speke would see little of the war in his posting with a Turkish regiment. "I was more of a sportsman and traveller than a soldier," he later wrote, "and I only liked my profession when I had the sport of fighting."

While still on his way to the war, Speke befriended a young man on board his steamship named Laurence Oliphant, who was, in many ways, a kindred spirit. Although twenty-six years of age, just two years younger than Speke, Oliphant also remained closely tied to his patrician parents. His father, Sir Anthony Oliphant, was a member of the Scottish landed gentry and had served as chief justice in Ceylon, now Sri Lanka, with Laurence as his private secretary. Laurence now lived with both of his parents in London, in a house on the city's famous Half Moon Street, and his father was his companion on board the ship. Like his new friend, however, Oliphant had ambitions beyond his aristocratic family. He had published a pamphlet titled *The Coming Campaign,* in which he had laid out a plan to relieve the Turkish-held town of Kars in western Armenia, then under siege. He had also been angling to be sent alone into the Caucasus Mountains to meet with a Muslim leader named Schamyl, who was waging a guerrilla war against the Russians.

The war, in fact, was where Oliphant's interests diverged with Speke's. While Oliphant had immersed himself in battle-field strategy, Speke's thoughts had been far from the conflict in Crimea. Despite his near-death experience in Africa, which was by then widely known, he told Oliphant that he planned to return to the continent at the first opportunity. "Of course he is dying to go back and try again," Oliphant wrote home soon after meeting Speke, "but is going to take a turn to Sebastopol first." What Speke wanted to "try again," however, was no longer merely hunting in East Africa. He now coveted for himself the same prize that he knew Burton was chasing.

•

Burton, six years older and with far more miles on his battered body, had not recovered from the attack in Somaliland as quickly as Speke. After returning to England, he had needed the help of doctors and dentists before his jaw had finally begun to heal. When he was able to speak again without excruciating pain, he gave a talk before the Royal Geographical Society on his expedition to Harar and then took some time to see his scattered family, visiting his brother and sister in Boulogne, his father in Bath, and his mother's grave in Walcot cemetery. In the eyes of his adoring niece Georgiana Stisted, Burton remained "stalwart, erect, sound in wind and limb, in no particular had he the physique of one who had knocked at death's door more than once during the past twelve months." The trials he had endured, however, were still written upon "his handsome face," she wrote mournfully, which "was scarred by the lance which had transfixed his jaw and palate."

Although there was little Burton could do to fix his scarred face, he had done his best to seek retribution for his lost friend. Before leaving Aden, he had written to the government, asking them to avenge not just the expedition's losses but Stroyan's murder. "Lieutenant Burton," Speke later wrote, argued "that a ship should be sent to blockade their [the Somalis'] coast, with a demand that they should produce for trial in Aden the living bodies of the two men who so cruelly killed our lamented friend, and so wantonly endeavoured to dispatch me." The new political resident in Aden, Coghlan, had consequently laid out the terms of peace, which demanded that "the traffic in slaves through the [Somali] territories, including the port of Berbera, shall cease for ever," but also that the Somalis would "use their best endeavours to deliver up Ou Ali, the murderer of Lieutenant Stroyan."

Finally ready to try to put the tragedy behind him, Burton turned his attention to the war, although he had more contempt for Britain's own commanders and their allies than he did for the enemy. His country, he argued, was fighting largely because "a long sleep of peace" had made "England, at once the most unmilitary and the most fighting of peoples, 'spoil for a row.'" Two years into the war, Burton believed, they had not only been forced to play "second fiddle" to France, their long-loathed enemy from the Napoleonic Wars, but, worse, had lost "for ever the affection of Russia, our oldest and often our only friend amongst the continentals of Europe."

He would only spend four months in the Crimean War, arriving after the cruel winter of 1854 and leaving just before the war's end, but Burton would witness enough incompetence and corruption, from the buying of promotions to blatant favoritism for the British elite, to confirm his long-standing disdain for the military command. After a brief stop at the point from which Florence Nightingale had sailed to the Barrack Hospital only seven months earlier, Burton set out for Balaklava. The Sanitary Commission had been there a month before, attempting to clear the harbor of the infected and decaying amputated limbs that had been left behind in the wake of the infamous Battle of Bala-klava, during which more than 1,200 men had died in a single day.

It was during that battle that a unit of the British light cavalry was so ravaged by the enemy's guns that it inspired Tennyson's wrenching poem "The Charge of the Light Brigade." The brigade, led by James Brudenell, 7th Earl of Cardigan, had been sent on a suicidal mission that had left nearly half of its six hundred men either dead, captured, or wounded. Cardigan, who had paid tens of thousands of pounds for his appointment, the equivalent of millions of pounds today, not only survived the charge without injury but returned home to a hero's welcome. Boasting of feats of bravery that were later found to be largely untrue, he retired on his sprawling, fourteenth-century family estate. The men who had been under his command, however, had always known the truth. By the time Burton arrived in Crimea, the cavalry officers he met were "violently excited by reports that Lord Cardigan was about returning to command," he wrote, "and I heard more than one say, 'We will not serve under him.'"

To the people at home, Cardigan and men like him were portrayed as war heroes, and their fame was used not just to boost morale and encourage support for the war but to sell products. The Industrial Revolution that had fueled British economic power in the previous century had given way to what became known as the Second Industrial Revolution, which was now manufacturing everything from mass-produced firearms to cutlery and portable stoves. The latter could be used at home, manufacturers assured the British public, as could the new styles of clothing that were created for the men fighting on the front. Despite his men's disdain for him, an open-fronted wool vest that buttoned closed was christened "cardigan" in honor of the Earl of Cardigan, and a distinctive style of sleeve designed by the coat manufacturer Aquascutum for the British commander in chief, FitzRoy Somerset, 1st Baron Raglan, became known as the "raglan sleeve." Stretching in one continuous, diagonal piece from the cuff to the collar, rather than ending at the shoulder, the raglan sleeve allowed Raglan, who had lost his right arm forty years earlier during the Battle of Waterloo, to more easily swing his sword. Years later it would be adopted in the United States for baseball.

Raglan died in his tent the same day Burton reached Balaklava. "The unfortunate Lord Raglan, with his *courage antique,* his old-fashioned excess of courtesy, and his nervous dread," was, Burton wrote, "exactly the man *not* wanted." Raglan had never recovered from the infamy of letting thousands of men freeze and starve to death the previous winter. "It did not occur to the Government of the greatest engineering country in the world," Winston Churchill would write in disgust a hundred years later, "to ease the movement of supplies from the Port of Balaclava to the camp by laying down five miles of light railway." After issuing the order, tragically misconstrued, that precipitated the charge of the light brigade, Raglan sent thousands of young men, fresh from training, to their death at Sebastopol. "I could never return to England now," he had told an aide. "They would stone me to death."

After being turned away by Raglan's successor, General Sir James Simpson, Burton found a position as chief of staff to General W. F. Beatson, who had created a cavalry unit of Turkish irregulars that became known as Beatson's Horse. Although he liked Beatson, Burton saw nothing but dejection and a stunning lack of discipline among the men he met. "You cannot conceive of the miserable apathy, the ne'er do wellness of the Crimea," he wrote confidentially to Norton Shaw, secretary of the Royal Geographical Society. "Our poor fellows are sensibly dispirited." Beatson would later be accused of mutiny.

After doing what he could to improve the unit, establishing everything from saber training to daily drills, Burton began to look for ways to be useful to the war effort at large. Although he had no way of knowing it, two of the possibilities that occurred to him were the same ideas that Laurence Oliphant, the aristocratic young man Speke had met on the steamship, claimed as his own. Approaching the British ambassador to the Ottoman Empire, Lord Stratford de Redcliffe, Burton laid out a plan for the relief of Kars, which had been the subject of the pamphlet Oliphant had published before leaving for the war. Stratford in turn suggested to Burton that he enlist the help of the Muslim leader Schamyl, whom Oliphant had been trying for months to visit on behalf of the British military. Burton was at first interested in the expedition, but after learning that he would not be able to extend Schamyl any financial or military support, he turned down the offer, writing that Schamyl would "infallibly set me down for a spy, and my chance of returning to Constantinople will be uncommonly small."

Oliphant, on the other hand, although he had never been given permission to pursue either of his plans, had not given up. Still feeling ownership over the ideas, he was taken aback when Burton published a letter in *The Times* about Schamyl, which read, Oliphant's biographer would later write, "as if he were the only person ever to have thought of a diversion in the Caucasus." For Oliphant, this was just one more in a series of intersections with Richard Burton, who was already living the life that Oliphant, a budding linguist, writer, explorer, and even student of Islam, envisioned for himself.

Burton had never paid much attention to the admiration others felt for him, nor noticed how easily it turned to envy. Just as he was unaware of the resentment Speke had been nurturing since Somaliland, it did not occur to him that Oliphant, or anyone, might think that he had somehow stolen their ideas. It was this inability to see the jealousy directed toward him, or, if seen, to give it more than a moment's thought, that would in the end be more dangerous to him than any expedition he would ever take, and would lead to incalculable loss. "The tragedy again and again repeated of a great life maimed and marred by envious, eyeless mediocrities," one of his early biographers would lament. "What might have been, what would have been."

CHAPTER SEVEN

What a Curse Is a Heart

In August of 1856, four months after the signing of the Treaty of Paris ending the Crimean War, Burton's life took another dramatic turn. This time, however, instead of plunging into feverish study, far-flung exploration, or a continental war, he was astonished to find himself falling in love with a young woman he had met six years earlier. Her name was Isabel Arundell, and she was everything he was not—religious and aristocratic, pale-haired and blue-eyed, young and naive. He, on the other hand, was everything she wanted to be.

Born ten years almost to the day after Burton—his birthday was March 19, 1821, hers March 20, 1831—Isabel had been raised in a family that had deep roots in British history and held an iron grip on her young life. She was very aware of being an Arundell of Wardour, a devout Catholic family that could trace its lineage back to the Normans and was "one of the oldest and proudest houses of England," her biographer would later write, quoting the old song, "Ere William fought and Harold fell/There were Earls of Arundell." Her ancestry included a long list of famous names, from Sir Thomas Arundell, who was both a distant cousin to Henry VIII and related by marriage to both of the wives he had had beheaded, Anne Boleyn and Catherine Howard; to Henry, third Baron Arundell, who was imprisoned in the Tower of London for five years after being accused of involvement in the "Popish Plots" against King Charles II.

Isabel had been named for her father's first wife, who had been a close friend of her mother's and had died not long after giving birth to a little boy. After her death, Isabel's father, Henry Arundell, "a country gentleman pure and simple," as his daughter later described him, married Elizabeth Gerard, with whom he had eleven children. They were "great and small," Isabel explained. "I mean that some only lived to be baptized and died, some lived a few years, and some grew up." Although her father doted on her, calling her a "bit of 'perfect nature,'" her mother's love was more demanding and severe. "We trembled before her," Isabel wrote, "but we adored her."

While Burton had been largely left to his own devices as he was shuttled across Europe, Isabel had been raised in strict British discipline and structure. "Great attention was paid to our health, to our walks, to our dress, our baths, and our persons," she wrote. "Our food was good, but of the plainest; we had a head nurse and three nursery-maids.... The only times we were allowed downstairs were at two o'clock luncheon (our dinner), and to dessert for about a quarter of an hour if our parents were dining alone or had very intimate friends.... We were not allowed to speak unless spoken to; we were not allowed to ask for anything unless it was given to us. We kissed our father's and mother's hands, and asked their blessing before going upstairs, and we stood upright by the side of them all the time we were in the room." From the ages of ten to sixteen she attended school at a convent in Chelmsford, about forty miles outside of London, after which she moved back home to Essex.

The Arundell family home, Furze Hall, embodied the calm, quiet British life that Burton had never had. "It was a white, straggling, old-fashioned, half-cottage, half-farmhouse, built by bits...buried in bushes, ivy, and flowers," Isabel would fondly recall. "Creepers covered the walls and the verandahs, and crawled in at the windows, making the house look like a nest." Just under her bedroom window was a "pretty honeysuckle and jessamine porch," she wrote, "in which wrens and robins built their nests, and birds and bees used to pay me a visit on summer evenings." Most days, she would walk to the woods just down the lane, book in hand. "As far as books were concerned, I brought myself up," she said. Her favorite was *Tancred,* a religious novel by Benjamin Disraeli, "with its glamour of the East." "I used to think out after a fashion my future life, and try to solve great problems," she wrote. "I was forming my character."

Isabel was torn between her religious convictions and filial obedience, and a growing desire for a larger, less conventional, more adventurous life than she was expected to live. Early on, she found a way to escape from her predictable world and her mother's tightening grip by befriending a group of Romani who had set up camp near her home. She knew that her mother would be furious if she found out, but to Isabel the pull of the Romani was irresistible. "I was enthusiastic about gypsies," she later wrote, "and everything Eastern and mystic, and especially about a wild and lawless life." She visited them as often as she dared, helping when she could, if they were sick "or got into a scrape with the squires anent poultry, eggs, or other things." Eventually, she developed a close relationship with a tall, refined-looking woman named Hagar. "When they were only travelling tinkers or basket-menders, I was very obedient," she wrote, "but wild horses would not have kept me out of the camps of the oriental, yet English-named, tribes." Hagar herself, who had nicknamed Isabel "Daisy," had an English last name that would later have profound meaning for her young friend: Burton.

One day when Isabel visited the Romani camp, Hagar told her that they were about to leave. She had, however, cast Isabel's horoscope, and she wanted to share it with her. Translating it from Romani for Isabel, she said, "You will cross the sea, and be in the same town with your Destiny and know it not. Every obstacle will rise up against you, and such a combination of circumstances, that it will require all of your courage, energy, and intelligence to meet them. Your life will be like one swimming against big waves; but God will be with you, so you will always win. You will fix your eye on your polar star, and you will go for that without looking right or left." The horoscope contained everything Isabel had ever wanted for her life: excitement, adventure, the unknown. Instead of the tradition and discipline that had constricted her since childhood, it promised her a life of challenges and dangers, a chance to live by her own strength and wits.

Years later, Isabel would insist that Hagar had then added to her prediction, with a specificity that would astonish her by its accuracy: "You will bear the name of our tribe," she said Hagar told her. "You shall have plenty to choose from, and wait for years; but you are destined to him from the beginning. The name of our tribe shall cause you many a sorrowful, humiliating hour; but when the rest who sought him in the heyday of his youth and strength fade from his sight, you shall remain bright and purified to him as the morning star." Although the Romani Burtons were leaving Furze Hall, their name, Hagar promised, would one day belong to Isabel. "The name we have given you will be yours, and the day will come when you will pray for it, long for it, and be proud of it."

•

Isabel did not leave England for the first time until she was nineteen years old, when she traveled with her family to Boulogne. Having lived her entire life in what, for her, had been the gentle, protecting arms of England, she had the opposite feeling Richard and Edward Burton had had years earlier, when they had finally been freed from their hated boarding school to return to Europe. As Isabel watched the white cliffs fade from view, she had, she later wrote, "never felt so patriotic." At the same time, she was thrilled by her first taste of adventure. Sitting on the deck of her ship, she was reminded of the words of Hagar Burton. "I remembered that Hagar had told me I should cross the sea," she wrote, "and then I wondered why we had chosen Boulogne."

For the rest of Isabel's life, she would believe that the answer to that question came walking toward her the day she visited the city's famous ramparts. As she studied the ancient stone fortifications, she was startled to see a man looking straight at her. "He had very dark hair...a brown, weather-beaten complexion; straight Arab features; a determined-looking mouth and chin, nearly covered by an enormous black moustache," she wrote. "But the most remarkable part of his appearance was two large, black, flashing eyes with long lashes, that pierced one through and through. He had a fierce, proud, melancholy expression; and when he smiled, he smiled as though it hurt him." He was, she realized, "the vision of my awakening brain."

After her first season as a debutante, when she had been introduced to the suffocating world of chaperones, haughty footmen in powdered wigs, and enormous, layered dresses, Isabel had learned something about herself: She would much sooner live the life of a spinster than marry one of the simpering, soft-handed "mannikins" she had met in London. "I sometimes wonder if they are men at all, or merely sexless creatures—animated tailors' dummies," she had written with disgust.

Whatever her mother's expectations, Isabel knew that on this one point she would not give in. She would choose a husband for herself. "As God took a rib out of Adam and made a woman of it, so do I, out of a wild chaos of thought, form a man unto myself," she had written, and then proceeded to describe this ideal man in minute detail: "black hair, a brown complexion... large, black wondrous eyes.... He is a soldier, and a man; he is accustomed to command and to be obeyed.... He is a man who owns something more than a body; he has a head and heart, a mind and soul. He is one of those strong men who lead, the mastermind who governs."

As clearly as she could see this man in her mind's eye, Isabel had always believed him to be merely a "myth of my girlhood." That changed the day she met Richard Burton on the ramparts. He seemed to have stepped out of her diary, created from the words she had written to describe the only man she would marry. When she saw Burton standing before her, she was "completely magnetized," she later wrote. "He looked at me as though he read me through and through in a moment." Turning to her sister, she whispered, "That man will marry me."

Isabel returned to the ramparts the following day, and so did Burton. When she and her sister stopped on the stone promenade, he walked up to them holding a piece of chalk and wrote on the wall: "May I speak to you?" Picking up the chalk that he had left for her, she wrote in reply: "No; mother will be angry." She was right. Her mother found out about Isabel's brief, scrawled conversation with Richard Burton, and she was not only angry but determined to keep her daughter as far as possible from this dangerous man.

Burton was the last man Elizabeth Arundell wanted for a son-in-law. Not only was he ten years older, with a shockingly wide range of experiences, while her daughter was young, sheltered, and naive, but he was poor and unconnected. Although, as a Catholic, Elizabeth knew what it was like to be shunned by British society, she had raised Isabel to marry into that world, to be the wife of "a wealthy peer." She refused to admit that her daughter was falling in love with a penniless explorer. When Isabel turned "red and pale, hot and cold, dizzy and faint, sick and trembling" each time she saw Burton, her mother would bring in a doctor, insisting that her daughter's "digestion was out of order." The doctor would dutifully prescribe a pill for Isabel, which she would throw into the fire at the first opportunity.

Before Isabel's family returned home to London after their two-year sojourn in Boulogne, her cousins threw a party, inviting everyone they knew, among them Richard Burton. "He waltzed with me once," she wrote years later, still holding tight to the memory, "and spoke to me several times." Afterward, she carefully laid aside the sash and gloves she had been wearing that night because he had touched them while they danced. "I never wore them again," she wrote. On the journey back to London, she wrapped herself in a cloak, climbed into one of the lifeboats that was tied to the side of the ship, and thought about how different she was from the girl who had left England two years earlier, and "how much of my destiny had been fulfilled."

•

Four years would pass before Isabel saw Burton again. Instead of losing interest, however, her obsession only grew. She prayed for him every night, carefully kept the gloves he had once touched, and filled her diary with thoughts of him. She also watched him from afar, reading everything he wrote and every article written about him, hungrily taking in the adventures he was having, the great things he was accomplishing, without her. "Richard has just come back with flying colours from Mecca; but instead of coming home, he has gone to Bombay to rejoin his regiment," she wrote in her diary two years after leaving Boulogne. "I glory in his glory." A year later, she worried as he set off again, this time for East Africa. "And now Richard has gone to Harar, a deadly expedition or a most dangerous one, and I am full of sad forebodings," she wrote. "Will he never come home?"

Isabel wanted Richard to come home not so she could settle down with him but so that, when he left again, he would take her with him. Marrying Richard Burton was her only hope of escaping the small, stifling life her mother had planned for her. "I should love Richard's wild, roving, vagabond life.... I long to rush around the world in an express; I feel as if I shall go mad if I remain at home," she wrote. "What others dare I can dare. And why should I not? Who misses us? Why should we not have some useful, active life? Why, with spirits, brains, and energies, are women to exist upon worsted work and household accounts? It makes me sick, and I will not do it."

Growing up, Isabel had wanted not just to marry an adventurous man, but to be one. Her father, she said, had "brought me up like a boy, teaching me to ride and shoot, everything, in fact that would suit me for my after life of adventure and peril." She "worship[ped] ambition," she wrote, and dreamed of being her own driving force, of having "the will and power to change the face of things." Isabel feared that both her father's lessons and her own dreams would be wasted on a life of quiet, womanly work. Burton, she had realized as soon as she met him, could change that. "I wish I were a man; if I were, I would be Richard Burton," she wrote in her diary. "But as I am a woman, I would be Richard Burton's wife."

The only problem was that Burton seemed not only completely unaware of her fervent devotion to him, but, she thought, uninterested in a girl like her. She knew that he had already had many romances with exotic, experienced women, who, as his niece would later write, were either "pretty or handsome... ugly ones he wouldn't look at." In Boulogne, he had carried on a "serious flirtation" with a strikingly pretty cousin of Isabel's named Louisa, which it had been agony for her to witness. Isabel considered herself to be in "the ugliest stage of my life," she wrote. "I was tall, plump, and meant to be fair, but was always tanned and sunburnt.... I was too fat to slip into what is usually called 'our stock size,' and my complexion was by no means pale and interesting enough to please me.... I used to envy maypole, broomstick girls, who could dress much prettier than I could. I was either fresh and wild with spirits, or else melancholy and full of pathos." She could not imagine that Burton would ever fall in love with her, but neither could she imagine living without him. "What a curse is a heart!" she scrawled in her diary.

Isabel still clung to the dream that Burton might one day notice her, but in the meantime she refused to simply wait in her room, hoping he would come home. During the Crimean War, she repeatedly begged to be made a battlefield nurse, working under the guidance of Florence Nightingale, but she was turned away each time. "How I envy the women who are allowed to go out as nurses!" she wrote. "I have written again and again to Florence Nightingale; but the superintendent has answered me that I am too young and inexperienced, and will not do." Finally she decided that, if she could not help the soldiers themselves she would help their wives, many of whom had been left nearly destitute in England while their husbands were away fighting. "My plan was to be some little use at home," she wrote. "We started a subscription soup-cauldron and a clothing collection.... No destitute woman was to be left out, nor any difference made on account of religion.... Lodging, food, and clothes were given according to our means, and words of comfort to all." The roughly 150 women who joined the club Isabel founded, the Stella Club, made their rounds twice a week, not only bringing provisions but visiting the sick and dying, reading to them, and writing letters to their loved ones. Isabel would never forget the wretchedness she witnessed during that time. "I cannot attempt to describe the scenes of misery we saw," she later wrote, "nor the homes that we saved, nor the gratitude of the soldiers later when they returned from the war and found what we had done."

After Burton had himself returned from the war, Isabel was at the famous Ascot Racecourse in Berkshire when she was stunned to see an old friend: Hagar Burton. After clasping Isabel's hand, Hagar asked her, "Are you Daisy Burton yet?" Shaking her head, Isabel replied, "Would to God I were!" Hagar's face, Isabel later wrote, lit up. "Patience," she said. "It is just coming." At that moment, Hagar, who, as a Romani, was often treated with arrogant disrespect and even violence, was forced to hurriedly wave goodbye to her friend as she was shoved away from a carriage. "I never saw her again," Isabel wrote.

Two months later, as she was walking through London's Botanical Gardens with her sister Blanche and a friend, Isabel saw the man she had been thinking and dreaming of since the day they had met six years earlier. This time, Burton was not alone. With him was the "gorgeous creature of Boulogne," Isabel later wrote, Louisa, the pretty cousin she had then been so jealous of, but who was now married to someone else. "We immediately stopped and shook hands, and asked each other a thousand questions of the four intervening years, and all the old Boulogne memories and feelings which had lain dormant, but not extinct, returned to me," she wrote. Burton then asked Isabel if she came to the gardens often. "Oh yes," she replied, "we always come and read and study here from eleven to one, because it is so much nicer than staying in the hot rooms at this season." "That is quite right," Burton said, then asked her what she was studying. Isabel showed him the book she was carrying—Disraeli's *Tancred,* which Burton then proceeded to explain to her. Isabel listened intently although she had been reading *Tancred,* "the book of my heart and tastes," since childhood. As she walked away, Isabel heard Burton say to Louisa, "Do you know that your cousin has grown charming? I would not have believed that the little schoolgirl of Boulogne would have become such a sweet girl." Her cousin's only reply, Isabel later wrote, was "'Ugh!' with a tone of disgust."

When Isabel returned to the gardens the following day, Burton was there, alone this time, working on a poem. Looking up, he said teasingly, "You won't chalk up 'Mother will be angry' now, will you?" As the days passed, they continued to meet. Walking through the gardens together, Isabel "trod on air." After two weeks, Burton put his arm around her waist, pressed his cheek to hers, and proposed. "Could you do anything so sickly as to give up civilization?" he asked. "And if I can get the Consulate of Damascus, will you marry me and go and live there?" Not knowing that Isabel had thought of little else than marrying him for the past six years, he then said, "Don't give me an answer *now,* because it will mean a very serious step for you—no less than giving up your people, and all that you are used to."

So overcome with emotion was Isabel that, for a moment,

she could not speak. "It was just as if the moon had tumbled down and said, 'I thought you cried for me, so I came,'" she later wrote. Misunderstanding her silence, Burton said, "Forgive me! I ought not to have asked so much." But Isabel, in a rush of words, finally replied, "I don't want to 'think it over'—I have been 'thinking it over' for six years, ever since I first saw you at Boulogne on the ramparts. I have prayed for you every day, morning and night. I have followed all your career minutely. I have read every word you ever wrote, and I would rather have a crust and a tent with you than be Queen of all the world." When Burton, who had no illusions about what Isabel's mother thought of him, said, "Your people will not give you to me," Isabel, now twenty-five years old and with a far greater understanding of her place in the world, answered swiftly and confidently, "I know that, but I belong to myself—I give myself away."

•

Isabel had always known that Burton would leave again. He had made no secret of the fact that he had returned from the war with plans to "turn his attention to the 'Unveiling of Isis,'" as she put it, "discovering the sources of the Nile." One afternoon in October, a few months after their engagement, which they had kept a secret, he drew for her a simple sketch of what he thought the Lake Regions of East Africa would look like. In return, she reached up and secured a steel chain around his neck, dangling from which was a medal of the Blessed Virgin, "which we Catholics commonly call 'the miraculous medal,'" she wrote.

That night Isabel could not sleep. Around 2:00 in the morning, she saw what she later claimed was an apparition. It was Burton, opening her bedroom door and stepping inside. "A current of warm air came towards my bed. He said, 'Goodbye, my poor child. My time is up, and I have gone, but do not grieve. I shall be back in less than three years, and I am your destiny. Goodbye.' He held up a letter—looked at me with those Gypsy eyes, and went slowly out, shutting the door." Jumping from her bed, Isabel raced into the hall but found it empty. Going to her brother's room, she sat down and began crying, insisting that Richard was gone. "Nonsense," he told her, "you have only got a nightmare."

The next morning, Isabel, who had spent most of the night curled up in a chair in her brother's room, looked up as her sister Blanche walked in, holding a letter. In the mail that morning she had found an envelope addressed to her and was surprised to find inside two letters from Burton. The first letter was for Blanche, asking her to break the news of his leaving for Africa gently to her sister and to give Isabel the second letter. That letter "assured me," Isabel wrote, that "we should be reunited in 1859." Placing the letter in a small bag, Isabel tied it onto a chain which she then slipped over her head, proudly wearing Burton's message as he did her miraculous medal.

CHAPTER EIGHT

Horror Vacui

When John Hanning Speke returned home from the Crimean War in February of 1856, the first thing he did after meeting with Richard Burton was to visit the map room of the Royal Geographical Society. The Society had yet to find a permanent home, beginning life more than a quarter of a century earlier in a few rooms at the Horticultural Society on Regent Street before moving to a slightly larger space ten years later and then, in 1854, leasing its current apartment at 15 Whitehall Place. The five-story, white stone building was chosen primarily for one reason: It could hold the Society's rare and extensive map collection, which extended "from the earliest period of rude geographical delineations to the most improved of the present time."

Among the founding aims of the Society, the collection included thousands of maps, atlases, globes, and charts, sketched on scraps of paper, hand printed in bound journals, and engraved on yellowing cloth. It was largely because of this fascinating collection, which was open to the public and "daily visited by intelligent strangers," that the Royal Geographical Society received government funding. Although the vast majority of its members were well-to-do, or at least well connected, not many actually paid their dues, leaving the Society to rely on government aid not just to fund expeditions but to pay rent. The annual grant of £500 provided by Her Majesty's Treasury was used to cover the new accommodations and to hire the map collection's first curator, Trelawney Saunders.

The collection that Saunders oversaw was useful to future expeditions, but it also charted one of the most important advances in the history of cartography: Not the filling in of blank spots on maps, but the creation of them. Before the eighteenth century, many European mapmakers had what art historians refer to as *horror vacui,* a fear of leaving empty spaces. When drawing parts of the world for which they had no firsthand information, they relied on rumor, conjecture, or their own imaginations, adding to their maps sea monsters and mythical islands, decorative creatures and imaginary mountains. As cartography entered the Age of Enlightenment, however, it moved from the realm of art into that of science. Limited to using only information for which they had reliable, eyewitness evidence, modern European mapmakers had no choice but to leave blank large sections of the world, especially when drawing the continent of Africa.

Between the fifteenth and nineteenth centuries, European depictions of Africa changed dramatically. One of the oldest known maps of the continent, created in the mid-sixteenth century by a German mapmaker who later died of the plague, features a drawing of a naked, one-eyed giant where Nigeria and Cameroon should be. Roughly a hundred years later, the Dutch mapmaker Willem Janszoon Blaeu attempted to camouflage his ignorance of the continent by filling the interior of his map with illustrations of some of Africa's most famous animals, from lions and elephants to ostriches, and the oceans surrounding it with Dutch ships sailing among mythical creatures such as a half horse, half sea serpent. By 1805, however, British cartographer John Cary openly admitted on his map of Africa all that he did not know, leaving blank nearly everything below the equator besides a few small features hugging the coastline. Nearly fifty years later, just five years before Speke walked into the Royal Geographical Society for the first time, the editor R. Montgomery Martin wrote a note to accompany a map that was exhibited at London's Great Exhibition of 1851 and featured large expanses of blank space in both equatorial and southern Africa. "More than five-sixths of the region are still unknown to European Geographers," he explained. "Of the alleged Mountains of the Moon we know nothing." It was one of the central constructs of Western cartography: Until a region had been mapped by Europeans, even if it had been occupied by millions of people over millennia, the land and everything in it was considered a mystery.

Of course, African land was not a mystery to the people who lived there, but not only was information obtained from widely traveled Africans, from merchants to messengers, largely dismissed, but so were their own forms of cartography. Little has been written about early African mapmaking, but it ranged widely from rock art to schematic maps to scarification. Ephemeral maps, often drawn on the ground, were occasionally described in journals or sketched on paper by foreign travelers, but rarely did they make the transfer to European or North American maps with attribution and without alteration.

•

One map in particular stood out among the many that adorned the walls of the Royal Geographical Society. On loan from the Church Missionary Society, it had been drawn two years earlier by the German missionaries Jakob Erhardt and Johannes Rebmann, after their flash of insight concerning the source of the White Nile. Immediately exciting interest in scientific communities across Europe, the map had already been printed in several publications, from the missionary magazine *Das Calwer Missionblatt* to the scholarly *The Athenaeum,* before reaching the Royal Geographical Society in the summer of 1855.

A simple sketch of East Africa without embellishments, the map was notable only for a single feature: a great blue "inland sea," which Erhardt and Rebmann had drawn where most mapmakers believed a desert to be. Not only was the body of water enormous, eight hundred miles long by three hundred miles wide, beginning at the equator and stretching to the 14th degree of south latitude, but it was so strangely shaped that even the most experienced geographers struggled to describe it. Burton referred to it as a "hideous inflated leech," but for most who saw the map, the word "slug" leapt to mind. "In this section-map, swallowing up about half of the whole area of the ground included in it, there figured a lake of such portentous size and such unseemly shape, representing a gigantic slug, or, perhaps, even closer still, the ugly salamander, that everybody who looked at it incredulously laughed and shook his head," Speke later wrote. "It was, indeed, phenomenon enough in these days to excite anybody's interest."

The appearance of Erhardt and Rebmann's "slug map" had caused an immediate stir at the Royal Geographical Society. It had brought a deep sense of satisfaction to the revered armchair geographer William Cooley, who, Burton later wrote, "still stood upon his 'Single Sea,' and considered any one who dared to make two or three of it his personal enemy." It had also given a sense of urgency to the Society's long-held but largely latent interest in finding the source of the White Nile.

The formation of the East African Expedition, as it came to be known, found the support of one of the Society's most esteemed members, Admiral Sir George Back. A legendary explorer himself, Back had been on John Franklin's first Arctic expedition as a very young man nearly forty years earlier, and, later, on the infamous voyage of the HMS *Terror,* which had been trapped in ice so thick it was rumored to have squeezed the turpentine from the ship's planks. Now sixty years old, Back wanted someone to solve the greatest geographical mystery of his age. Richard Burton, he believed, was the man for the job.

Burton himself had already suggested a similar expedition to the Society. Although his proposal had outlined a journey to the Lake Regions of East Africa, to be the first European to study "the limits of the 'Sea of Ujiji,' [also known as Lake Tanganyika] and secondarily to determine the exportable produce of the interior and the ethnography of its tribes," he had known as well as Back did what his real job would be. "In these days every explorer of Central Africa is supposed to have set out in quest of the coy sources of the White Nile," he wrote, "and when he returns without them, his exploration, whatever may have been its value, is determined to be a failure." When Burton received his official instructions from the Royal Geographical Society, therefore, he was not surprised to find among them the order to march north to "the range of mountains marked upon our maps as containing the probable sources of the Bahr-el-Abyad [White Nile], which it will be your next great object to discover."

What Burton needed now was a second in command, and, despite their painful past, he turned to Speke. He chose Speke, he would later explain, because he "had suffered with me in purse and person at Berberah, and because he, like the rest of the party, could obtain no redress." Speke, knowing that he had no ability to put together such an elaborate expedition on his own, had originally decided to return to the Caucasus Mountains. Although he had left his friend Edmund Smyth in the lurch two years earlier, when he had gone to Somaliland with Burton instead of traveling with Smyth as planned, he wrote to him again, suggesting that they resurrect their abandoned hunting trip. Smyth had quickly agreed and the two had begun making plans, even buying guns and other equipment for their journey. Speke had then written to Norton Shaw at the Royal Geographical Society, asking for help in acquiring passports that would allow them to cross into Russia. In reply, Shaw had not only warned Speke that he would have little chance of entering Russia so soon after the war but had informed him that Richard Burton was returning to Africa. The same day that Shaw's letter arrived, Speke also received one from Burton himself, inviting him to join his expedition. "This settled the matter. Without a second thought I disposed of my Caucasian equipments," Speke wrote, apparently unconcerned that in the process he had also, once again, disposed of Smyth.

For Speke, Erhardt and Rebmann's strange slug map that he saw at the Royal Geographical Society represented not just an oddity or a mystery, but potentially valuable insight into the mission he was about to undertake with Burton. "Here was revealed to me, for the first time," he wrote, "the great objects designed for the expedition in question." Although he would much rather be leading his own expedition, and he had grave doubts about the man who would be commanding this one, he was willing to take nearly any chance if it meant being sent to search for the source of the White Nile.

Although the Society had chosen Burton to lead the expedition and agreed to let him use its name and connections, it was able to offer little of what he needed most: funding. Thanks in large part to the substantial personal connections of the Society's current president, Sir Roderick Murchison, the Foreign Office had agreed to provide the expedition with a £1,000 grant, although with great reluctance. The East India Company had at first promised to match these funds but in the end had backed out, offering Burton only two years' leave of absence and a free ride to Zanzibar. Burton knew that the funding was not nearly enough for the type of expedition he was expected to carry out, but he also knew that, no matter how persuasive his arguments, he would not receive a shilling more.

The year before, Jakob Erhardt had requested little more than £200 to hire twenty porters for a four-hundred-mile march into the East African interior. Erhardt's woefully inadequate estimate, Burton wrote, "was highly injurious to future travelers; either he knew the truth, and he should have named a reasonable estimate, or he was ignorant of the subject, and he should have avoided it." Either way, the result was that Burton had been given only £1,000 to fund an expedition that would easily cost five times as much.

When Speke learned how severely underfunded the expedition would be, he nearly pulled out. Agreeing that the expedition to Somaliland had caused him significant suffering even beyond his eleven stab wounds, he had written angrily to Robert Playfair, assistant resident in Aden, that he had been "a great loser by reputation as well as by pocket in consequence of the failure." The only reason he now agreed to continue with the

East African Expedition, he later claimed, was not because he needed Burton but because Burton needed him. "Captain Burton...knew nothing of astronomical surveying, of physical geography, or of collecting specimens," Speke wrote, "so he pressed me again to go with him, and even induced the President of the Royal Geographical Society to say there need be no fear of money if we only succeeded."

·

Burton looked forward to the expedition with a singular relish. "Of the gladdest moments in human life, methinks, is the departure upon a distant journey into unknown lands," he wrote. "Shaking off with one mighty effort the fetters of Habit, the leaden weight of Routine." Before he could sail to Africa, however, he had to make an overland journey to Bombay to secure Speke's leave. The two men only stayed in India for a week, but while there they were able to stock up on scientific instruments and hire two young Goanese men, Valentine Rodriguez and Gaetano Andrade, as cooks for the expedition. As promised, the East India Company then gave them a ride to Zanzibar on the *Elphinstone*, a 387-ton sloop-of-war named for the governor of Bombay.

On the way to Africa, they stopped in Aden, where Burton hoped to convince Dr. John Steinhaüser, who was stationed there as a civil surgeon, to join the expedition. Burton had met Steinhaüser in India years earlier, when they were both taking language exams, and he had visited him after his journey to Mecca, when the two men had discussed collaborating on a "full, complete, unvarnished, uncastrated" translation of *The Arabian Nights*. Steinhaüser was a "sound scholar, a good naturalist, a

skillful practitioner," Burton wrote, but he was also "endowed ...
with even more inestimable personal qualities." Steinhaüser
immediately agreed to join the expedition, but he would have
to wait for approval from the British East India Company before
leaving for Zanzibar.

Back on board the *Elphinstone,* Burton spent most of the
more than two-week journey reading everything he could about
the island where their expedition would finally begin. He and
Speke also examined the equipment—sextants, barometers, and
thermometers—that they had picked up in Bombay and would
rely on to take scientific measurements. His experience on the
ship, compared to nearly any sea journey Burton had taken in
the past, was a pleasure. "The order, coolness, and cleanliness of
a ship of war," he wrote, "no rattling, heaving throbs ... no cabins
rank with sulphuretted hydrogen, no decks whereon pallid and
jaundiced passengers shake convulsed shoulders as they rush to
and from the bulwarks and the taffrail." By the time he looked up
from his books and his notes, Zanzibar lay before them.

Part of an archipelago consisting of a series of small islands
as well as two main islands—Zanzibar itself, more formally
known as Unguja, and Pemba—Zanzibar had been occupied
for at least seventeen thousand years before the first European,
the Portuguese explorer Vasco da Gama, landed there in 1498.
Searching for a sea route between Europe and India, da Gama
realized what the Africans and Arabs had long known—with a
harbor that was both protected and easily defended, Zanzibar
was the perfect launching pad for both trade and exploration.
Two hundred years later, the Sultanate of Oman defeated the
Portuguese, taking control of the island and large swaths of the
Swahili coast, developing clove plantations, and creating one of
history's most infamous slave markets. European explorers soon
realized that here they could find everything they would need—

from food and local currency, usually beads and cloth, to porters and guides—for their long journeys into the interior.

From the sea, Burton's first impression of Zanzibar was of peaceful, languid beauty. Surrounded by sapphire blue waters and blindingly white beaches, the interior of the six-hundred-square-mile limestone island was made green and shady by a profusion of coconut palms and mango trees, first brought from India. "Truly prepossessing was our first view of the then myste-rious island of Zanzibar, set off by the dome of distant hills, like solidified air, that form the swelling line of the Zanzibar coast," he wrote. "Earth, sea, and sky, all seemed wrapped in a soft and sensuous repose, in the tranquil life of the Lotus Eaters." As it grew dark, the beach sparkled with a profusion of tiny lights that looked to the men on the ship like glowworms. The screams and shouts of the red colobus monkeys, endemic to the island, drifted toward them, as did the rich, spicy scent of the island's famous clove plantations.

Burton knew, however, that the people harvesting the cloves had arrived in a reeking, pitching, perilously overcrowded slave boat that bore no resemblance to the comfort and safety of the *Elphinstone*. Like others at the time, Burton and Speke were unapologetic in their racism, with all of its attendant arrogance and ignorance, but they were sickened by the slave trade, which, Burton wrote, "had made a howling desert of the land," and took great pride in their country's efforts to end it. But although Britain had passed the Abolition of the Slave Trade Act fifty years earlier and had begun to patrol the Indian Ocean near Zanzibar, looking for slave ships, little had changed in East Africa, where the shackling and selling of human beings was still a common and daily occurrence. "Zanzibar is a peculiar place," Burton wrote to a friend. "An admirable training ground for damnation."

•

When the small boat that had taken them to shore landed on the island, the men made their way toward the British consulate, crossing a wide stretch of beach to what looked to Burton like a "claret-chest, which lay on its side, comfortably splashed by the sea." There, greeting them with a warm but wan smile, was Lieutenant Colonel Atkins Hamerton, a tall, dark-eyed Irishman who had been the British consul in Zanzibar for the past fifteen years. Hamerton looked older than his fifty-two years, with fully white hair and beard and a complexion that Burton once knew to be "fair and ruddy" but was now "bleached ghastly pale by ennui and sickness." Although he was "full of amusing anecdotes" and eager to help, it was obvious to Burton that Hamerton was dying. "The worst symptom in his case—one which I have rarely found other than fatal," Burton wrote, "was his unwillingness to quit the place which was slowly killing him."

Recently, Hamerton had been doing his best to navigate a particularly difficult transition in Zanzibar, following the death only two months earlier of its most recent sultan, Saʿīd ibn Sulṭān. The sultan, who had ruled over both Zanzibar and Oman, had been succeeded by his son, Sayyid Majid, one of the oldest of his father's twenty-five sons and multitude of daughters, all born to concubines. Majid's older brother, Thuwaini bin Said, however, believed that the inheritance should rightfully have been his. In compensation, the sultanate was divided. Thuwaini was made the sultan of Muscat and Oman, a much weaker, poorer realm than that of his younger brother, and Majid promised to pay him an annual tribute.

Hamerton now told Burton and Speke with sympathy that not only was there political upheaval but they had chosen the worst time of year to arrive in Zanzibar for an expedition such as theirs. Burton had known that this would be the case when they left England but believed that he had to set out immediately or risk having no expedition at all. Now in Zanzibar, they were not only in the middle of the dry season, when it was almost impossible to find water in large stretches of the terrain through which they'd be traveling, but just about to enter the vernal monsoon, "when everything," Speke wrote, "would be deluged."

They would not be able to leave for the interior until June, Burton realized, which was six months away. It would take at least a month to organize the expedition, hiring guides and porters, buying supplies and pack animals. Burton decided to use the remaining time to explore as much of the East African coast as possible, taking exhaustive notes about the region along the way—thousands of pages on everything from the local languages to the animal and plant life, politics, climate, geography, and ethnography. He would also take advantage of the opportunity to meet with Johannes Rebmann.

Before leaving London, Burton had visited the Church Missionary Society at its headquarters in Salisbury Square, offering to deliver a message for them to Rebmann. The missionary had been gone from Europe for years and, lately, had stopped answering their letters. The society now wanted to know, Burton wrote, why Rebmann had not acknowledged "in any way, either by letter or message, the communication of his employers." The Royal Geographical Society had also encouraged Burton to meet with Rebmann, who had not only helped to draw the famous "slug map" but was familiar with the terrain and knew several of the local languages. The Geographical Society hoped that he might be willing to accompany the expedition into the interior, but Burton hoped that he would turn them down. "I am resolved not to take Mr. Rebmann," he wrote to George Back, the explorer who had chosen him to lead the expedition. "He would never stand the climate, suffers from spleen and appears to have a kind of longing for martyrdom which you know would not suit the R.G.Soc."

A few weeks after arriving in Zanzibar, early in the new year, Burton, Speke, and a small crew set out for the coast in a rented dhow, pulling behind them a corrugated iron lifeboat. The dhow was rotting and crawling with rats and cockroaches, but the crew much preferred it to the lifeboat, which Burton had ordered from a company in the United States and had assembled, with some difficulty, in Zanzibar. He had named it the *Louisa,* presumably for his friend, the pretty cousin that Isabel had envied, but his men called it the *Sharrádeh,* or runaway mare. Burton admitted that it "was indeed sadly given to breaking her halter and to bolting," but argued that it was also "graceful, fireproof, wormproof, and waterproof, incapable of becoming nail-sick or water-logged."

They headed north, hugging the coast of East Africa, pulling in and out of coves, and stopping on islands. Burton took every opportunity to inspect Portuguese and Persian ruins, which held no interest for Speke, while Speke grew increasingly frustrated that Burton, "being no sportsman, would not stop for shooting." As they had plenty of time, Speke wrote with irritation, "I thought it would be much more agreeable to spend it in hippopotamus-shooting." Burton, however, pushed on. Finally, on January 17, they reached Mombasa, and, after a seven-hour journey by rowboat, an uphill hike, and a five-mile walk, all of it through pelting rain, they finally arrived at the Kisuludini mission house, where Johannes Rebmann lived with, in Speke's words, his "amiable English wife."

Rebmann was welcoming when they arrived at his mission, and concerned for their safety, but, to Burton's relief, he deflected any suggestion that he join the expedition. It was readily apparent that Burton, although respectful, was not eager to have him and would, moreover, never let him proselytize on their journey through the interior. Every man was entitled to his own religion, Burton believed, or none at all, and he refused to allow his expedition to be used in the name of Christian conversion. Rebmann's "presence would give a Missionary semblance to the Expedition," he wrote to the Royal Geographical Society, "and prove a real calamity."

Burton did, however, allow Rebmann to give him some advice. The dry season that year had been particularly devastating, the missionary told him, resulting in a drought that had led to widespread famine. It had also killed several hundred head of cattle that belonged to the Maasai, a nomadic tribe that lived largely on the meat, milk, and blood of their cows. Now struggling to survive, they had set off on a warpath, stealing cattle, pillaging villages, and attacking even the largest caravans.

Knowing that Burton had planned to travel through the Maasai plains on his march west into the interior, Rebmann advised him to follow the less direct but far safer caravan route, which would take him through the Arab town of Kazeh. Agreeing that it would be foolish to tempt the Maasai, Burton altered not only his path into the interior but his plans to visit Mount Kilimanjaro before returning to Zanzibar from their coastal excursion. Instead, they would travel south from the mission and explore the Pangani River. Speke, annoyed that they had "frittered away so much time at Mombas, and in inspecting ruins," thought that there was now no reason to change their plans simply because of the Maasai, claiming that he was personally unconcerned about the potential danger. "I, on the other hand, did not see any cause of alarm," he later wrote, "for I thought we could easily have walked round the Masai party."

•

Since arriving in Zanzibar, Burton's relationship with Speke had grown increasingly tense. "I could not but perceive that his former alacrity had vanished," Burton wrote. "He was habitually discontented with what was done; he left to me the whole work of management, and then he complained of not being consulted." With no idea why Speke was disgruntled, Burton had become used to just ignoring his obvious unhappiness. The situation did not overly concern him, but it was a disappointment, especially as John Steinhaüser, the one friend he had counted on having with him on the overland journey, had been forced to pull out at the last minute. "His presence," Burton wrote, would have been "no small comfort." Although Elphinstone had agreed that Steinhaüser would be a valuable addition to the expedition and had recommended him for the job, permission had been delayed. In the meantime, the surgeon had fallen ill and, to Burton's immediate and lasting regret, was now too weak to travel from Aden to Zanzibar, much less into the interior. With only Speke left, Burton wrote, he now had "with me a companion and not a friend, with whom I was 'strangers yet.'"

Although Speke had yet to tell Burton how offended he had been by his admonishment during the attack in Somaliland, he had begun to openly express his disdain for his commander to other people. Simmering with resentment, he painted Burton as everything he himself feared being: a coward and a fraud. "I have now had ample analogous proof that B never went to Mecca & Harar in the common acceptance of that word, but got artful natives to take him to those places, & I would swear he did many a trick at their instigation," he wrote to his mother, Georgina Speke, from Zanzibar. "Wishing I could find something more amusing to communicate than such rot about a rotten person."

Finally, as they made their way along the coast, Speke, bored and frustrated, allowed his anger to boil over, admitting to Burton one of the reasons he was so unhappy. It had been wrong, Speke said, to use his diary and his natural history collection from the Somali expedition. It was an "unfair appropriation of *my* remarks appearing in print as *your* remarks," he insisted. Burton, surprised, responded that it had been a legitimate and common use of the material, explaining that commanders often published their subordinates' work following an expedition. Everything he said, however, only managed to outrage Speke even further. Burton's defense of his actions, Speke later wrote, "added Gall to it."

Even now, Burton did not understand the depth of Speke's anger toward him, but it was clear that his subordinate now felt that he rather than Burton should be in command of the expedition. "Much of the change he explained to me," Burton later wrote, "by confessing that he could not take an interest in an exploration of which he was not the commander." Burton was beginning to realize that he had invited onto his expedition a man who had a "habit of secreting thoughts and reminiscences till brought to light by sudden impulse. He would brood, perhaps for years, over a chance word, which a single outspoken sentence could have satisfactorily settled." Speke's quiet, gentle demeanor, his "almost childlike simplicity of manner," Burton now believed, belied an "immense and abnormal fund of self-esteem, so carefully concealed, however, that none but his intimates suspected its existence." Although outwardly he seemed far more modest and self-effacing than Burton, who was often criticized for his arrogance, in truth Speke took great pride in his own abilities and was affronted by the suggestion that anyone, especially his commander, was more accomplished, capable, or brave. "He ever held, not only that he had done his best on all occasions," Burton wrote, "but also that no man living could do better."

When they reached the Pangani River, Burton was able to mollify Speke somewhat by finally giving him an opportunity to do what he loved best: hunt. "The river was extremely tortuous and filled with hippopotami," Speke wrote. "They could not resist continually popping up their heads and apparently inviting us to take a shot, which, as may readily be imagined, I lost no opportunity in complying with." The hippos, irritated but unafraid, snorted at the men in their small, fragile boat. The huge riverine animals, which might charge at any moment or simply surface, easily upending their boat, were a genuine danger, even more so than the crocodiles, which, Burton wrote, "terrified by the splash of oars, waddled down with their horrid claws, dinting the slimy bank, and lay like yellow logs, measuring us with small, malignant, green eyes, deep set under warty brows."

As it grew dark, Burton sat down to his notes but found it difficult to resist the beauty that surrounded him, the quickly vanishing fireflies, the murmuring of the black river at his feet. "All around reigned the eternal African silence, deep and saddening, broken only by the curlew's scream, or by the breeze rustling the tree-tops, whispering among the matted foliage," he wrote. "We sat under a tree till midnight, unsatiated with the charm of the hour. The moon rained molten silver over the dark foliage of the wild palms, the stars were as golden lamps suspended in the limpid air, and Venus glittered diamond-like upon the front of the firmament."

CHAPTER NINE

Bombay

A few days later, the expedition stopped in Chogué, a small military station established by the Sultan of Zanzibar on the Pangani River. Hoping to add a few men to their ranks, Burton and Speke announced that they were hiring. "Volunteers were now called for to accompany us, who would carry each his arms, a little food, and such baggage as might be necessary," Speke wrote. "Five men were readily enlisted; besides these, they supplied four slave-servants, and two men as guides." Most of the men at the station were Baloch, described by Burton and Speke as "Beloch," from regions in and around Iran. Speaking several different languages, their families had settled in Zanzibar and the surrounding area in the 1820s, most taking jobs as soldiers. They were strong and experienced travelers, and Burton believed that they would be able to keep the expedition safe.

One man at the station, however, stood out among all the

others. He was not a Baloch but a Yao. Enslaved for much of his childhood and young adulthood, he was now a free man, able to make his own choices, fulfill his own destiny. Small and thin, with teeth filed to a sharp point and large, intelligent eyes, he was about to become, Burton later admitted, "the gem of the party." His name was Sidi Mubarak Bombay.

Bombay had little that he could call his own. Even his name had been carelessly assigned to him by the man who had bought and enslaved him in India when he was still a child. His African name was long forgotten, taken from him decades ago along with his family and his childhood in a single, terrifying night. He would never forget the day he had been kidnapped from his village in the Yao territory, on the border of modern-day Tanzania and Mozambique, although at the time it had been a bewildering blur of sickening screams, pounding feet, and slashing swords. "A large body of Wasuahili merchants and their slaves, all equipped with sword and gun, came suddenly," he would later recall. "Surrounding our village, [they] demanded of the inhabitants instant liquidation of their debts... advanced in former times of pinching dearth, or else to stand the consequences of refusal." The men who had descended on Bombay's village had once been enslaved themselves, an experience that had taught them not only the horrors of slavery but what might be gained by tricking, capturing, and selling another human being.

The Yao, part of the Bantu-speaking peoples of East and Central Africa, were not naive. Their name is the plural form of "cao," which means "treeless place," and they are believed to have originated in the mountainous area east of Lake Malawi, from where they had dispersed, dividing into subtribes and migrating both north and south. Sophisticated agriculturalists, the Yao grew plentiful sorghum, maize, and manioc, which they supplemented with hunting using bows and arrows but also traps, nets, and dogs. Living in a land rich in iron ore and, at one time, elephants, they were also highly skilled iron smiths and active ivory traders. Since 1800, the Yao had been working with Arab traders, bringing them ivory but also, with the growth of the slave trade, enslaved people from the interior to sell on the coast.

Bombay's village, which he called Uhiyow, was made up of a poor, isolated subgroup whose little interaction with the outside world had come from the men who tempted them with cloth and beads, slowly leading them into increasingly deeper debt and, ultimately, to this tragic moment. "As all the residents had at different times contracted debts," Bombay said, "there was no appeal against…this sudden demand, but no one had the means of payment." With no guns of their own and no way to fight back, they were left with little choice. "The whole village," he said, "took to precipitate flight."

In the resulting chaos of the attack on his village, Bombay had suddenly found himself alone. Although he had never really known his mother, who had died when he was an infant, until that night he had had a father, a family, and friends. For the rest of Bombay's life, his father's fate would remain a mystery. He assumed that he had either died trying to defend himself or had run, escaping into the surrounding landscape, perhaps eventually building a new life. "I never more gained any intelligence," he said. Nor would he ever again call this village home. Along with everyone else who had not escaped or died in the attack, Bombay was tied with rope and chains and forced to begin a brutal journey across hundreds of miles of land to Kilwa, a small island south of Zanzibar and a launching point for the slave trade.

•

Of the hundreds of thousands of people captured and dragged from their homes in the African interior, Bombay was at least among those who reached Kilwa alive. Many either succumbed to wounds they had sustained during their capture or died from disease, starvation, or sheer exhaustion, having been forced not only to walk barefoot in chains but often to carry elephant tusks, staggering in small groups under the crushing weight of a hundred or more pounds of ivory. Those who survived the journey to Kilwa were put in dhows, small sailboats so tightly packed with people that many more died and were thrown overboard during the more than two-hundred-mile trip to Zanzibar. Bombay, alone and scared, endured this additional misery on the Indian Ocean only to be led to an underground prison made from coral blocks and lime cement after landing on the island. Thick-walled and low-ceilinged, with little air or light and reeking of blood, sweat, sewage, and death, the prison was just steps from the open market, where Arab slave traders waited impatiently in the bright equatorial sun.

The slave trade in East Africa had, in a limited way, likely been going on for several centuries, but it reached its height in the nineteenth century, with the rise of Zanzibar as a central slave market. By that time, between eight and ten thousand people were brought to the island in chains every year, most of them from Kilwa. Their abject misery was made all the more horrifying when set against the gentle beauty of Zanzibar's white beaches and swaying palm trees. It was a scene of such cruelty and heartbreak that it sickened even the most jaded traveler. Twenty years before Bombay's arrival, a Briton named Thomas Smee, who commanded a research ship that had docked in Zanzibar harbor, described watching as a line of men, women, and children, bedecked in gold jewelry and gems to catch the buyer's eye, their skin gleaming with coconut oil, were paraded through the town in single file, blinking in confusion and terror. "At the head of this file, which is composed of all sexes and ages from 6 to 60, walks the person who owns them," Smee wrote. "When any of them strikes a spectator's fancy, the line immediately stops, and a process of examination ensues, which, for minuteness, is unequalled in any cattle market in Europe.... From such scenes one turns away with pity and indignation."

On Zanzibar in the mid-1800s, slave traders paid on average £4 to £5 for a man, slightly more for a woman. Bombay, still just a child, was bartered away, his young body exchanged for a few lengths of cloth. The coveted cotton of Gujarat, a large state in western India known for its brightly colored and intricately woven textiles, was often traded in the markets of Africa for silver, ivory, and people. When the transaction was complete, Bombay, understanding little of what was happening to him and helpless to prevent it even if he did, found himself aboard a ship that would carry him thousands of miles from his home and family. At the end of the journey, he would complete the circle of trade, with the cloth now in Africa and he in Gujarat, where he would live in slavery for the next twenty years.

•

Although at twelve years old Bombay had already experienced more tragedy and terror than most people would in a lifetime, he had been given at least one small reprieve from misfortune: His ship had sailed east from Africa rather than west. In the United States, where slavery had become a part of the economy, enslaved people were often condemned to working in fields on large plantations. In India, people of lower castes were already forced to do most of the domestic and agricultural work, so owning a person from Africa was largely considered a status symbol for the elite or a means of protection for the powerful. The maharajas, who were often at war with each other, preferred to have Africans rather than Indians in military positions—from soldiers to bodyguards to palace guards—believing that they not only had greater physical strength but were more likely to remain loyal.

These military, and in some cases administrative, positions gave enslaved people in India a path not only to freedom but to wealth and power. Some even ruled kingdoms of their own. In 1490, an African guard named Sidi Badr seized control of Bengal, where he ruled for three years before he was assassinated. In the late sixteenth century, Malik Ambar, who had been born in Harar, Ethiopia, and, like Bombay, was sold into slavery as a child, became one of the most famous rulers in the Deccan, in southern India. Ambar had begun his steady climb to power as soon as he was freed after the death of the man who had owned him. After he took a position in Bijapur in the northwestern Deccan, which placed him in charge of a small contingent of troops, his followers quickly grew in number until he had seven thousand soldiers, at which point he joined the ongoing fight for control of the neighboring Ahmadnagar kingdom. When he met a young man in Bijapur who was related to the Ahmadnagar royal family, he used him as a secret weapon, marrying him to his own daughter, installing him as sultan, and then making himself the sultan's regent, from which position he ran the kingdom.

Whether enslaved or free, powerful or poor, most Africans in India were given one of two titles: Habshi, which is Persian for Abyssinian, a region that now encompasses Ethiopia; or Sidi, possibly derived from the Arabic word "Saiyid," meaning "lord" or "master." The title Sidi was most commonly used on the western coast, attached as a prefix to a person of African descent, which is how the young East African who arrived in Gujarat in the 1830s, stripped not just of his freedom, family, and religion but even of his own name, became known as Sidi Mubarak Bombay.

Later in life, Bombay would explain that, because he was so young when he was enslaved, he did not remember many of the important dates that made up his life—his birth, capture, or liberation. He did, however, know one thing with certainty: Like the famed Malik Ambar, he was given his freedom when the man who owned him died. "I served with this master for several years, till by his death I obtained my liberation," he said. Unlike Ambar and Sidi Badr, however, Bombay saw his freedom not as a path to power in the country that had enslaved him but as a chance to finally make his way home. He chose to return to Africa, if not to the life that he might have had, at least to a world that he had once known. "My next destination," he said, "was Zanzibar."

•

Bombay had quickly found work in East Africa, but it was dreary toil in the army of the sultan, who died soon after Bombay returned from Gujarat. The job required little work and offered even less pay, forcing him to pass his days, he later recalled, "in half-starved inactivity." Beyond working in a clove field, however, or becoming the monster he had once feared by capturing villagers to sell in the slave market, there was little other work to be found. One possibility, although remote and infrequent, was to be hired onto a European expedition, which, while dangerous, paid slightly better than the sultan's army and held the promise of achievement, if not recognition.

Although they would rarely admit it, European explorers

came to Zanzibar looking not just for men who could carry their supplies although those were vitally important roles to fill for any expedition, but for those who could help them chart their course, and get them there and back alive. "Native testimony," as it was known derisively in England, was instantly dismissed as highly suspect if not completely worthless by armchair geographers and gentlemen scientists, the assumption being that anyone who actually lived in the region explored could not possibly have any useful knowledge of it. The explorers themselves, however, knew that their most reliable sources of information were the local inhabitants they hired to take them into the interior. Their first mission, therefore, after landing on Zanzibar was to find men capable of leading their caravans. They needed people who possessed multiple talents, able to find reliable porters and healthy pack animals; gather supplies, from food to weapons to medicine; and help plan their path. Once the expeditions began, these men would have to oversee the porters, serve as negotiators and interpreters, administer medical care, and navigate safe passage through hundreds of miles of unmapped land. It was a difficult job, and those who accepted it did not always make it home alive.

Bombay was not dissuaded by the dangers these expeditions posed. He had faced worse, and he had been alone. He had, moreover, as good a chance as any man and better than most of not only surviving the journey but distinguishing himself on it. Although he was small in stature, lacking the physical strength that Indians had long attributed to East Africans, and was not yet qualified to serve as a guide after having lived in India for so long, he had other qualities that were especially valuable on an expedition. He spoke several languages, was loyal and hardworking, clever and brave. Even after what he had endured as a child, he was not bitter but surprisingly softhearted. Most important, he was trustworthy. "His good conduct and honesty of purpose," Speke would quickly learn, "are without parallel."

·

So impressed was Burton with Bombay that soon after arriving in Chogué he asked him to leave his position as a soldier for Prince Majid and join the expedition as its head gun carrier. "We thought…so highly of his qualifications," Burton wrote, "that persuasion and paying his debts induced him, after a little coquetting, to take leave of soldiering and follow our fortunes." Along with daily rations and "an occasional loin-cloth covering whenever his shukka might wear out," Burton offered Bombay 5 dollars per month, to be paid in full upon their return to Zanzibar, assuming he survived the journey. The dollars Burton carried on the expedition were Maria Theresa thaler, silver bullion coins commonly referred to as "dollars" and used in international trade for more than a hundred years.

For Burton, Bombay's cheerful attitude, honesty, and admirable work ethic were his most valuable qualities. "He works on principle," Burton wrote, "and works like a horse." For Speke, it was more personal. Before they met Bombay, Burton was the only person in the expedition that Speke could talk to, and he had little interest in talking to Burton. Although Speke insisted that it did not bother him that he did not speak Arabic or any African languages, the fact that Bombay, who spoke Hindi, could understand the Anglo-Hindi that Speke had learned in India was a great relief for him from the loneliness that he had felt since arriving in Zanzibar. "I do not…feel so much pleasure in solitude," he would later tell a friend. "My only [motivation] for having travelled so much alone was for the better prosecution of my end in view—otherwise I like to share enjoyment being not quite so selfishly constituted."

After just a day at Chogué, Burton and Speke left with their new recruits. That night, as darkness fell, Speke realized that he had left his compass at their last campsite and wanted to return to retrieve it. Refusing to turn back for a single instrument, Burton insisted on continuing northward. When they finally reached a village on the riverbank where they decided to spend the night, to "revel on a feast of milk and flesh," Speke announced that he was going to return for his compass, even though it was now fifteen miles away. "I called on volunteers to forsake these festivities and follow me back to get it," he wrote. "Bombay of all the party was the only man who could be induced to go."

Not only did Bombay agree to make the additional thirty-mile round-trip journey with Speke, but he did so willingly and cheerfully. He was "ever ready to do anything for anybody," Speke wrote with affection. As the two men walked, Speke talked about his interest in the area's flora and fauna, discussing everything they happened to see, from river shells to birds, and Bombay shared stories from his own life and memories of the wildlife his father had shown him. After returning to their previous campsite, they quickly found the compass and turned back around, allowing no time for rest. "Cheerily did we trip along, for Bombay...seemed to me a surprisingly indefatigable walker," Speke wrote, "for he joked and talked and walked as briskly at the end of thirty miles as he did at starting."

By the time they made it back to the village where Burton and the other men were waiting, Speke had, he would later write, "become much attached to Bombay." He wanted the newest member of the expedition not only to join them on their overland journey but to serve as his personal translator and servant—"a regular Friday." Although he was daily hardening his heart toward Burton, searching for shortcomings in his commander and turning over and over in his mind any perceived slights, he saw in Bombay someone he could talk to, someone he could trust. What Burton had lost in Steinhaüser, Speke had found in Bombay.

CHAPTER TEN

Death Was Written

When they returned to Zanzibar on March 6, Burton had to be carried onto the island, too ill to walk, with Speke hobbling behind. Not long after leaving Chogué, the two explorers and Valentine, one of the expedition's young Goanese cooks, had suffered a fever so debilitating that it not only cut their coastal expedition short, it nearly killed them. Speke referred to it as a "violent bilious fever," which had turned them all a shade of yellow so startlingly bright it reminded him of a guinea coin. "Had we been able to perspire," he wrote, "I have no doubt we should have sweated out a sort of yellow ochre which a painter might have coveted." They had likely contracted typhoid fever, which is common in East Africa and affects the liver, often causing jaundice. "Jack Speke & I look like ghosts enjaundiced," Burton wrote to a friend when he was again well enough to hold a pen, "if English has such a word and ghosts such a disease."

The onset of the illness had been marked by weakness and a heavy, debilitating fatigue, but it had quickly progressed. Not only had the men suffered splitting headaches and vomiting so severe they could hardly stand, but their eyes had grown "hot, heavy, and painful," Burton wrote, "the skin...dry and burning, the pulse full and frequent, and the tongue furred." He had not eaten for a week and had rarely slept, falling into a miserable state of anxiety, depression, and delirium. He had a supply of quinine, a malaria drug that had been derived from the bark of the cinchona tree only a few decades earlier, but it had to be carefully administered. "This drug...has killed many," Burton warned, "especially Frenchmen, who, by overdosing at a wrong time, died of apoplexy."

Having gotten word that Burton and Speke were dangerously ill and had resorted to "physicking ourselves," as Speke put it, Hamerton had chartered a boat to pick them up and bring them back to Zanzibar. The consul, although so ill himself he "lived only in the evening," did everything he could to help the men, treating them "like sons," Burton wrote gratefully, "rather than like passing visitors." Hamerton also did his best to impress upon them how dangerous the expedition that lay ahead would be. Beyond the threat of illness, they faced the serious risk of angering, alienating, foolishly tempting, or unknowingly threatening the people they would encounter along the way. "The Consul had also warned me," Burton wrote, "that my inquiries into the country trade, and the practice of writing down answers—without which, however, no report could have been compiled—were exciting ill will."

Burton did not take Hamerton's admonishments lightly, especially knowing that the consul had also tried to warn the French explorer Eugène Maizan. Before Maizan had left Zanzibar in 1845, Hamerton had "cautioned him to no purpose,"

Burton wrote, "that his glittering instruments and his numerous boxes, all of which would be supposed to contain dollars, were dangerous." Maizan had refused to listen, and his murderer, after dismembering and beheading him, had turned his gutted gold chronometer into a tobacco pouch and the gilt knob from his tent pole into a neck ornament.

As a harsh reminder of Maizan's fate, Hamerton had even taken Burton to Zanzibar's fort so that he could see for himself the man who had beaten the war drum during the murder. Although it was widely believed that the actual murderer was still at large, this man had been convicted of killing Maizan and chained in front of the French consulate for two years before being dragged to the fort, where for the past eight years he had been "heavily ironed to a gun under a cadjan shed," Burton wrote, hardly able to "stand or lie down." Burton pitied both Maizan and this innocent man, who had been subjected to years of torture, but he refused to be dissuaded. He would not carry gilded instruments into the interior, but neither would he abandon his expedition before it had even begun. "Rather than return to Bombay," he wrote, "I would have gone to Hades."

•

Burton was not about to be frightened off, but as he now waited for the end of the Masika, the long rainy season, he found himself constantly on edge. The fever had clung to him longer than it had to Speke, leaving him, he wrote ruefully, "in the condition of a bed-ridden old woman." The rain pounded down for days on end, flooding large parts of the island and turning its sunny, tropical beauty into a bleak landscape that, mixed with the crack of lightning and boom of thunder, felt ominous. Speke noted that Burton seemed jittery, complaining "of the shock his nerves had received since the Somali encounter," but Speke felt it too. "The atmospheric air's being so surcharged with electricity was palpably felt by the nervous system," he wrote. "I experienced a nervous sensibility I never knew before of being startled at any sudden accident. A pen dropping from the table even would make me jump."

The Masika had begun early that year, and was expected to last several months. "For this to subside," Speke wrote, "we had now to wait here as patiently as we could, occupying the spare time so forced on us in purchasing an outfit and in preparing for the journey." They had brought to Zanzibar some of what they needed, picking up scientific instruments in Bombay and carrying from England their own clothing and personal gear. Although both men had with them only one extra pair of clothing, Burton had chosen his carefully, knowing from experience that it could greatly affect not just his comfort but his chances of survival. After warning that the color red "should ... be avoided, the dye soon turns dark, and the appearance excites too much attention," he wrote that, "besides shirt and trowsers, the only necessary is a large 'stomach-warmer' waistcoat, with sleeves and back of similar material, without collar—which renders sleeping in it uneasy—and provided with four-flapped pockets." Burton filled his pockets with everything from note- and sketch-books to a watch, compass, thermometer, and knife. The knife itself was an extremely useful, multipurpose tool, which "should contain scissors, tweezers, tooth-pick, and ear-pick, needle, file, picker, steel for fire, turnscrew, watch-spring saw, clasp-blade, and pen-blade."

The expedition still needed supplies, however, not only rations but, nearly as important, *kuhonga,* or gifts. Burton referred to *kuhonga* as "blackmail, so much dreaded by travelers," but it had long served as an important entry fee into East Africa, obliging explorers to at least acknowledge their trespass into foreign lands. The most common *kuhonga* at that time were cloth, beads, and brass wires. Called *masango,* the wires were available in Zanzibar "when cheap, for 12 dollars," Burton found, "and when dear for 16 dollars."

As Burton had long known, and Speke had learned from painful experience in Somaliland, some forms of *kuhonga,* like any trade good, were preferred while others were completely unacceptable. Failure to understand the difference, or to keep up with the ever-shifting markets, could spell the end of even the most carefully planned and well-funded expedition. On his first trip to Aden, Speke had brought with him "all manner of cheap and useless chow-chow, guns and revolvers, swords and cutlery, and beads and cloths," Burton recalled with exasperation, noting that it "would have [been] rejected with disdain."

Cloth was more useful than wire, but it was difficult to carry and easy to choose the wrong kind. Burton was on a tight budget with his underfunded expedition, but he knew that while he could buy cheap cloth to give to his porters, it would be foolish to try to pass it off as *kuhonga.* "In some regions," he wrote, "the people will not sell their goats and more valuable provisions for plain piece-goods.... Often, too, a bit of scarlet broadcloth thrown in at the end of a lengthened haggle, opens a road and renders impossibilities possible." The most varying and complicated *kuhonga* were beads, which were roughly equivalent to the copper and silver coins of Europe, although more beautiful in their shimmering variety. There were about four hundred different types of beads, or *ushanga,* in East Africa, and the importance of buying the right ones, Burton warned, could not be overstated. "Any neglect in choosing beads, besides causing daily inconvenience, might arrest an expedition on the very threshold of success," he warned. "Toward the end of these long African journeys, when the real work of exploration commences, want of outfit tells fatally."

Burton knew that, after buying supplies and *kuhonga*, he would have little left over to pay his men. Fortunately, several of them were servants of the sultan, "in his pay and under his command." The head clerk of the Zanzibar customs house, Ramji, agreed to go with them and allowed Burton to hire as guards and porters ten men whom he enslaved but referred to as his sons. Burton agreed to pay each of Ramji's "sons" 5 dollars a month. He promised the same amount to the eight Baloch soldiers whom he had hired in Chogué, along with their *jamadar*, or military commander, agreeing to pay them six months' wages up front, before they had left Zanzibar.

Burton thought the arrangement fair, and all he could afford on his limited budget, but to his surprise, Hamerton stepped in. The British consul "offered to defray, from public funds, which he understood to be at his disposal, certain expenses of the expedition," Burton wrote, "and he promised, as reward to the guide and escort, sums of money, to which, had I been unfettered, I should have objected as exorbitant." To Said bin Salim, the expedition's *ras kafilah*, or caravan guide, Hamerton gave 500 dollars to cover his family's expenses while he was away. Said, whom Burton described as a "timid little man, whose nerves were to weeping-point," had agreed only with great reluctance to join the expedition, so Hamerton also promised him a thousand dollars and a gold watch if it was successful. The consul's promises, however, were "purely conditional," Burton insisted, "depending entirely upon the satisfactory conduct of those employed."

•

On June 16, after the rains had abated and Burton had gathered most of the supplies they would need, he was finally ready to leave Zanzibar and sail to the mainland. The expedition then included sixteen men: Burton, Speke, and Bombay as well as the cooks Valentine and Gaetano, the eight Baloch soldiers, and a few porters. The sultan of Zanzibar had loaned them a small three-masted, eighteen-gun corvette or warship called the *Artémise* that was to take them to the mainland. Hamerton, despite the fact that he daily appeared to draw closer to death, insisted on accompanying them. "Though almost lethargic from the effects of protracted illness," Burton wrote, Hamerton "had deemed it his duty to land us upon the coast, and to superintend our departure from the dangerous sea-board." Mr. Frost, the apothecary who had been overseeing the consul's care, traveled with him.

The *Artémise* landed on the coast of East Africa at Wale Point, across from Zanzibar and a few miles from a small settlement called Kaole, from where the expedition planned to set off into the interior. Before they could leave the ship, however, they had to wait for the caravan leader Said bin Salim and the customs clerk Ramji, both of whom had left for the mainland two weeks earlier to try to hire more men. The African caravans, which made the long trip from the interior every year following the rainy season, had not yet reached the coast, making it much harder to find available porters. Burton, who expected to be gone for as long as two years, thought that they would need at least 170 men. As well as tents, mosquito nets, air pillows and blankets, a table and chairs, eating and cooking utensils, camp beds and carpets, the expedition had seventy loads of *kuhonga* and enough ammunition to last two years, which amounted to forty boxes weighing forty pounds each.

While they waited at Wale Point, Speke took advantage of the opportunity to hunt more hippopotamuses. "The ivory of these animals is more prized than that of the elephant," he wrote, "and, in consequence of the superior hardness of its enamel, it is in great requisition with the dentist." Speke's interest, however, was less in the animals themselves than in the thrill of the hunt. "The best time to catch the hippopotamus is when the tide is out and the banks are bared, for then you find him wallowing in the mud or basking on the sand," he wrote. "I especially mention this, as it is quite labour in vain, in places where the water is deep, to fire at these animals unless you can kill them out right, as they dive under like a water-rat, and are never seen more if they are only wounded."

These hunting trips, although a delight to Speke, were at times a danger to the expedition. When the hippos were partially submerged, Speke liked to shoot at their ears, trying to bait them into charging the canoes, a tactic that occasionally worked too well. During one hunt, a male hippopotamus "drove a tusk clean through the boat with such force that he partially hoisted her out of the water," Speke later recalled. On another occasion, a female came up under them so quickly that Speke was sent flying backward, and one of the men actually fell out of the canoe and onto the hippopotamus's back, quickly scrambling back in. One of Burton's elephant guns also went overboard and could not be recovered. Speke deeply regretted the loss, although he argued that his commander's firearms were only "used for display to amuse the Arabs."

Burton found Speke's enthusiasm for hunting a distraction and an annoyance, not to mention a cruelty if not necessary for food. He especially disapproved of elephant hunting, writing angrily of men who "have made it their sport, to murder elephants." He did notice, however, that his companion was particularly careful when holding a loaded gun. "He was ever remarkable for the caution with which he handled his weapon," Burton noted. As someone who saw guns only as a means of protection or a guard against starvation, he appreciated that Speke at least understood and took seriously the danger they posed. "I ever make a point of ascertaining a fellow-traveller's habits in that matter," Burton explained, "and I observed that even when our canoe was shaken and upthrown by the hippopotamus he never allowed his gun to look at him or at others."

·

Ten days after the expedition had left Zanzibar, Said and Ramji finally arrived at Wale Point. They had with them, however, far fewer men than the expedition needed. Burton had hoped to hire 170 porters; they had brought thirty-six. Ramji had initially hired more men, he told Burton, but "hearing that their employer was a muzungu, a 'white man,'" they had "at once dispersed."

Ladha Damha, Zanzibar's collector of customs who had joined them on the coast a few days after they arrived, suggested that, as there were not enough men to carry their supplies, they hire donkeys. They soon learned, however, that finding good donkeys was almost as difficult as finding men. "Thirty animals, good, bad, and indifferent," Burton wrote, "were fitted for the roads with large canvass bags and vile Arab pack-saddles, composed of damaged gunny-bags stuffed with straw." Knowing that they would be overburdened, he reluctantly left behind 359 dollars' worth of goods, as well as his beloved iron lifeboat, the *Louisa,* which he knew he would sorely regret when they finally reached Tanganyika—the lake that they would be the first Europeans to see and which Burton hoped might be the source of the White Nile. He hired twenty-two men to follow them with the rest of the baggage in ten days. The expedition would not see these men, or their desperately needed supplies, for nearly a year.

Burton also found that, no matter his personal objections to slavery, there was little he could do to prevent having enslaved men in his expedition. "For the evil of slave-service there was no remedy," he wrote, "so that I paid them wages, and treated them as if they were free men." He also refused the gifts of enslaved people that were offered to him, and he asked the men he had hired not to use their wages to buy enslaved people for themselves. They, however, objected to their commander's request, pointing out that they were "allowed by our law to do so." "All I could do was to see that their slaves were well fed and not injured," Burton wrote.

Even Bombay bought an enslaved man to travel with him on the expedition, although he treated this man better than he did himself. His name was Mabruki, and like Bombay he was a Yao. Bombay showed Mabruki not just kindness but deep affection, referring to him as his brother. Mabruki "had been selected by his fellow-tribesman Bombay at Zanzibar," Burton wrote. "He was the slave of an Arab Shaykh, who willingly let him for the sum of five dollars per mensem." Mabruki appeared to Burton and Speke to be as coldhearted as Bombay was warm. "His temper is execrable, even in extremes," Burton wrote, "now wild with spirits, then dogged, depressed, and surly, then fierce and violent." Bombay, however, who understood what it meant to be enslaved, the rage and humiliation that accompanied that condition, "was warmly attached" to him, Speke wrote, though, in his opinion, "Mabruki had no qualifications worthy of attracting any one's affections."

•

Little more than a week after they arrived at Wale Point, Frost, the apothecary who had accompanied Hamerton to the main-land, told Burton that it was time for them to return to Zanzi-bar. "With brow severe and official manner," Burton wrote, "he informed me that the state of Lieut. Colonel Hamerton's health forbade a longer stay near the coast." Burton agreed with him that the consul should go home, had thought him too ill to make the trip in the first place, but he strongly disagreed with Frost's use of "minute doses of morphine and a liberal diet of sugar" to treat what appeared to Burton to be a "fatal liver-complaint." The apothecary argued that the doses of morphine were "little ones," and as such harmless to Hamerton, but it was clear that neither were they helpful.

Before Burton stepped off the *Artémise,* Hamerton gave him one last piece of advice: Trust your instincts, and don't listen to the armchair geographers. "March straight ahead," he said, ignoring "'velvet-slipper men,' who afford opinions." Burton then "took melancholy leave of my warm-hearted friend, upon whose form and features death was written in legible charac-ters." He knew that this might be the last time he saw Hamer-ton, and although the consul knew it too, he assured Burton that he was not worried. "He looked forward to death with a feeling of delight, the result of his religious convictions," Burton later recalled. "This courage was indeed sublime. Such examples are not often met with among men."

Knowing that he would need Hamerton's help while he was in the interior, Burton worried about the consul's health nearly as much for his own sake as for his friend's. So feared was the land through which they were about to travel that his men were already getting nervous. A Baloch named Zahri, who had been to the interior before, insisted that they could not travel with less than 150 guns and several cannon. Another man warned that they would pass through a land in which men sat in trees shooting poison arrows at strangers, and rarely missed. "He strongly advised them, therefore, under pain of death to avoid trees," Burton wrote with frustration. "No easy matter in a land all forest." The men told each other tales of herds of elephants attacking men as they slept, rhinoceroses that could kill two hundred men at a time, and hyenas that were more dangerous than Bengal tigers. There was little Burton could do to calm their fears. "In vain I objected that guns with men behind them are better than cannon backed by curs, that mortals can die but once, that the rations might be carried where not purchasable, and that powder and ball have been known to conquer rhinoceroses, elephants, and hyenas," he wrote. "A major force was against me."

One night after Hamerton had left, Burton brought Ladha, the customs collector, and his clerk, Ramji, to a local church to discuss their plans for the expedition. He insisted that they include on their list of necessary items a boat, explaining that, as they had been forced to leave the *Louisa* behind, he did not want to search for one when they reached Lake Tanganyika, or, as it was locally known, the Sea of Ujiji. Ladha then turned to Ramji, speaking to him in Kutchi, a dialect from the area surrounding the Gulf of Kutch, of which, Burton wrote, "he assumed me to be profoundly ignorant." "Will he ever reach it?" Ladha asked. "Of course not," Ramji replied with disdain. "Who is he?" Burton said nothing at the time, but later, to Ladha's shock, he told him that he fully intended to explore the Sea of Ujiji—and that he knew Kutchi.

As the three men stood talking, they were suddenly startled into silence by a sickening cry. "The loud wail of death rang wildly through the grave-like stillness of night," Burton wrote.

They ran to the door of the church, where they learned that the only son of a highly respected local chief had been killed along with two of his men after a hippopotamus had upended their boat. Turning angrily to Burton, Ladha laid the blame for the tragedy at his feet. "Insaf karo! be honest!" he cried, "and own that this is the first calamity which you have brought upon the country by your presence."

Burton objected, but when Ladha left, he wrote, "my spirits went with him." As he stood alone in the church, the long series of disappointments, mishaps, and tragedies that had already beset the expedition came rushing back to him. They had been delayed for months by both a devastating dry season and a fierce monsoon. They had neither enough supplies nor enough men. Steinhaüser had fallen ill, Speke was disgruntled, and Hamerton was on the verge of death. None of his men believed that the expedition could succeed, or that they would even survive. "In the solitude and the silence of the dark," Burton wrote, "I felt myself the plaything of misfortune."

CHAPTER ELEVEN

An Old Enemy

Following a blood-red flag, the East African Expedition finally set out for Lake Tanganyika on the morning of June 27, 1857. The men "in bravery of shield, sword, and dagger," Burton wrote with pride, "hurried in Indian file out of the Kaole cantonments." An hour earlier, the morning stillness had been rent by a blaring, banging cacophony that had quickly grown, goading even the most resistant man into action. Beating drums, lilting pipes, and braying horns were punctuated by cries of "Kwecha! Kwecha! Pakia! Pakia! Hopa! Hopa!," which Burton translated as "Collect! pack! set out!"

In Swahili, Burton would later write, the word for *caravan* is "safari," from the Arabic *safar,* meaning journey. For a man without a country, who had felt at home in any land but England, studying any language and culture but his own, it was a word that had long stirred both his mind and his emotions, bringing with it visions of adventure, opportunity, even hope. Later, thinking of all that an expedition meant to him, he would quote the old adage, "The world is a great book, of which those who never leave home read but a page." Now, however, the journey ahead offered him a more immediate gift: relief from the bleak thoughts of the night before and his fears for the future of his expedition. "The excitement of finding myself on new ground," he wrote, "and the peculiarities of the scenery, somewhat diverted melancholy forebodings."

The *kirangozi,* or guide, leading the caravan held the expedition's flag. Although it would soon be torn to tatters by whipping wind and snagging thorns, its vivid red color proudly announced that they were from Zanzibar. Behind the *kirangozi* was a high-ranking *pagazi* or porter, striking a kettle drum and looking regal in a long, narrow swath of scarlet broadcloth and a headdress made from the hide of a black-and-white monkey, topped with the towering, golden plume of the crested crane. Next in line came the pack animals, each assigned two men, one to lead and one to drive; then the porters, "mostly lads, lank and light," Burton wrote, "with the lean and clean legs of leopards," carrying long cylindrical packs, roughly six feet in length, two in diameter, on top of their heads or across their narrow shoulders. Bringing up the rear were the gun carriers, who were given lighter loads but were expected to be ready at all times to defend the expedition.

If Burton could have seen the land through which he was about to travel from above, laid out before him like a modern-day satellite picture, even he would have been struck dumb by its extraordinary beauty. As soon as he left the green-blue waters of the Indian Ocean, the terrain would begin to shift, from march to march, mile to mile. Much of the ground below their feet was stiff, dense red clay, but at other times it was the bright white of granite or even the glittering silver of mica. There were broad plateaus that suddenly dropped down into vast, cauldron-like basins filled with fog and mist; thin, winding rivers; thick forests; golden fields; and wide savannas. The trees, some standing alone, others huddled together as if in solemn assembly, ranged from emerald leaved and pink flowered to limbs so heavy and wide they cast a circular shadow whose perimeter, Burton swore, was no less than five hundred feet in the mid-day sun. The East African skies, he would later write, dazzled by the mere memory, were "purer and bluer than I had ever seen in Greece or Italy."

As the long line of men and donkeys wound "like a monstrous land-serpent over hill, dale, and plain," Burton knew that there was always the possibility of meeting a slave or ivory caravan along the way. In most instances, there would be little interaction beyond an initial, wary greeting. Each caravan's *kirangozi* would slowly approach and quickly size up the other, before suddenly launching what seemed to be a violent attack. "Their example is followed by all with a rush and a crush, which might be mistaken for the beginning of a faction," Burton wrote, "but it ends, if there be no bad blood, in shouts and laughter." Trouble—someone accidentally killed in the melee, or the good-spirited shoving growing more serious, heated, and dangerous—was rare. If it happened, however, the expedition had a plan: The agreed-upon signal for any kind of danger was three gunshots, which would instantly bring the gun carriers to the front of the caravan, prepared to fight.

The assumption was not only that there would not be violence between caravans, but that they would help each other if the opportunity arose. As Burton and his men made their way to the first stop on their route, a small village called Kuingani, the porters left signs on the trails for future travelers. Although the sandy path leading to Kuingani demanded their constant attention, littered as it was with thick, ragged plants and thorns that sliced open the porters' bare feet and tore at the legs of their donkeys, the men looked for ways to leave messages for anyone else who might come this way. Using everything from broken pots to a pile of snail shells or an animal skull, they would indicate that water was nearby, or, with a broken branch or a line drawn in the sand, leave behind a warning not to use a dangerous path. If there was time, they would even try to add a little humor to their messages. "Here and there a little facetiousness appears in these erections," Burton wrote, "a mouth is cut in the tree-trunk to admit a bit of wood simulating a pipe."

Most of the paths that the expedition would follow over the next nine months had been made by African traders, later followed by Arab slavers. While they forced their human cargo toward the coast, many of these men ate the mangoes that they had brought with them from Arabia, spitting the seeds at their feet as they walked. Soon, wide-armed, fragrant mango trees, their long-stemmed fruit hanging like ornaments, lined this path of human misery. The contrast was a stark reminder of the painful pairing of beauty and sorrow that defined so much of the region. "The demon of Slavery reigns over a solitude of his own creation," Burton later wrote. "Can it be, that by some inexplicable law, where Nature has done her best for the happiness of Mankind, Man, doomed to misery, must work out his own unhappiness?" Although he felt helpless to counteract the despair that he saw, a few weeks later Burton would have the opportunity to help free five people who, like Bombay, had been kidnapped when their village was attacked. He did no more than anyone with a heart and guns might do, but he was able to restore at least this small group "to their hearths and homes," he wrote.

·

The great East African kingdoms through or near which the expedition was about to travel were large, powerful, and politically complex. Among the best known of the first dynasties was that of the Chwezi people. Believed to have ruled modern-day Western Uganda and, later, parts of Kenya and Tanzania, the Chwezi are associated with some of the most stunning early earthworks on the continent, including a six-and-a-half-mile-long ditch system that encircled a riverbank grazing area. Possibly around the turn of the fifteenth century, the Chwezi were replaced in the south by the Hima people and in the north by the Luo, who ruled over vast stretches of the region until they eventually became part of the Bantu populations.

By the nineteenth century, there were many autonomous kingdoms in the region. Among the most important kingdoms in the west were the Kingdom of Loango, which had been founded by the Vili people, likely in the fifteenth century, and Karagwe, an agricultural kingdom ruled by King Rumanika. In the north, the largest kingdom was Buganda, which had been founded nearly five hundred years earlier when the ruler of the Ganda people extended his control over the region. When Burton and Speke arrived in Zanzibar, the current king of Buganda, Mutesa I, had just come into power. During his twenty-eight-year reign, Mutesa I would reform and expand Buganda's military and keep a tight rein on Arab traders, foreign missionaries, and European explorers.

Although Arabs had been trading in the region for centuries, they were taking advantage of a system that had already been well established by East Africans, particularly the Nyamwezi. Part of a strong agricultural empire that grew everything from corn and millet to rice, the Nyamwezi had also developed a wide-ranging trade network that stretched from the region surrounding Lake Tanganyika to the coast, the very path Burton's expedition would be traveling. They had a collaborative and mutually beneficial working relationship with Arab traders that was occasionally strengthened through marriage. In fact, Fundikira, the chief of Unyanyembe, the most important of the Nyamwezi chiefdoms, had allowed his daughter to marry Muhammad bin Juma, an Omani Arab. Burton had been fortunate enough to hire several Nyamwezi for his expedition, a significant stroke of luck as they were the most highly sought after guides and porters in the region.

After passing through a muddy swamp choked with long, tangled grass, Burton and his men could finally see the village of Kuingani in the distance. A collection of "bee-hive huts," Kuingani was surrounded by rice fields and dotted with cocoa and mango trees, basil bushes, and wild, towering hibiscus. There was little to do there but rest and prepare for the next stage of the expedition. Burton, however, still haunted by doubts and seeing his own worry reflected in the eyes of his men, took advantage of the opportunity to invite a *mganga,* or medicine man, into his tent to give him a prophecy.

Although he was a man of science, Burton, like many Britons born into the Victorian Age, also had a deep interest in the supernatural. He had tried everything from hypnosis, which, with his riveting black eyes, he was said to be alarmingly good at, to crystal gazing. Before traveling to Mecca, he had befriended a man named Frederick Hockley, a well-known British occultist who practiced what was known as "scrying," peering into some medium, in Hockley's case crystals, to find clues about the future. Hockley wrote that Burton had been "desirous of taking with him a crystal and mirror" to Mecca, and Hockley had given him a "small, oval, mounted crystal" and a black mirror, which he later used to try to follow Burton's progress. "Emma my seeress (who was then fourteen years old)," Hockley had written with excitement, "inspected and said—'Now it's light; I see some sand. Now I see some camels.'" Burton, far more skeptical than Hockley, was harder to impress. Later writing to a friend, he complained that he had been told that his crystals "contain a 'good spirit,' which," he grumbled, "is not interesting."

Burton was also more than willing to try hallucinogenic drugs, thinking that at best they might open a window into the cultures he was studying, or, at the very least, provide an interesting experience. In India he had smoked opium and drunk bhang, a form of cannabis, which, he wrote, made him "suspect treachery everywhere, and in the simplest action detect objects the most complexedly villainous. Your thoughts become wild and incoherent, your fancy runs frantic." In East Africa, he had tried pombe, made from malted millet, which can be extremely potent. He had also chewed khat, a stimulant taken from the leaves of the *Catha edulis* or Flower of Paradise. Burton was disappointed that, on him, khat seemed to have little effect. "I once tried in vain a strong infusion," he wrote. "The Arabs, however, unaccustomed to stimulants and narcotics, declare that, like opium eaters, they cannot live without the excitement."

The medicine man in Kuingani offered Burton and his men not excitement but something more valuable: reassurance. After accepting as payment one dollar and a skullcap that Burton had bought in Surat, the man shook a large gourd filled with pebbles and pieces of metal and waved before him two goat horns tied together by a snake skin and decorated with bells. "When fully primed by the spirit of prophecy, and connected by ekstasis with the ghosts of the dead, he spake out pretty much in the style of his brotherhood all the world over," Burton wrote. "The journey was to be prosperous. There would be much talking, but little killing.... Happy return to wife and family."

Although Burton put as little faith in the medicine man's

prophecy as he did in any religious ceremony, he accepted it as a small source of comfort in the face of an expedition that, with each passing day, seemed increasingly likely to fail. For the first week after leaving Kaole, Burton listened for the reassuring sound of the *Artémise*'s gun, which rang out every evening, traveling for miles across the quiet landscape. Hamerton had insisted on staying near the coast until the expedition had made it past the region where Maizan had been murdered, and the gun had been a nightly reminder that his friend was still nearby and that, if needed, "refuge was at hand." After a few nights, however, the reports suddenly ceased, leaving Burton to wonder why. Finally, one of his men "hardened his heart" and approached him with disturbing news. A trader traveling from the coast had spread a rumor among the porters that Hamerton was dead. Not knowing what to believe, Burton consulted with Said bin Salim, who told him that he "fully trusted in the truth of the report." Worse, every man on the expedition agreed, persuading themselves, Burton wrote, "that Lieut. Colonel Hamerton's decease had left me without support from the government of Zanzibar."

Soon after, the expedition, which already had far too few men, began to suffer a string of devastating desertions. Porters near the back of the caravan would quietly drop their pack and slip off into the woods. Others would leave during the night or when the other men were distracted, as happened during an attack from a swarm of bees. "During our eighteen months of travel," Burton later wrote, "there was not an attendant, from Said bin Salim to the most abject slave, who did not plan, attempt, or carry out desertion." By late July, they had lost nine porters to desertion, one of whom had been carrying a portmanteau that held most of the expedition's pens, ink, and paper, their surveying books, and the *Nautical Almanac* of 1858. It was, Burton wrote, an "irreparable loss."

Born in Devon but raised in Europe, Richard Burton regarded England with the same distaste and skepticism that many of his countrymen felt for him. After engineering his own expulsion from Oxford, where he was ridiculed and bored, he joined the British East India Company before becoming a famed explorer, writer, poet, and anthropologist as well as one of the world's most accomplished linguists, speaking more than twenty-five languages and at least another dozen dialects.

In 1855, Burton, who studied every religion and respected none, became the first Englishman to enter Mecca disguised as an Arab. Even though he spoke Arabic with near perfect fluency and could recite a quarter of the Koran, he knew that it would be easy to make a mistake that could cost him his life. "A blunder, a hasty action, a misjudged word," he wrote, "and my bones would have whitened the desert sand."

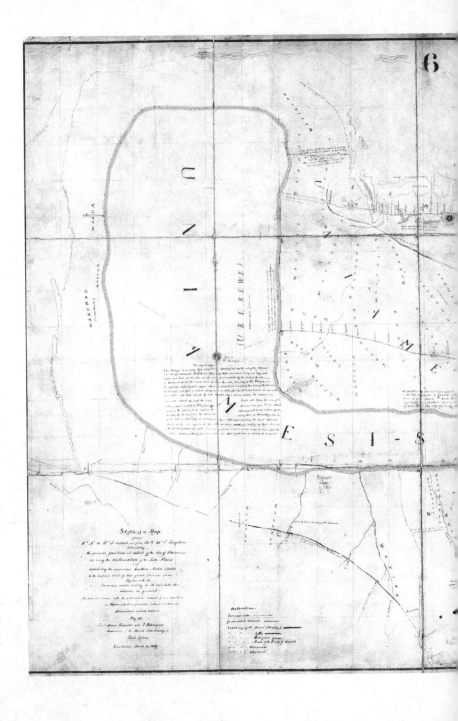

Long determined to solve the geographical mystery that had fascinated philosophers and geographers for millennia—finding the source of the White Nile—the Royal Geographical Society was intrigued in 1855 by a highly unusual map of East Africa drawn by German missionaries. Although ridiculed for its enormous sluglike shape, the map's single inland lake inspired the Society to sponsor an expedition to the region led by Richard Burton and his second in command, John Hanning Speke. *[Lake's outline enhanced for clarity]*

A member of the British aristocracy, John Hanning
Speke was born and raised at Jordans, his ancestral
estate in Somerset, where he became an enthusiastic and
highly skilled hunter. After joining the Bengal Native
Infantry and moving to India, he took every opportunity
to explore, map, and add to his growing natural history
collection. His life as an explorer began in earnest while
on leave in Aden, where he met Richard Burton and
joined his expedition.

Lying twenty miles off the coast of East Africa, the island of Zanzibar had been occupied for thousands of years before the first Europeans landed there in 1498, followed soon after by British traders and explorers. When Burton and Speke arrived in 1856, they went directly to the British consulate, where they found Colonel Atkins Hamerton, who was eager to help but clearly gravely ill. The consul's once "fair and ruddy" face, Burton wrote with concern, was now "bleached ghastly pale."

A stark contrast to the natural beauty of Zanzibar were the horrors of the island's slave market, where men, women, and children were sold into a life of captivity. Most had been captured in the East African interior, chained and dragged hundreds of miles to the coast, and then forced into small, overcrowded boats that took them to Zanzibar, from where they were sent to Arabia or India. The infamous slave market was finally closed in 1876 and a museum commemorating its victims built on its site 137 years later.

Kidnapped from his village in East Africa and sold
for cloth in Zanzibar when he was just a child, Sidi
Mubarak Bombay was enslaved in western India
for twenty years. Finally freed when the man who
owned him died, Bombay made his way back to the
continent of his birth, where he met Burton and
Speke just as they were about to set off in search
of the source of the White Nile. Quickly coming
to admire Bombay's "unwearied activity, and . . .
undeviating honesty," Burton acknowledged him as
"the gem of the party."

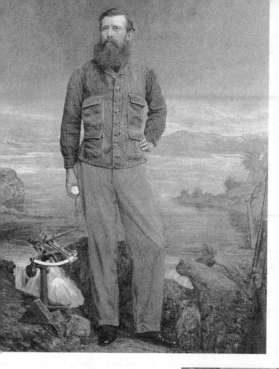

After a long and difficult journey to Lake Tanganyika, which he hoped was the source of the White Nile, Burton lay paralyzed with malaria while Speke and Bombay traveled north to another lake: the Nyanza. Although he saw only a small portion of the lake, Speke was stunned by its beauty and elated by stories of its seemingly endless shores, which he was told "probably extended to the end of the world." Certain that he had "discovered" the illusive source, Speke named the largest lake in Africa for his own queen: Victoria.

Soon after Burton's expedition left for the interior, Atkins Hamerton died and Christopher Palmer Rigby was appointed the new British consul at Zanzibar. A distinguished linguist in his own right, Rigby had long competed with Burton for recognition within the British military. Alarmed when he heard that his old nemesis was now in a unique position to either help or hinder his expedition, Burton worried that he could not trust him, writing that Rigby's name "was not nice in the nostrils of men."

Reaching England before Burton, who was not yet well enough to travel, Speke quickly laid claim to one of the greatest discoveries in the history of exploration. The day after he arrived, he met with Sir Roderick Murchison, president of the Royal Geographical Society, to describe the Nyanza and make a case for returning to East Africa as the leader of his own expedition. After listening with enthusiasm to Speke's story, Murchison said simply, "Speke, we must send you there again."

Born in the Scottish Highlands, James Augustus Grant first met Speke in the Indian Army. Twelve years later, when he learned that Speke was returning to East Africa in an effort to prove his claims about the Nyanza, Grant offered to travel as his subordinate. Although often sidelined during the expedition, denied even a chance to see the Nile as it rushed from the Nyanza, Grant remained fiercely loyal to Speke for the rest of his life, insisting that "not a shade of jealousy or distrust, or even ill-temper, ever came between us."

Although his own expedition was severely underfunded, John Petherick, a Welsh trader and consul to Khartoum, agreed to meet Speke and Grant with boats and supplies at the end of their journey. When Petherick was delayed by hardship, illness, and the death of two of his men, Speke angrily refused his help and later accused him of participating in the slave trade, a baseless claim that severely damaged Petherick's reputation and led to the loss of his consulship. "The blow," Petherick admitted, "was as hard as I could well bear."

After Speke sent the Royal Geographical Society a historic telegram from Egypt, announcing that "the Nile is settled," Murchison invited him and Grant to give a talk upon their return to London. So much excitement surrounded the event, which was held at the Burlington House on Piccadilly, that a surging crowd shattered windows in the palatial building. Inside, a standing-room-only audience included everyone from the Count of Paris to the Prince of Wales.

Isabel Arundell was raised by a controlling mother in a strict, aristocratic Catholic family whose ancestors included Sir Thomas Arundell *(below)*, distant cousin of Henry VIII. Isabel was deeply religious, but she dreamed of an adventurous life, free from the suffocating restrictions placed on Victorian women. "I wish I were a man," she wrote; "If I were, I would be Richard Burton. But as I am a woman, I would be Richard Burton's wife."

Despite Speke's telegram, the source of the Nile was far from settled, and the battle between Burton, Speke, and their supporters continued unabated, carving an ever-widening gulf between the two men. Finally, a highly anticipated "great Nile debate" was scheduled to take place on September 16, 1864, at the Royal Mineral Water Hospital in Bath. As he stepped into the lecture hall the day before the debate, Burton saw Speke for the first time in years. "I shall never forget his face," Isabel later wrote of the man whom she believed had betrayed her husband. "It was full of sorrow, of yearning, and perplexity."

Quickly fleeing the hall, Speke set out for Neston Park, his uncle's vast estate just a few miles outside of Bath. There, he knew, he would find solace in hunting with his cousin, George Fuller. Sensing that Speke was unusually agitated that day, Fuller kept his distance in the wide, open field until he heard the report of a gun. Turning, he was shocked to see his cousin falling from the low stone wall he had been climbing. Fuller ran to help him, but Speke died soon after of a self-inflicted gunshot wound to the chest.

No one was more horrified or haunted by Speke's sudden death than Burton, who lived another twenty-six years, his once strong body slowly betraying him as his sharp mind kept spinning. His final years were spent in Trieste, most days at his desk translating ancient Arabic texts, from the *Kama Sutra* to *The Scented Garden*. Although Isabel worried about the controversial books, Burton took great satisfaction in knowing that the British public would find them equally shocking and irresistible.

Early on the morning of October 20, 1890, Isabel found Burton dead at the age of sixty-nine, his final translation unfinished. To the outrage of his family and friends, she insisted on a Catholic funeral for her irreverent and openly agnostic husband. Burton's body was then shipped from Trieste to England, where he was buried in a granite and marble tomb that Isabel had designed to look like an Arab tent.

After losing Burton, the man whom she called her "earthly god and king" and to whom she had devoted the great majority of her life, Isabel believed that she must now do what she could to save his soul. Sitting before a fire, she fed his last great literary work, his painstaking translation of *The Scented Garden,* to the flames. "Sorrowfully, reverently, and in fear and trembling," she later wrote, "I burnt sheet after sheet."

Although he had put the source of the White Nile on the map of the world, solving the mystery that had captivated men for millennia, Speke was largely forgotten after his death. His friends and supporters did their best to keep his memory alive, placing a small memorial in the stone wall where his life had ended and erecting a larger obelisk in Kensington Gardens. Few visitors, however, stop to read the words etched into its granite base.

Having been the object of intense curiosity, envy, suspicion, and fear for most of his life, Burton found himself in his later years poor and powerless. After his death, however, his many books, poems, and translations, perhaps even more than his legendary travels, gave him a measure of immortality. Burton's obituary in the London *Times* hailed him as "one of the most remarkable men of his time," and his portrait, painted in 1872 by the famed artist Sir Frederic Leighton, now hangs in London's National Portrait Gallery, among those of his country's most revered citizens.

Living to the age of sixty-five, Bombay became one of the most widely traveled men in Africa. He had not only traveled with Burton and Speke to the Tanganyika, Speke and Grant to the Nyanza, and Henry Morton Stanley to find David Livingstone, but he and Verney Lovett Cameron were the first to cross the entire continent, from east to west. By the end of his life, having covered some six thousand miles, mostly by foot, Bombay had secured his place among the most accomplished guides in the history of African exploration.

The remaining men, moreover, sick, exhausted, scared, and longing for home, had already begun to fight. Burton believed that it was "usually better to let these quarrels work themselves out; if prematurely cut short, the serpent, wrath, is scotched, not slain." Speke, however, claimed that he alone was always left to deal with any arguments that broke out among the men, separating the combatants and doling out punishments. One day, he wrote, after a group of men refused to work, "an altercation took place which I had to settle, as was invariably the case when any difficulties arose in the camp."

In truth it was Bombay who most often soothed tensions, reprimanding but also reassuring the men and getting everyone back to work. He had quickly become a favorite among the other men in the expedition, who had given him affectionate nicknames that ranged from Pombe, meaning small beer, to Mamba, or crocodile, in reference to the sharply filed teeth he so often flashed at them with his wide smile. Although he never hesitated to give orders, directing porters to pick up the pace, guards to take their fair share of the loads, he worked harder than any of them. This was especially true of his own enslaved servant, Mabruki. "He toiled like a char-woman to raise our tents and to prepare them for habitation," Burton wrote, "while his slave... sat or dozed under the cool shade." Bombay, Speke believed, was one of the most generous men he had ever met. "He would do no wrong to benefit himself," he wrote. "To please anybody else there is nothing he would stick at."

Burton liked to complain that Bombay was forgetful and clumsy, but, like Speke, he had come to rely on his kind, calm demeanor, his fervent loyalty, and his eagerness to help. He would long remember in particular Bombay's kindness toward him during a grueling march, when neither he nor Speke was strong enough to walk. Speke was able to ride on one of the donkeys, Bombay leading him, but the rest of the pack animals were needed to carry cargo, leaving Burton to hobble as best he could on his own, trembling legs. Forced to lie down to rest every half hour, he finally looked up to find Bombay smiling down at him. "I saw with pleasure the kindly face of Seedy Bombay," he wrote, "who was returning to me in hot haste, leading an ass, and carrying a few scones and hard-boiled eggs."

Bombay's generosity also served as an inspiration or, in some cases, a bruising lesson to the other men. One night, as they made preparations to rest after a long march, Burton and Speke realized that their tent had yet to arrive with the rest of the caravan. Turning to Said bin Salim, their caravan leader, they asked him to lend them half of the length of canvas that served as his tent so that they could have some shelter from the elements. When Said refused, Bombay, outraged, lashed out at him, shaming him in front of the other men. Said finally gave in, grudgingly handing over the canvas. When Burton tried to give it back the next day, however, he "testily refuse[d] the half returned to him."

·

In the first eighteen days of the expedition, the caravan covered only 118 miles, a dangerously slow pace. It was not for lack of trying. Most days began at 4:00 a.m., with the piercing cry of one of the expedition's several, carefully cared for roosters. "The red-faced, apoplectic chanticleer...flaps his wings and crows a loud salutation to the dawn," Burton wrote. "He is answered by every cock and cockerel within earshot." Gaetano and Valentine would then build a fire, shivering in what seemed to the young men from Goa to be intolerable cold, and make breakfast for Burton and Speke. While the expedition's leaders began the day with tea or coffee, if they had it, along with rice-milk and whey cakes or porridge, their men prepared for the long march ahead by eating meat that they boiled in a cauldron over an open fire.

On a good day, the expedition would leave an hour later, the men filing into their respective places in the long, undulating caravan line. On a bad day, marked by excruciating illness or simply paralyzing fatigue, they were unable to even contemplate a long march, reduced to lying in their tents, delirious with fever or lucid enough to fear for their own survival. "We were wretched," Burton admitted. "Each morning dawned with a fresh load of care and trouble, and each evening we knew that another miserable morrow was to dawn, but I never relinquished the determination to risk everything, myself included, rather than to return unsuccessful."

By now, Burton had been able to add a few more men to the expedition, so that they numbered one hundred and thirty-two in total. Besides Bombay and Said bin Salim, among the most essential members of the party were the interpreter Muinyi Wazira, who spoke five different African dialects; the cooks Valentine and Gaetano; and Mallock, who was the *jemadar*, leader of the soldiers. Mohammed was the expedition's oldest soldier and Shahda its youngest. Khudabakhsh was tall and strong but hottempered, Burton wrote, "formed by nature to be the best man of the party; he has transformed himself into the worst." Of the other guards, Burton referred to Ismail as a "confirmed invalid" and Belok as a snob but admitted that Darwash conducted himself with decorum. He seemed to admire Gul Mohammed but could not decide whether to trust him. He is "brave and treacherous, fair-spoken and detractive, honorable and dishonest, good-tempered and bad-hearted," he claimed. Keeping track of all of the men and keeping them alive, he knew, would be his greatest struggle.

The donkeys alone represented a seemingly insurmountable challenge. "Kicking and plunging, rearing and pawing," they resisted any attempts at taming with a ferociousness that defeated even the men who had been hired to handle them. It was almost impossible to secure their loads, each of which weighed roughly two hundred pounds and were tied on with rope that had already begun to rot. During a march they were, if possible, even more difficult to handle. "The asses shy, stumble, rear, run away, fight, plunge and pirouette when mounted," Burton wrote with exasperation. "They hog and buck till they burst their girths; they love to get into holes and hollows; they rush about like pigs when the wind blows."

As the days passed, the motley assortment of donkeys quickly shrank from thirty to half that number. One was accidentally left behind after a hurried exodus from camp. Two wandered off when no one was looking, and another so strained its back that it could barely hobble along much less carry the awkward, impossibly heavy packs. A notoriously vicious donkey known as the "one-eyed fiend" because it had lost an eye at some point, simply lay down on the ground and refused to move. Finally, he was "cast adrift in the wilderness," Burton wrote, "because no man dared to load and lead him." One night, the men were woken from their sleep by the screams of three donkeys that were being attacked by a hyena, which tore ragged pieces of flesh from their flanks. "These, however, were the animals brought from Zanzibar," Burton noted. The donkey from the mainland "defends itself successfully against its cowardly assailant with teeth and heels."

The weather was as unpredictable and temperamental as the donkeys. It alternated between a scorching heat that seared their faces and sapped their strength and brutal, drenching storms that turned the swollen clouds a dark, bruised purple, dragging them across the sky. "Furious blasts battered rain-drops like musket bullets," Burton wrote. "The tall stiff trees groaned and bent before the gusts; the birds screamed as they were driven from their perching-places; the asses stood with heads depressed, ears hung down, and shrinking tails turned toward the weather, and even the beasts of the wild seemed to have taken refuge in the dens." The ground, already saturated from days of monsoon rains, sucked at their feet, slowing the expedition to a crawl and casting a pall over everyone and everything. "The earth... emits the odor of sulphureted hydrogen," Burton wrote, "and in some parts the traveler might fancy a corpse to be hidden behind every bush."

Even when it was not raining, everything the expedition owned was damp, dripping, rotten, or rusted. From scientific equipment to personal gear, it quickly began to disintegrate. "The humidity of the atmosphere corrodes every thing with which it comes in contact," Burton complained. "The springs of powder-flasks exposed to the damp snap like toasted quills; clothes feel limp and damp; paper, becoming soft and soppy by the loss of glazing, acts as a blotter; boots, books, and botanical collections are blackened; metals are ever rusty; the best percussion caps though labeled water-proof, will not detonate unless carefully stowed away in waxed cloth and tin boxes." Wood mildewed, match heads shrank and crumbled, cardboard boxes dissolved into paste, and sodden gunpowder refused to light.

As he had always done, Speke prided himself in working in nearly any weather. Sitting under a dripping tent or on a rise of scorched earth, he taught himself how to use the sextant. Struggling to make the most of the broken, damaged equipment, he stopped to take measurements as the expedition staggered up mountains or thrashed its way through jungles. "Night after night, at the end of the burning march, he sat for hours in the chilling dews," Burton would later recall, "practising lunars and timing chronometers." Although he suspected that Speke was eagerly looking for any fault in him, Burton openly admired his young companion's discipline and fortitude, later even writing about his travels through the Himalayas. Speke had there "led the hardest of lives," Burton would write. "He rose with the freezing dawn, walked in the burning sun all day... passed the biting nights in the smallest 'rowtie' tents, often falling asleep before finishing his food."

Despite his own recurring fevers, Burton had also found a way to keep working. Most nights after the caravan had stopped to rest, he wrote reports for the Royal Geographical Society and added to the voluminous notes that he had started in Zanzibar. He had already filled several notebooks, crowded with detailed descriptions of everything he had seen and experienced, his obsessive nature and deep fascination with Africa propelling his pen across page after page. "No apology is offered for the lengthiness of the ethnographical descriptions," he would later write. "The ethnology of Africa is indeed its most interesting, if not its only interesting feature. Every thing connected with the habits and customs, the moral and religious, the social and commercial state of these new races, is worthy of diligent observation, careful description, and minute illustration."

Both Burton and Speke also daily struggled with the expedition's scientific equipment, which, even when untouched by damp or donkey, rarely worked. Among the supplies they had brought from Bombay were a six-inch sextant, two prismatic compasses, five thermometers, two pocket chronometers, protractors, and a patent log, a mechanical device that was usually used on ships to measure the speed and distance traveled by water but which Burton and Speke hoped to use on land. "My first occupation was to map the country," Speke wrote. "This is done by timing the rate of march with a watch, taking compass bearings along the road, or on any conspicuous marks—as, for instance, hills off it—and noting the watershed—in short, all topographical objects."

Although the hundreds of miles that the caravan was covering by foot was sparsely populated, it was immensely varied. Over the course of the expedition, the men would cross high, open grasslands, tangled, thorny scrub brush, waste-deep bogs, and a waterless, sandy wasteland. The flora and fauna, in turn, were equally, even spectacularly diverse—in size, beauty, and complexity, as well as in the benefits they offered and the dangers they posed.

For the hungry men, the grassy plains provided the best hunting grounds as well as a distraction from the expedition's grinding misery. There, they found a multitude of birds, from partridges and green pigeons to guinea-fowl, which looked to Burton like "large blue-bells upon the trees." They passed herds of quietly grazing zebra, "the most graceful of animals," Burton wrote admiringly, and single leopards sitting high in gnarled trees, their sleek, spotted bodies slumped over thick branches. Giraffes galloped jerkily by, tails wagging, heads bobbing, impossibly long legs seemingly dislocated at their knobby joints. There were several species of antelope, including the long-necked kudu and the large, heavily maned wildebeest, which "the porters regard with a wholesome awe," Burton wrote, "declaring that they are capable of charging a caravan."

The jungles, with their dense vegetation, were the most difficult terrain for the caravan to pass through. It was also far harder to hunt here, with the animals able to use camouflage or simply deathlike stillness to hide in plain sight. The only animals they saw with any frequency were small black-faced monkeys, which stared at them with open curiosity before bounding away. Even elephants seemed to prefer the jungles, where they could "wallow in the pools and feed delicately upon succulent roots and fruits, bark, and leaves," Burton wrote, and where it was harder for ivory hunters to reach them.

The only thing the elephants had to fear in the jungles were the minuscule creatures teeming at their feet. Among the twisted vines and rotting leaves, the land hummed with life, home to dozens of different species of ants, a danger to even the largest of animals if sick or injured. The longhorn crazy ant spun in erratic, un-antlike patterns, spraying formic acid from its curved abdomen. An ant that Burton simply called the "pismire," an archaic word for ant, had a "bulldog head and powerful mandibles," he wrote, giving it a bite that "burns like a pinch of a red-hot needle. When it sets to work, twisting itself round, it may be pulled in two without relaxing its hold." Most infamous was the coppery brown safari ant, a genus of the army ant that moved by the millions, swarming over any possible prey or perceived threat. Tight columns crossed the expedition's path, attacking "man and beast ferociously," Burton recalled, "causing the caravan to break into a halting, trotting hobble, ludicrous to behold."

Many nights during their long journey, as the men lay in their flimsy tents, they heard the one sound that never failed to make their hearts pound with fear: the low, throaty roar of a lion. The lions themselves were not always nearby—their roar could travel for miles—and even if they were, Burton insisted, they were rarely man eaters. "This peculiarity," he argued, "being confined to old beasts whose worn teeth are unfit for fight." Most of the men in the expedition, however, had likely known someone who had been mauled or even eaten by a lion. Burton himself knew a man who had survived a lion attack: Britain's most famous and revered explorer, David Livingstone, who had been exploring Southern and Central Africa for more than a decade but whose principal goal was the eradication of the slave trade.

When Livingstone was a young man, he had worked as a missionary in Bechuanaland, now Botswana. A lion had eaten several cattle owned by a nearby village, and Livingstone—foolishly, he would later admit—had set off alone with only one gun to kill it. He had shot at it twice, missing both times, and was reloading his gun when he heard several men from the village frantically shouting to him. He looked up just in time to see the lion leaping onto his back. "He caught my shoulder as he sprang, and we both came to the ground below together," he recalled. "Growling horribly close to my ear, he shook me as a terrier dog does a rat." Although the villagers quickly shot at the lion, scaring him off and leaving Livingstone with little more than a torn shoulder, he would never forget the near death experience, or how surprisingly little fear he had felt. "The shock produced a stupor similar to that which seems to be felt by a mouse after the first shake of the cat. It caused a sort of dreaminess, in which there was no sense of pain nor feeling of terror, though quite conscious of all that was happening," Livingstone later wrote. "It was like what patients partially under the influence of chloroform describe, who see all the operation, but feel not the knife.... The shake annihilated fear, and allowed no sense of horror in looking round at the beast. This peculiar state is probably produced in all animals killed by the carnivore; and if so, is a merciful provision by our benevolent Creator for lessening the pain of death."

•

Animal attack was always possible during an expedition, but far more deadly were the multitude of diseases that lurked in their water, their food, and the insects that swarmed in the air around them. Although later in the expedition Speke would complain to Norton Shaw that "Burton has always been ill," he was the first and hardest hit by illness. He came to fear most the painful, potentially fatal fevers, which, he wrote, "attack the brain, and often deprive one of one's senses. Then there is no rallying from the weakness they produce." The symptoms, moreover, were as varied as they were alarmingly strange. "When lying in bed, my toes have sometimes curled round and looked me in the face," he later recalled. "At other times, when I have put my hand behind my back, it has stuck there until, with the other hand, I have seized the contracted muscles, and warmed the part affected with the natural heat, till, relaxation taking place, I was able to get it back."

The painful contortions and forced idleness were bad enough, but for Speke the fact that Burton was well while he was ill was nearly as unbearable as the illness itself. "Unaccustomed to sickness," Burton noted, "he could not endure it himself nor feel for it in others." Speke, however, was not the only sick member of the expedition for long. The caravan leader, Said bin Salim, the cooks Valentine and Gaetano, and several of the expedition's porters quickly fell prey to fevers, as did Burton. While Speke's fever contorted his body, Burton's played havoc with his mind. "I had during the fever-fit, and often for hours afterward, a queer conviction of divided identity, never ceasing to be two persons that generally thwarted and opposed each other," he later described. "The sleepless nights brought with them horrid visions, animals of grisliest form, hag-like women and men with heads protruding from their breasts."

The expedition was also threatened by a smallpox contagion that had cruelly claimed the lives of many of the men in the caravans they passed. One of the most lethal diseases of the eighteenth century, smallpox had been largely eradicated in Britain by the mid-1800s, but it remained a significant danger in Africa, where few people had been vaccinated. "A single large body, which had lost fifty of its number by small-pox, had passed us but yesterday on the road, and the sight of their deceased comrades recalled to our minds terrible spectacles," Burton would later write. "The wretches would not leave the path, every step of failing strength was precious; he who once fell would never rise again; no village would admit death into its precincts, no relation nor friend would return for them, and they would lie till their agony was ended by the raven and vulture, the fisi and the fox." Burton's men turned away in sorrow and fear as they passed the dead bodies lying on or near the path. A few contracted the disease themselves, and, unable to keep up with the caravan, soon fell behind before disappearing altogether. The expedition doubled back to search for them but found no signs that might lead them to the dying men.

•

On September 10, nearly three months after the expedition had left the coast, the men reached what Burton referred to as the "Pass Terrible." After entering the forested Rubeho Mountains, which rose to more than 7,000 feet, they steeled themselves for what lay ahead. "Trembling with ague, with swimming heads, ears deafened by weakness, and limbs that would hardly support us, we contemplated with a dogged despair the apparently perpendicular path ... up which we and our starving drooping asses were about to toil," Burton wrote. "We hardened our hearts, and began to breast the Pass Terrible."

It took them six hours to reach the summit. Burton was weak but lucid. Speke was barely able to walk let alone climb a mountain, needing the help of three men just to keep upright. "He ... advanced mechanically," Burton wrote, "almost in a state of coma." When they finally reached the other side, they were forced to stop. Speke's fever had boiled over into a delirium so violent that they had to remove his weapons for fear he would hurt himself or someone else. Burton worried that Speke's attack might have a "permanent cerebral effect," or that he might not survive it at all. "Death," he wrote, "appeared stamped upon his features."

Two days later, Speke was finally well enough to be carried in a hammock. Burton, however, had emerged from his own fever-induced stupor only to realize that his expedition was in immediate danger. He had assumed that the hundreds of pounds of supplies that he had brought from Zanzibar would last them at least until they reached Lake Tanganyika. Instead, it was already nearly gone. "For the first time since many days I had strength enough to muster the porters and to inspect their loads," he wrote. "The outfit, which was expected to last a year, had been half exhausted in three months."

With this shocking discovery, Burton realized that they had added the threat of starvation to that of disease. As they trudged west toward Lake Tanganyika, struggling with their mutinous donkeys, sagging under the weight of their heavy packs, and weak with fever and fatigue, they saw the bodies of men who, they assumed, had died not just because they had contracted smallpox but because they could not find anything to eat. "We were saddened by the sight of the clean-picked skeletons," Burton wrote, "and here and there the swollen corpses, of porters who had perished in this place of starvation."

The region was reluctant to provide for those who were simply passing through. "The land is stony and rugged, with a few fields scattered in a thick bushy jungle," Burton wrote. "The ground is red, and cultivation alternates with scrub and forest full of wild fruit—some edible, others poisonous." Even if they could find people with whom to trade, they had little of value to offer in return for meat or milk. Burton had been able to afford little of the high-quality *kuhonga* sold in Zanzibar, and much of what he had bought had already either been given away or taken by his men during the march. "Said bin Salim, to whom it had been intrusted, had been generous, through fear," Burton bitterly complained. "Moreover, while too ill to superintend disbursements, he had allowed his 'children,' aided by the Baloch and the 'sons of Ramji' to 'loot' whatever they could seize and secrete."

Aware of the looming danger and knowing that both Burton and Speke were perilously ill, the expedition's men, far from home, had little choice but to take what they could when they could, and to find ways to feed themselves. Whenever an easily edible animal, from a hare to an antelope, crossed their path, they immediately dropped their packs and chased it with their spears. Within minutes, it would be dead, torn to pieces, and eaten raw. Even ants were satisfying sources of protein, and eating them a small act of vengeance for the irritation and pain they had caused. "Man revenges himself upon the white ant, and satisfies his craving for animal food," Burton wrote, "by boiling the largest and fattest kind, and eating it as a relish with his... porridge."

Unsure if they would be able to replenish their supplies at the next town they reached, or if they would even make it to the next town, Burton knew that his best hope lay with the consulate in Zanzibar. Speke, finally well enough to think clearly again, agreed, equally worried that the expedition was in grave danger and determined to send a letter with the next trade caravan they passed that was returning to the coast. "I calculated our rate of expenditure, found we had not enough for the necessities of the journey, and prevailed on Captain Burton to write back for more, notwithstanding our Government subsidy was out," he wrote. "I could not brook the idea of failure." The question was, who would help them?

Nearly a month earlier, Burton had written confidently to Hamerton, politely but urgently requesting aid. "We are still suffering from consequences of fever," he informed him, "and look with horror upon our diminishing medicine." Having neither heard back nor received additional supplies, Burton had finally and reluctantly come to the conclusion that the rumors had been true and that his friend was dead. Now, "with swimming head and trembling hands," he took a piece of the expedition's precious remaining paper and began to write to the unknown consul who had replaced Hamerton in Zanzibar. "Sir, I have taken the liberty to address you without even knowing your name. Our necessities may excuse this proceeding," he wrote, editing as he went. "Since the death of our lamented friend Col. Ham., we have been entirely neglected by those who promised fairest. Not a letter or paper has reached us, altho' Arabs & others have repeatedly received theirs from the coast.... We are ever suffering from fever, and our ~~supply of~~ Quinine is so low, that we must reserve it for emergencies. In conclusion Sir I have the honour to express ~~my hope~~ my conviction that you will not allow 2 officers esp. employed under the patronage of H.R.M.'s Foreign Office, to suffer any longer from such undeserved & disgraceful neglect."

The letter, carried back by Yaruk, the expedition's *jemadar*, on a perilous, lonely journey, would eventually reach Zanzibar, as the East African Expedition continued to limp toward Lake Tanganyika. No one, however, would be there to receive it for nearly eight months. When the man appointed to replace Hamerton finally reached the island, moreover, he would be little help to Burton. The newest British consul at Zanzibar was none other than Colonel Christopher Palmer Rigby, the ambitious linguist who had been bested by Burton in the Gujarati exam more than a decade earlier, and had subsequently been president of the committee that had failed him in Arabic. As Burton fought his way toward what he hoped was the source of the White Nile, he knew only that his friend, the man who had treated him with such kindness and concern and on whose help he had been able to rely, was gone. What he did not know was that an old enemy had taken his place.

——— ◆◆◆ ———

CHAPTER TWELVE

Tanganyika

It took the expedition 134 days to travel roughly six hundred miles. By the time they reached Kazeh, one of the most important trading depots in the region and a critical juncture for the expedition, they were almost three quarters of the way to Lake Tanganyika. With more than 250 miles to go, however, their need for provisions had grown even more desperate. They planned to rest for a few days in Kazeh, hoping that supplies from Zanzibar would find them there. Five weeks would pass before they were able to set out again.

One of the first things Burton did after arriving in Kazeh was to hire a man named Shaykh Snay bin Amir. Not only was Snay well connected and hardworking, taking charge of the expedition's supplies, helping them hire porters, and finding a place for them to stay, but he was exceptionally knowledgeable about the region. "Snay had travelled as much as, or more than, any person in this land," Speke wrote admiringly. "And from being a shrewd and intelligent inquirer, knew everybody and everything."

So wide-ranging had Snay's travels been throughout East Africa that Burton and Speke realized he might be able to shed some light on one of their most pressing questions. Spreading before him their copy of the strange map drawn by Rebmann and Erhardt, they asked him about the enormous, sluglike lake that dominated the page. Snay's confident reply stunned them. Rebmann and Erhardt had gotten it wrong. "The missionaries had run three lakes into one," Speke wrote. In reality, there was not a single, sprawling inland lake but three separate ones, each larger than the last: Nyasa to the south, Tanganyika to the west, and Nyanza, also known as Ukerewe, to the north. After examining the map, Snay expressed surprise that they were continuing west toward the town of Ujiji, which lay on the banks of Lake Tanganyika, rather than north toward the Nyanza. "He strongly advised us," Speke later wrote, "if our only motive in coming here was to look at a large piece of water, to go to it instead of on to Ujiji."

Feeling "great glee at this," Speke immediately suggested to Burton that they change their route. Instead of "journeying westward to the smaller waters of Ujiji," he argued, they should turn their sights to this larger lake to the north. After all, the Nyanza, he would later insist, was greater not only in size but "in every respect than the Tanganyika." Although Burton wrote that he "saw at once that the existence of this hitherto unknown basin would explain many discrepancies promulgated by speculative geographers," he was not about to give up on the Tanganyika. He had invested too much time, effort, health, and hope in it to turn away now.

•

The expedition would not be going anywhere soon. A week after they arrived in Kazeh, nearly every man, from the *kirangozi* to the cooks, again fell ill. Valentine and Gaetano were the first to get sick. Then Mabruki and Bombay, who was "laid up by a shaking ague," Burton wrote. The "sons" of Ramji were weak with fever, and Ismail, one of the Baloch soldiers, was dying of dysentery. Speke had finally recovered and was now stronger than he had been for much of the journey, but he was one of the few members of the expedition still on his feet.

Burton, too, had fallen ill and, a month later, was so weak that Speke convinced him to let him temporarily take over the leadership of the expedition. "I thought Captain Burton would die if we did not make a move," Speke later wrote, "so I begged him to allow me to assume the command pro tem, and I would see what I could do to effect a move." On December 5, Speke led any man who was well enough to walk and half of their baggage to the next town, Zimbili. Although he would remain in Kazeh, Snay promised to forward their letters and papers with the next caravan heading back to Zanzibar, and, more critical, to hurry on the "lagging gang" that was carrying the provisions they had been forced to leave behind at the coast and which they desperately needed.

Three days later, Burton, "in truth, more dead than alive," followed. This order of procession continued through December. Speke would set out for the next stop ahead of Burton, prepare lodging for the expedition, and then the two men would be reunited a few days later. The only way to move Burton was to carry him in a hammock. As the expedition already had too few men, they could only spare two when at least four were needed to support Burton's prone body, even after it had been whittled away by weeks of illness. On the last march before Christmas, Said, the caravan leader, walked by Burton in silence, without giving his prostrate commander a backward glance. "Doubtlessly impressed with the belief that my days were numbered," Burton wrote, he "passed me on the last march without a word."

By mid-January, six months after they had left the coast, Burton was almost completely paralyzed, unable even to use his hands. His arms and legs had suddenly begun "to weigh and to burn as if exposed to a glowing fire," he wrote. By the time the sun set that night, he agreed with Said: He must be dying. "The attack had reached its height. I saw yawning wide to receive me, 'Those dark gates across the wild/That no man knows,'" he later recalled. "The whole body was palsied, powerless, motionless, and the limbs appeared to wither and die; the feet had lost all sensation, except a throbbing and tingling, as if pricked by a number of needle-points; the arms refused to be directed by will, and to the hands the touch of cloth and stone was the same. Gradually the attack seemed to spread upward till it compressed the ribs; there, however, it stopped short." Burton would remain in this state of near total paralysis for nearly a year.

The expedition, Burton knew, was at least two months from any medical help. They still had hundreds of miles to go before they would even reach the lake, where, he wrote, "the principal labor of the expedition [was] still in prospect!" It seemed unlikely that the men would be able to carry him that distance, especially as they were all weak from their own repeated illnesses, punishing work, and meager rations. Burton had undertaken the expedition "with the resolve to do or die," he wrote. "I had done my best, and now nothing appeared to remain for me but to die as well."

Speke, although he had often been surly and distant, now showed genuine concern for Burton's health. Over the course of the long journey, the two men had had moments of closeness, spending quiet, congenial evenings together. Sitting in their tent after a long march, Burton writing reports, letters, and notes for his next book, Speke had worked on his own sketches and writing, occasionally showing his accounts of their journey to Burton, asking for advice that Burton readily gave. They had also shared the small collection of books that Burton had allowed himself to bring on the expedition. "The few books—Shakespeare, Euclid, and so forth—which composed my scanty library," Burton wrote, "we read together again and again."

Now, Burton took comfort in the knowledge that, whatever happened to him, Speke would carry on. "If one of us was lost," he hoped, "the other might survive to carry home the results of the exploration." Although Speke wanted Burton to live, and was doing his best to save him, Burton knew that his subordinate hungered to have the expedition under his own command. Burton wanted to find the source of the White Nile himself, but he was grateful that, at the very least, the young man he had taken under his wing would do everything in his power to see the expedition through to the end.

Even Speke, however, was not wholly well. He had regained his strength, but he had lost something equally valuable: his sight. The fever that had nearly killed him had left behind a cruel and frightening legacy. "My companion, whose blood had been impoverished, and whose system had been reduced by many fevers," Burton wrote, "now began to suffer from 'an inflammation of a low type affecting the whole of the interior tunic of the eyes, particularly the iris, the choroid coat, and the retina'; he describes it as 'an almost total blindness, rendering every object enclouded as by a misty veil.'" Valentine had been struck by the same condition, describing it as an "inky blot" on his eyes, "which completely excluded the light of day." The blot, the renowned British ophthalmologist Sir William Bowman would later explain in a letter to Speke, was caused by "inflammation of the iris, known as iritis, there being a deposit of some of the black pigment of the iris on the front of the lens.... They may in time disappear, but I do not know that the medical art can supply any remedy for them."

The condition, known generally as ophthalmia, was not uncommon in the nineteenth century. Burton and Speke had both suffered from it at various times in their lives, Burton in India and Speke at home in England. Two attacks of ophthalmia during Speke's childhood had "rendered reading a painful task," which, Burton suspected, explained his "devotion to bird-nesting and his hatred of 'book-learning.'" The men who had fought Napoleon in Egypt had also suffered from the disease, which caused not only pain and inconvenience but a terrifying loss of what they held most dear. "In the case of ophthalmia, the anguish of the affected part is acute nearly to delirium," early-nineteenth-century historian Lieutenant Colonel Robert Wilson wrote in his seminal *History of the British Expedition to Egypt.* "When the beauties of nature, the wonders of the universe, the objects of dearest affections can no longer be gazed on, that darkness is surely more painful to a soldier than the tranquil gloom of the grave."

•

On February 10, as a storm brewed, the men forded a river before fighting their way over a succession of high, steep hills thickly carpeted in long tiger and spear grasses, reeds, and ferns. They had added two men to the detail carrying Burton's hammock, but they all sweated, limped, and tripped as they climbed the hills, swatting away the grasses and nervously glancing at the roiling sky above, "purple-black with nimbus." Peering into the distance, however, they could see hope shining through the clouds. "Walls of sky-blue cliff with gilded summits," Burton wrote, "were as a beacon to the distressed mariner."

Three days later, they crested yet another hill, its incline so steep that the donkey Speke was riding on died halfway up. As they paused to rest on the summit, something in the distance caught Burton's eye. Although he had avoided a full-blown case of inflammatory ophthalmia by, he believed, treating his eyes with "camel medicine," he suffered from what he referred to as "webs of flitting muscae [that] obscured smaller objects and rendered distant vision impossible." Now, wincing against the glare of the sun and blinking his infected eyes, Burton turned to Bombay and asked, "What is that streak of light which lies below?" Bombay answered simply, "I am of opinion that that is the water." What he was seeing, Burton suddenly realized, was Lake Tanganyika.

Burton's first reaction to the lake was not elation but bitter disappointment. "I gazed in dismay," he later wrote. "I began to lament my folly in having risked life and lost health for so poor a prize, to curse Arab exaggeration, and to propose an immediate return, with the view of exploring the Nyanza, or Northern Lake." As the porters carried him closer, however, past a veil of trees, his eyes mercifully clearing, "the whole scene," he wrote, "suddenly burst upon my view, filling me with admiration, wonder, and delight." Before him lay the longest and second deepest freshwater lake in the world, slicing through more than four hundred miles of the Western Rift Valley. Like a jagged blue crack in the face of the earth, the massive body of water was flanked by stony, forested land that rose steeply from its shores.

Later, remembering this moment and the stunning beauty of the lake and the land that surrounded it, Burton would overflow with a gushingly vivid, almost feverish description of the Tanganyika. "A narrow strip of emerald green, never sere and marvelously fertile, shelves toward a ribbon of glistening yellow sand, here bordered by sedgy rushes, there cleanly and clearly cut by the breaking wavelets," he wrote. "Farther in front stretch the waters, an expanse of the lightest and softest blue … sprinkled by the crisp east wind with tiny crescents of snowy foam. The background in front is a high and broken wall of steel-colored mountain, here flecked and capped with pearly mist, there standing sharply penciled against the azure air." It was everything he had dreamed of and more, worth even the frail and paralyzed body that he now inhabited. "Forgetting toils, dangers, and the doubtfulness of return," he wrote, "I felt willing to endure double what I had endured."

•

Standing next to Burton, Speke squinted into the distance, his obvious annoyance a startling contrast to Burton's rapture. By now almost completely blind, Speke felt robbed of the verdant and azure beauty—"one of the most beautiful inland seas in the world," he would later write—which was spread out before nearly every man in the expedition but him. "You may picture to yourself my bitter disappointment," he wrote, "when, after toiling through so many miles of savage life, all the time emaciated by divers sicknesses and weakened by great privations of food and rest, I found, on approaching the zenith of my ambition, the Great Lake in question nothing but mist and glare before my eyes."

Carefully making their way down the other side of the steep hill, the men soon reached the edge of the lake. After hiring a canoe, they crossed to the province of Ujiji, where they would stay while they explored the Tanganyika, hoping to find a river flowing out of its blue depths. After a journey of nearly eight months, Burton and Speke were the first Europeans to reach the lake, but Arabs had been there for nearly two decades, using Ujiji as a depot from where they bought ivory and enslaved people from the surrounding region. In Zanzibar, the traders would sell those they had kidnapped for a nearly 500 percent profit, which was why, Burton noted dismally, it was so difficult to abolish the slave trade.

After reaching Ujiji, Burton quickly found lodgings in an Arab *tembe*, a circular hut with eaves held aloft by large poles. The roof was covered with mud and tall grass to keep out the rain, and inside clay benches lined the curved walls. For furniture, Burton also had a cartel, which was an iron bedframe that could be used as a bed, chair, or table and had been made without joints, nuts, or screws that might be lost along the way. As most of their candles and lanterns had already been used, broken, or lost, they used "dips" to light the dark interior, ladling hot wax and tallow from a cauldron over homemade wicks, then setting them into chipped pots filled with palm oil.

Several different peoples lived along this stretch of the Tanganyika, including the Wakaranga, the Wavinza, and the Wajiji. The expedition had the most interaction with the Wajiji, whom Burton admiringly described as "almost amphibious." They were "excellent divers," he wrote, "strong swimmers and fishermen, and vigorous ichthyophagists all." He filled his notebooks with detailed descriptions of their lives on the lake, watching riveted as they glided through the rough waters with the same ease that he walked on land and, using a variety of tools, from hooks to baskets to rope nets, effortlessly caught enough fish to fill their boats.

As Burton had known it would be, the first and greatest challenge facing the expedition now that it had reached the Tanganyika was to find a way to sail on it. The options were few as most of the peoples who lived along the lake were at war with one another and so unable or unwilling to rent out their larger and sturdier boats. All that was available in Ujiji were "little cockle-shell canoes, made from the hollowed trunks of trees," Speke wrote, which were "not only liable to be driven ashore by the slightest storm, but are so small that there is but little stowage-room in them for carrying supplies." Although Burton had had no choice but to leave his American lifeboat, the *Louisa,* behind, he regretted the decision now more than ever. "The first aspect of these canoes made me lament the loss," he wrote. "Regrets, however, were of no avail. *Quo-cumque modo.*" He would find a way to explore the lake—*in any way.*

Since reaching Ujiji, Burton had been told by several locals that a large river flowed out of the lake's northern reaches. The possibility that the river might feed into the White Nile, and that he had only to find it to confirm that the Tanganyika was its source, tormented him as he lay in his *tembe,* too sick to sit up much less to travel for weeks in a rough and cramped canoe. "I lay for a fortnight upon the earth," he wrote, "too blind to read or write except with long intervals, too weak to ride, and too ill to converse." The only answer, he realized, was to wait in Ujiji while one of his men visited an Arab who lived on the western shores of the lake and who, they had been told, had a dhow that was large and safe enough to carry them on a complete survey of the enormous lake.

The plan at first was to send Said to negotiate, but, as with anything that the expedition tried to do, the preparations alone took far longer than they had expected or could afford. "First a crew had to be collected, and when collected to be paid, and when paid, the boat was found to be unseaworthy, and must be plugged," Speke wrote in frustration, "and so much time elapsed, and plans were changed." In the intervening weeks, while Burton lay nearly lifeless in his *tembe,* Speke slowly began to heal. After arriving in Ujiji, as well as being nearly blind, he had suffered from a strange, disfiguring fever that had resulted in a "curious distortion of face," Burton wrote, "which made him chew sideways, like a ruminant." Unlike Burton, however, the younger man's body was growing stronger. With the help of Bombay, Speke used the time while they waited for the canoes to swim in the lake and walk to the market, protecting his eyes from the sun by carrying an umbrella and wearing "stained-glass spectacles."

By early March, Speke was ready to set out for Kasengé, the village on the west bank of the lake where he hoped to obtain the dhow. He had gathered twenty-five men for the voyage, among them Bombay, Gaetano, two soldiers, a man to navigate the boat, and twenty sailors. Their canoe, while insufficient for an extended survey of the lake, would have to do for this shorter voyage. It was exceptionally long and narrow, hollowed out of a single, enormous tree trunk taken from a grove of towering trees on the western side of the lake. Wooden planks were tied across the opening and covered in blankets for seating. Inside, along with their food, fuel, and cooking utensils, they packed sixty pounds of cloth, a magazine of powder, a large load of blue beads and another of *kitindis* or coil bracelets, which they hoped to use to pay for the dhow. When they had finished packing, the canoe was so crowded that Speke doubted that they could all fit inside without sinking. "I litter down amidships, with my bedding spread on reeds, in so short a compass that my legs keep slipping off and dangling in the bilge-water," he wrote. "The cook and bailsman sit on the first bar, facing me; and behind them, to the stern, one half the sailors sit in couples; whilst on the first bar behind me are Bombay and one Balooch, and beyond them to the bow, also in couples, the remaining crew. The captain takes post in the bows, and all hands on both sides paddle in stroke together."

Despite Speke's initial enthusiasm and improved health, the journey, which proceeded in stages along the long, ragged shore, was a disaster from the start. A storm immediately overtook the small expedition, terrifying the men as they labored in their crowded, unwieldy canoe to navigate the heaving waters. So broad and deep was the Tanganyika, moreover, deeper than only one other freshwater lake in the world, that it seemed like they were navigating not a lake but a sea. The storm, Speke wrote, was "an ocean-tempest in miniature."

Should their canoe sink or the men simply be cast out into the pitching lake, they feared not only drowning but being eaten alive. Having lived their entire lives on the lake's shores, where it was not uncommon to be caught in a crocodile's jaws, the crew was constantly on the lookout for the stealthy predators. They refused even to dip a pot into the lake for water, fearing that the ripples would catch the attention of a pair of green, slit-pupiled eyes. When Speke carelessly tipped the leftover scraps from his meal overboard, his men immediately and angrily complained, insisting that he drop them in the bottom of the boat instead. "The traditions of Tanganyika hold...that the ravenous hosts of crocodiles seldom spare any one bold enough to excite their appetites with such dregs as usually drop from those utensils; moreover, they will follow and even board the boats, after a single taste," Speke wrote. "The sailors here have as great an aversion to being followed by the crocodile as our seamen by a shark."

Even when they stopped to rest along the shore, Speke was not safe from attack. One night, another violent storm beat on his tent with such fury that the howling wind ripped it from its pegs. After the wind had finally died down, Speke lit a candle so that he could put his tent back in order. "In a moment, as though by magic," he wrote, "the whole interior became covered with a host of small black beetles, evidently attracted by the glimmer of the candle." He desperately tried to fight them off, brushing them from his clothing and bedding, crushing them under his feet, and knocking them from the sides of the tent. The beetles, however, refused to leave, seeming to only grow in number and intensity as Speke flailed his arms, feeling them crawling through his hair, down his legs, and up his sleeves. Finally, exhausted, he gave up, extinguishing the candle and lying down, fragile wings whirring around his head, tiny, sticky feet climbing over his face as he fell into an uneasy sleep.

Later, awoken by an odd sensation that was not on his head but in it, Speke realized to his horror that one of the beetles had crawled deep into his ear canal. "He went his course, struggling up the narrow channel, until he got arrested by want of passage-room," he later wrote. "This impediment evidently enraged him, for he began with exceeding vigour, like a rabbit at a hole, to dig violently away at my tympanum." At first, Speke was tempted to react in the same way that the expedition's donkeys had when a swarm of bees had set upon them, running around in circles, racing blindly under bushes, frantically trying anything to rid themselves of the menace. Instead, forcing himself to remain calm, he tried every remedy he could think of, desperately searching for something—salt, oil, tobacco—that he could pour into his ear to chase the beetle and its sharp, black mandibles out. Finally, he resorted to melted butter, coaxing the sticky liquid down his ear canal. When that didn't work, he picked up his penknife. "I applied the point of a penknife to his back, which did more harm than good," he wrote. "Though a few thrusts kept him quiet, the point also wounded my ear so badly, that inflammation set in, severe suppuration took place, and all the facial glands extending from that point down to the point of the shoulder became contorted and drawn aside, and a string of boils decorated the whole length of that region. It was the most painful thing I ever remember to have endured."

For the next few days, Speke could not even open his mouth and was able to consume nothing more than broth. He was now, moreover, not only nearly blind but partially deaf. The infection left behind by the beetle and his penknife "ate a hole between that orifice [his ear] and the nose," Speke wrote, "so that when I blew it, my ear whistled so audibly that those who heard it laughed." To his surprise, however, as the days passed he found that the attack had actually helped to improve his sight. "It was not altogether an unmixed evil," he wrote, "for the excitement occasioned by the beetle's operations acted towards my blindness as a counter-irritant by drawing the inflammation away from my eyes." The beetle itself, dead but still stubbornly lodged in Speke's ear, remained with him until, some six months later, a leg, a wing, and a few other tiny body parts were carried out in the wax.

•

Eight days after leaving Ujiji, Speke and his men finally reached Kasengé. The Arab Shaykh Hamed bin Sulayyim, who owned the dhow they hoped to rent, was warm and welcoming but frustratingly evasive. "The dhow I had come for, he said was lying at Ukaranga, on the eastern shore," Speke wrote, "but was expected in a day or two, and would then be at my service." When the dhow arrived a few days later, Speke watched it enviously from the shore. "She looked very graceful in contrast to the wretched little canoes," he wrote, "and came moving slowly up the smooth waters of the channel decked in her white sails, like a swan upon 'a garden reach.'" He looked forward to sailing it back to Ujiji, from where they would finally be able to survey the length of the lake.

As the days passed, however, the Shaykh had one reason after another that he could not let Speke take the boat. It needed repairs, he said, or he could not find enough sailors to man it. Speke tried everything he could think of to persuade him, presenting him with the *kuhonga* he had brought from Ujiji, inviting him to a private meeting with Bombay as the interpreter, offering him money, guns, and his powder magazine, which he had noticed the Shaykh admiring. After two weeks of being offered food, gifts, promises, and excuses by his host, seemingly everything but the dhow, Speke finally gave up, realizing that he had neither the supplies nor the patience to wait any longer. "Feeling now satisfied that nothing would prevail upon the Shaykh to let us have the dhow," he wrote, "I wished to... return to Ujiji."

For Speke, the journey back to Ujiji, where Burton waited expectantly, was even worse than the trip there. Once again, he had been humiliated. It was as though he were repeating his degrading expedition to the Wady Nogal, when Sumunter had taken advantage of his naïveté, and he had failed to accomplish the principal task that Burton had set for him. Now he had to tell his commander that he had been unable to get the one thing the expedition needed most, and without which all of their work and sacrifice would be wasted.

On March 29, nearly a month after Speke had left Ujiji, Burton heard the rattle of matchlocks outside his *tembe*, signaling that the men had arrived. Expecting a triumphant return, he was astonished to see Speke standing before him downcast, exhausted, bedraggled, and drenched. The men had endured another storm on the way back, more powerful than the one that had ushered them to Kasengé. Even worse, they had no dhow to show for their troubles. "I never saw a man so thoroughly moist and mildewed; he justified even the French phrase 'wet to the bone,'" Burton wrote. "His paraphernalia were in a similar state; his guns were grained with rust, and his fire-proof powder-magazine had submitted to the monsoon-rain." Burton was sympathetic but made no effort to hide his frustration. "I was sorely disappointed; he had done literally nothing."

Speke did, however, bring Burton something that he had wanted almost more than the dhow. The Shaykh had told Speke that, on a journey to the northern end of the lake, he had seen a large river flowing out of it. "Although I did not venture on it," the Shaykh said, "I went so near its outlet that I could see and feel the outward drift of the water." At the time, he claimed, he had been under attack by an armada of some forty canoes, but he had "felt the influence of a large river, which drains the water northward." While Burton had waited for Speke to return, another man at Ujiji had told him a similar story. "When we compared statements," Burton wrote, "we saw what was before us—a prize for which wealth, health, and life were to be risked."

Determined to see the river for himself, Burton found fifty-five men and two large canoes and insisted that he be helped into one of them. He knew that both he and the canoes might not be strong enough to survive the journey, but after waiting for nearly a month in Ujiji he was willing to take that chance. "We had no other resource left us but to proceed with the investigation of the Lake in common canoes; for we could not wait any longer, as our supplies were fast on the wane," Speke wrote. "I was sorry for it, as my companion was still suffering so severely, that anybody seeing him attempt to go would have despaired of his ever returning. Yet he could not endure being left behind."

Two weeks later, after facing storms so fierce their canoes

were repeatedly swamped and nearly sent whirling to the bottom of the lake, they arrived at Uvira, the northernmost trading center on the Tanganyika. Burton's hopes, however, were dashed almost immediately. The son of a local sultan visited the men and, upon hearing that they were looking for a large river that issued from the lake, told them that he knew the river, which was called the Rusizi, and could take them to it, but that it flowed into, not out of, the Tanganyika. The news, Burton later wrote, left him feeling "sick at heart."

Later, Burton would realize that none of the sources he had depended on for information about the river had been reliable, including Speke himself. After asking Bombay about Speke's conversation with Hamed bin Sulayyim, Bombay told him that Speke, in his excitement, had misunderstood the Shaykh, who had actually said that the river poured into the lake. Bombay, moreover, did not think that Hamed bin Sulayyim had ever been anywhere near the river. It was, he believed, all a ruse to impress Speke. Later, Burton would also question the man in Ujiji who had told him that he had watched the Rusizi's direction for two days. Now, he "owned that he had never been beyond Uvira, and that he never intended to do so," Burton wrote. "Briefly, I had been deceived by a strange coincidence of deceit."

Burton was still determined to explore the lake, with or without a dhow, in good health or in bad. While on the journey to the Rusizi, he had developed an ulcer on his tongue that was so severe he could barely talk or eat, adding to his frailty. After living on nothing but milk for seventeen days, however, his tongue had healed, and although his legs were still swollen and weak, his hands were no longer numb, making it possible for him to again read and write. Speke was still deaf in one ear, and would be for the rest of his life, but his vision had cleared. They were strong enough now, Burton believed, to return to Ujiji, stock up, and survey the lake in its entirety.

What they found in Ujiji, however, ended all hope of a long survey. Their already meager supplies had been reduced to almost nothing. Before leaving, Burton had placed Said in charge of the cloth that was so vital to everything they did, from buying food to paying local chiefs. Now, of the 120 *shukkah* or feet of cloth that they had left behind, only ten remained. "I naturally inquired what had become of the 110 others which had thus prematurely disappeared," Burton wrote. "Said bin Salim replied by showing a small pile of grain-bags, and by informing me that he had hired twenty porters for the down-march." Neither had Burton heard back from Snay bin Amir in Kazeh, to whom he had written repeatedly, hoping to hear that the new consul in Zanzibar had sent lifesaving provisions. "Old Want began to stare at us," Burton wrote. "Nowhere might a caravan more easily starve than in rich and fertile Central Africa."

Their last hope lay in the rumors that they had been hearing for days of a large caravan headed their way. Burton was skeptical—"not sanguine enough to expose myself to another disappointment," he wrote—but to his surprise, a week after they had returned to Ujiji he heard musket shots in the distance, announcing the arrival of strangers. By noon, his *tembe* was surrounded by boxes, packages, and men, part of a caravan led by an Arab trader named Mohinna whom they had met in Kazeh and who had agreed to bring with him the supplies they had left behind in the care of Snay bin Amir. "Had this timely supply not reached us," Speke wrote, "it is difficult to conceive what would have been our fate."

As welcome as the caravan was, it had also brought with it news from a world that seemed impossibly far away and had somehow continued to revolve without them for the past year. Among the packages were letters that had been sent to Burton from Zanzibar but also from Europe and India. "They were the first received after nearly eleven months," Burton wrote, "and of course they brought with them evil tidings."

For the first time, the men learned that a mutiny in India had started nearly a year earlier. Although it was unsuccessful, India's First War of Independence was the first concerted effort to shake off the British Empire's imperialist rule and would, ninety years later, finally bring about independence. Burton had warned of the simmering resentment in India years earlier in his book on Mecca, writing that Indians would soon decide that "the English are not brave, nor clever, nor generous, nor civilised, nor anything but surpassing rogues...and look forward to the hour when enlightened Young India will arise and drive the 'foul invader' from the land." Now, however, his thoughts were not with the British or the Indians but with his younger brother, Edward, who had been his closest companion in childhood and who was now a surgeon-general in Ceylon. One of Speke's brothers, also named Edward, was in India as well. Edward Speke, they would later learn, had been killed during the mutiny. Edward Burton had survived, but would return home a deeply, tragically changed man.

In the parcel from Zanzibar was also news of a loss that Burton had expected, had even assumed, but for which he mourned nonetheless. A letter from Frost, the apothecary who had been overseeing Hamerton's care, confirmed his fears. His friend had died little more than a week after leaving the expedition, while still aboard the *Artémise* as it bobbed in Zanzibar harbor. "He was a loss to his country," Burton wrote. "His honor and honesty, his gallantry and determination, knew no bounds; and at heart [he was] a 'sad good Christian'—the heavens be his bed!" The death of Hamerton was also, Burton knew, a loss to him personally and to his expedition. In fact, they had been lucky that he had survived as long as he had. "The consul's death," he wrote, "might have proved fatal to the expedition had its departure been delayed for a week."

Already feeling cut off from the world, Burton absorbed this news as yet another in a series of painful blows. "Such tidings are severely felt by the wanderer who, living long behind the world, and unable to mark its gradual changes, lulls, by dwelling upon the past, apprehension into a belief that his home has known no loss," he explained, "and who expects again to meet each old familiar face ready to smile upon his return as it was to weep at his departure." As he continued to inspect the supplies, moreover, he realized that they were not the godsend that he and Speke had at first believed them to be. Among the boxes that the porters had carried into Ujiji were packages of ammunition that the expedition did not need, broken bottles of cognac and curry powder, nearly empty canisters of coffee, tea, and sugar, and cloth and beads of the most inferior kind.

They now had enough food and *kuhonga* to get them to Kazeh, but they would have to leave Ujiji immediately. Their departure, Burton wrote, "was fated to resemble a flight more than the march of a peaceful expedition." There was no longer any possibility of exploring the rest of the lake. With his men's lives hanging in the balance, he had no choice but to head back to the coast and, from there, to Zanzibar. Burton still believed that, had they had more time to explore, they might have found the White Nile flowing out of the Tanganyika, but he knew that without proof he was just another explorer, vainly flailing at the edges of an ancient mystery.

CHAPTER THIRTEEN

To the End of the World

Before they had even left Ujiji, Speke began to argue that, instead of going directly to Zanzibar, they should make a detour north, to the Nyanza. "I was all the while burning to see it," he wrote. They could march to Kazeh first, he suggested, and if Burton was still not well enough, Speke would take a smaller contingent and go without him. "You can employ the time in taking notes from the travelled Arabs of all the countries round," he told Burton, knowing that the idea would appeal to him. Burton, still unable to walk and concerned that even in Kazeh they would not find enough supplies to justify an additional, unplanned journey, resisted the idea.

Burton's mind was still on the Tanganyika. As the caravan set out for the coast, leaving Ujiji behind, he took one last look at the long, shimmering lake. Later admitting that "the charm of the scenery was perhaps enhanced by the reflection that my eyes might never look upon it again," he described the setting with even more exuberance than he had used when recalling his first glimpse of it from the hills. "Masses of brown-purple clouds covered the quarter of the heavens where the sun was about to rise," he wrote. "Presently the mists, ruffled like ocean billow and luminously fringed with Tyrian purple, were cut by filmy rays, while, from behind their core, the internal living fire shot forth its broad beams, like the spokes of a huge aerial wheel, rolling a flood of gold over the light blue waters of the lake."

Three weeks later, on June 20, 1858, the expedition was back in Kazeh. On the way there, by a rare stroke of good luck, they had crossed paths with another caravan that was carrying some of the supplies that they had left behind when leaving the coast a year ago. Among the boxes were more letters, which, as always, brought more loss. "Almost every one had lost some relation or friend near and dear to him," Burton wrote. "Even Said bin Salim's hearth had been spoiled of its chief attraction, an only son." For Burton himself, there was news of a death that was even more personal and painful than that of Hamerton. As he had made his way toward the Tanganyika, he now learned, his father had died in England. While Hamerton's death had left Burton more alone in Africa, his father's death left him more alone in the world. Burton's father had never been a warm, reassuring presence in his life, but he had been a symbol of strength and the kind of thirst for adventure and knowledge that had defined his oldest son. It would have been a blow at any time, but it was particularly poignant now, as he was still so sick and so far from any semblance of home.

In Kazeh, to his surprise, Burton felt a weight begin to lift. Not only was his health slowly improving, but the doubt that had haunted him since they landed on the coast had finally receded. "Stronger than any physical relief, in my case, was the moral effect of success, and the cessation of the ghastly doubts and cares, and of the terrible wear and tear of mind, which, from the coast to Uvira, had never been absent," he wrote. "I felt the proud consciousness of having done my best, under conditions from beginning to end the worst and the most unpromising, and that whatever future evils Fate might have in store for me, it could not rob me of the meed won by the hardships and sufferings of the past."

Speke, on the other hand, was unhappy and restless. While Burton settled into the work he loved best, losing himself in voluminous, minutely detailed notes on the language and life of the people they had met, Speke could not sit still a moment longer. "This is a shocking country for sport there appears to be literally nothing but Elephants," he complained in a short letter to Shaw at the Royal Geographical Society, hardly bothering with punctuation. "There is literally nothing to write about in this uninteresting country nothing could surpass these tracks, jungles, plains etc. for dull sameness, the people are the same everywhere in fact the country is one vast senseless mass of sameness." Even the work that did interest him, taking scientific measurements, was impossible because he needed help, and Burton, he grumbled, was useless. "Up to the present time I have failed being able to take them simply from want of an assistant to take the time," he told Shaw. "For Burton has always been ill; he won't sit out in the dew & has a decided objection to the sun, moreover when there happens to be a good opportunity for taking a Lunar his eyes become bad & so I always get disappointed."

Burton noticed, once again, that Speke was "a little sour," but he believed it was because he did not speak Arabic and so felt lonely and left out of the animated conversations that Burton was having with the Arab traders in Kazeh. It was "partly why he wished to have an expedition of his own," Burton guessed.

Speke did want an expedition of his own, and he did not want to wait for it. He now reminded Burton of the conversation they had had before leaving Ujiji. "I should proceed alone [to the Nyanza]," he argued, "and satisfy the Royal Geographical Society's desires as far as possible about all the inland seas, the object for which they sent us."

Not only was Speke eager to set out on his own expedition, his interest in the Nyanza had grown since their return to Kazeh. With the help of Burton and Bombay, he again questioned Snay bin Amir, the Arab who had first told them that there were three large inland lakes, not one, and advised that they travel to the Nyanza instead of to the Tanganyika. Snay had also mentioned that he knew of two rivers that ran out of the northern lake, which he called the Katonga and the Kitangura. Now, however, after explaining his own journey to the Nyanza, stage by stage, he told Speke that there was another river farther north. He had not seen it himself, but an enslaved man now living in Kazeh was a Wanyoro, the people through whose land this river flowed. "This man called the river Kivira, and described it as being much broader, deeper, and stronger in its current than either the Katonga or Kitangura river," Speke wrote with excitement. "It came from the generally acknowledged direction of the lake."

It did not take much convincing for Burton to agree to let Speke travel without him to the Nyanza. "My companion, who had recovered strength from the repose and the comparative comfort of our head-quarters, appeared a fit person to be detached upon this duty," Burton wrote. "Moreover, his presence at Kazeh was by no means desirable." Speke would later claim that Burton had stayed behind in Kazeh because he was "most unfortunately quite done up." Burton, believing that he would have another chance to return to East Africa and explore the Nyanza, wrote that he now had "more important matters to work out" to ensure their return to the coast. He also later admitted that it was a relief when Speke left as he was a liability among the Arabs, on whose help the expedition depended. "The difficulty was exaggerated by the Anglo-Indian's complete ignorance of Eastern Manners and customs," he wrote, "and of any Oriental language beyond, at least, a few words of the debased Anglo-Indian jargon."

Speke was again quick to rebuff any suggestion that he dress like an Arab on his journey. "The Arabs at Unyanyembé [near Kazeh] had advised my donning their habit for the trip, in order to attract less attention," he wrote, "a vain precaution, which I believe they suggested more to gratify their own vanity in seeing an Englishman lower himself to their position, than for any benefit that I might receive by doing so." Later, when Burton saw what Speke had written, he would declare it just another example of the young man's profound ignorance, scoffing at the idea that any Arab would envy an Englishman. "What knowledge of Asiatic customs can be expected from the writer of these lines?" he sneered. "This galimatias of the Arabs!—the haughtiest and the most clannish of all Oriental peoples."

Speke, however, did want the help of their Arab caravan leader, Said. "I begged for leave to take Sheikh Said with me," he wrote. "I argued that the road was dangerous, and without him I thought I could not succeed." Burton wanted to keep Said with him in Kazeh but finally relented, with the stipulation that Speke had to first convince Said himself, who was under no obligation to go anywhere but the agreed upon round-trip journey to the Tanganyika. When Speke approached Said, the caravan leader at first tried to put him off and then, when pressed, simply refused. Speke, he said, was not his chief. Frustrated, Speke argued with Said, insisting "that it was as much his duty as mine to go there" and threatening to take away the reward that Hamerton had promised if the expedition was a success. When Said would not change his mind, Speke blamed Burton, later claiming that Burton had "positively forbade his going." After learning of this accusation, Burton would only shrug, writing that he had done his best not to influence Said either way.

Soon after word got out that Said had refused to join Speke's expedition, the other men began to resist as well. The *kirangozi* insisted that he could not go because regional wars had made the roads impassable and it was now too dangerous. The guards at first objected and then began to bargain, refusing to be forced into an additional march of more than four hundred miles without fair compensation. Even Bombay insisted that he be compensated for the risk as well as the time and energy it would take to march to the Nyanza and back. "The old and faithful servant 'Bombay'...required instant dismissal unless he also received cloth before the journey," Burton wrote. "He was too useful to my companion as interpreter and steward to be lightly parted with." Speke would have given in anyway, willing to do almost anything to keep Bombay, but his heart softened when he found out that the cloth was for Mabruki, the man Bombay had bought as a slave but treated as a brother. "It was for this youth, and not himself, he had made so much fuss and used so many devices to obtain the cloths," Speke wrote. "Indeed, he is a very singular character, not caring one bit about himself, how he dressed, or what he ate; ever contented, and doing everybody's work in preference to his own."

•

Told that it would take him roughly sixteen marches to reach the Nyanza, Speke packed enough supplies for six weeks. Besides Bombay, he brought along Mabruki and Gaetano, one *kirangozi*, twenty *pagazis,* and ten guards. Each guard had a gun, one of which was Burton's double rifle. Speke also brought along Burton's five-bore elephant gun, the only one that hadn't been lost on the journey to the Tanganyika, as well as his own four-gauge rifle. To help carry their provisions, they used two of the expedition's least problematic donkeys: Ted and Jenny.

As Speke had expected after traveling to the Tanganyika, every day brought a near disaster. Every man but Bombay made clear their resentment at being pulled away from family and the rest that they had earned after a year of hard and dangerous travel, trudging dejectedly and complaining openly. The *pagazis* soon held a strike, demanding more cloth before they would take another step. Speke had brought the wrong kind of beads, which made it infinitely harder to buy the things they could not carry. "The white beads which I have brought have no value with the natives," he wrote in frustration. "Such a rage for coloured beads, that if I had brought some, I might purchase anything." One sultan whose land they passed through, the first female sultan that the expedition had encountered, forced a long delay. Another, believing that Speke was a magician, insisted that he predict the future. He "begged that I would cast his horoscope, divine the probable extent of his father's life, ascertain if there would be any wars, and describe the weather, the prospects of harvest, and what future state the country would lapse into," Speke wrote. "The shrewd Bombay replied, to save me trouble, that so great a matter required more days of contemplation than I could afford to give."

Although Speke's eyes had healed enough to at least lift the veil that had clouded them for so long, they were still profoundly sensitive to light. To protect them from the searing sun, he wore a "wideawake," a broad-brimmed felt hat that had gained popularity in Victorian England but had been worn in

Europe for centuries, best known for sitting atop Rembrandt's head in his seventeenth-century self-portraits. Speke also had sunglasses—"French grey spectacles"—but they had caused such a stir among the people he met, who were determined to get a closer look at his "double eyes," that he had been forced to take them off during the journey.

When the men reached the Nyanza on July 30, a month after leaving Kazeh, Speke had to peer at the lake from beneath his wideawake. Unlike his and Burton's first view of the Tanganyika, however, it was immediately apparent to Speke that not only was the Nyanza well worth any trouble it had taken to reach it, but that it was the most extraordinary lake he had ever seen. "The vast expanse of the pale-blue waters of the Nyanza burst suddenly upon my gaze," he wrote. "The view was one which, even in a well-known and explored country, would have arrested the traveller."

Covering an area of nearly 27,000 square miles, the Nyanza is the largest lake in Africa and the second largest freshwater lake in the world. Looking out over its seemingly endless, sparkling waters, Speke marveled at it, wondering just how far it stretched, a question that, through Bombay, he asked nearly everyone he met. When he interviewed a woman who had been born much farther north on the Nyanza, she told him that, as far as she knew, there was no end to the lake. "If any way of going round it did exist," she said, "she would certainly have known it." Another man, who had traveled extensively on the Nyanza as a fisherman, agreed with her. In answer to Speke's question, he turned to face north and began nodding his head and snapping the fingers of his right hand as he repeatedly thrust it forward, trying, Speke thought, "to indicate something immeasurable." Finally looking at Speke, he said that no one knew where the lake ended, but "it probably extended to the end of the world."

If the Tanganyika was a crack in the face of the earth, the Nyanza was a vast, jagged-edged hollow. Although it was more than twice the size of the western lake, at just 270 feet deep it was far shallower, especially compared to the nearly five-thousand-foot-deep Tanganyika. Over its relatively short lifespan of only 400,000 years, the Nyanza had already dried up three times. Now, however, two hundred different species of fish swam in its waters and nearly a thousand islands broke its surface. Its irregular edges were rimmed with everything from papyrus swamps to evergreen forests, three-hundred-foot-tall cliffs, and rich rain forest.

Speke would later insist that, even as he squinted beneath the dark brim of his slouching hat, he immediately knew that he was looking at the source of the White Nile. He had no proof, had not even been within hundreds of miles of the northern stretches of the lake, but he was certain that he was right. "I no longer felt any doubt that the lake at my feet gave birth to that interesting river," he wrote, "the source of which has been the subject of so much speculation, and the object of so many explorers." He, not Burton, had answered the age-old question. He, not Burton, had found the lake that they had all dreamed of. "This is a far more extensive lake than the Tanganyika," he wrote proudly. "So broad you could not see across it, and so long that nobody knew its length."

Speke spent only three days at the Nyanza before returning to Kazeh. In his mind, however, this enormous, ancient lake, which had been home to countless peoples over hundreds of thousands of years, now belonged to him. Again and again, for the rest of his life, he would refer to the Nyanza as "my lake." His only regret was that he had to leave it. "I felt as much tantalised as the unhappy Tantalus," he wrote, "and as much grieved as any mother would be losing her firstborn."

·

While Speke was gone, Burton's health had continued to improve. He had used the time without his sullen companion to work on his ethnological and geographical notes but also to prepare the expedition for its final push to the coast. Using Indian cotton-tape, he had patched the hammocks, which were vital to his survival during his long paralysis. He had hired a traveling tinker to mend a damaged kettle and asked the endlessly talented and resourceful Snay bin Amir to transform an old pair of iron hoes into two coveted pairs of stirrups. Their tents had been shored up with double cloth, blue cotton curtains, and strong, careful stitches. Valentine had made leather-soled green baize slippers for Burton, overalls for Speke, and several items stitched from indigo-dyed cotton for himself and Gaetano. Burton himself had revamped his umbrella, "ever an invaluable friend in these latitudes," he wrote, by "removing the rings and wires from the worm-eaten stick, and by mounting them on a spear, thus combining with shelter a staff and a weapon."

On August 25, just when Burton had finished his projects and was beginning to weary of Kazeh, eager to begin the final leg of their expedition, he heard cries and gunshots in the distance. Speke had returned. As the relatives of the men in his caravan rushed out to greet them, deeply relieved that their loved ones had returned safely, Speke was gratified to see the Arabs warmly welcoming him back. Burton too was waiting, happy to see his companion looking well and whole, and interested to hear what he had learned.

When Burton sat down the next morning to share breakfast with Speke and to discuss his journey, however, Speke shocked him with a stunning announcement. I "expressed my regret that he did not accompany me," Speke wrote, "as I felt quite certain in my mind I had discovered the source of the Nile." Expecting Burton to be thrilled by the news and impressed by his achievement, Speke was taken aback by his commander's obvious and heavy skepticism. "It was an inspiration perhaps: the moment he sighted the Nyanza," Burton would later write, baffled. "The fortunate discoverer's conviction was strong; his reasons were weak." The Nyanza certainly could be the source, Burton thought, but they needed much more than a hunch. Speke had spent only a few days at the lake, seen only a fraction of its immense waters, and taken no serious scientific measurements. The few interviews that he had conducted, moreover, had, of necessity, been filtered through layers of translation. "Jack, wholly ignorant of Arabic, was obliged to depend upon 'Bombay.' Bombay misunderstood Jack's bad Hindustani," Burton later wrote. "My experience is that words in journeys to and fro are liable to the severest accidents and have often bad consequences.... It is easy to see how the blunder originated."

Speke, shocked and angry that Burton did not immediately take his word for fact, grew increasingly resentful, insisting that he had discovered the source of the White Nile and that he had all the proof he needed. "After a few days it became evident to me that not a word could be uttered upon the subject of the lake, the Nile, and his *trouvaille* generally without giving offense," Burton wrote. "By a tacit agreement it was, therefore, avoided." Speke, moreover, was not only deeply offended by Burton's reaction but increasingly suspicious that his commander was downplaying the discovery because he wanted to claim it as his own. In an attempt to appease Speke, Burton had assured him that, although he was still too ill and the expedition too depleted to return to the Nyanza now, they would later explore the lake together. "We will go home," he said, "recruit our health, report what we have done, get some more money, return together and finish our whole journey."

Speke had other plans. Burton may be the commander of the expedition, but he had not found the source of the Nile. That honor, Speke believed, belonged to him, and it would dramatically change the balance of power between them. Later, in a draft of an article for the Royal Geographical Society, Speke would write that, although he had had to leave the Nyanza before exploring it, he had "resigned myself to my fate feeling confident as soon as I returned to England and made all the circumstances of my discovery known, that I should soon return again." In the end, he crossed the sentence out, but not before adding a final thought: "I was not wrong."

Part Three

Fury

CHAPTER FOURTEEN

The Knives Are Sheathed

Soon after they left Kazeh in the fall of 1858, Speke fell ill again, nearly dying as they neared the end of the expedition. He had begun to show signs of fever on the second march, trembling in the "cruel easterly wind." By the time they reached the next village, Hanga, he was complaining of a mysterious, shifting pain that felt like a branding iron was being pressed just above his right chest. The sensation then moved to the left, spreading across his heart in sharp, pulsating jabs before clutching his right lung and finally settling like a malignant cloud over his liver.

They had nowhere to stay in Hanga but a small shelter that had apparently been used to house cows. It was "full of vermin," Burton wrote, "and exposed directly to the fury of the cold gales." As the days passed, Speke grew progressively worse. One morning, he woke suddenly from a nightmare in which he was being dragged by a pack of tigers and leopards harnessed to iron hooks. Sitting on the edge of his bed, gripping the sides with both hands, "half stupefied by pain," he cried out for Bombay.

As soon as he saw Speke, Bombay knew that he was suffering from what was known locally as "little irons," an agonizingly painful disease for which they had neither cure nor comfort. As another series of violent spasms racked Speke's thin body, Bombay took his right arm and helped him bend it backward until he was holding his left ear behind his head, "thus relieving the excruciating and torturing twinges by lifting the lung from the liver," Burton wrote. The spasms, however, kept coming, each one more painful and horrifying to behold than the last. "He was once more haunted by a crowd of hideous devils, giants, and lion-headed demons, who were wrenching, with superhuman force, and stripping the sinews and tendons of his legs down to the ankles," Burton wrote. "With limbs racked by cramps, features drawn and ghastly, frame fixed and rigid, eyes glazed and glassy, he began to utter a barking noise, and a peculiar chopping motion of the mouth and tongue, with lips protruding—the effect of difficulty of breathing—which so altered his appearance that he was hardly recognizable, and completed the terror of the beholders."

Shocked by Speke's suffering, Burton stayed by his side, doing what he could to help. Knowing that the Arabs had their own treatment for the little irons, he sent for Snay bin Amir, who coated Speke's side with a poultice of powdered myrrh, mung bean, and egg yolk. When that had no effect, Snay insisted that they bring in a medicine man. The ligature that the man wrapped around Speke's waist, however, not only failed to ease his pain but pressed so agonizingly against his tortured organs that the patient soon ripped it off.

As he twisted and writhed in pain, Speke fell into a near constant state of delirium. To Burton's surprise, his babblings became an angry string of accusations against his commander. "He let out all his little grievances of fancied wrongs, of which I had not had even the remotest idea," Burton wrote. Not only railing against Burton for stealing his diary and natural history collection from Somaliland, Speke now laid bare his most deeply buried resentments. "He was awfully grieved because in the thick of the fight at Berberah, three years before, I had said to him, 'Don't step back, or they will think we are running,'" Burton wrote, amazed that the simple words spoken in a moment of extreme peril had so wounded his companion that he had spent years turning them over and over in his mind. "I cannot tell how many more things I had unconsciously done, and I crowned it by not accepting immediately his loud assertion that he had discovered the Sources of the Nile," Burton later recalled, stunned by the extent of Speke's bitterness. "I never should have known that he was pondering these things in his heart, if he had not raved them out in delirium."

In the wake of another jolting spasm, Speke, believing that he was dying, cried out for pen and paper. "Fearing that increased weakness of mind and body might presently prevent any exertion," Burton later recalled, "he wrote an incoherent letter of farewell to his family." That spasm, however, mercifully marked the beginning of the end of the little irons, after which Speke slowly began to recover. Several weeks would pass before he could again lie on his side, but he was finally able to sleep sitting up, propped on pillows, the pain, although still present, fast fading. Unaware of the long-hidden fury that he had revealed in his delirium, Speke looked at Burton, relieved and exhausted. "The knives," he said, "are sheathed."

•

By the time Speke was strong enough to continue their march, the expedition had a new caravan leader. Having lost his patience with Said, Burton decided to replace him with Bombay. "Said bin Salim had long forfeited my confidence by his carelessness and extravagance," he wrote, "and the disappearance of the outfit committed to him at Ujiji." Calling Said over, Burton tried to break the news to him as gently as he could, keeping in mind the Persian proverb that warns, "fell not the tree which thou hast planted." "Being now wiser in East African travel than before," he told Said, he "intended to relieve him of his troublesome duties." Said received the news with the "wryest of faces," but he was even more aggrieved when he learned that Bombay would now be in charge of the coveted cloth. From that moment on, Said tried everything in his power to discredit Bombay. "If an evil tale ever reached my ear its subject was the innocent Bombay," Burton later recalled. "Its object was to ruin him in my estimation." Bombay, however, had nothing to fear, having long ago earned his commander's trust not just by his "unwearied activity," Burton wrote, but by his "undeviating honesty, and his kindness of heart."

In early December, the expedition met a caravan coming from the coast and carrying mail addressed to Burton and Speke. The men in the caravan, "after receiving and returning news with much solemnity," Burton wrote, "presently drew forth a packet of letters and papers, which as usual promised trouble." Although, unlike the others, this caravan did not deliver news of another death, another loved one lost, it did, for Burton, bring with it an immediate and heavy sense of foreboding. Handed a letter, he saw that it had been written by the newly appointed

British consul in Zanzibar: Christopher Palmer Rigby. "That name," Burton wrote, "was not nice in the nostrils of men."

•

On February 2, 1859, the men of the East African Expedition saw the coast again for the first time in a year and a half. "Jack and I caught sight of the sea," Burton wrote. "We lifted our caps, and gave 'three times three and one more.'" After requesting and receiving a small boat from Zanzibar to explore the Rufiji River, whose course was then unknown to Europeans, they stopped at Kilwa, the island that Bombay had been dragged to as a child before reaching the slave markets at Zanzibar. In the end, however, they were unable to explore the Rufiji because of a devastatingly widespread outbreak of cholera. "We lost nearly all our crew by the cholera, which, after ravaging the eastern coast of Arabia and Africa, and the islands of Zanzibar and Pemba, had almost depopulated the southern settlements on the main land," Burton wrote. "No man dared to take service on board the infected vessel."

A month later, the men once again landed on Zanzibar. Although they were thrilled to be back, it was immediately apparent that the island was, as Burton wrote, "in the height of confusion." The cholera epidemic had devastated the population, killing some 250 people a day. "The dead are buried amongst the living," Rigby had written in his diary on February 1, "by the roadsides in long lines or shallow graves, the earth scarcely covering the toes." Zanzibar was also in political turmoil. Thuwaini bin Said, the sultan of Oman and brother of Majid, the sultan of Zanzibar, had sent a fleet of gunships to invade the island. Angered that his brother had stopped sending the financial tribute that he had promised little more than two years before, he had vowed to take what he believed was rightfully his. Coming to Majid's aid, Rigby had ordered a British cruiser to repel the attack before Thuwaini's ships reached Zanzibar.

Too weak to give much thought to what was happening around them, Burton and Speke went directly to the British consulate. For Burton, however, the large white building facing the sea, where Hamerton had so warmly greeted him two years earlier, had changed fundamentally and irrevocably. "Sick and way-worn, I entered the house connected in memory with an old friend, not without a feeling of sorrow for the change," he wrote. "I was fated to regret it even more." Suddenly, he was weighed down with a heavy feeling of fatigue and sorrow that had little to do with the long journey he had just completed or the illnesses he had suffered. As had always happened to him following an expedition, the more successful the journey, the more difficult the end. "The excitement of travel was succeeded by an utter depression of mind and body," he wrote, "even the labor of talking was too great."

Wanting only to lick his wounds and hide away with cheap French novels, *"à vingt sous la pièce,"* Burton did his best to avoid the new consul. Rigby, in turn, was not eager to spend time with Burton and had, besides, a busy schedule, having only been in Zanzibar for seven months. In March of the previous year, while Burton and Speke had been trying to hire a boat to explore the Tanganyika, Rigby had been thrown from a runaway carriage in Bombay. He had received word of his new appointment while confined to bed for two months, during which time he had nearly lost both of his legs to amputation. Though still thin and weak, he had finally been well enough to leave for Zanzibar in late June, only arriving at the consulate in July, where the British flag had been hoisted for the first time since Hamerton's death.

As soon as Burton arrived, it was clear that old resentments had not been forgotten. "The consulate was no longer bearable to me," Burton wrote. "I was too conversant with local politics, too well aware of what was going on, to be a pleasant companion to its new tenant." It did not help that Burton openly visited and spoke warmly of the French consul, Ladislas Cochet, with whom Rigby had already had a diplomatic dispute. "Contrast Rigby's scruples as a host," Rigby's daughter would write in anger years later, "with Burton's absence of proper feeling as a guest when he foregathered on friendly terms with a man not on visiting terms with the said host, viz. M. Cochet."

In stark contrast to his own tense relationship with the consul, Burton noticed with chagrin that Speke and Rigby became fast friends. "Arrived at Zanzibar, he fell into bad hands," Burton later wrote, "and being, like most ambitious men, very apt to consider himself neglected and ill-treated until crowned by success, he was easily made sore upon the point of merits not duly recognized." Still clutching his deep sense of aggrievement and his wounded pride, Speke quickly found common cause with Rigby, enumerating the ways in which Burton had injured him. The slights and insults were all the more outrageous, Speke argued, because Burton would have been lost without him. "Had I not been with him," he wrote, "he never could have undergone the journey."

Speke would later insist that even Hamerton had warned him about Burton. He claimed that the late consul had praised his ability before they had even left Zanzibar, suggesting that only he could save the expedition. "When I had reason to ask him confidentially if I could leave Burton with propriety . . . he said, no for God's sake do not, or you will hazard the success of the Expedition," Speke told Rigby. "He felt certain from what he had already seen that he, Burton, would fail, but at the same time he said, 'I must say you are lucky in having Speke with you, and I hope you will get on well together.' At the time that he said this to Burton, he said to me 'Speke, I am sorry to part with you, for I fear this Expedition will fail. Do you know I would not myself go with that man Burton on any condition.'"

For Speke, Rigby proved a sympathetic listener, taking in with concern every criticism and claim his new friend had to offer against his old enemy. "Speke is a right good, jolly, resolute fellow," Rigby wrote to a friend a few weeks later. "Burton is not fit to hold a candle to him and has done nothing in comparison with what Speke has." The consul, in turn, fed Speke's greatest fear: That Burton would steal from him again, this time not just his diary but his greatest discovery. "Speke is a modest, unassuming man, not very ready with his pen," Rigby wrote. "Burton will blow his trumpet very loud and get all the credit of the discoveries. Speke works. Burton lies on his back all day and picks other people's brains."

•

Even before he had learned that Rigby would be Hamerton's replacement in Zanzibar, Burton had feared that his friend's death would bring with it not just personal sorrow but professional peril. Eight months earlier, he had written to Shaw at the Royal Geographical Society, worried that he would not be able to honor the promises the consul had made to his men. "The late Lt. Col. Ham...advanced out of the public money no less a sum than $500 to our guide & promised him an ample reward & a gold watch, in case he brought us home alive, an event then considered highly improbable," Burton had written. "These are sums which we could not afford, nor can we on our return pay the high salaries promised in our presence to these men.... I venture to urge, most forcibly, this subject upon the Exp. C. of the R.G.S. as, unless Col. Ham.'s promises be fulfilled by his successor, we shall be placed in a most disagreeable position at Zanzibar." Burton and Speke had by then already spent hundreds of pounds of their own money just to make it to the Tanganyika. Speke had also written to Shaw with the same concerns seven months earlier, when he had "addressed to you a letter urging the necessity of arrangements for rewarding our guide & attendants," Burton had reminded Shaw. The Society had yet to respond to either man.

Now forced to ask Rigby to honor Hamerton's commitments, Burton was not surprised when the new consul refused. "As it appeared to me that Colonel Hamerton had received no authority from government to defray any part of the expenses of this expedition," Rigby would later explain to the British government in Bombay, "and probably made these promises thinking that if the exploration of the unknown interior were successful a great national object would be attained, and that the chief man who conducted the expedition would be liberally rewarded, and as Captain Burton had been furnished with funds to defray the expenses, I told him that I did not feel authorized to make any payment without the previous sanction of government." As Rigby must have known, however, and the Bombay government and the Royal Geographical Society certainly did, Burton had not been given enough funds even to meet the expedition's most basic needs, much less to cover the promises that Hamerton had made on the government's behalf.

Having by now used £1,400 of his own money to help finance his woefully underfunded expedition, Burton did not have any left to give as an additional payment to the men who had traveled with him. He did not, moreover, think that they deserved it even if he had. "Our followers were to receive *certain pay* in *any case*, which they *did* receive, and a reward in case they behaved well," he argued. "Our asses, thirty six in number, all died or were lost; our porters ran away; our goods were left behind and stolen."

Bombay received all that he had been promised, but the rest of the men, who if at times had been frightened or frustrated during the journey had nonetheless risked their lives to bring it to a successful conclusion, now found themselves summarily dismissed. Speke, who had earlier threatened Said with the loss of his reward when he refused to travel with him to the Nyanza, made no effort now to secure additional payment for any of the men. "Jack agreed with me thoroughly that it would be an act of weakness to pay the reward of ill-conduct," Burton wrote. "Instead of putting it down to generosity, they would have put it down to fear, and they would have played the devil with every future traveler." Neither did Rigby, after refusing to use the government funds that had been promised by his predecessor, insist that Burton somehow personally honor Hamerton's commitments. Instead, Burton later claimed, he agreed "that the 500 dollars originally advanced were sufficient."

Burton had planned to stay on the island, hoping to let his body heal and convince the government to give him more leave and additional funding so that he could continue exploring. Rigby's obvious "desire to see me depart," however, and Speke's "nervous hurry to hasten home" left him little choice. "I was unwilling to leave the field of my labors while so much remained to be done," he wrote. "But the evident anxiety of my host to disembarrass himself of his guest, and the nervous impatience of my companion—who could not endure the thought of losing an hour—compelled me, sorely against my wish, to abandon my intentions."

Reluctantly, little more than two weeks after returning to

Zanzibar, Burton joined Speke on the *Dragon of Salem,* a British sailing ship heading to Aden. Rigby declined to accompany the men on board to say his goodbyes, although it was "a mark of civility usual in the East," Burton would later comment, certain that the slight had been intentional and directed at him. Bombay, however, was there when they needed him, as he had been since their first meeting two years earlier. Rigby's "place... was well filled up by Seedy Mubarak Bombay," Burton wrote, "whose honest face appeared at that moment, by contrast, peculiarly attractive."

·

In Aden, both Burton and Speke stayed with Burton's old friend, Dr. John Steinhaüser, who had been unable to join the expedition. As Burton was still sick, complaining that "the fever... clung to me like the shirt of Nessus," Steinhaüser advised that he stay in Aden until his health improved. While there, Burton later wrote, Steinhaüser, a surgeon, not only did what he could to help him recover his health, but worried that his friend was heading into unforeseen trouble. Steinhaüser "repeatedly warned me," Burton would later write, "that all was not right."

On April 18, a Royal Navy frigate, the HMS *Furious,* pulled into Aden. On board was the 8th Earl of Elgin, son of the 7th Earl, for whom the Elgin Marbles, now known as the Parthenon Sculptures, had been named. Traveling with him was his private secretary, Laurence Oliphant. Oliphant happened to be at a particularly difficult and vulnerable time in his life. He had spent months traveling with Elgin, to and from China, and he had recently learned of the sudden and unexpected death of his beloved father. After leaving China, Oliphant had woken from a vivid dream and, finding his friends, told them that "he had seen his father, and that he was dead." Soon after, the ship had stopped in Galle, Ceylon, where he learned that his father had died from a heart attack on the same night as his dream.

Despite his fresh grief, Oliphant was pleased to be reunited with Speke, whom he had befriended four years earlier on a ship heading to the Crimean War. He was also interested in hearing about his travels with Burton, having, unbeknownst to Burton, vied with him in the past for military assignments and public acclaim. Lord Elgin offered both men a ride home aboard the *Furious*. Believing Burton too ill to travel, Steinhaüser insisted that he stay in Aden a few weeks more. Speke, however, quickly accepted, so eager to return to England, Burton later wrote, that he "did not take leave of his host."

Before Speke left, Burton spoke to him one last time, wishing to take a moment to mark the end of their extraordinary expedition. Although the relationship between the two men had been strained for most of the journey, and Speke's bitter ravings during his most recent illness had laid bare the extent of his resentment, still they had spent two years together, nursing each other in illness, calming each other's fears, sharing books and ideas, disappointment and elation. As the *Furious* prepared to leave, Burton told Speke that he would quickly follow him home. "I shall hurry up, Jack," he said, "as soon as I can." Speke, he would later claim, replied with warm reassurance: "Goodbye, old fellow; you may be quite sure I shall not go up to the Royal Geographical Society until you come to the fore and we appear together. Make your mind quite easy about that."

Left behind in Aden, Burton wrote again to the Royal Geographical Society, this time to tell them about the Nyanza. Before Speke and Bombay's journey, and even after their return, Burton had openly considered the possibility that the northern lake, rather than the Tanganyika, might be the source of the

White Nile. Now, although he still held out hope for the Tanganyika, he wrote to the Society of Speke's trip to the Nyanza, urging its members to pay close attention. "Capt. Speke...will lay before you his maps & observations & two papers, one a diary of his passage of the Tanganyika between Ujiji & Kasenge, and the other, his exploration of the Nyanza," he wrote. "To which I would respectfully direct the serious attention of the Committee, as there are grave reasons for believing it to be the source of the principal feeder of the White Nile."

On board the *Furious,* however, Speke's softened feelings toward Burton quickly changed, as did his plans. "He was persuaded to act in a manner which his own moral sense must have afterwards strongly condemned," Burton would later write, "if indeed it ever pardoned it." As he had shared his anger and fear with Rigby at Zanzibar, Speke now confided in Oliphant, who, like the consul, had felt wronged by Burton in the past and advised Speke to be wary of him now. Years later, Speke would recall the conversation that he had had with Oliphant as they sailed to England aboard the HMS *Furious,* and the advice that his friend had given to him. "Burton was a jealous man, and being Chief of the expedition he would take all the glory of Nyanza," Oliphant warned him. "If he were in Speke's place he would go up to the Royal Geographical Society at once, and get the command of the second expedition."

CHAPTER FIFTEEN

'Twas Me He Shot

After three weeks aboard the HMS *Furious*, Speke wasted no time in laying claim to the discovery of the source of the White Nile. The day after he arrived in Plymouth, he traveled to London, checking into Hatchett's Hotel in Piccadilly, where he received a letter from the Royal Geographical Society's secretary, Norton Shaw, welcoming him home. Speke's reply was delivered the same day. "I may have told you before, I believe most firmly that the Nyanza is one source of the Nile, if not the principal one," he wrote, the only time he would admit to even the slightest doubt. That night, explaining that Speke "wanted advice," Shaw took him to meet with Clements Markham, who would one day become one of the Society's best known and longest serving presidents. "We talked the whole matter over for some time," Markham would later write of his conversation with Speke, "but I rather misdoubted his want of loyalty to Burton."

Whatever his personal feelings about Speke, the next day Markham traveled with him to Belgrave Square. The grandest building in Belgravia, one of the most elite districts in central London, Belgrave Square would one day house embassies and ambassadors, dukes and princesses, and was now home to the current president of the Royal Geographical Society, Sir Roderick Impey Murchison. Speke brought with him a map that he had sketched of his travels to the Nyanza, eager to make his argument to Murchison that this lake, and not the Tanganyika, was the source of the White Nile, but also that he, and not Burton, should command the next expedition to East Africa. "Sir Roderick," Markham noted, "at once took him up."

Like Speke, Murchison belonged to the British aristocracy. Born to wealthy parents at Tarradale House, built on the site of Scotland's storied Tarradale Castle, he had attended the Royal Military College before entering the army. After turning to the life of a country gentleman, he had devoted much of his time to Speke's favorite pastime: hunting. He had also become an extremely skilled and knowledgeable geologist, creating both the Silurian and Devonian systems based on his detailed research of the geology of South Wales, southwestern England, and the Rhineland. By 1859, Murchison had already been elected president of the Royal Geographical Society three times—in 1843, when he had succeeded William Richard Hamilton, who had brought the Rosetta Stone from Egypt; again in 1851; and most recently in 1856, when Burton and Speke had left for Zanzibar.

Murchison had been chosen as president not only for his geological accomplishments but for his social connections. Soon after its founding in 1830, the Royal Geographical Society had fallen on hard times. In what became known as the "hungry forties," membership had been so low that the Society's Council had even considered inviting women to join. They had avoided that extreme measure by doing two things that were nearly as controversial: insisting that members begin paying their dues and, thanks largely to Murchison, shifting the Society's attention away from the serious but staid work of the scientist in favor of the glamorous world of the explorer. The move had alienated many of the country's most celebrated scientists, from Alfred Russel Wallace to Charles Darwin, who would publish *On the Origin of Species* just a few months after Speke's return from East Africa. At the same time, however, the emphasis on exploration had attracted the attention of the press, and a much wider array of paying members.

During his second term, Murchison had even created a new section within the British Association for the Advancement of Science, an organization that often worked in collaboration with the Royal Geographical Society. Known as Section E, it separated geography from what had once been its companion subject, geology. In the past, geology had been considered more serious, and as such more important, than geography. After Murchison began allowing explorers to speak at the meetings, Section E quickly overshadowed every other section. It was "second in popularity and utility to no other," Murchison wrote. By 1856, the beginning of his third term as president, the Royal Geographical Society had two thousand fellows, far more than any other scientific society in London.

To keep the Society strong, Murchison realized, he needed an explorer who would appeal to a wide audience. "These were the days when the Society in question could not afford to lack its annual lion," Burton would later sneer, "whose roar was chiefly to please the ladies and push the institution." For many years, Murchison's friend David Livingstone had filled that role, as loved and admired for his fight to end the slave trade as he was for his feats of exploration. Livingstone, however, had by then been in the public eye for nearly twenty years and was nearing fifty, his hair growing gray and his years of injuries and illnesses beginning to tell on his once strong body. The Society needed a fresh face.

Murchison had been interested in Speke even before he returned home. Nearly a year earlier, he had convened a meeting to discuss a field book that Burton had sent, along with a map that Speke had sketched of the early stages of their travels. After sharing the book and the map, Murchison had directed the Society's attention to Burton's young and relatively untested companion, John Hanning Speke. "Many of us are well acquainted with the previous remarkable exploits in foreign travel which Captain Burton has performed," he said, "and he is now associated with a man who seems to be his equal." It was Speke's proposed journey to the Nyanza, aligned as it was with Murchison's own suppositions about the geography of East Africa, that most captured his interest. "God grant that Captain Speke may return from the hazardous expedition he is making to try and reach the more northerly and great lake," he said. "Hitherto there has been much mystery respecting the so-called interior sea."

By the time Speke visited Belgrave Square, he had no trouble convincing Murchison that he was deserving of his own expedition. "Sir Roderick, I need only say, at once accepted my views," Speke would later write, thrilled to have found an ally in this powerful man, "and, knowing my ardent desire to prove to the world, by actual inspection of the exit, that the Victoria N'yanza was the source of the Nile, seized the enlightened view that such a discovery should not be lost to the glory of England and the society of which he was president." Murchison, nearing seventy and with no children of his own, regarded with pride the fine-boned, well-bred young man sitting before him, fresh from his adventures in Africa. "Speke," he said, "we must send you there again."

•

In late May of 1859, two weeks after Speke's meeting with Murchison, Burton arrived in London. While his subordinate had been treated as "the hero of the hour" since his return, Isabel would bitterly note, there was little fanfare for the expedition's commander. Quietly making his way to London, he was stunned to find that Speke had not only gone directly to the Royal Geographical Society without him but had already given a lecture to that august body—"much against my own inclination," Speke would later insist. Astonished, Burton wrote that he "found the ground completely cut from under my feet." As he struggled to understand what had happened to his expedition while he was still in Aden, one thing became painfully clear: Speke was no longer his friend and protégé but his adversary. "My companion now stood forth in his true colours," Burton wrote, "an angry rival."

Despite his astonishment at Speke's actions in his absence, Burton defended him. He continued to openly admire his best traits, later writing that "no man can better appreciate the noble qualities of energy, courage, and perseverance which he so eminently possessed than I do." And he insisted that, had Speke not fallen under the malignant influence of men like Rigby and Oliphant, their friendship could have survived their journey. "Jack is one of the bravest fellows in the world," Burton would later tell Isabel, who was outraged on his behalf. "If he has a fault it is overweening vanity, and being so easily flattered; in good hands he would be the best of men. Let him alone; he will be very sorry some day."

Two days after his return home, the Royal Geographical Society presented Burton with the Founder's Medal, one of its most prestigious awards. Grateful for the recognition and still feeling an obligation to Speke, he used his acceptance speech in part to praise his companion. "You have alluded, Sir, to the success of the last expedition. Justice compels me to state the circumstances under which it attained that success," Burton said, addressing Murchison. "To Captain J. H. Speke are due those geographical results to which you have alluded in such flattering terms. While I undertook the history and ethnography, the languages and the peculiarities of the people, to Captain Speke fell the arduous task of delineating an exact topography, and of laying down our positions by astronomical observations—a labour to which at times even the undaunted Livingstone found himself unequal."

Murchison could not have agreed more. About to hand over the presidency to his successor, the politician and diplomat Lord Ripon, he had lobbied the Society to present Speke with the Founder's Medal at the same time that it was awarded to Burton. When the Council demurred, Murchison was determined nevertheless to use this meeting, meant to honor Burton, to shine a spotlight on Speke. "I must also take this opportunity of expressing to you my hearty approbation of the very important part which your colleague, Captain Speke, has played in the course of the African expedition headed by yourself," Murchison said in his opening remarks. In his own address to the Society, he intended to "dwell upon the discovery of the vast interior Lake of Nyanza, made by your associate when you were prostrated by illness, a discovery which in itself is also, in my opinion, well worthy of the highest honour this Society can bestow." True to his word, Murchison not only praised Speke in his own speech but argued that he should be given command of the next expedition. "Let us hope that when re-invigorated by a year's rest, the undaunted Speke may receive every encouragement to proceed from Zanzibar to his old station," he urged the Society, "and there carry out to demonstration the view which he now maintains, that the Lake Nyanza is the main source of the Nile."

Speke's triumph was nearly complete. He had not only claimed for himself one of the greatest prizes in geographical history but had successfully painted the expedition's commander as a pathetic figure, limping behind the bold young hero. A few weeks later, after hearing a discussion of both the Tanganyika and the Nyanza at a June meeting of the Royal Geographical Society, a reporter for *The Examiner* would come away with the impression that only one mattered. "We shall confine our notice to the lake Nyanza, as the most important," he wrote. "This was visited by Captain Speke only, his companion having been prevented by heavy sickness from accompanying him."

Later that month, the Royal Geographical Society met again, this time to consider competing proposals from both Burton and Speke for a return expedition to East Africa. The meeting was called by the Society's Expedition Sub-Committee, which included Laurence Oliphant, who had been invited to join the Council after returning to England with Speke, and Francis Galton, who was Charles Darwin's cousin. Galton would later not only coin the phrase "nature versus nurture" but, influenced by his cousin's theory of natural selection, develop the dangerous and discredited practice of eugenics. An explorer and mathematician, Galton also wrote a popular book called *The Art of Travel,* which offered explorers practical information such as a formula for determining the trajectory of a charging animal and advice to hire women for expeditions, explaining that they like to carry heavy objects and cost little to feed because they can just lick their fingers while cooking. Later, in his memoirs, Galton would sum up Burton's and Speke's strengths as explorers and differences as men. "Burton was a man of eccentric genius and tastes, orientalised in character and thoroughly Bohemian," he wrote. "Speke, on the other hand, was a thorough Briton, conventional, solid, and resolute."

Burton knew that while he was more qualified than Speke to lead the next expedition, he was a difficult, even controversial figure, a hedonistic man in a puritanical age. The British government had just passed the Obscene Publications Act, outlawing the sale and distribution of any material that it judged to be inappropriate. The novelist George Eliot was harshly criticized in *The Saturday Review* for mentioning pregnancy in *Adam Bede*, and her own publisher complained when, in another novel, she dared to describe an orphan in need of a bath. "I do not recollect of any passage," he wrote to her, "that moved my critical censorship unless it might be the allusion to dirt in common with your heroine." England, moreover, was far from alone in its censorship. In the United States, Walt Whitman's *Leaves of Grass* was declared "too sensual." Most libraries refused to buy a copy, Whitman was fired from his job as a clerk in the Bureau of Indian Affairs, and the president of Yale declared the book to be little better than "walking naked through the streets." Even in France, Gustave Flaubert was tried for obscenity after publishing his debut novel, *Madame Bovary*, and Baudelaire was fined for "offending public morals" because of the sexual imagery in *Les Fleurs du mal*.

Not only did Burton treat puritans with contempt, he surrounded himself with men whose interests were considered nothing if not obscene. Among his closest friends was the poet politician Richard Monckton Milnes. A member of Parliament, Milnes was known for his enormous library, filled with rare and beautiful books as well as a large, and now illegal, collection of erotica that included the complete works of the Marquis de Sade. Milnes would in turn introduce Burton to the man who supplied most of his collection, Frederick Hankey, son of the governor of Malta and a former Guards officer now living with his mistress in France. Hankey, who had his own collection, largely composed of tools of sexual torture, would later proudly show Burton one of his prized possessions: a book made from human skin. His only regret was that the skin had been taken from a man already dead. For years, as Burton continued to travel the world, Hankey would beg him to bring home the skin of someone who had been flayed alive. "Not a man killed nor a fellow tortured. The canoe floating in blood is a myth of myths," Burton would later write to Milnes from West Africa. "Poor Hankey must still wait for his peau de femme."

To some degree, Burton had only himself to blame for his reputation. He enjoyed watching "polite society" flush with outrage and excitement, eyes widening and mouths dropping open as he told stories from his travels, allowing them to believe nearly anything of him, from sexual exploits to murder. "He took great delight in shocking goody people, and in effecting his purpose he gave free rein to his imagination. People who knew Burton partially, from meeting him at public dinner or in clubs, have generally a number of gruesome stories to retail about his cruelty and immorality. They often say truly that Burton told the horrible stories against himself," a friend of his would later write. "I have no doubt he did.... At the same time I am certain that Burton was incapable of either monstrous cruelty or gross immorality. I knew Burton well... and I have noticed that acts of cruelty and immorality always drove him into a white heat of passion." Burton found it interesting, moreover, that while his lies were always accepted, his honest tales rarely were. "He said it was so funny to be believed when you were chaffing," Isabel would recall, "and so curious never to be believed when you were telling the truth." Burton was still invited to parties, but he was often treated as a curiosity, and with caution. "His usual conversation in those days," Galton explained, "was not exactly of a stamp suitable to Episcopal society."

·

Speke's proposal to the Sub-Committee—that he return to the Nyanza by the same route he had taken before—was immediately accepted. Confident now of his place of privilege within the Society, he asked for £5,000, five times as much as Burton had received four years earlier, and passage to Zanzibar in a warship befitting the expedition's prestige. Although the Society expressed doubt that he would need quite that much funding, it did eventually agree to £2,500, a sum that, had Burton received it in 1856, would have saved him needless budgeting, haggling, and worry and made it possible for him to fully explore both the Tanganyika and the Nyanza. The committee also tentatively approved a proposal from Burton to resume his search for the source, although it was clear to everyone concerned that he would not be well enough to leave anytime soon. After funding Speke's expedition, moreover, there would be no money left for another.

Speke, finding himself suddenly a star, soaked up the Society's approval and the public's excitement. "My dear Rigby, I transmit by post through Aden the proceedings of the R.G. Society, to show you what interest my discoveries have created in this land," he crowed in a letter to the consul. "Since I came home

I have had...[no] rest, being giddily hauled about from right to left and back again. The Gaiety is such as I never dreamed or ever thought of." He had not only returned a hero, but was now being sent back a leader—at the helm of his own expedition, better funded and more closely watched than Burton's had ever been.

For Speke, the approval of his proposal had meant not only a victory for himself but a defeat for Burton. Having stayed in frequent communication with Rigby after leaving Zanzibar, Speke wrote to him again, exulting in the fact that Burton had tried and failed. "On proposing to go to the Lakes again I mentioned the circumstances to Burton that he might have a fair chance with me which I am happy to say he took advantage of by sending in the following day his papers also proposing himself for my scheme," he wrote. "Well, I say I am glad because in the Elections by the council the preference was given to me in consequence of my having done the scientific part of the last one." Burton might be brilliant and famous, writing acclaimed books and speaking dozens of languages, but Speke had gotten there first—to the lake, to England, and to the Royal Geographical Society. "Sir R. Murchison," Speke wrote with relish, "is my patron this time."

Speke was also being wooed by one of the most successful publishers in the United Kingdom: John Blackwood. Blackwood's father had founded William Blackwood and Sons more than fifty years earlier. Although he was the sixth son, John was particularly skilled at cultivating new literary talent. Since taking over the publishing house seven years earlier, he had won over a wide array of celebrated writers, including Mary Ann Evans, whose first work under the pen name George Eliot had been published in *Blackwood's Magazine* just two years earlier. *Blackwood's* would also later publish Anthony Trollope, E. M. Forster, and, forty years after Speke, would be the first to publish Joseph Conrad's *Heart of Darkness.*

Laurence Oliphant had known John Blackwood for years, occasionally writing for him and frequently bringing him new talent. Now he brought him John Hanning Speke. Speke and Oliphant were already in Scotland, giving speeches to the British Association for the Advancement of Science, when Blackwood invited the young explorer to his summer home in Gibleston, Fife. "We have had a very interesting visitor, Captain Speke, lately from the Mountains of the Moon, and what he believes to be, I think with good grounds, the fountains of the Nile," Blackwood wrote to George Eliot in August. "He is a fine, manly, unaffected specimen of an Englishman.... He has gone through dangers and suffering enough to disgust any ordinary man with the mere thoughts of Africa, but he is determined to go back and carry out his discovery, and has got a grant for the purpose. His reply to my remonstrance against his going again was unanswerable—'Fancy my disgust if any vapouring, boasting Frenchman went and got the credit of this discovery for France.'"

The benefits of publishing his travels in *Blackwood's* were not lost on Speke. In fact, he had begun corresponding with John Blackwood soon after returning to England. Although Murchison had expected Speke to give his papers to the Society's *Journal* for publication, as was customary for a Society-funded expedition, Oliphant had convinced him that his story deserved a wider audience than the Society could give it. "As a great number of friends, both here and in India, have expressed a warm desire to be made acquainted with my late journeyings in Africa, as well as with the social state and general condition of the people whom I found there, I send for publication in your

Magazine the accompanying Journal, which I kept when travelling alone in Africa," Speke had written to Blackwood, ignoring the contributions of Bombay and the dozens of porters, guards, and guides who had made his journey possible. "Very numerous inquiries have been addressed to me by statesmen, clergymen, merchants, and more particularly geographers; and I hope the appearance of the Journal in your widely-circulated pages will convey to them the desired information."

While Speke wanted his travels to appear in *Blackwood's*, however, he did not want the scientific community to turn its attention back to Burton. After learning that the Royal Geographical Society had decided, for the first time, to devote an entire edition of its *Journal* to Burton's recounting of the East African Expedition, Speke wrote a bitter letter to Norton Shaw, claiming that publishing with *Blackwood's* instead of the Society had been not his idea but Shaw's. Burton "tells me that he has written a very long report for the Society's journals which rather surprises me for if you remember I offered the Society, through you, all the MS. Which I had written in Africa for the benefit of the Society," he complained. "When you told me not to be so liberal but to profit myself by publishing a book the same as everybody else does."

Winning was no longer enough. Burton, even with broken health and little hope of finding support for an expedition of his own, was still a danger. Burton had made the initial introductions for Speke to the Royal Geographical Society, encouraging him in his desire to become a member. Now, Speke wanted not just to be lauded by that Society but for it to exclude Burton from any recognition. In letters to both Rigby and Shaw, Speke told them that Lord Elphinstone, the governor of Bombay, had expressed "his regret that the gold medal was not given to me instead of to Burton." Even the fact that Burton had led the last expedition had become intolerable to Speke. "I am sure every-body at Zanzibar knows it," he later insisted to Rigby, "that I was the leader and Burton the second of the Expedition."

•

At the same time that Speke was writing to Rigby to tell him of his successes in England, he was encouraging the consul to make an official accusation against Burton. Burton, he argued, had acted unfairly, even cruelly, toward his men by not giving them a reward. He knew that Hamerton had made the promise, that Rigby had refused to use government funds to honor it, and that Burton had long before run out of the expedition's money and had spent more than £1,000 of his own just to get them back to the coast. Nevertheless, as soon as he left Zanzibar, Speke had written to Rigby, accusing Burton of cheating Ramji, whom Burton had paid at the outset for the help of his enslaved men. "I consider it positively iniquitous that Ramjee should be cheated, and told Burton so more than once when talking over affairs inland," Speke had written while still sailing to Aden. "You heard yourself how Burton disposed of the subject at your breakfast table one day, and I think now that you are fully aware of the whole matter you are in duty bound to see justice done to this unfortunate man. Excuse my saying so, for I thought you did not properly understand me at Zanzibar when telling you of the circumstance, or that you must have considered you had no right to interfere."

After Speke returned to England, neither he nor Rigby mentioned their concerns to Burton. Instead, writing up a list of accusations, they sent them where they knew they would do the most damage: to the British government in Bombay and the Royal Geographical Society in London. "Captain Speke since his departure from Zanzibar, having written me two private letters, pointing out so forcibly the claims of these men, the hardships they endured, and the fidelity and perseverance they showed... I deem it my duty to bring their claims to the notice of government," Rigby wrote, not mentioning his own role in refusing to honor his predecessor's commitment. "For I feel that if these men remain unpaid, after all they have endured in the service of British officers, our name for good faith in these countries will suffer."

When Norton Shaw received Rigby's letter to the Royal Geographical Society, he showed it to Burton. Although Burton found himself blindsided yet again, this time he defended himself with the most powerful weapon he had: his pen. "I must express my extreme surprise that Capt. Speke should have written two private letters forcibly pointing out the claims of these men to Captain Rigby, without having communicated the circumstance in any way to me, the chief of the expedition," he wrote to the Bombay government. "I have been in continued correspondence with that officer since my departure from Zanzibar, and until this moment I have been impressed with the conviction that Captain Speke's opinion as to the claims of the guide and escort above alluded to was identical with my own.... I regret that Captain Rigby, without thoroughly ascertaining the merits of the case (which he evidently has not done), should not have permitted me to record any remarks which I might wish to offer, before making it a matter of appeal to the Bombay government."

Then Burton turned his pen on the consul himself. From the moment he had learned of Rigby's appointment to replace Hamerton, Burton had known that he would not receive a warm welcome in Zanzibar. As he had sailed to Aden, however, he had believed that he was leaving the dangers of petty jealousy behind. Once again, he had been wrong. His response to Rigby now was barely contained fury.

> Sir,—I have been indebted to the kindness and consideration of my friend Dr. Shaw, for a sight of your letter addressed to him the 10th of October last from Zanzibar. I shall not attempt to characterize it in the terms that best befit it. To do so, indeed, I should be compelled to resort to language "vile" and unseemly as your own. Nor can there be any necessity for this. A person who could act as you have acted must be held by everyone to be beneath the notice of any honourable man. You have addressed a virulent attack on me to a quarter in which you had hoped it would prove deeply injurious to me: and this not in the discharge of any public duty, but for the gratification of a long-standing private pique. You sent me no copy of this attack, you gave me no opportunity of meeting it; the slander was propagated as slanders generally are, in secret and behind my back. You took a method of disseminating it which made the ordinary mode of dealing with such libels impossible, while your distance from England puts you in a position to be perfectly secure from any consequence of a nature personal to yourself. Such being the case, there remains to me but one manner of treating your letter, and that is with the contempt it merits.

As a result of Speke's and Rigby's accusations, Burton received an apology, of sorts, from the Royal Geographical Society and a reprimand from the Bombay government. An Expedition Committee led by George Everest, for whom Sagarmartha, the world's highest mountain, would be named six years later, admitted that Burton's expedition, which "achieved results of such importance, would have warranted the Expenditure of even a larger sum." When Burton asked for their help in recovering the money he had been forced to spend, however, he was informed that, not only would the Society itself not reimburse him, but, "in the opinion of the Committee, the Society has no claims on the Foreign Office for any sum beyond the £1,000 already advanced."

From Bombay, Burton was stunned to find that Rigby's and Speke's word had been accepted over his own, and that, after years of effort and sacrifice, he had earned not gratitude but censure. "Having taken into consideration the explanation afforded by you . . . together with the information on the same subject furnished by Captain Speke, he [the secretary of state for India] is of the opinion that it was your duty . . . not to have left Zanzibar without bringing these claims before the consul there," a representative of the government wrote to Burton. "Had this course been followed, the character of the British government would not have suffered." Refusing to simply take the blow, Burton responded immediately. "I represented the whole question to Captain Rigby, who, had he then—at that time—deemed it his duty to interfere, might have insisted upon adjudicating the affair with me, or with Captain Speke, before we left Zanzibar," he pointed out. "I venture to express my surprise, that all my labors and long services in the cause of African exploration should have won for me no other reward than the prospect of being mulcted in a pecuniary liability incurred by my late lamented friend, Lieut. Colonel Hamerton, and settled without reference to me by his successor, Captain Rigby."

Now that Burton had been not only defeated but humiliated, Speke professed regret that it had to be done. In a letter to Rigby, he insisted that the whole affair had caused him great pain. "Of all the painful things that I have ever had to undertake the severest and most painful as to my feelings I concluded yesterday," he wrote. "This was...to write my opinions versus Burton's and now the matter is lying before the Gov't." At the same time, he asked Rigby to protect their personal correspondence so that Burton would not see the extent to which they had jeered at him in their letters, laughing at his "weak legs and rotten gut" and the "loathing" that they felt for him. "Burton I believe will require my letters to you," Speke wrote. "If this be the case grant him a sight of them, after erasing all matter which does not relate to the subject at issue—but give up those only which induced you to act against him."

To Burton, what was more baffling even than Speke's betrayal was his righteous anger. Even after he understood the extent of Speke's ambition and the depth of his resentment, Burton had found it difficult not to think of him as the young man whom he had invited onto his expeditions, introduced to scientists, explorers, and patrons, advised when he was unsure and nursed when he was unwell. "He had doubtless been taught that the expedition had owed to him all its success: he had learned to feel aggrieved," Burton wrote, trying to make sense of what had happened. "No one is so unforgiving, I need hardly say, as the man who injures another." Now when he thought of the time he had spent with Speke in Africa, Burton was reminded of a couplet he had learned in Arabic years ago:

I taught him archery by day—
when his arm waxed strong, 'twas me he shot.

CHAPTER SIXTEEN

An Exile's Dream

As Speke rose on the heady current of his newfound fame, Burton descended into despair. The depression that had always followed his every triumph now loomed even larger, casting a long shadow over all that he had accomplished, and all that he had hoped to do. Although he had crossed hundreds of miles of land unmapped by Europeans, reaching the Tanganyika and winning the Founder's Medal, his defeat at the hands of the man he had mentored, and whom he had believed to be his friend, sullied every achievement.

The only bright spot in Burton's life was Isabel, but even she now seemed unattainable. They had been separated for three years, and she had not heard from him for nearly as long, but her devotion had never wavered. She had written to him faithfully since the night he had left England without saying goodbye, sending him long letters every two weeks, filled with newspaper clippings, descriptions of books she was reading, news of their friends and family. In return, she had received four letters from Richard, and then nothing more.

While Burton had been risking his life in a desperate attempt to solve an ancient mystery, Isabel had traveled to Europe with her family, the only adventure she was allowed. Even then, wherever she went, her thoughts had never been far from the man she yearned to marry. In Italy, she had been amazed to find his name carved into the Leaning Tower of Pisa and had scratched her own next to it. "How curious it would have been if while he was doing it he could have said, 'My future wife will also come and chisel hers,' so many years later, in remembrance of me," she wrote. In Switzerland, she had received two offers of marriage, neither of which she had even considered accepting. She would marry Richard Burton or no one at all.

Isabel had been back in England for a year when she heard of Speke's triumphant return from Africa. There had still been no word, however, either public or private, from the man to whom she had remained not just faithful but fervently devoted. Just as she was considering giving up altogether and joining a convent, an anonymous letter arrived from Zanzibar. The envelope had been addressed to her, but inside it held nothing but a small poem on a single sheet of paper.

TO ISABEL
That brow which rose before my sight,
As on the palmer's holy shrine
Those eyes—my life was in their light;
Those lips my sacramental wine;
That voice whose flow was wont to seem
The music of an exile's dream

Two days later, Isabel read in the newspaper that Burton was finally on his way home. "I feel strange," she wrote in her diary, "frightened, sick, stupefied, dying to see him, and yet inclined to run away lest, after all I have suffered and longed for, I should have to bear more." The next day she was visiting a friend, waiting in an upstairs parlor, when she heard the doorbell ring, announcing another visitor. After the door was opened, she heard a man's voice drifting up the stairs. "I want Miss Arundell's address." It was a voice that, she later wrote, "thrilled me through and through." Moments later Isabel heard the door to the parlor open behind her and turned around, astonished to find Richard Burton standing in the doorway. "For an instant we both stood dazed," she wrote. "I felt so intensely, that I fancied he must hear my heart beat, and see how every nerve was overtaxed."

Completely forgetting the friend she was there to see, Isabel had immediately followed Burton out of the parlor, down the stairs, and into a cab. "I felt quite stunned," she wrote. "I could not speak or move, but felt like a person coming to after a fainting or a dream; it was acute pain, and for the first half-hour I found no relief." So shocked was Isabel that she had been unable even to cry, her eyes wide, dry, and staring, her heart painfully pounding. Struggling to recover, she had pulled from a pocket the picture of Burton that she had carried with her for three years, an icon, a talisman, a symbol of hope. Without hesitating, he had reached into his own pocket and taken out a picture of her. Both pictures, Isabel would later insist, were in perfect condition, showing "how carefully we had always kept them."

As overwhelmed as Isabel had been to finally see the man who had for years filled her dreams, even she could not help but notice how profoundly he had changed since she had seen him last. "He had had twenty-one attacks of fever—had been partially paralyzed and partially blind," she later wrote, horrified by the memory. "He was a mere skeleton, with brown-yellow skin hanging in bags, his eyes protruding, and his lips drawn away from his teeth.... He was sadly altered; his youth, health, spirits, and beauty were all gone for the time." Although Isabel's heart broke at the memory of the man who had once radiated strength and vigor, now thin, pale, and weak, her desire and determination to marry him was, if anything, even stronger. "He was still... my earthly god and king, and I could have knelt at his feet and worshipped him," she wrote. "I used to like to sit and look at him, and think, 'You are mine, and there is no man on earth the least like you.'"

•

As desperate as Isabel was to finally marry Burton, she still had one immovable obstacle: her mother. Eliza Arundell had been searching for a suitable match for her oldest daughter for ten years, but not only did Richard Burton not fit that description, he was as far from the ideal suitor as she could imagine. When Isabel had told her that she wanted to marry Burton, Eliza's response had been cold, unbending, and stunningly harsh, even for a mother who had always demanded complete obedience from her children. Isabel would never forget it. "When I came home to you in an ecstasy and told you that I had found the Man and the Life I longed for... what did you answer me?" she later wrote. "'That he was the *only* man you would never consent to my marrying; that you would rather see me in my coffin.'"

Burton was everything Eliza did not want in a son-in-law. He was well known, but in the worst possible way. Scandalous rumors about him flew in every direction, and he was rarely seen in the Arundells' elevated social circles—although, as Isabel would finally find the courage to point out to her mother, the last place Burton wanted to be was in her parents', or anyone's, social circle. He had very little money and even fewer prospects. The Bombay government had reprimanded him, and the Royal Geographical Society, after awarding him its highest medal, now ignored him, showering all of its attention and funding on the man who had been his subordinate. To a woman who wanted for her daughters not just social standing but financial stability, Burton seemed the worst possible choice.

What made Burton completely unacceptable to Eliza, however, was the fact that not only did he not share her religious beliefs, he apparently had no religion whatsoever. Isabel would spend the rest of her life gently but firmly trying to convert Burton to Catholicism, refusing to give up even as he lay on his deathbed. Georgiana Stisted, Burton's niece, would later claim that he had been a Deist for most of his life, but Burton himself, while studying nearly every religion, disavowed them all. Organized religion, he believed, brought only unhappiness to both its practitioners and those they professed to "save." "I begin to believe that the only safe belief is a thorough disbelief in what ones neighbours believe," he wrote to a friend. "Hoping that we shall meet at the next séance."

Despite Eliza's deep and open dislike for Burton and her absolute refusal to allow him to marry her daughter, Isabel continued to try to convince her. A few months after her fiancé returned from Africa, she wrote her mother a long, carefully reasoned, strongly argued letter. Before laying out her case, however, she began with a warning. "My dear Mother, I feel quite grateful to you for inviting my confidence. It is the first time you have ever done so, and the occasion shall not be neglected. It will be a great comfort to me to tell you all," she wrote. "But you must forgive me if I say that I have one tender place too sore to be touched, and that an unkind or slighting word might embitter all our future lives." Then she set out to address her mother's concerns, point by point, hoping to prove how unfair and illogical they were. "It surprises me that you should consider mine an infatuation, you who worship talent, and my father bravery and adventure, and here they are both united," she argued. "Look at his military services—India and the Crimea! Look at his writings, his travels, his poetry, his languages and dialects. Now Mezzofanti is dead he stands first in Europe; he is the best horseman, swordsman, and pistol shot. He has been presented with the gold medal, he is an F.R.G.S. [Fellow of the Royal Geographical Society], and you must see in the newspapers of his glory, and fame, and public thanks.... I could tell you such adventures of him, and traits of determination, which would delight you, were you unprejudiced." After reminding her mother of Burton's many accomplishments, Isabel insisted that he was also a thoroughly good man, despite what she may have heard to the contrary. "He is not at all the man...that people take him to be, or that he sometimes, for fun, pretends to be," she wrote. "Any evil opinions you may have heard...arise from his recklessly setting at defiance conventional people talking nonsense about religion and heart and principle."

On the subject of religion, Isabel rushed to reassure. "He leads a good life, has a natural worship of God, innate honour, and does unknown good," she wrote. Isabel was confident, moreover, that with time and calm, gentle guidance—not unlike what she was currently applying to her mother—she could bring him around. "At *present* he is following no form; at least none that he *owns* to," she admitted, but there were already signs, she believed, that he would eventually come around to their way of thinking. "He wishes to be married in the Catholic Church, says that I must practise my own religion, and that our children must be Catholics, and will give such a promise in writing." There were plenty of men who professed to be God-fearing Catholics, Isabel reminded her mother, but few, she argued, were as genuinely good as Burton. "I myself do not care about people *calling* themselves Catholics, if they are not so in actions," she wrote, "and Captain Burton's life is far more Christian, more gentlemanly, more useful, and more pleasing to God—I am sure—than many who *call* themselves Catholics, and whom we know."

Although Isabel used every resource at her disposal, from her sharp mind to her heaving heart, to convince her mother to accept Burton, Eliza would not be moved. "The only answer to this letter was an awful long and solemn sermon," Isabel would later recall. "Telling me, 'that Richard was not a Christian, and had no money.'" Burton advised her to give up, certain that she would never be able to change her mother's mind about him. They both had "the noble firmness of the mule," he said. The only option left them, he believed, was to marry without her blessing. Isabel, however, resisted. Although she was by now nearly thirty years old, she still could not bring herself to disobey her mother.

•

Burton's life had suddenly, inexplicably fallen apart. Everything he had dreamed of, worked for, repeatedly risked his life in the pursuit of, had vanished, leaving him with no idea where to turn next. Even those few parts of his life on which he had always been able to rely had crumbled. Both of his parents were dead, and his younger brother, Edward, who had been a mainstay throughout his life, the best friend of his peripatetic childhood, had changed completely, tragically, and irrevocably. Edward Burton had survived the Indian Mutiny two years earlier, during which Edward Speke had been killed, but had been sent home after suffering severe sunstroke. The sunstroke, it was believed, coupled with an attack three years earlier during which he had been beaten by an angry mob, had led to what could only be described as a complete mental collapse. "His mind slowly gave way," Georgiana Stisted would later write, "and never recovered." The brave, handsome young man who had followed his brother in every youthful rebellion, even managing to be expelled from Cambridge after Richard was asked to leave Oxford, was now an inmate in the Surrey County Lunatic Asylum. He had not spoken since being brought home, and but for a single exception, little more than a murmur, would not speak again for the rest of his life, nearly forty years. The severity and mystery of Edward's illness left him utterly, hopelessly isolated from the world around him, impossible even for his brother to reach.

Eager to forget everything that had happened since his return, Burton left London at the first opportunity. Restlessly moving from place to place, he attempted to both cure his broken body and free his tortured mind. "I was driven out of town by an intense longing for cool air and a weight upon the mind— something like what conscience must be," he wrote to Monckton Milnes from Dover, where he had gone to take "the water cure." Milnes then invited him to spend a week at his country manor, Fryston Hall, where he hosted everyone from Henry Adams to Tennyson, who nicknamed the drafty old estate "Freezetown." Milnes himself lovingly referred to it as Aphrodisiopolis, in reference to his large collection of erotica. From Fryston Hall, Burton traveled to Boulogne, where he had first met Isabel nearly ten years earlier, stopping in Paris to visit Hankey.

Even Milnes and Hankey, however, with their rare collections and outrageous suggestions, could not take Burton's mind off what he had lost. When he visited his family, his young niece, Georgiana, could not help but see that her once vibrant uncle had changed, and she was not alone. "Everybody remarked he looked ill and depressed," she wrote. It was not just that he was frail and weak. His heart was broken. "Speke's strange breach of faith affected him more than he would confess to," Georgiana later recalled. "So affectionate a nature could not fail to keenly feel the complete severance of a long friendship." Georgiana and her parents doted on Burton, taking him on long walks and to family dinners, and ensuring that he had time and solitude to write and think, but nothing seemed to help. "All that summer he seemed ailing and despondent," Georgiana wrote. "In his family the expression, 'an unlucky Burton,' is proverbial, and certainly at times his ill-luck was almost inveterate enough to terminate his career. Even a good thing would come to him like a scorpion, with a sting in its tail."

CHAPTER SEVENTEEN

Hard as Bricks

Comfortable and content in his ancestral home at Jordans, Speke moved forward with plans for his own expedition. The decisions that seemed to most absorb his thoughts, however, involved not what supplies he would bring or even the route he would take but whom he would hire. From his own recent experience, Speke knew that choosing the men with whom he would travel through East Africa was a vitally important, potentially dangerous decision. He would not make it lightly.

Loyalty became central to Speke's decisions. The one person he knew without question that he had to have with him on his expedition was Sidi Mubarak Bombay. "Tell Bombay I was swelling him all over the world," he wrote to Rigby, "and have created so much interest here about his hire, that the next time I must bring him home with me." With Bombay by his side, Speke knew, he would have not only a translator and guide, but a trust-worthy companion. He would never be lost nor lonely.

Far more difficult for Speke was choosing his second in command. The Royal Geographical Society had already received several applications for the position, but Speke wanted someone he knew personally and trusted. His first thought was Edmund Smyth. He had already let Smyth down twice in the past: First in 1854, when he had chosen to sail alone to Aden rather than to travel with Smyth as they had planned, and then again two years later, when he had abandoned their plans to go hunting in the Caucasus Mountains after receiving Burton's invitation to join the East African Expedition. But Speke was confident that Smyth would not hold the past against him, and he felt that, even in the most difficult of situations, he could rely on his old friend. He was "a chap who won't go to the devil, full of pluck and straight-head foremost," he wrote, "a man of precisely my habits, and one entirely after my own heart." Smyth had served in India with the 13th Bengal Native Infantry, fighting in the battles of Chenab and Gujrat in the Second Anglo-Sikh War. He had hunted with Speke in the Himalayas, explored the mountains of Kumaon and Garhwal, and opened a path on the upper reaches of the Ganges that had been long closed to travelers. Two years earlier, the writer Thomas Hughes, who had attended the Rugby School with Smyth, had even created a character based on him in his popular novel *Tom Brown's School Days*. "The queerest, coolest fish in Rugby," Hughes had written of the Smyth character, Crab Jones. "If he were tumbled into the moon this minute, he would just pick himself up without taking his hands out of his pockets."

After inviting Smyth to go with him, however, Speke changed his mind yet again. Suddenly deciding that his old friend was no longer tough enough to travel with him, he rescinded his offer.

"I hear Smyth is feverishly inclined," he wrote dismissively to Shaw. "I won't have him with me.... I am as hard as bricks." Speke was looking for someone who was smart and strong but also, and perhaps more importantly, unshakably loyal. He needed someone who would never betray him, envy him his position as commander of the expedition, or vie for his place in history as discoverer of the source of the Nile.

In the end, the perfect companion presented himself when James Augustus Grant wrote to Speke, offering to accompany him to East Africa. The son of a parish minister, Grant had been born in the Scottish Highlands and educated in Aberdeen before joining the Indian army, where he had met Speke twelve years earlier. Grant had all of the qualities that Speke was looking for in a second in command, few of which could be used to describe either Burton or Speke himself. Grant was modest, self-effacing, and happy to play second fiddle. "Mother thinks no end of our friend Grant and is immensely pleased with the idea of my having such a companion," Speke wrote to Shaw from Jordans, his family estate. With Grant, Speke knew, he would never be in danger of having to share the spotlight. "I feel I never shall be robbed of the discovery of the Nile," he wrote contentedly to Rigby.

•

While claiming to have discovered the source of the White Nile had come easily to Speke, proving it would be far more difficult. Although he had already been to the Nyanza, he had never before led an expedition of this size. All of the difficult decisions for which he had criticized Burton would now be his to make. The Royal Geographical Society, moreover, would be of little help. Expecting Speke, like all of their explorers, to take matters into his own hands, they did not even send instructions until a month before he and Grant were scheduled to leave England. When the instructions did finally arrive, Speke found that they offered little guidance. Beginning in Zanzibar, the expedition was to travel directly to the northern reaches of the Nyanza, find the point at which the White Nile issued from the lake—thus proving that it was the principal source—and follow the river north to the German mission of Gondokoro on the east bank, in what is today South Sudan. All of which would be accomplished, the Society expected, by the end of 1861, in little more than a year.

Speke knew that by the time his expedition reached Gondokoro it would be in trouble, with little or no supplies and no way to get a boat to take it to Khartoum, from where it was supposed to return home. He needed someone willing to meet him with boats and supplies. With Murchison's help, he found just the right man. John Petherick knew the region near Gondokoro as well as nearly any explorer and better than most. A Welsh mining engineer, he had searched in vain for coal deposits in Egypt and Sudan before giving up and becoming an ivory trader in the Nile Valley. While there, he had explored the Nile's tributaries and become the first European to map the Bahr el-Ghazal, a river whose drainage basin is the largest of the Nile's ten sub-basins. After being appointed the British vice-consul in Khartoum, he had returned to England in 1859 and sought out Murchison, whom he had known for years. Murchison, in turn, introduced him to Speke.

Over the next few months, Speke worked hard to forge a friendship with Petherick. After seeing a map that he had drawn of the upper Nile, Speke had pronounced it "a most valuable production" and Petherick "the greatest traveller in that part of Africa." Petherick enjoyed exploration but was happy in his anonymity. Speke urged him to consider how famous he might become. "It was far from my thoughts to court notoriety either as a traveller or as an author," Petherick wrote. "One of the most urgent of my new acquaintances to induce me to overcome my prejudices with respect to publishing was Captain Speke." Speke encouraged Petherick not just to publish his travel journals but to do as he had done and hand them over to *Blackwood's*. "The interest... is much more intense than you suppose, or I am sure you would not withhold from the public what they want so much, and which is now kept secret within yourself," he urged Petherick. "The Royal Geographical Society has not the means of spreading anything about whereas Blackwood has a larger circulation than anyone else. Again, the Royal Geographical Society are slothful to the last degree, but Blackwood does not want a week to produce a map, a paper, or anything else."

Speke even invited Petherick to join him at Jordans. "I have asked Petherick to come here for a few days," he wrote to Shaw at the Royal Geographical Society, "that we may make arrangements for ripping open Africa together." While Speke's mother highly approved of Grant for his obvious loyalty to her son, his sisters preferred Petherick, if for no other reason than he made them laugh. Short and stocky with an unruly beard and a head full of wild curls, Petherick was more at home in a camp in Africa than a British estate. He bumbled around their delicate furniture and fine china "like a rampant hippopotamus," Speke wrote. His sisters loved watching the burly man struggle to figure out how to fit in and what he was supposed to be doing. "Petherick much to the amusement of the girls," Speke wrote to Blackwood, "could not find his place in the books at church today."

Petherick, however, for all his awkwardness among aristocrats, was smart. He wanted to return to the Nile, and he was cheerfully willing to set aside his own ambitions to help Speke achieve his, but he was concerned that he would not have the funding necessary for such a difficult undertaking. Even Speke had only received £2,500, and much of that had been a result of Murchison's direct appeal to his friends at the Treasury. To do what Speke and the Royal Geographical Society were asking of him—to travel south from Khartoum while Speke was heading north from Zanzibar, and then to wait in Gondokoro with three boats stocked with supplies for Speke and his men—Petherick would need a grant that was commensurate with Speke's. "The expense of such an expedition would amount to about £2,000," Petherick explained to the Society. "In the event of so large a sum not being available, I would then propose to place two well-provisioned boats, under the superintendence of one of my own men, on whose integrity I could confidently depend, to await the arrival of the expedition.... The expense would be, on a moderate calculation, £1,000."

Petherick was right to worry. The Royal Geographical Society attempted only to have his consular salary raised by £300 a year, and the government refused even that request. "I must say," the under secretary to the Treasury complained, "the Geographical Society draws largely on us." Murchison did what he could to raise the money himself, finally convincing the Society and the Foreign Office to give £100 each, contributing £20 of his own money, and urging his fellow Society members to do the same. "Consul Petherick could hardly be expected to do this at his own expense," he chided them. In the end, however, Petherick still found himself far short of the £2,000 he knew he needed. Despite the fact that he repeatedly tried to explain that what they were asking him to do was impossible with the funds they had given him, Francis Galton, who served on the Society's Expedition Sub-Committee, issued instructions ordering Petherick to be waiting for Speke in Gondokoro by November of 1861, and, if necessary, to remain there until at least June of 1862.

While Petherick struggled to make the Society pay attention, Speke and Grant prepared to leave. Galton invited both men to his home to wish them a bon voyage. Years later, he would recall the visit, during which he was struck by Grant's obvious devotion to Speke. "I may say," he later wrote, "that the attachment of Grant to Speke was most remarkable for its loyalty and intensity." Even with Grant, however, Speke was unwilling to take any chances. Clearly recalling his tortured relationship with his own commander, he wrote an unapologetically severe contract for his modest, unassuming second in command, asking him to sign it the night before they left for East Africa.

> I hereby agree to accompany Captain J. H. Speke in his expedition to Eastern Central Africa on the following conditions: That I shall be no expense to the Expedition throughout its whole journey and that I devote my entire services and abilities to the Expedition and renounce all my rights to publishing or collections of any sort on my own account until approved of by Captain Speke or the R.G.S.
>
> On the other hand Capt Speke agrees to make Captain Grant a part of the Expedition upon the conditions above stated.
> *J. A. Grant*
> *J. H. Speke*

•

Finally confident that he would never find himself in the same position he had placed Burton, Speke began to feel some regret for the way things had turned out. Burton used to infuriate him with his supreme confidence, his disinterest in anyone else's opinion, and his certainty that, no matter the situation, he could rely solely on his own intellect. What had really enraged Speke, however, was the fact that Burton had been neither impressed nor threatened by him. "He used to snub me so unpleasantly when talking about anything that I often kept my own council [*sic*]," Speke had complained to Shaw. "Burton is one of those men who never *can* be wrong, and will never acknowledge an error so that when only two are together talking becomes more of [a] bore than a pleasure."

Now, however, as he prepared to take command of his own expedition, Speke's feelings had begun to shift from resentment to magnanimity. "Burton and I met at the R.G. Society today," he admitted in a letter to Rigby, "but he did not speak to me for we have had a little difference of opinion after which he desired that all private correspondence should cease." The letters between the two men, which had continued since Speke left Aden, had grown increasingly cold as the extent of Speke's betrayal was slowly revealed. What had begun in the most familiar of terms, two friends addressing each other with respect, even warmth, had quickly devolved into crackling tension and then barely concealed fury. "My dear John" quickly became "My dear Speke," which was then shortened to "Speke," and finally to the barest minimum required by civil correspondence in the Victorian Age: "Sir." In the end, Burton asked Shaw to act as mediator between them, explaining that he did not "wish to have any further private or direct communication with Speke."

Two days before Speke was to leave on his expedition, he wrote to Burton one last time. "My dear Burton," he wrote, attempting to return to a friendlier tone. "I cannot leave England addressing you so coldly as you have hitherto been corresponding the more especially as you have condescended to make an amicable arrangement with me about the debt I owe you." Burton, however, refused to accept Speke's offer of conciliation. He had been too injured, had lost too much. His feelings for Speke could never be mended. "Sir, I have received your note of the 16th April," he replied tersely. "With regard to the question of debts I have no objection to make. I cannot however accept your offer concerning me corresponding less coldly—any other tone would be extremely distasteful to me." "I am Sir," he wrote, leaving the letter unsigned.

Part Four

———◆◆◆———

The Malignant
Tongues of Friends

CHAPTER EIGHTEEN

The Prince

The first person to welcome Speke back to Zanzibar in the fall of 1860 was the last person he had seen as he left the island more than a year earlier. Neither Speke nor Burton would ever forget the sight of Sidi Mubarak Bombay standing on the shore, wishing them a fond farewell as their ship had sailed out of the harbor. Now that Speke was back, Bombay was waiting, still steadfast, honest, and brave. Ready to return with him to the Nyanza.

After being reunited with Bombay, Speke was eager to see the man with whom he had formed a long-distance alliance over the past year. Quickly leading Grant to the British consulate, he found Rigby waiting for them there. "He was delighted to see us," Speke wrote, "and in anticipation of our arrival, had prepared rooms for our reception, that both Captain Grant and myself might enjoy his hospitality until arrangements could be made for our final start into the interior." The consul also pulled Speke aside to show him what he believed was an ancient Hindu map that had been published some sixty years earlier and which he thought might support Speke's argument that the Mountains of the Moon were south of the Nyanza, and so could not cut off the Nile from the lake as some of his critics had suggested. "Colonel Rigby now gave me a most interesting paper, with a map attached to it, about the Nile and the Mountains of the Moon...from the 'Pŭrans' of the ancient Hindŭs," Speke wrote. "It exemplifies, to a certain extent, the supposition I formerly arrived at." The real source of ancient knowledge about East Africa, Speke now believed, was not the Egyptians but the men who had drawn this map. "All our previous information concerning the hydrography of these regions, as well as the Mountains of the Moon, originated with the ancient Hindŭs, who told it to the priests of the Nile," he argued. "All those busy Egyptian geographers, who disseminated *their* knowledge with a view to be famous for *their* long-sightedness, in solving the deep-seated mystery which enshrouded the source of their holy river, were so many hypothetical humbugs."

So confident was Speke in his own first impressions of the region, he not only believed that he had found the source of the White Nile but had already renamed it. After returning to England, he had bestowed upon the largest lake in Africa the name of a British queen: Victoria. "I christened the Lake after the Queen," he had explained to a friend, "because she asked so politely after my health on my return." The Nyanza, of course, already had a name. In fact, it had several. As well as its Swahili name, those living nearest the lake, who spoke the Bantu language Luganda, called it Nalubaale, attributing to the lake, which provided so much for their community, the spirit of a woman or mother. The Luo people, living in what is today Kenya and Tanzania, called it Nam Lolwe, in the Dholuo dialect, which means an endless lake or body of water. None of these people knew or cared that in the Western world their lake had suddenly become known as the Victoria Nyanza, soon to be anglicized even further to Lake Victoria.

Speke was certainly not the first, nor would he be the last, explorer to name a geographical feature that belonged to another continent. Lakes, mountain ranges, island archipelagoes, even entire countries were named for men who had visited them only once or never at all. Those who lived beside them, grateful for the food, water, shelter, or beauty they provided, occasionally regarding them with fear and always with respect, were rarely if ever consulted. Not every explorer, however, approved of the practice. Burton had found the renaming of the Nyanza not just presumptuous but preposterous, as he did Speke's decision to designate features of the Tanganyika "Speke Channel" and "Burton Point." "My views... about retaining native nomenclature have ever been fixed, and of the strongest," Burton wrote, going on to quote the geographer James Macqueen that "nothing can be so absurd as to impose English names on any part, but especially upon places in the remote interior parts of Africa."

To Speke, the lake was already the Victoria Nyanza, and his only job now was to prove its—and his—place in geographical history. In order to do that, he needed to hire as many men as he could find. As the caravan leader, he once again hired Said bin Salim, despite the fact that he had sold most of their supplies while they were on Lake Tanganyika and Burton had been forced to replace him with Bombay. As his factotum, translator, and companion, Speke would not consider any man but Bombay. Bombay in turn chose as his own companion Mabruki, the enslaved man he had bought three years earlier to bring with him on Burton's expedition. Just as Speke could not imagine traveling in East Africa without Bombay, Bombay would not leave Zanzibar without Mabruki.

As Murchison had in England, Rigby did all he could to help Speke in Zanzibar. Having criticized Burton for not honoring the promises Hamerton had made to his men, and refusing to use his powers as Hamerton's replacement to honor them himself, Rigby now made careful note of every agreement Speke entered into. "The payment of these men's wages for the first year, as well as the terms of the agreement made with them, by the kind consent of Colonel Rigby were now entered in the Consular Office books," Speke wrote, "as a security to both parties, and a precaution against disputes on the way."

Speke was thrilled not only to be reunited with Rigby and Bombay, but to be traveling with Grant. "He is a very dear friend," he wrote, "and being a good sportsman we get through our days wonderfully." Grant heartily agreed, later writing that "not a shade of jealousy or distrust, or even ill-temper, ever came between us." There was, however, from the beginning not just an easy camaraderie between the two men but also a clear understanding of their relative positions within the expedition. They were the same age—in fact, Grant was a few weeks older than Speke—and had had very similar military careers, but there was never any question that Speke was the commander and Grant his subordinate. Grant never chafed at the distinction, as Speke had under Burton, nor did he ever forget the agreement he had signed before leaving England. A highly skilled artist, he had brought with him to Zanzibar his sketchbook, inside of which he wrote, "Notice. If I die this book is to be given, with Speke's permission, to my sister."

Before leaving Zanzibar, Speke was invited on a hippopotamus hunt. He left Grant, also an experienced and enthusiastic hunter, behind. As he patiently awaited Speke's return,

Grant was invited to witness the execution of two men accused of murdering the German explorer Dr. Albrecht Roscher near Lake Nyasa only a few months earlier. After a long delay in the execution orders from the sultan, one man in the crowd finally addressed Grant. "Might it commence?" he asked. "Yes," Grant replied, "certainly; proceed," and then watched as the two prisoners, one after the other, were nearly decapitated by a sword. "Both appeared as if in a sweet sleep; two chickens hopped on the still quivering bodies, and the cows in the open space lay undisturbed," Grant later wrote. "I left the spot, hoping never to witness such another scene; but I had the satisfaction of feeling that justice was carried out, and that had I not been present those murderers would have escaped punishment."

·

Eager to reach the Nyanza, and expecting to meet Petherick in Gondokoro in just a year and a half, Speke sailed for the mainland little more than a month after arriving in Zanzibar. He "set out on the march," he wrote, "perfectly sure in my mind that before very long I should settle the great Nile problem for ever." To his great frustration, however, as soon as his expedition began, so did the desertions. "I started from Zanzibar with 200 followers," he complained. "We had only 40 men of the 200 when we reached Kazeh, 430 miles west of the sea-coast. Three-fourths had deserted us." Although he had accused Burton of being too harsh when refusing to reward those who had deserted his expedition, Speke now demanded a far more serious punishment for his own men. "The Sultan's men slip away and leave us in the lurch. I have told the Sheikh to indite a letter to the Sultan complaining of them, and asking that severe penalties may be instituted for such demeanour to deter any others from following their example," he wrote to Rigby. "They virtually are thieves, made worse because they swore allegiance to me, and I wish them to be so served.... I send a list of the 17 men who have bolted so that you can do as you think best." His warning to the men who remained was clear: At risk was not just their reward, but their freedom. "Should they desert," he told them, "they would find my arm long enough to arrest them on the coast and put them in prison."

Speke wanted obedience among his men, but more than that he wanted to keep moving. At every point, his expedition was frustratingly, even dangerously slowed. In Kazeh, the trading post where he and Burton had been forced to spend five weeks because of Burton's illness, Speke was detained by illness, logistics, and negotiations for nearly twice as long. When he finally set out again, he was stopped almost immediately in the kingdom of Uzinza, where its chief, Lumeresi, insisted that he stay for nearly three months. By then it was October, nearly a year after the expedition had left Zanzibar and only a few months before they were supposed to meet Petherick, and they still had hundreds of miles to go.

The expedition was quickly running low on provisions. Writing in desperation to Rigby, Speke admitted that he was deeply concerned, "scarcely knowing what to do." The men relied heavily on foraging and hunting small game, usually sparrows and doves. "We had to trust to chance and our rifles," Grant wrote. "One night our entire dinner consisted of two ears of Indian corn, eaten with salt." While the others hunched dejectedly over their tin-lid plates, perched on top of wooden boxes, Bombay slipped away, later returning with a dead, "very small, and awkwardly flattened out" chicken. Then he disappeared again, somehow finding five live chickens, which fed them for the next two days.

Nearly every man had also already been sick. Speke and Grant fell prey to diseases that turned their strong, healthy bodies into limping, coughing, shivering shells. Speke developed such a severe cold that he could hardly sleep or stand. "The symptoms, altogether, were rather alarming," he later admitted. "The heart felt inflamed and ready to burst, pricking and twingeing with every breath, which was exceedingly aggravated by constant coughing, when streams of phlegm and bile were ejected." Finally, as he had on the Tanganyika when a beetle crawled into his ear, Speke attempted to take matters into his own hands. "Thinking then how I could best cure the disease that was keeping me down," he wrote, "I tried to stick a packing needle, used as a seton, into my side." Too weak to force the dull point through his flesh, he asked one of the men to do it, but even he was unable.

Grant suffered from frequent fevers, but his most crippling complaint was an infection in his right thigh, which became "deformed with inflammation." For months, he had no idea what was causing the extreme swelling, or how to treat it. The "intense pain . . . was relieved temporarily by a deep incision and copious discharge," he wrote. "Fresh abscesses formed, and other incisions were made. . . . Daily, to bring out the accumulated discharge, I stripped my leg like a leech." The men, seeing Grant's intense suffering, did everything they could to relieve it. Bombay made him a poultice of cow dung, salt, and mud, but nothing seemed to help. His leg only grew worse.

•

To add to Speke's fears and frustrations, news reached him of the release of *The Lake Regions of Central Africa,* Burton's book about the East African Expedition. Although Burton had acknowledged his companion's courage and strength, he had also described his every failing and shortcoming, from the fact that he did not speak Arabic or any African languages to his inability to acquire boats on the Tanganyika. After hearing about Burton's book and the accusations in it, Speke's irritation turned to rage, and he vowed revenge. "I have heard today from Rigby...that Burton has published some bitter things concerning myself in allusion to the lake expedition, and I must now say that if he had been impinging my honor in any way, I shall be very sorry that I have glossed over many of his transactions in the late papers which I sent to you for publication," he wrote to his publisher, John Blackwood. "Indeed I shall much regret their being published during my absence if you can possibly keep the public in suspense until my return without injury to yourself." Blackwood, who had already advised Speke to temper his attacks on Burton in his articles for the magazine, would urge him to not make any changes to his book. Even Speke's mother would write to Blackwood, asking him to prevent her son from bringing his feud with Burton into the open. "We have been so strongly recommended to dissuade Hanning from ever bringing before the public that altercation, that we wish to put it out of his power to do so," she wrote, "and Mr. Speke and my other sons all think it would be advisable to have his book published as he left it."

Speke, unaware of his family's concerns or his publisher's reluctance, continued to rail against Burton from East Africa. "All right & ready to fight," he wrote to Blackwood, having begun to formulate his response. "I could stand it no longer, so I have let fly at Burton's eye, and I think he had got it, as richly as he deserves." Grant, Speke told him, had been equally incensed by Burton's book. "Old Grant says the man ought to be hung," he wrote, "an opinion I must say I long ago arrived at." Knowing that he would also have a receptive audience in Rigby, Speke filled his every letter to the consul with bitter complaints about Burton. "If the Society only knew him as I know him and could see what dupes they had been made to his insane vanity, his journal never would have been accepted from him," he wrote in a long, rambling letter that moved from old wrongs to future plans for revenge and back again. "You are right in calling him a mean & malignant wretch and I long to return to England and to have a counter out against him. He printed my Somali diaries without asking my leave to swell his 'First Footsteps'—promising to repay me for the expenses I was put to on going into the Somali country alone.... Selfishness alone was the root of all his evils, it led to Vanity, the deceit, and every other abomination of which he was, is, and ever, I am afraid, will be master of.... Burton's saying I acted in a 'subordinate capacity' only shows how he stings under the impression that people have arrived at the right conclusion that I and not he conducted all the work of the late Expedition. Never was there a row in camp but Burton called on me to settle it as he felt himself incapable. What was the use of saying I knew neither Arabic or French, and that my want of knowledge in manners and customs was a good reason for sending me away from Kazeh."

●

By now only two kingdoms lay between the expedition and the Nyanza, but they were two of the largest and most powerful in East Africa—Karagwe and Buganda, home to modern-day Kampala, the capital of Uganda. Hoping to receive better accommodations and more respect from their kings, Speke pretended to be royalty himself. When he was offered the usual lodgings reserved for Arab traders, he claimed to be insulted, insisting that he was not a trader but a prince. "I struck out on my claim as a foreign prince," he wrote, "whose royal blood could not stand such an indignity. The palace was my sphere." When made to wait for hours to see the king, as was customary, he roared in anger, threatening to leave. "I had made up my mind never to sit upon the ground as the natives and Arabs are obliged to do," he explained, "nor to make my obeisance in any other manner than is customary in England." With Bombay as his interpreter, he offered his *kuhonga* while sitting on an iron stool, holding an umbrella to protect himself from the sun. "I could neither sit in the sun nor live in a poor man's hut," he wrote. "It was unworthy of my dignity."

As heavily as he relied on Bombay, and as devoted and irreplaceable as Bombay had repeatedly proved himself to be, Speke had allowed a rift to open up between them. It had begun with the always simmering, occasionally erupting tension between Bombay and one of the other members of the expedition, a highly skilled but arrogant and ambitious man named Baraka who had long been jealous of Bombay's position of power. Speke knew that Baraka had "incessantly bullied" Bombay, doing all that he could to turn the other men, especially the Wanguana porters, against him, but he was furious when Bombay, out of desperation, turned to a medicine man for help. Exchanging precious beads for a concoction that he hoped might "affect the hearts of the Wangŭana so as to incline them towards him," Bombay had poured it into a pot of *pombe* and placed it near Baraka. When Baraka found out that the pombe had been contaminated, he accused Bombay of trying to kill him. Furious with Bombay for "his belief in such magical follies," Speke punished him by showing favoritism to Baraka, taking him instead of Bombay whenever he visited the king. This one act, "little as it might appear to others," Speke knew, "was of the greatest consequence to the hostile parties."

In his restlessness and impatience to reach the Nyanza, Speke even lashed out at Bombay himself. One morning when their regional guide did not show up, Speke ordered Bombay to strike the camp. "How can we go?" Bombay asked, knowing that they were already far behind schedule and that they risked losing their way in territory that none of them knew. Without answering him, Speke simply repeated his order: "Strike the tent." Unwilling to blindly follow orders when he was concerned about their consequences, Bombay questioned Speke again. "Who will guide us?" he asked. Speke answered only with another curt command to strike the tent. When Bombay still did not set to work, Speke, in a fury, called some of his men over and pulled the tent down himself, covering Bombay in its folds. Bombay finally "flew into a passion," Speke later recalled, "abusing the men who were helping me, as there were fires and powder-boxes under the tent. I of course had to fly into a passion and abuse Bombay." After shouting that they could blow up the entire camp, Bombay stood stunned as Speke angrily replied, "If I choose to blow up my property, that is my look-out; and if you don't do your duty, I will blow you up also." Furious, Bombay said that he refused to be insulted. In response, with all of his men watching, Speke hit Bombay. And then he hit him again. And again. Dripping blood, Bombay walked away, vowing to never again work for Speke, a vow that he would not keep.

Despite the violence and humiliation of this moment, Bombay forgave Speke, returning to their camp and continuing the march. Speke never admitted remorse for his actions, seeming to believe that what had been at risk was not Bombay's safety and self-respect, his friendship with Speke, or even his continued loyalty to the expedition, but Speke's own dignity. "It was the first and last time I had ever occasion to lose my dignity by striking a blow with my own hands," he later wrote. "But I could not help it on this occasion without losing command and respect; for although I often had occasion to award 100 and even 150 lashes to my men for stealing, I could not, for the sake of due subordination, allow any inferior officer to strike Bombay, and therefore had to do the work myself."

•

As intent as Speke was on reaching the Nyanza and proving that it was the source of the White Nile, he was not worried about missing Petherick in Gondokoro. The trader, he believed, would wait for him however long it took, setting out in search of him if necessary. Having left England before Petherick, Speke assumed that he had received the funding he needed. More than that, he believed that Petherick was obligated to give him whatever assistance he might require, no matter how inconvenient, costly, or dangerous it might be to Petherick himself. In January, Speke had been thrilled to hear that "foreign visitors" had been spotted on the Nile, certain that they were Petherick and his men. "The new year was ushered in by the most exciting intelligence, which drove us half wild with delight," he wrote, "for we fully believed Mr. Petherick was indeed on his road up the Nile, endeavoring to meet us."

A few months later, after Speke had reached Buganda, news came again, this time of a bearded white man, seen by the scouts of Mutesa, the kingdom's powerful ruler. Speke was elated but also concerned. Petherick, he suddenly realized, might inadvertently ruin his ruse, revealing that he was not royalty. Deciding to send Baraka to try to find Petherick, Speke wrote a letter to send with him. "My dear Petherick," he wrote. "You will have to drop your dignity for the present, and to look upon me as your superior officer." He explained that he had told Mutesa that

Petherick was his subordinate, and that "I ordered you to come up the Nile to look for me and bring me away, and that three vessels were mine as well as their contents, and you could not disobey my orders." It was also important, he urged, that Petherick not appear dressed as an officer. "Don't bring uniform, for I have none," Speke wrote. "But bring a lot of common red cloth and fez caps for my men to wear as a guard of honour."

Another difficulty was Grant. Not only had his leg not healed, it had grown worse, slowing down the expedition even further. "One thing only now embarrassed me—Grant was worse, without hope of recovery for at least one or two months," Speke wrote. "To get on as fast as possible was the only chance of ever bringing the journey to a successful issue." The only answer, Speke finally decided, was to send Grant ahead with the baggage to the palace of King Kamrasi in Bunyoro, north of the Nyanza, while he continued east without him, marching until he reached the Nile and, he hoped, the point at which it issued from the Nyanza. Although Speke's decision would later be questioned for its fairness to Grant, Grant defended Speke to the last. "At the time I was positively unable to walk twenty miles a-day, especially miles of Uganda marching, through bogs and over rough ground. I therefore yielded reluctantly to the necessity of our parting," Grant explained. "I am anxious to be explicit on this point, as some have hastily inferred that my companion did not wish me to share in the gratification of seeing the river. Nothing could be more contrary to the fact." Whatever the reason for Speke's decision, both men knew that the result would be the same. Grant, who had shared in the difficulties, expenses, and dangers of the expedition, would be deprived of both the thrill of the moment—seeing the Nile as it rushed from the Nyanza—and the glory that was to come.

Three weeks after leaving Buganda and separating from

Grant, Speke and his men reached Urondogani, where they finally saw the White Nile. "Here at last I stood on the brink of the Nile," he wrote. "Most beautiful was the scene, nothing could surpass it!" Turning to Bombay and the others, he urged them to "shave their heads and bathe in the holy river, the cradle of Moses." Bombay politely declined. "We don't look on those things in the same fanciful manner that you do," he explained to Speke. To Speke, the land that surrounded the Nile was the perfect place not just for European commerce but for Christian conversion. "What a place, I thought to myself, this would be for missionaries!" he wrote. Just as the Nyanza already had a name, however, Bombay gently reminded Speke that he and the other men in the expedition already had a faith, and it was as strong and deep as Speke's own. "We could no more throw off the Mussulman faith," Bombay told him, "than you could yours."

A week later, Speke and Bombay stood before a roaring waterfall, roughly sixteen feet high and nearly a thousand feet wide. As they watched, Africa's largest lake gave birth to the world's longest river, lifeblood to millions of people over thousands of miles. Speke did not have the scientific measurements or completed navigation that he would need to definitively prove that the Nyanza was the source of the White Nile, nor did he now have the supplies or time to get them, but he was satisfied that he had accomplished what he had set out to do. "The expedition had now performed its functions. I saw that old father Nile without any doubt rises in the Victoria Nyanza, and, as I had foretold, that lake is the great source of the holy river," he wrote with satisfaction. "I felt I ought to be content with what I had been spared to accomplish; for I had seen full half of the lake, and had information given me of the other half, by means of which I knew all about the lake, as far, at least, as the chief objects of geographical importance were concerned."

After deciding to name the falls Ripon Falls, in honor of the 1st Marquess of Ripon, who had been president of the Royal Geographical Society when the expedition began, Speke returned to Urondogani, where he had first seen the Nile, bought five wooden boats, and set sail on the river. Doing what he could with the limited time and resources he had, he noted the longitude and latitude, the elevations of the river itself and the hills surrounding it. His boat avoided hippopotamuses and crocodiles as his men fished for six-foot-long Nile perch with large, gaping mouths and silvery stomachs. Looking around him, Speke took a moment to appreciate not just the river's potential for commercial wealth or Christian conversion but simply its beauty. He felt, he wrote, "as if I only wanted a wife and family, garden and yacht, rifle and rod, to make me happy here for life."

·

In February, thirteen months after he was supposed to meet Petherick in Gondokoro, Speke's expedition finally reached the German mission. Along the way, he had reunited with Grant in Bunyoro and stopped in a camp that he thought might be Petherick's. Instead, it had belonged to Petherick's trading rival, a Maltese named Amabile Musa de Bono. De Bono was no friend of Petherick's. Not only were the two men competitors in the ivory trade, but Petherick as consul to Sudan had arrested de Bono and one of his most senior men, Kurshid Agha, for slave trading. In fact, a friend of Petherick's had recently warned him that de Bono had been trying to get rid of him, even spreading rumors that Petherick himself had been involved in the slave trade. De Bono's men now told Speke that, having heard about his expedition, de Bono had sent them to help him. They must have been the white men Mutesa's scouts had seen near the Nile,

Speke now realized. He was grateful to de Bono, but where, he asked them, was Petherick. The response, he later wrote, was "a mysterious silence."

As he walked along the river in Gondokoro, passing the mission's empty church and a few boats lined up on the bank, Speke suddenly saw a man hurrying toward him. Even from a distance, he could tell that it was an Englishman, but when the man drew near, it was clear that, once again, it was not Petherick. Instead, Speke's friend Samuel Baker seized his hand in his strong, leathery grip. "What joy this was I can hardly tell," Speke wrote. "We could not talk fast enough, so overwhelmed were we both to meet again."

An engineer, explorer, and big game hunter, Baker had for years been trying to organize an expedition of his own to find the source of the White Nile. The Royal Geographical Society, in an effort to keep him from competing with Speke and Grant, had tried to talk him into exploring the Sobat River in southern Sudan instead. Baker, however, would not be dissuaded. "I had a wild hope, mingled with humility," he wrote, "that, even as the insignificant worm bores through the hardest oak, I might by perseverance reach the heart of Africa." Knowing that he would not receive any help from either the Royal Geographical Society or the government, Baker used his own money, which he had earned building a railway and bridges in Eastern Europe. It was there that he had also met his exceptional young wife, Florence, in a slave market in Romania. Born in Hungary, abandoned in a refugee camp as a child, and sold to an Armenian slave trader, Florence spoke Turkish, Arabic, and English. Baker was at least twice her age, but she had insisted on traveling through Africa with him, even dressing as he did in heavy hunting clothes, although she drew crowds whenever she tried to wash her long, blond hair in the river.

Having heard rumors that Petherick had died, the Royal Geographical Society had asked Baker to help Speke at Gondokoro. Baker had agreed, but he and Florence were still there not because they were willing to wait for years for Speke but because they were trying to hire some of de Bono's men for their own expedition. After Baker had shared with Speke everything that had happened in the Western world since his departure nearly three years earlier, from the death of Prince Albert, Queen Victoria's husband, to the beginning of the American Civil War, Speke asked him if he knew what had happened to Petherick. Baker replied that before leaving England Petherick had been given £1,000 from a subscription raised for him to help Speke, and that he was now trading ivory at a post about seventy miles west of Gondokoro.

As he listened to Baker, Speke's confusion turned to irritation. "I naturally felt much annoyed at Petherick," he later wrote, "for I had hurried away from Uganda, and separated from Grant...solely to keep faith with him." Three of the boats that he had seen tied along the riverbank belonged to Petherick, he learned, and had been left there for him, filled with provisions and guarded by Petherick's own men. It was the absence of Petherick himself, however, that angered Speke. As his expedition was severely depleted, he grudgingly accepted ninety-five yards of cloth from Petherick's men, but only "the commonest stuff," he insisted, "as a makeshift for mosquito-curtains for my men, besides four sailor's shirts for my head men." The rest he refused, taking instead the supplies and boats that Baker offered.

Four days later, Petherick and his wife, Katherine, arrived in Gondokoro. Their journey, which was supposed to have taken six weeks, had lasted seven months and had cost Petherick not twice what the Royal Geographical Society had given him but five times that amount. He and his wife had barely survived, and several in their expedition had not. Petherick's botanist, James Brownell, and his young assistant, Foxcroft, had both died of fever. They had been shipwrecked, had hauled boats across hundreds of miles of barren land and waist-high marsh, had lost nearly all of their provisions, and had staggered into the trading post at Wayo starving and in rags. They had been there not to trade, as Baker had implied and Speke believed, but in a desperate attempt to find food and medical aid. Although the brutal journey had transformed Petherick from a strong, healthy explorer to "a helpless invalid," he had never given up, determined "to vanquish every obstacle, and keep my appointment with Speke at whatever hazard."

Before he even stepped out of his boat at Gondokoro, Petherick saw Speke standing on the shore. Surprised and relieved to see the man whose health and well-being had been his primary concern and principal objective for the past seven months, Petherick was at first eager to show him all that he had provided for his expedition. His excitement, however, soon turned to shock. Speke immediately made it clear that not only was he not grateful for what Petherick had endured to help him, he thought that he had not done enough. "Instead ... of the cordial meeting I had anticipated from the ardently sought-for, and now successful, travelers," Petherick wrote, "we were met with coolness." Petherick urged Speke to take all that he wanted from the supplies he had left for him, but Speke refused. He would not "partake of more of our stores or assistance than would satisfy their most urgent requirements, and that elsewhere could not be obtained," Petherick wrote in astonishment. He no longer needed his help, Speke told Petherick. "Baker has offered me his boats."

That night, Speke agreed to dine with Petherick and his wife, but Katherine would never forgive the disdain with which he treated them both. They had brought with them from

England a large ham, hauling it for hundreds of miles, keeping it while losing so many precious supplies, and refusing to eat it when they had so little else to keep them alive. They had told each other that they would save it to celebrate with Speke when they were finally reunited with him in Gondokoro. As they ate, Katherine, as her husband had done earlier in the day, pleaded with Speke to accept their help. "But," she later recalled with disgust, "he drawlingly replied, 'I do not wish to recognize the succor dodge.'" Barely able to contain her outrage, she left the table, refusing to ever again share a meal with him. Months later, still sickened by the memory, she wrote a letter from Khartoum, describing Speke's behavior when they arrived in Gondokoro. "After all our toil!" she wrote. "Never mind, it will recoil upon him yet, his heartless conduct."

CHAPTER NINETEEN

Damn Their Souls

While Speke had marched steadily toward the Nyanza with a single, unwavering ambition, Burton had seemed to spin in circles. Shifting from continent to continent, idea to idea, he had become what he feared, "a blaze of light, without a focus." The searing intellect that had for so long fueled his study of languages and religions, foreign cultures and distant lands was suddenly without direction or purpose. He was frustrated with himself and furious with everyone else. "What a misanthrope I am," he wrote.

One of the few people Burton still trusted after a year of being blindsided and betrayed was his friend John Steinhaüser, the Swiss civil surgeon in Aden. "He was one of the very few who, through evil as well as through good report," Burton wrote, "disdained to abate an iota of his friendship, and whose regard was never warmer than when all the little world looked its cold-

est." He had long regretted the fact that Steinhäuser had fallen
ill and been unable to join the East African Expedition, certain
that, had he been there, "in all human probability Lieut. Speke
would have escaped deafness and fever-blight, I paralysis."
More than Steinhäuser's medical skill, however, Burton valued
his friendship. Steinhäuser was "a man of literary tastes and of
extensive reading, and better still, a spirit as staunch and determined as ever attempted desperate enterprise," Burton wrote.
"No unkind thought, much less an unfriendly word, ever broke
our fair companionship." When the two men had met again at
a bistro in Boulogne, Steinhäuser had told Burton that he had
an idea. "I'll tell you what it is I have in mind," he said. Burton
would later remember his friend throwing wide his hands and,
with what looked like divine inspiration flooding his face, saying,
"I'll go to America! Yes, I'll go to America."

Burton and Steinhäuser had set sail for North America in
the spring of 1860, just a year before the start of the American
Civil War. They traveled together from Canada to Boston, New
York, and Washington. Then Burton, determined to see the
American West, boarded a stagecoach alone, riding from St.
Joseph, Missouri, to San Francisco. His travels were propelled,
as they so often had been in the past, by a fascination with other
cultures. In the American West, he set out to study the Mormon
church and Native American tribes, who had long been fighting
Europeans for their land and their lives.

Since his journey to Mecca, Burton's nascent form of
anthropology, born from a natural love of learning and a genuine interest in other cultures, had begun to transform into something new, not just tainted by imperial arrogance but infected
by personal bitterness. As he had everywhere he had traveled,
Burton studied the languages he encountered among Native
Americans, particularly sign language, and he compared tradi-

tions, rites, and religions to those that he had either observed or read about in other cultures. Fascinated by scalping, he argued that it had originated not in North America but in northeastern Asia. "The underlying idea," he wrote, "is doubtless the natural wish to preserve a memorial of a foeman done to death." But his descriptions of Native Americans were often callous and cruel, devoid of compassion or even honest perspective. In *The City of the Saints,* his book about his travels through North America, he characterized Native Americans not simply as members of a different culture, deserving of respect and protection, but as a different species. "I do not believe that an Indian of the plains ever became a Christian," he wrote in a discussion of American missionaries. "He must first be humanized, then civilized, and lastly Christianized; and, as has been said before, I doubt his surviving the operation."

Burton had long derided the desperate efforts of Christian missionaries to "save the savages." Speke, who frequently described Africans as children, admired the work of missionaries, insisting that "to instruct him is the surest way of gaining a black man's heart, which, once obtained, can easily be turned in any way the preceptor pleases." Burton, on the other hand, despite Isabel's best efforts, had little time for religious men, especially missionaries. He had seen them at work in Africa and found their methods at best ineffective and hypocritical, at worst brutal. He dryly pointed out that, while missionaries often flew into a fury over talismans of other religions, they encouraged reverence for Christian symbols and objects, from medals to palm leaves. "Priests may be good servants, but they are, mundanely speaking, bad masters. The ecclesiastical tyranny exercised upon the people from the highest to the lowest goes far to account for the extinction of Christianity in the country where so much was done to spread it," Burton wrote. "Whilst the friars talk of 'that meekness which becomes a missioner'...they issue eight ordinances or 'spiritual memorandums' degrading governors of cities and provinces who are not properly married, who neglect mass, or who do not keep saints' festivals. Flogging seems to have been the punishment of all infractions of discipline." In much of East Africa, Burton enjoyed telling his readers, evil spirits were white.

Despite their deep religious beliefs and devout commitment to missionary work, Burton seemed to have more tolerance for Mormons. They reminded him in some ways of the Muslim men he had met and admired in both Arabia and Africa. He was especially impressed by their charismatic president, Brigham Young. Stopping in Salt Lake City, he spent an hour with Young, who had taken over the leadership of the church after the murder of its founder, Joseph Smith. "The first impression left upon my mind by this short séance was, that the Prophet is no common man," Burton later wrote, "and that he has none of the weakness and vanity which characterize the common uncommon man." Burton was not, moreover, offended by the Mormons' most controversial practice: polygamy. Speke, who would never marry, believed that "all those who have many wives, seem to find little enjoyment in that domestic bliss so interesting and beautiful in our English homes." Burton, though, had studied polygamy in the Muslim religion and saw some value in it. "The literalism with which the Mormons have interpreted Scripture has led them directly to polygamy," he wrote. "The texts promising to Abraham a progeny numerous as the stars above or the sands below...induce them, his descendants, to seek a similar blessing." Even women, he insisted, benefited from the practice, especially if they were living in rural Utah. "Servants are rare and costly; it is cheaper and more comfortable to marry them," he argued. "Life in the wilds of Western America is a course of severe toil: a single woman can not perform the manifold duties of housekeeping, cooking, scrubbing, washing, darning, child-bearing, and nursing a family. A division of labor is necessary, and she finds it by acquiring a sisterhood."

•

While Burton had been contemplating the virtues of polygamy in Utah, Isabel had been at home, preparing to become his wife. She would later claim that, after he had left for North America, once again disappearing without saying goodbye, she had known that he was gone without being told. "I was walking out with two friends," she wrote, "and a tightening of the heart came over me." Returning home, she had been in the process of telling her baffled sister that she somehow knew she would not see Richard again for some time, when there had been a knock on the door. "A note with the well-known writing was put into my hand," she wrote. "I knew my fate, and with deep-drawn breath I opened it. He had left."

In his letter, Burton had told Isabel that he would be gone for nine months, and that he would expect an answer when he returned. Would she, at long last, defy her mother and marry him? "If I had not the courage to risk it," she knew, "he would go back to India, and from thence to other explorations, and return no more." Isabel spent the next six weeks in bed, a series of confused and concerned doctors treating her for "influenza, mumps, sore throat, fever, delirium, and everything that I had not got," she wrote, "when in reality I was only heartsick, strug-gling for what I wanted, a last hard struggle with the suspense of my future before me, and nothing and nobody to help me." By the time she finally pulled herself out of bed and sent the doc-tors away, Isabel had made up her mind. She was "going to marry a poor man, and also to fit myself for Expeditions," she wrote, so she had better get to work.

Over the next few months, Isabel devoted herself to learning everything she might need to know as Richard Burton's wife. Although she wrote that she could not "live like a vegetable in the country...in a white apron, with a bunch of keys, scolding my maids, counting eggs and butter," she fled the city for a friend's farmhouse, where she learned not only how to cook but how to care for horses, feed chickens, and milk cows. Returning to London, she asked a friend to teach her how to fence. When he asked her why, she was astonished by the question. "Why?" she said. "To defend Richard, when he and I are attacked in the wilderness together."

Finally beginning to feel physically prepared, Isabel sat down to write a list of seventeen "Rules for my Guidance as a Wife," which she hoped would help her to keep Burton not just happy, but at home. "Let your husband find in you a companion, friend, and adviser, and *confidante,* that he may miss nothing at home," she wrote to herself. "Attend much to his creature comforts; allow smoking or anything else; for if you do not, *somebody else will.*" Having always dreamed of an adventurous life, she looked forward to being ready to "rough it like a man" and to "let nothing ever be at a standstill." "Nothing," she knew, "would weary him like stagnation." At the same time, she admonished herself to always be "cheerful and attractive" and to "improve and educate yourself in every way...that he may not weary of you." She should "never refuse him anything he asks.... Keep up the honeymoon romance, whether at home or in the desert." She would of course never question or criticize him, but more than that, she would not allow herself to even "answer when he finds fault" with her. Above all, she would "never permit any one to speak disrespectfully of him," and she would "hide his faults from *every one.*" She did add that, "with his particular temperament," there may be times when she should "advocate peace," but only if it was "consistent with his honour before the world."

By the time Burton returned to England, Isabel was ready. Approaching her parents, she asked once again for their blessing. Her father, who had long been fascinated with Burton, told her, "I consent with all my heart, if your mother consents." Her mother's reply was a short, sharp "Never!" Isabel, however, if not past caring, was at least done waiting. "I cannot sacrifice our two lives to a mere whim, and you ought not to expect it," she told her mother. "I am going to marry him, whether you will or no." Although, like her father, Isabel's siblings "said they would receive him with delight," it was finally decided that she would marry Richard in a small ceremony, with only a few friends to witness the event.

Three weeks later, Richard and Isabel were married at the Bavarian Catholic Church on Warwick Street in London. Wearing a white bonnet and a fawn-colored dress and filled with religious solemnity, Isabel met Richard at the door to the church. As they stepped inside together, she was thrilled to see him touch the basin of holy water and make "a very large sign of the Cross." He had promised both her and the cardinal who had agreed to let them marry that Isabel would always be free to practice her religion. "Practice her religion indeed!" he had said. "I should rather think she *shall.*" Despite this cheerful concession to his wife's religion, Burton was not about to change his own opinion of the church, nor would he make any effort to redeem his reputation in the eyes of London society. After their wedding, Richard and Isabel attended a breakfast at the home of their mutual friend George Bird, a physician who had also served as Isabel's fencing instructor while Burton was gone. Unable to resist teasing Burton about the wild rumors that had for so long swirled around him, Bird said, "Now, Burton, tell me; how do you feel when you have killed a man?" Looking up at the doctor in mock surprise, Burton replied, "Oh, quite jolly! How do you?"

•

Not long after his wedding, Burton lost nearly everything he owned in a fire. Before leaving for North America, he had given his possessions to his agents, Messrs. Grindlay, to store in their warehouse and had yet to remove them. The blaze consumed "all we possessed in the world," Isabel wrote, "except the few boxes we had with us." Most painful for Burton were the rare manuscripts and personal writings that he had stored for safe-keeping, not trusting them to his travels. Trying to make light of the loss, he joked, "I dare say that the world will be none the worse for some of those manuscripts having been burnt." He did marvel, though, when a clerk, having explained that the Grindlay brothers had been insured but Burton had not, then asked if he had lost anything of value, such as jewelry. "On my saying 'No,'" Burton later recalled, "the change in his face from sympathy to the utter surprise that I could care so much for any other kind of loss, was amusing." It did not matter anyway, he said, as no money could replace what he had lost.

Early in 1861, Burton was finally offered a consular appointment. It paid only £700 a year and was on the West African island of Bioko, then known by the Portuguese name Fernando Po and considered to be the "Foreign Office Grave." Burton knew, however, that he could not refuse it. "Needless to say I have gratefully accepted it," he wrote to Milnes. "The dog that refuses the Governmental crumb shall never be allowed by a retributive destiny to pound with his teeth the Governmental loaf." He had hoped for something better, believed that his years of service if not his dozens of languages and encyclopedic knowledge of Asia and East Africa, would warrant it, but he had known that it would probably never happen. Years later, the Irish-American journalist Frank Harris would ask Lord Lytton, the Viceroy of India, why Lytton had never recommended Burton for the post. "They'd never send him," Lytton had cried. "He's not got the title or the position; besides, he'd be too independent. My God, how he'd kick over the traces and upset the cart!"

Isabel, however, was offended for her husband. "He, who in any other land would have been rewarded with at least a K.C.B. [Knight Commander] and a handsome pension, was glad to get his foot on the lowest rung of the ladder of the Consular service," she complained. "At the age of forty he found himself at home, with the rank of Captain, no pay, no pension, plenty of fame, a newly married wife, and a small Consulate in the most pestilential climate." She was even more unhappy when she learned that he would not take her with him, certain that she would not survive the climate. "Under normal circumstances Equatorial Africa is certain death to the Englanderin," Burton wrote. "I am surprised at the combined folly and brutality of civilized husbands who, anxious to be widowers, poison, cut the throats, or smash the skulls of their better halves. The thing can be as neatly and quietly, safely and respectably, effected by a few months of African air at Zanzibar or Fernando Po."

Burton was worried about dying not of disease in Fernando Po but of boredom. In an effort to fend off monotony and perhaps even achieve something worthwhile, he filled every day with frenzied activity. He wrote his best-known epic poem, *The Kasidah*, which he signed as F.B., using the pseudonym Francis Baker—his middle name paired with his mother's maiden name—and pretended to have translated it from Arabic. He took 2,500 pages of notes and collected enough native proverbs to fill a 450-page book, which he published as *Wit and Wisdom from West Africa*. He explored the Niger River delta and the Bonny River; searched for gorillas along the Gabon River; and climbed Mount Cameroon, then known to Europeans as Mount Victoria, claiming to be the first European to reach its summit. "To be first in such matters is everything," he wrote, "to be second nothing." He also twice visited the Kingdom of Dahomey, then known for its human sacrifices, admiring the "protracted reigns of a dynasty, whose eight members have sat upon the throne 252 years, thus rivalling the seven Roman monarchs whose rule extended over nearly the same period." As he left, having witnessed a mass ritual execution, Burton shook hands with the Dahomey king. "You are a good man," the king told him, "but too angry." Burton could not help but agree. "Travelers like poets," he admitted, "are mostly an angry race."

Nothing Burton did seemed to free him from the anger and depression that had gripped him since his return from East Africa. In a letter to Blackwood discussing his travels through North America and his plans for a book about them, he wrote hopefully, "I must keep my hand in as regards Africa." Fernando Po, however, was not what he had in mind. Despite all that the island had offered him in inspiration and adventure, he found it oppressive, later admitting that soon after arriving he had been "uncommonly suicidal." He felt like "a caged hawk," he wrote, "a Prometheus with the Demon Despair gnawing at my heart."

•

By the end of 1862, Burton's heart was not only consumed by despair, it had begun to rot. On trips home from Fernando Po, he had attended meetings of the Ethnological Society of London, which had been established twenty years earlier to "confirm by inductive science the cherished unity of mankind." There had been a schism within the society, however, dividing those who believed in monogenism, that all human beings shared a common ancestry, from those who argued for polygenism, the belief that different races had different origins. The polygenists left the society, among them Richard Burton, who now placed his powerful intellect and years of research at the service of a pseudoscience so twisted, destructive, and vile it would do incalculable damage for years to come.

In 1863, the same year that Abraham Lincoln issued the Emancipation Proclamation, Burton, on leave from his consular post, became a founding member of the Anthropological Society of London. The society was the brainchild of Dr. James Hunt, a well-known speech therapist who included among his patients Leo Tennyson, son of Alfred, Lord Tennyson, and the mathematician and writer Charles Dodgson, known by the pen name Lewis Carroll, author of *Alice's Adventures in Wonderland*. Hunt professed to be antislavery, but so extreme were his views on race that he was later accused of collaborating with American Confederates, paid by them to influence Britons in their favor. To both Hunt and Burton, monogenism was an antiquated religious concept, used by men like Speke, who believed that Africans were the descendants of Noah's second son, Ham, and were thus "condemned to be the slave of both Shem and Japeth." With the 1859 publication of Darwin's *On the Origin of Species*, however, the foundation of monogenism had begun to shift from biblical theories to human antiquity, from the realm of religion to that of science.

Burton cared less about the fight raging between the monogenists and the polygenists than being free to study and say whatever he wanted. "I cannot but congratulate ourselves," he said in his first address to the society, "upon the fact that we find in the room a liberty of thought and a freedom of speech unknown, I may assert, to any other society in Great Britain." Soon after that meeting, however, Burton found even this new society too restricting. "Hardly had we begun when 'Respectability,' that white sepulcher full of uncleanness, rose up against us," he sneered. "Propriety cried us down with her brazen, blatant voice and the weak-kneed brethren fell away."

In a back room of Bertolini's, a restaurant near Leicester Square, Burton started his own, secretive society: the Cannibal Club. Surrounded by white men in black top hats and tails, Burton called the meetings to order using a mace carved to look like the head of an African man with a human thighbone in his mouth. No subject was taboo at the Cannibal Club, but its specialty was pornography, which drew to it men like Burton's old friend, the poet parliamentarian Monckton Milnes. It also attracted Milnes's most promising young protégé, Algernon Charles Swinburne. A petite, frail man with a small mouth, a strikingly large head framed by loose curls, and a nervous temperament, Swinburne had been born into a wealthy Northumbrian family and attended Eton and Oxford before, like Burton, leaving without a degree. He now devoted most of his time to drinking himself unconscious, engaging in self-flagellation, and writing intensely lyrical but, for Victorian England, shockingly explicit poetry. Only twenty-seven years old when he joined the Cannibal Club, Swinburne would go on to become one of the most noted British poets of the nineteenth century, nominated for the Nobel Prize in Literature every year from 1903 to 1909, the year of his death.

For Burton, Swinburne wrote what became known as the Cannibal Catechism. Before each meeting, as the men laughed and leered, eager to drink themselves sick, one member would recite the first stanza of Swinburne's poem, which had been written to mock the holy sacrament of the Eucharist. It was bawdy and blasphemous, the perfect balm for Richard Burton's ravaged heart.

> *Preserve us from our enemies;*
> *Thou who art Lord of suns and skies;*
> *Whose meat and drink is flesh in pies;*
> *And blood in bowls!*
> *Of thy sweet mercy, damn their eyes;*
> *And damn their souls!*

CHAPTER TWENTY

Neston Park

The Royal Geographical Society was not prepared for the crowd that gathered outside Burlington House, home to the Royal Society, for its special meeting on June 23, 1863. Accustomed to a small, mild-mannered audience of gentlemen scientists, it was suddenly inundated with a surging throng so enormous and determined it shattered windows in the palatial building on Piccadilly. Inside, dignitaries from the Count of Paris to the Prince of Wales entered the dark-paneled lecture theater, filling its tiered rows of curved and cushioned seats. Many would linger after the lecture, examining the drawings and specimens that had been carefully arranged on a table. Others would be disappointed altogether, forced to stand outside the packed lecture hall hoping to hear what was said inside. From royalty to shopkeepers, they were all there to hear the honored speaker of the night, John Hanning Speke.

Two months earlier, Speke had sent a telegram to Murchison from Alexandria, Egypt. In words that had reverberated through the halls of the Society and out into the wider world, he had announced that "the Nile is settled." News had traveled far faster than Speke himself, and by the time he and Grant returned to London, excitement had built to a fevered pitch. "To have solved the problem of ages, to have travelled through Africa from the Indian Ocean to the Mediterranean, to have followed the great Father of Waters from its head among the Mountains of the Moon to its mouth on the coast of Egypt, is a feat which will make the names of Speke and Grant for ever memorable in the annals of geographical discovery," one reporter marveled. "Mystery is no longer attached to the origin of the Nile, for the problem on which Homer has spoken, on which Herodotus speculated, which baffled Alexander, and gave occupation to Nero, has at last been settled by the skill, the perseverance, and the energy of a couple of English officers."

Before leaving Egypt, which he had traveled to by boat on the Nile from Gondokoro, Speke had rewarded the final nineteen members of his expedition, whom he referred to as "my faithful children." Appointing Bombay captain of the "faithfuls," he asked the Royal Geographical Society to give him a silver medal and the rest of the men bronze. Each man also received a monetary award. "I had promised to give them all, provided they behaved well upon the journey . . . a purse of money," Speke wrote, "to begin a new life upon, as soon as they reached Zanzibar." Those who had deserted and were found again in Zanzibar, however, he arranged to have imprisoned, as promised.

Speke and Grant now struggled to make their way through the crowd to the platform, where Murchison was waiting. Although it was not yet 8:00 p.m., the appointed hour for the meeting to begin, Murchison stood, announcing that "he was sure the impatient audience would not be loth to take the acquaintance of Captain Speke and Captain Grant at once." The audience erupted into long and raucous cheers. Finally, prepared to tell his story, Speke spoke. "In the year 1858, when I discovered the Victoria Lake...I at once felt certain in my own mind it was the source of the Nile," he told his rapt audience. "A doubt still existed in every body's mind but my own as to the origin of the Nile, which no one would believe until I went again and turned the river down from head to mouth." The mystery of the source of the Nile was now solved, he said, but it could have been settled years ago if not for the resistance of one man. "Had I been all alone in this first expedition I should have settled the Nile in 1859," he said, "but, my proposal [had] been negatived by the chief of the expedition, who was sick at the time and tired with the journey."

•

Murchison could not have been prouder of his protégé. Along with his glittering reception at Burlington House, the Royal Geographical Society had awarded Speke one of its highest honors, the Founder's Medal, which he had long coveted. He had also received gold medals from the kings of France and Italy— the Italian medal inscribed with the words *Honor est a Nilo,* Honor is from the Nile—as well as congratulations from Queen Victoria, for whom he had named the Nyanza. He had not only earned the admiration and adoration of thousands across the Western world, but had renewed interest in the Society itself.

The pleasure that Murchison took in Speke's fame, however, was short-lived. The explorer, he soon learned, planned to give the full account of his expedition not to the Royal Geographical Society, but to Blackwood. Murchison had been surprised and disappointed when, four years earlier, Speke had published his journal in Blackwood's magazine, but he had decided to let the matter drop. Speke had not led that expedition, and Burton had given the Society a lengthy manuscript to which they had devoted an entire edition of their *Journal.* Now, however, Speke was not only the commander of a Society-sponsored expedition but had been handpicked by Murchison himself to search for the source of the White Nile. The idea that he would treat the Society and the men who had supported and encouraged him with such casual disregard and disrespect astonished Murchison. "The Council," he confided to Grant in typical Victorian understatement, "are displeased with him."

Finally, after months of urging, complaining, and demanding, the Royal Geographical Society did receive a short article from Speke. The article, however, was so disappointing that Murchison dictated a terse letter to the man he had once enthusiastically championed, complaining of its "very brief and imperfect character." The ruling members of the Society then convened a committee to consider how they should respond. In the end, they came to the conclusion that they would have to publish the article, but they would preface it with a highly unusual note. "The council regret that so very important a subject should be illustrated, in their Journal, only by this short memoir," the note began. "As the author has not transmitted ... any other materials or diary of his travels, the reader must look for further information in the published work of Captain Speke, respecting the important expedition with which he was entrusted, and in which he has been supported throughout by the President and Council of the Society." The Society also added footnotes, correcting mistakes and, even more painfully, comparing the detail and precision of Burton's previous work to the apparent inattention of Speke's.

John Blackwood, who had won the right to tell the story the world was waiting to hear, also had serious concerns. He was astonished to find the article that Speke gave him riddled with errors that could, Blackwood knew, "discredit the whole book." Even Grant, who defended Speke against any accusation, admitted that he hoped that he would "consent to have certain alterations made.... It strikes me he sadly wants the advice of a friend." Speke, however, brushed aside all well-meaning advice. "Don't fear critics," he wrote to Blackwood. "We will put them to shame if they wag their tongues."

Blackwood, however, worried not only that critics would find errors in Speke's account but that they would not be able to read it at all. While Burton could produce hundreds of pages of prose sitting in a tent, fighting a fever, Speke struggled to put pen to paper in his room at Jordans. "He writes in such an abominable, childish, unintelligible way that it is impossible to say what anybody could make of them," Blackwood wrote in frustration to his nephew, William, who also worked for the family publishing house. "And yet he is full of matter & when he talks and explains all is right." Speke was trying, he knew, but the result was so garbled that even the man who had been hired to typeset the book, referred to as "Mr. B.," was baffled. Speke's manuscript "never would do to go before the public," William told his uncle. "It would be the death of Mr. B were he to attempt to correct it. The Boy that has been going over it with me has been nearly in fits with laughing." As he often did in his letters, Speke used little punctuation in his manuscript, his thoughts rambling across the page, seemingly written as they occurred to him. In one passage, about the kingdom of Buganda, he wrote, "Then ordering the return home much to my delight, for though beautiful the

N'yanza was the want of consideration for others peoples comfort, the tiring incessant boating all day long and every day, as well as Mtesa's hurry scurry about everything."

Finally, out of desperation Blackwood decided to hire a ghostwriter. Speke had an astonishing tale to tell, he knew, one that thousands of people were eager to read. He just did not know how to tell it. "There is not a doubt of its being most interesting and full of curious and novel scenes some of which though seem most childish," William Blackwood wrote to John. "Someone must be found to fashion his remarkable work." His uncle agreed. Speke, they determined, needed a full-service editor, one who would not just clean up his manuscript but largely write it. "The thing would be for the Editor to read it over with Speke," John explained, "put questions to him & afterwards write out as nearly in his language as presentable English will permit."

Speke went along with the plan, but his pride was wounded. It could not have helped, moreover, that the man Blackwood had chosen to rewrite his book had a surname that made Speke's blood boil: Burton. John Hill Burton was a well-known and respected author in his own right, having written a literary biography of David Hume as well as a seven-volume history of Scotland. "Burton is a thorough good fellow," John Blackwood wrote, "& if we could only get Speke to comprehend the infernal absurdity & incomprehensibility of the style in which he expresses himself the two would suit each other & work well together as they are both gentlemen." Speke moved into Burton's Edinburgh home, where he spent day after day working closely with him on the manuscript. The collaboration was respectful and productive, but far from happy. Burton described Speke's prose "like an endless thread [that] required no end of breaking," and Speke, bored and frustrated, complained to Blackwood that he was "sick of proofs."

Journal of the Discovery of the Source of the Nile was finally released in December of 1863. It was an instant sensation, selling out as soon as it hit the shelves. Despite the best efforts of Blackwood and John Hill Burton, however, the book also immediately came under attack. Speke had been proud of the fact that he had served as cartographer on both expeditions, but his maps were shockingly wrong. A third of the Nyanza's massive western shoreline was too far to the east; the water levels were not even close; and based on his calculations, the Nile ran uphill for ninety miles. Even Rigby criticized the book, writing to Grant that "Speke tells far too much of his disputes...and not enough about the country, and his account is so vague that you cannot follow him." Rigby's criticism must have been particularly galling when Speke learned that he was also being ridiculed for his reverential reference to the "ancient Hindu map" that Rigby had shown him in Zanzibar. Unknown to either man, the map was a famous fraud, long dismissed in geographical circles. Humiliated, Speke asked Blackwood to remove it from future printings, but the damage had been done.

Speke was also pilloried for attacking the men who had helped him—in this case, Petherick. Months earlier, he had sent Petherick a letter from Khartoum, assuring him that if he would just explain the circumstances that had caused him to arrive late in Gondokoro, all would be forgiven. "My dear Petherick," Speke had written, "Should you feel inclined to write a full statement of the difficulties you had to contend with in going up the White Nile, it would be a great relief to the mind of every person connected with the succouring fund, and also to myself, as people's tongues are always ready in this meddling world." After he had returned to England, however, Speke's righteous anger seemed to have once again grown. Blackwood had advised him to tone down his denunciation of Petherick in his book, pointing out that Speke had "met and dined with him, not quarreling or showing that you were offended, and then when you come home you publish a statement or rather expression which is infinitely more damaging than if you had cut him on the spot. Consult your brothers or anyone about this and I am sure they will agree with me." Speke had given in, including only "two chilly lines" about Petherick, but soon after the book's release, he gave a speech on Christmas Eve that caused far more harm than any of his complaints about broken promises or stolen supplies. Spreading the rumor that he had heard in Gondokoro from Petherick's trading rivals, men whom Petherick had arrested for selling enslaved people, Speke suggested that the consul himself had taken part in the slave trade.

For Petherick, the repercussions were immediate and devastating. "The blow," he wrote, "was as hard as I could well bear." Although there was no proof to support such serious allegations, the Foreign Office, eager to avoid any controversy, revoked his consulship. Still in Khartoum, he did what he could to defend himself, professing his innocence in letters to anyone who would listen, even beginning legal proceedings against Speke, but to no avail. His wife too, astonished by Speke's accusations, wrote home from Khartoum. "Is it possible that Speke can so have acted? It seems incredible that he should impugn the honour and integrity of Petherick," she wrote. "My heart is filled with bitterness." Speke, irritated by these efforts to answer his accusations, regretted not his own actions but that he had ever had any association with Petherick. "I wish to God I had never seen the beast," he complained, "for both he and his wife are writing against me in the most blackguardly style."

After carelessly destroying the reputation of an innocent man, Speke found the adulation that had surrounded him since his return to England begin to fade. Even Murchison felt moved to come to Petherick's defense, telling a meeting of the Royal Geographical Society that the accusations had been "most unjustly brought against M. Petherick," and writing to Grant that Speke had sent him a "most *violent* telegram [about Petherick]. So violent that if I had made it public he could have been very injured." Burton railed that Petherick had been "thrown overboard without pity, his private fortune wasted, the health of himself and his heroic and attached wife, altogether and perhaps irretrievably ruined, and his character as a merchant and a public servant blasted in the eyes of his countrymen and of the civilized world, by being charged with a dereliction of duty, and with the crime of slave dealing, at the moment he was doing everything in his power to put it down."

Bruised by what seemed to him unfair and unwarranted criticism, Speke believed that he had himself been wronged. "I have been accused in the public press," he complained, "as being ungenerous." He was even frustrated and angry with those closest to him, bitter that Blackwood had been so critical of his manuscript and that Grant, then in Edinburgh working on his own account of their journey, had not come to London for the publication of his book. Murchison believed Grant wise to have kept his distance, writing to him that he was fortunate to be "clear of this row [with Petherick]. Everyone says that your name should have been inscribed with that of Speke in the pages of his book. Now it is lucky that he left you out, indicating that you are not responsible for any indiscretion of his." Speke, unrepentant, vowed that he would rely only on himself. "I shall never travel with a male companion again in wild country," he wrote to Blackwood, "and certainly shall never again think of writing a personal narrative since it only leads to getting abused." He was also still furious with Burton, arguing that his publisher should not be "afraid on my account of what I have written for it only exists between Burton . . . and myself whether we will fight it out with the quill or the fist. . . . I think I have been very mild considering the amount of injustice he has done to me."

Restless and eager to escape his critics, Speke left for France, bringing Laurence Oliphant with him. In Paris, he met with Emperor Napoleon III, nephew of Napoleon I, and his wife, Empress Eugénie, whom, Speke wrote, seemed "delighted with the prospects" of another expedition to Africa. Speke planned to cross the continent from east to west, gathering Christian converts along the way. It was an expedition, he argued, that only he would be able to complete.

Murchison, however, having gotten word of Speke's efforts, made it clear that the Royal Geographical Society would not be involved. "As I saw that some people thought that Speke's Expedition Appeal came from *us*," he wrote to Austen Henry Layard, permanent under-secretary at the Foreign Office, "I thought it my duty to undeceive his Lordship." He was also, he told Layard, concerned about Speke's state of mind. "Speke sent me telegrams from Paris denouncing Petherick, but which I could not read or produce so intemperate were they. They are tied up and docketed with others as 'Speke visions'!" he wrote. "I have deeply regretted these aberrations as Speke has, in other respects, the qualities required to ensure success as a bold explorer."

•

In August, Speke traveled home from France and Burton returned from Fernando Po. It was the first time in many years that they had been in England at the same time, and neither man knew what his future held. Although they had each commanded a successful expedition to Africa, they had little hope of leading another. At least for the time being, the Royal Geographical

Society had had enough of both of them. "I understand from Murchison," the foreign secretary, Lord John Russell, wrote that summer, "that…the Geographical Society are anxious to break off all connections with Captain Speke." Instead, Murchison had placed his trust once again in the hands of his old friend and the Society's most experienced explorer, David Livingstone. In December, just before Speke gave his speech attacking Petherick, Murchison had written to Livingstone, proposing that he return to Africa to circumnavigate the Nyanza and confirm, or repudiate, Speke's theory. Livingstone, although by then fifty-one years old, had accepted the offer.

The Society, however, had not forgotten Burton and Speke. Murchison, who had built a large and enthusiastic following around the famed Section E of the British Association for the Advancement of Science, wanted to generate excitement for the association's 34th annual meeting, which was to be held that September in Bath. Livingstone would be there, giving one of the keynote speeches, but he dreaded the event, as he did all public speaking. "A cold shiver comes over me when I think of it," he wrote to a friend. "Ugh!" The association needed another way to draw people to Bath. The answer was a debate between two of the most famous and controversial explorers of the day, each arguing his case for the most mysterious and explosive of subjects: the source of the White Nile.

At first, Burton had little interest in what quickly became known as "the great Nile debate." He knew that Speke did not have enough evidence to prove his assertions about the Nyanza, and he had already agreed to speak about Dahomey, which he was confident would be one of the most popular lectures at the conference. Not only was Dahomey a subject of great fascination to many of those attending the meeting, but Burton himself was a famously electrifying speaker. "He had both a fine imaginative power and a memory richly stored not only from study but from personal experience," Bram Stoker would later write. "As he talked, fancy seemed to run riot in its alluring power; and the whole world of thought seemed to flame with gorgeous colour." Burton knew that he needed neither a debate nor a controversy to draw a crowd, and he certainly did not need John Hanning Speke.

Just as Burton still believed that the Tanganyika might be the source of the White Nile, moreover, Isabel still held out hope that he and Speke might reconcile. She had a personal connection to Speke that had nothing to do with her husband: A hundred years earlier, the Spekes and the Arundells had been related by marriage. Isabel and John also had a mutual friend, Countess Kitty Dormer, who had once been engaged to Isabel's father and was now willing to facilitate a meeting between her and Speke. They met only once, Isabel wrote, but exchanged several messages. At one point, she later recalled, Speke apologized to her for his falling out with Burton. "I am so sorry," she said he told her. "I don't know how it all came about. Dick was so kind to me... and I used to be so fond of him; but it would be too difficult for me to go back now." Isabel believed that no matter how shattered the relationship between the two men was, it might still be mended. "We nearly succeeded in reconciling Richard and Speke," she insisted, "and would have done so, but for the anti-influences around him."

Isabel knew that the most malignant of those influences now was Laurence Oliphant. Oliphant, who had just returned from the trip to France with Speke, had long known exactly how to enflame his friend's hatred of Burton. "Such a breach once made," Burton knew, "is easily widened." Now Oliphant turned his attention to Burton, casually mentioning that he had had a conversation with Speke about the proposed debate. Speke, he claimed, had said that "if Burton appeared on the platform at Bath he would kick him." Burton reacted exactly as expected. "Well, that settles it!" he spat. "By God, he shall kick me." Witnessing the conversation, Isabel was surprised neither by her husband's reaction nor Oliphant's meddling. Oliphant, she knew, had a "habit of sundering friends."

Years later, Isabel would claim that Oliphant, following a strange and extreme religious conversion, would come to regret the damage he had done, not just to Burton's relationship with Speke but also with the British-American explorer Henry Morton Stanley. "He worked upon Speke until he planted the seed of bitter enmity against Richard to the end," Isabel wrote. "I mentioned this to Mr. Stanley...and he replied, 'How very odd; he did exactly the same to me!'" When Isabel finally confronted Oliphant, she said that he offered no denial or defense. "Forgive me," he said simply. "I am sorry—I did not know what I was doing."

While Speke appeared to be looking forward to the debate with relish, attempting to convince Oliphant that he was confident of success, anyone who knew the two men understood that it would be far from a fair fight. Not only was Burton an extraordinarily skilled public speaker who derived immense pleasure from verbal sparring, tying his enemies into twisting, writhing knots, but Speke was as hopeless at the podium as he was with the pen. Now partially deaf, his hearing having never recovered after the beetle had burrowed into his ear, he found it at times difficult to follow even a quiet conversation, much less a lightning-fast, subtly shifting attack. By then, he was also known to be, in the words of the Irish journalist Sir John Gray, "a very poor and unready speaker." Like Livingstone, he had never enjoyed public speaking, a fact that was painfully apparent to his audiences. Nor, Speke knew, would he have many friends in the audience at Bath. While Burton's supporters were looking forward to watching Speke fail spectacularly and publicly, many of Speke's friends seemed to have abandoned him altogether. Murchison was now reserved and distant, and even Grant preferred to stay out of the fight, sending his regrets when Speke invited him to stay with him at his brother's house in nearby Monks Park so that he could attend the debate.

·

On September 13, the day before the British Association began its annual meeting, Burton and Isabel checked into the Royal Hotel in Bath. Nearly 2,800 people converged on the quiet Somerset city, which had been founded in the first century CE by the Romans, drawn to its natural hot springs. The debate between Burton and Speke was to be held on the 16th at the Royal Mineral Water Hospital, a commanding, 122-year-old stone building that sat on a corner lot with long tunnels running beneath it, carrying hot water from the springs to the King's Bath.

Two days later, on September 15, Burton and Isabel arrived at the lecture hall for the opening day of Section E. As soon as they entered the hall, their eyes were drawn to a thin, blond man sitting quietly on the platform, to Murchison's right. Burton and Speke had not seen each other for several years and had not spoken for more than five, since the day they had parted ways in Aden. Now in the lecture hall, Burton and Isabel were forced to pass directly in front of Speke in order to reach their assigned seats on the platform. As he looked up, they silently returned his stare. For Speke, all the painful, conflicting emotions, which for years had simmered just below the surface, seemed to come rushing back in that instant of recognition. "I shall never forget his face," Isabel would later write. "It was full of sorrow, of yearning, and perplexity."

Burton too was struck by the startling changes he saw in the face of the man he had once known so well. "I could not but remark," he wrote, "the immense change of feature, of expression, and of general appearance which his severe labours, complicated perhaps by deafness and dimness of sight had wrought in him." After a long moment, someone called to Speke and the spell was broken. Speke's pale, stricken face, Isabel wrote, "seemed to turn to stone." Beginning to fidget in his seat, Speke suddenly "exclaimed half aloud," and to no one in particular, "Oh, I cannot stand this any longer." Lurching out of his chair, he started for the door. A man standing nearby called out to him, "Shall you want your chair again, Sir? May I have it? Shall you come back?" As he left the hall, Speke muttered only, "I hope not."

·

After Speke bolted from the lecture hall, he headed not to his brother's house in Monks Park but for the ancient Roman road that led to London. His destination was Neston Park, a vast estate in Wiltshire, about twenty miles east of Bath. Established in the fifteenth century, Neston Park was now owned by Speke's uncle, John Bird Fuller, who lived with his family in a grand, columned, stone house on the estate. Agitated by his unexpected meeting with Burton and the knowledge that he would have to face him in a debate in less than twenty-four hours, Speke fled to the estate, where he knew he would be able to hunt, the one thing that had never failed to bring him solace.

By 2:30 that afternoon, just an hour after he had seen Burton,

Speke and his young cousin, George Fuller, were already moving quietly but steadily across the wide, open grounds of Neston Park. With the house far behind them, they swept through tall grasses, passing small groupings of trees and occasionally raising their guns to take aim as flushed partridges exploded from a ground nest or the tangled branches of a hedge. Behind them walked Daniel Davis, Fuller's groundskeeper, marking the birds as they tumbled from the sky.

Both Fuller and Davis, however, kept their distance. "I was apprehensive of an accident," Fuller later admitted. He knew that Speke had years of shooting experience, hunting a wide range of animals in circumstances far more difficult than a quiet English field, and was, as Burton himself had noted in East Africa, especially careful with his gun. He also knew, however, that the following day, in less than twenty-four hours, his cousin would face Burton on the platform at Bath, adding extreme stress to a day that was already filled with sorrow as it was the anniversary of the death of Speke's brother, Edward, who had been killed seven years earlier during the Indian Mutiny. Watching Speke now, Fuller and Davis both noticed a "carelessness in the use of the gun by Hanning." It was unlike him, and it was unnerving. "We therefore avoided being very close to him when walking the fields," Fuller explained.

The three men had been shooting for about an hour and a half, Fuller some distance in front of Speke, Davis behind him, when Speke neared a stone wall. Davis watched as Speke, gun in hand, prepared to climb the loose flagstones, which stretched across the field and were, at that point, layered roughly two feet high. Returning to his work, Davis had shifted his gaze when he suddenly heard the report of a gun. Looking up again, he expected to see a falling partridge. Instead, he saw Fuller, frantically running in his direction.

When he had turned at the sound of the gun, Fuller had seen his cousin dropping heavily from the low stone wall he had been climbing. Racing across the field, the tall grass flattening beneath his boots, he reached the wall to find Speke lying next to it, blood blossoming across the left side of his hunting shirt. The shotgun, a double-barreled, breach-loading Lancaster with no safety catch, was lying on the ground near Speke, one barrel half-cocked, the other fully discharged. As Fuller bent over him, Speke had strength for only three words. "Don't move me." By the time Davis arrived, Fuller had his hand pressed against Speke's chest, desperately trying to stop the bleeding. Instructing his groundskeeper to stay with his cousin, he ran for help.

Fuller returned quickly with a local surgeon, Thomas Fitzherbert Snow. As soon as Snow saw the man lying pale and still upon the ground, however, he knew that he was too late. The charge released by Speke's own hand had torn upward through his chest toward his spine, lacerating his lungs and shredding the large blood vessels near his heart. "Such a wound," Snow knew, "would cause death." While Davis had watched over him, alone and helpless, John Hanning Speke died where he had fallen, having never uttered another word.

CHAPTER TWENTY-ONE

The Weary Heart Grows Cold

When Burton arrived for the debate on the morning of September 16, he found the lecture hall at the Royal Mineral Water Hospital already "crowded to suffocation." Standing near the platform with Isabel, he tried to avoid the crush of people while he waited for Speke to arrive and the debate to begin. The eager audience was at first patient, happy to have secured a place in the hall for the most anticipated event of the conference. As the time for the debate came and went, however, and the platform remained frustratingly empty, the crowd began to grow restless, giving vent "to its impatience," a reporter wrote disapprovingly, "by sounds more often heard from the audience of a theatre than of a scientific meeting."

In a nearby room, the Council of the Royal Geographical Society was meeting, as was customary, to discuss Society business and to choose which papers would be read the next day.

They were just wrapping up, listening to a final speech by the Scottish traveler Sir James Alexander, who was arguing that the Council should recommend Speke for a knighthood, when a messenger entered the room. Quickly finding Murchison, the man handed him a letter. Murchison read it without comment and then quietly passed it to Norton Shaw, the Society's secretary, who was on his left. After reading the note himself, Shaw passed it to the man seated next to him. As Alexander droned on, apparently oblivious to the growing unease slowly filling the room, the letter was passed from hand to hand, finally ending with Francis Galton. One of the last people Speke had visited before leaving for East Africa four years earlier, Galton was now the last man there to learn that his friend had fatally shot himself.

Still waiting in the lecture hall, Burton was as confused by the delay as was everyone around him. "All the great people were with the Council, I alone was uninvited," he wrote bitterly. "So I remained on the platform with my wife, notes in hand, longing for the fray." Finally his friend, the geographer Alexander George Findlay, called him into the room. With his wife standing just outside the door, watching quietly, Burton lifted the letter that had already been read by every other man in the room. As he absorbed the message, he "sank into a chair," Isabel later recalled, "and I saw by the workings of his face the terrible emotion he was controlling, and the shock he had received."

Stunned and solemn, the members of the Council finally filed into the lecture hall. Taking his place on the platform, Murchison spoke to the crowd before him. "I have to apologize but when I explain to you the cause of my being a little longer in coming to take the chair than I ought to have been, you will pardon me," he said. A hush fell over the audience as all eyes were trained on Murchison. "We have been in our committee so profoundly affected by the dreadful calamity that has suddenly befallen my dear friend Captain Speke, by which he has lost his life, that it is impossible for me to proceed to the business of to-day." The end of Murchison's sentence was swallowed by a wave of sound as the shocking words "lost his life" instantly created in the hall what one reporter could only call a "sensation." The Society's president, however, struggled on, expressing not just the sorrow of the British Association and the Royal Geographical Society but his own personal grief. "That loss is the more painful to me from the fact that it was only yesterday that I saw my eminent friend, Captain Speke, and he was to have come here to-day to speak to you on the subject of African discovery," he said, "and you may easily conceive, therefore, the effect which the announcement of his death has had upon me." Feeling that he owed the men and women before him some explanation, Murchison told them what he knew. "The circumstances of the accident have not been fully explained to me, but it seems that he was out shooting with one or two friends," he said. "They heard a report from his gun, as he was getting over a wall, and on going to him they found that his gun had gone off, that the shot had gone through him close to his heart, and he could have lived only a few minutes." The hall erupted once again.

There was little left to do but offer tribute. After the crowd had quieted, Murchison proposed a resolution in Speke's honor, "that their most heartfelt condolence be offered to his relatives on his being thus cut off in so awful a manner, in the fullness of his strength and vigour." When he finished speaking, every hand in the hall was raised in support. Later that day, Clements Markham, who five years earlier had taken Speke to tell Murchison about the Nyanza and who was now chairman of Section E, made an announcement on behalf of Burton. "Captain Burton was greatly affected by the frightful occurrence to which attention had been called," a reporter later explained, "and being unable to trust himself to the making of any observations, had requested the secretary to read out a few words he (Captain Burton) had penned." In the wake of Speke's sudden and violent death, which took place only a few miles away and just hours before they were to face one another in a tense debate, Burton now struggled to convey both raw emotion and simple honesty. "The differences of opinion that are known to have lain between us while he was alive," Markham read on his behalf, "make it more incumbent on me to publicly express my sincere feeling of admiration of his character and enterprise, and my deep sense of loss."

•

Eleven days later, Speke's family brought his body home. "The bones of the traveller rest, not beneath the cloistered shades of Westminster Abbey," one newspaper reported, "but in a family vault under the pretty little church of Dowlish Wake ... four [kilometers] from the family seat of the Spekes at Jordans." Three hundred years earlier, Speke's ancestor, George Speke, had built a chapel in the small stone church, and a brass effigy commemorating him had been set into the floor. After a long, clergy-led procession that wound through the village, Speke's coffin was slowly carried past his shocked and grieving family, his friends, and, but for one, the greatest British geographers and explorers of his day—Murchison, Livingstone, and Grant.

Sick with grief and guilt, Grant was tortured by the thought that he might have somehow prevented Speke's death. "Had I gone thither with my friend," he wrote, "this calamity might have been averted." Now, clutching a wreath made of delicate white mignonette and wild violets, he watched as Speke's coffin was lowered into the vault. Crying so loudly that his sobs "were audible over the whole of the sacred building," a reporter wrote, he reached out and "placed the wreath upon the coffin containing the gallant captain's remains."

After Speke's body was buried, one question above all others haunted those he had left behind: Had his death been accidental or intentional? Anxious to spare Speke's family further pain and to ensure that they and he would not be burdened with what was then considered to be the shame of suicide, little inquiry was allowed into the tragedy. A brief inquest was held in Monks Park, at the home of Speke's brother, William, during which George Fuller, Daniel Davis, and Thomas Snow were each deposed. Soon after, a jury convened to listen to the coroner's report and quickly gave a unanimous verdict. "The deceased," they determined, "died from the accidental discharge of his own gun." Long after the case had closed, however, uncomfortable questions lingered. Why would a man with as much hunting experience as Speke and who had always shown extreme caution when handling firearms, climb a loose stone wall holding a half-cocked shotgun pointed at his chest? Had the obvious agitation that had so concerned Fuller and Davis that afternoon led to carelessness, or had it been a manifestation of despair?

Even the obituary that ran in *The Times* three days after Speke's death raised the question that was on everyone's mind. "Speke was the last man who could have been expected to succumb to so poor a peril as this," the obituary read. "He was a veteran sportsman. Even his zeal for adventure sprang originally from his ardor for the chase.... Such a man must have lived always in the midst of dangers; firearms must have been to him familiar as the pen to the writer, or the brush to the painter. Perhaps it was the great familiarity which produced the momentary incaution which has had such fatal effect." The fact that the question was unanswerable did not make it any easier to bear, nor would the sickening feeling it left behind ever fade.

For Burton, the idea that Speke may have intentionally ended his own life seemed to have been not just a possibility but his first assumption. "By God," he was said to have muttered after reading the letter announcing Speke's death. "He's killed himself." Although he had managed to make it through the meeting that day, delivering with trembling voice his paper on Dahomey, as soon as he was home, he had given in to grief. "He wept long and bitterly," Isabel wrote, "and I was for many a day trying to comfort him." Burton's niece Georgiana was also struck by the force of her uncle's sorrow. Speke "was not easily forgotten by the companion of his many wanderings," she wrote. "Burton's emotion was uncontrollable." Not only was he stunned and sickened by Speke's sudden death, but he knew that his own fate would forever be linked with Speke's. "Nothing will ever be known of Speke's death," he wrote to a friend just a few months later. "The charitable say that he shot himself, the uncharitable that I shot him."

•

Although only Speke had died that day, Burton believed that his death had silenced them both. "The sad event," he wrote in a letter to *The Times,* "must seal my mouth concerning many things." He had seen the debate as an opportunity not just to defend himself but to question what he believed were Speke's unfounded assumptions about the Nile and the Nyanza. "Had we met at Bath the discussion which would have resulted must have brought forth a far more searching scrutiny as regards the late expedition than can now be expected," he wrote in frustration. "As it is, I must be dumb upon many points, of which, under other circumstances, I had a right to speak."

Burton was only forty-three years old, but the life ahead of him held little of the charm and possibility that had once defined it. He was finally moved from the consulate at Fernando Po to Santos, Brazil, where he and Isabel remained for four years. He spoke of expeditions that he might make, from climbing in the Andes to exploring Patagonia, but it was too late. "Physically," a young foreign officer wrote, Burton was "a broken man." After some pleading on Isabel's part, he was appointed consul in Damascus, where he was thrilled to be back in the Middle East. By the summer of 1871, however, his anger and bitterness, this time directed at the Jewish people of Syria, once again rose to destroy any hope he had, and he was forced out. "Dismissal ignominious, at the age of fifty, without a month's notice, or wages, or character," he wrote bitterly to Isabel. Her heart, even more than his, was broken. "The jackals," she wrote in anger, "are always ready to slight a dead lion."

Throughout their thirty-year marriage, Isabel would remain deeply, even obsessively devoted to her husband, eager to do anything he asked at a moment's notice. "I am glad to say there was only one will in the house, and that was his," she would later write. "I was only too lucky to have met my master." Burton had taught her to proofread his manuscripts, take care of his personal and professional business, and, in his words, "pack, pay, and follow" every time he either wished or was forced to move on to the next consulate, country, or continent. His control of his wife even extended to practicing on her his skills as a hypnotist, boasting, a friend later wrote, that "at the distance of many hundreds of miles he could will her to do anything he chose as completely as if he were with her in the same room."

At the same time that Burton's natural strength and confidence began to abandon him, however, Isabel's grew. She loved finally being able to travel with her husband, facing uncertainty, discomfort, and even danger. When not editing or promoting his manuscripts, she had even begun to work on her own, beginning with *The Inner Life of Syria, Palestine, and the Holy Land,* which grew from a close-kept journal to a two-volume best-seller. By the time they landed in Trieste, in what would be Burton's last consular post and final home, Isabel came closer than she had ever thought possible to realizing her greatest dream: living what had always seemed to her to be the free and unfettered life of a man. While riding with Burton in the mountains, she dressed in a baggy, dark blue riding habit tucked into tall boots, a revolver and bowie knife clipped to her belt, her hair tied on top of her head and covered by a tarboosh, a flat-topped felt hat. She was "very much amused, and very much pleased," she later wrote, "to learn that all along the road I have been generally mistaken for a boy."

Burton's own slow transformation was internal but equally visible. When he returned for visits to England, it was clear to anyone who knew him that he was not just dejected but ravaged. His niece Georgiana was sickened by the stark changes she saw in her once bright and charming uncle. "Never had we known him so wretched, so unnerved; his hands shook, his temper was strangely irritable, all that appreciation of fun and humour which rendered him such a cheery companion to old and young had vanished," she wrote. "He could settle to nothing; he was restless, but would not leave the house; ailing, but would take no advice."

The only activity Burton felt fit for was writing, but even that proved to be a source of wrenching pain and remembered resentments. After a mysterious eight-year absence, a lost manuscript on Zanzibar that he had entrusted to the consul apothecary to send to the Royal Geographical Society had suddenly reappeared, found buried in a strongbox in Bombay. Burton had blamed Rigby for its disappearance, an accusation that Rigby indignantly denied, but now that he had it back, ready to revise, he was overwhelmed with memories more bitter than sweet. "I could not have believed, before Experience taught me how sad and solemn is the moment when a man sits down to think over and to write out the tale of what was before the last Decade began," he wrote. "How many ghosts and phantoms start up from the brain—the shreds of hopes destroyed and of aims made futile.... How many graves have closed over their dead during those short ten years—that epitome of the past! 'And when the lesson strikes the head/The weary heart grows cold.'"

•

A single, dim hope still flickered in Burton's breast: That he might be proven right after all, that the Tanganyika, not the Nyanza, was the source of the White Nile. In its obituary for Speke, *The Times* had assumed that the long, bitter debate between Burton and Speke was now over. "Captain Speke and Captain Burton can no longer be pitted against each other for the gladiatorial exhibition," it read. "It must be very hard for Captain Burton, who has won so many laurels, to reflect that he was once slumbering under the shadow of the very highest prize of all while another, and less experienced hand reached over and plucked the fruit." To Burton, however, despite his complaint that he had been silenced by Speke's death, the fight was not over. "Why should 'the very controversy be allowed to slumber,'" he asked, "because the gallant Speke was the victim of a fatal mishap?"

By now, Burton knew that he would not solve the mystery

of the Nile, but it suddenly appeared that neither would David Livingstone. After leaving for East Africa on his own search for the source of the Nile, the missionary had seemed to disappear. Years had passed with no word from him, and men who had deserted his expedition claimed that he had been murdered. The Royal Geographical Society held out hope, sending two expeditions in search of him, but both returned without success. Burton found the frantic efforts laughable. Using an insider's Latin slang to describe what he saw as the indignity of attempting to find the country's most renowned missionary, he scoffed that it would be "rather *infra dig* to discover a miss."

Finally, to the Society's embarrassment and annoyance, a brash, Welsh-born, workhouse-raised American journalist named Henry Morton Stanley not only found Livingstone, but settled the question of the source of the Nile. He did not do it alone, however, having the backing of the *New York Herald* and the help of one man in particular: Sidi Mubarak Bombay. Bombay had been grief-stricken by the news of Speke's death, comparing the loss to having his right arm cut off and vowing to make a pilgrimage to his grave one day, but for now he remained in Africa, willing to help in the search for David Livingstone.

As devoted as Bombay had been to Speke, however, his relationship with Stanley was tense from the moment they met. "The famous Bombay made his appearance," Stanley sneered after meeting the man whom both Speke and Burton had so highly regarded. "That Captain Speke had spoiled him with kindness was evident." Stanley accused Bombay of encouraging a mutiny, and Bombay refused to push the porters as relentlessly and ruthlessly as Stanley demanded. Nonetheless, by the fall of 1871, Bombay had led the caravan to the Tanganyika, the lake Burton still insisted might be the Nile's source. There, Stanley found Livingstone on its shores and, he later claimed, uttered the four words that were to become more famous than either man: "Dr. Livingstone, I presume?"

Despite Stanley's inexperience, he would go on to accomplish what neither Burton nor Speke had been able to do. Together with Livingstone, he traveled to the head of the Tanganyika, confirming that the Rusizi River flowed into rather than out of the lake and ending Burton's hope that it might somehow be a feeder to the Nile. Then, a year after Livingstone was found dead, kneeling by his bed, presumably in prayer, Stanley circumnavigated the Nyanza, proving that it was, as Speke had insisted, the principal source of the White Nile. His expeditions did not bring Stanley respect, but they did bring him fame, a condition, he wrote in his diary, that "I detest & shrink from." The Royal Geographical Society awarded Stanley its Patron's Medal for finding Livingstone, but he found that, having achieved what the Society's own expeditions could not, his efforts were not universally appreciated. "My success," Stanley wrote to one of the Society's most distinguished members, "seems to have aroused considerable bitterness in the minds of those from whom I naturally expected a different reception."

Grant, on the other hand, openly and enthusiastically applauded Stanley's expedition. Nearly a decade after his death, Speke had finally been vindicated, and Burton proved wrong. In a speech to the Royal Geographical Society, Grant congratulated the controversial journalist-explorer and reprimanded all who had questioned Speke, especially Burton. Stanley "has confirmed the discoveries made by Speke ... and sent home a map, and descriptions so vivid and truthful that the most skeptical cannot fail to be satisfied," Grant said. "The foremost of unbelievers, and the one who appeared first in the field, was Captain Burton, the companion at one time of Speke. He did not seem to have any reason for his argument. He said there must be several lakes, lagoons; anything, in fact, except *the* Lake." Burton responded to Grant's attack in a long letter to *The Athenaeum*, addressing his criticisms point by point. By then, however, even he knew that the battle had been lost. Both the scientific community and the public at large had accepted that the source of the White Nile was the Nyanza, now known to the Western world as Lake Victoria.

•

There was by now little interest in anything Burton had to say, on any subject. After years of being the object of intense, often malignant attention, regarded with either fascination or fear, adulation or revulsion, considered a strange and possibly dangerous outsider, he was now something far worse: a forgotten man. Poor, aging, sick, and angry, he found himself with no one to fight and nothing to fight for. He continued to write books and articles, but they earned neither public acclaim nor financial reward.

To Burton's amusement, the only books of his that now captured the public's attention were those translations considered by Victorian England to be obscene. He and his old friend Foster Fitzgerald Arbuthnot became the first to translate into English the *Kama Sutra,* a fifth-century Sanskrit manual on the art of love. To circumvent British obscenity laws, Burton created a fictional publishing house called the Kama Shastra Society of London and Benares. The book, which became, in the words of one scholar, "one of the most pirated books in the English language," was as publicly vilified as it was privately devoured. Even the *Kama Sutra,* however, paled in comparison to the indignation and excitement that surrounded his release, two years later, of a ten-volume translation (with a supplementary six volumes later added), of *The Book of the Thousand Nights and a Night,* known popularly as *The Arabian Nights.* "Probably no European has ever gathered such an appalling collection of degrading customs and statistics of vice," the British journalist Henry Reeve wrote of Burton's translation in *The Edinburgh Review.* "It is a work which no decent gentleman will long permit to stand upon his shelves." Comparing Burton's work to that of earlier translators, Reeve sneered that "Galland is for the nursery, Lane is for the library, Payne for the study and Burton for the sewers." Having expected nothing better, Burton laughed off the criticism, all the way to the bank. "I have struggled for forty-seven years, distinguishing myself honourably in every way I possibly could. I never had a compliment nor a 'thank you,' nor a single farthing," he said wryly to Isabel. "I translate a doubtful book in my old age, and immediately made sixteen thousand guineas. Now that I know the tastes of England, we need never be without money."

As Burton delved even deeper into the sexual studies that had absorbed much of his time at the Cannibal Club, he began to pull away from the radically racist ideas promoted there. Finally abandoning polygenism, he admitted that Africans had "shown themselves fully equal in intellect and capacity to the white races of Europe and America." When a Sudanese man named Selim Aga wrote a memoir that was published in *The Geographical Magazine,* Burton defended him against those who refused to believe that he could be the author. Having hired Aga as his factotum and traveled with him for three years in West Africa, Burton knew that he had been educated in Scotland, spoke English with a Scottish accent, and was perfectly capable of the article's sophisticated prose. "Those who noticed the article generally declared that it had been written by a European, and not a few suspected that it was by myself," Burton wrote to the magazine, but there was no question, he assured its readers, "of its being written by any one but 'Selim Agha.'" Burton's dawning understanding, however, had come too late and was far too little to counteract his ethnological writings and his early support of polygenism. Not even a full-throated espousal of racial equality, much less a quiet, deeply qualified shift in thought, could have fixed the damage already done. The only small measure of redemption he found was in finally accepting the truth. "Lies are one-legged and short-lived," he wrote in his "Terminal Essay" for *The Arabian Nights*, "and venom evaporates."

•

One night not long after Stanley's triumphant return, a young American journalist named George Washburn Smalley rushed up a set of stairs in London, late for a fashionable dinner party. Focused on where he was headed, he did not notice the man sitting on the stairs until he stumbled into him. The man was holding in his hands a book and a pencil, so absorbed in his work that he did not even look up. Smalley, however, taking in the thick hair, the broad shoulders, the long, jagged scar etched into the brown, leathery cheek, stopped short. "It was Burton," he realized with astonishment.

A graduate of Yale and Harvard Law and one of the most accomplished journalists of the American Civil War, Smalley was not about to let this moment pass by without speaking to Richard Burton. Hearing a voice, Burton finally looked up with his famously dark, mesmerizing eyes, now temporarily clouded with confusion. "He woke up as if from a dream," Smalley later recalled, "with the dazed air of one not quite sure where he is." Consumed with curiosity and completely forgetting about the party to which he had been racing only moments before, Smalley asked Burton what he was reading. Burton answered that it was the epic poem *The Lusiads,* which tells the story of Vasco de Gama's discovery of the sea route around Africa to India. Burton had been slowly translating the poem, written in the sixteenth century by the Portuguese poet Luís de Camões, for nearly twenty years. Smalley commented that "it seemed an odd place for such work," to which Burton answered, "Oh, I can read anywhere or write anywhere. And I always carry Camoëns about with me.... I have done most of my translating in these odd moments."

Smalley had met countless famous men in his years as a journalist, from military heroes to icons of industry, but he had never met a man like Burton. "I looked at him with that sort of curiosity one has in the presence of a perfectly unique, or at any rate, original person, whose character and capacities are both evidently beyond the common," he later wrote. "Are you never tired?" he asked Burton. "Never," Burton answered. "What do you mean by 'never'?" Smalley said, shocked. "I mean," Burton replied, "that I cannot remember that I ever knew what it was to feel tired or to be unable to go on with any work I wanted to do."

Realizing that the young man before him was on his way to the party from which he had just escaped, Burton now gave him a cynical grin. "You will find plenty of dull people in the rooms above," he warned. Smalley listened now to the "roar of human voices" emanating from the party. Guests and servants walked by them on the stairs, "passing and repassing" through thick, drifting clouds of cigarette smoke. "And there in the centre of this steam and amid all the social hurly-burly sat Burton," Smalley marveled. "Indifferent to everything around him, forgetful of it, hearing nothing but the music of Portuguese verse." The poem was the work, Smalley realized, of a man whose life was not dissimilar to that of the legendary writer, explorer, and linguist sitting on the stairs in front of him now. Burton was "living over again the miserable yet heroic life of a poor poet," Smalley wrote, "who had been dead three hundred years."

When Burton's translation of *The Lusiads* was finally released, Isabel feared that, like her brilliant if deeply flawed husband, it would never be understood. "If a thousand buy it, will a hundred read it, and will ten understand it?" she wondered. "To the unaesthetic, to non-poets, non-linguists, non-musicians, non-artists, Burton's Lusiads will be an unknown land, an unknown tongue." Her husband, however, was not only unconcerned, he expected nothing more. He had faced critics and detractors his entire life, had been betrayed and forgotten, and had allowed his fury to infect his own work, causing lasting damage both to his innocent victims and to his own name. What did it matter now if this work near the end of his life was ignored? "If a concurrence of adverse trifles prevent my being appreciated now," he wrote from Cairo, "the day will come, haply somewhat late, when men will praise what they now pass by." The years he had devoted to this single translation, a homage both to exploration and to poetry, was not for the critics or for the public but for himself. Far more than any expedition or adventure, any long-sought geographical prize, this might serve as his legacy after death. If not, it was at least a comfort in old age. "I have spared no labor on the work; I have satisfied myself if not *Malebouche*," he wrote near the end of his preface to *The Lusiads*, braced once more for attack. "I repeat my motto: *poco spero, nulla chiedo*." Little I hope, nothing I ask.

Epilogue

ASHES

Although he had solved the mystery that had captivated philosophers and frustrated explorers for millennia—had answered, in the words of the Royal Geographical Society, "the problem of all ages"—John Hanning Speke was quickly forgotten. He had been lucky and he had been right, and he had clung to those facts, hoping that they would protect him from becoming lost in the long shadow of Richard Burton. In the end, however, being right had not been enough. While more than a dozen biographies would be written about his deeply troubled, endlessly fascinating nemesis, Speke would be the primary subject of only one slim volume, written more than a century after his death.

Murchison, despite his frustration with Speke near the end of his life, did what he could to keep his memory alive. In 1866, two years after Speke's death, he raised a subscription to build a memorial to him in Kensington Gardens. A red granite obelisk was quarried in Aberdeen, Scotland, not far from where Grant was born, and the words "In Memory of Speke/Victoria Nyanza and the Nile/1864" etched into its base. The monument still stands today, surrounded by a low wrought iron fence. The stone is polished, the surrounding grass trimmed, but traffic speeds past it, few stopping to read the name of the man who put the source of the Nile on the map of the world.

Although Speke would have seethed at the idea, Burton remembered him better and longer than most. Not only did he contribute to Murchison's fund for the memorial, but he helped in the creation of a bust of the fallen explorer. A few months after Speke's funeral, which he had not attended, knowing that he would not be welcome, Burton was invited to the studio of the sculptor Edgar George Papworth, the artist commissioned to make the bust. Papworth came from a long line of artists and builders, from his grandfather, the "master plaisterer" at both St. James's Palace and Kensington Palace; to his father, a builder and architect; to his son, Edgar George Papworth Jr., who was among the most admired sculptors of his generation. Papworth knew stone and clay as well as any man then living in Britain, but he did not know Speke. Worried that his bust would have none of the qualities that had animated his subject in life, he asked for help from the man whose name had been linked with Speke's for the past ten years. "I only took the cast after death and never knew him alive," he told Burton as they stood in his studio in Dorset Square, staring at the incomplete bust. "But you who lived with him so long can surely give me some hints."

Burton, intimidated neither by the art nor the artist, did not hesitate. Isabel, who was with him in the studio, later explained that her husband "had learnt something of sculpting when a boy in Italy." Taking Papworth's sculpting pencil from his hand, he immediately set to work. "With a few touches here and there," Isabel wrote, he "made a perfect likeness and expression." Isabel, who had watched as her husband carved life into the bust of a man who had been both his intimate friend and greatest foe, would later memorialize the moment in a poem she titled "Who Last Wins."

A Moulded mask at my feet I found
With the drawn-down mouth and the deepen'd eye,
More lifeless still than the marbles round—
Very death amid life's mimicry

Even Speke's most lauded accomplishment was muted over time. Although the Nyanza is the principal source of the White Nile, the lake itself is fed by many smaller rivers and streams, pouring into it from the surrounding mountains. In 2006, nearly 150 years after Speke and Bombay first saw the Nyanza, a British explorer named Neil McGrigor claimed to have made the first full ascent of the Nile from sea to source, and then to have traced the Nyanza's largest feeder, the Kagera River, which is now considered to be the most remote headstream of the Nile.

Tragically, Speke's most lasting legacy was neither his expeditions nor any memorial built in his honor but his reckless, baseless theories connecting race and religion. For Speke, "the history of Noah, and the disposition of his sons on the face of the globe" explained what he believed was a fundamental difference between races. When Bombay, the man upon whom he relied most heavily while in East Africa and to whom he owed so much, had asked him about "the origin of Seedis, his caste, and . . . by what law of nature I accounted for their cruel destiny in being the slaves of all men," Speke had confidently answered. Bombay, he said, was "of the black or Hamitic stock, and by the common order of nature, they, being the weakest, had to succumb to their superiors, the Japhetic and Semitic branches of the family."

Speke was far from the first to espouse the Hamitic Myth, which had been used for decades to justify slavery. His popularity in Victorian England, however, as well as his fervent belief in the myth and his eagerness to discuss it, led to its increased acceptance. The stunning achievements of the ancient Egyptians, which the British Empire had been so eager to study and appropriate, were explained away by yet another distinction, this time between the sons of Ham. Only the youngest, Canaan, had carried the curse of his father, the argument went, but Mizraim, the ancestor of the Egyptians, did not. By 1994, the Hamitic Myth would not only feed racial prejudice but give rise to one of the most devastating civil wars in African history: the Rwandan genocide. Speke's argument that the Hutu majority in the region were descendants of Canaan, "a primitive race," and that the Tutsi minority were the sons of Mizraim, descended from "the best blood of Abyssinia," had led to decades of discrimination. In the end, 800,000 people would die in the uprising, their lives lost to a hatred born of a myth perpetuated by a man to whom Africa meant little more than its potential for the British Empire and the fame it might bring him.

•

The East African to whom Speke first explained his theory about East Africans, Sidi Mubarak Bombay, would live a life that was longer, more eventful, and more accomplished than Speke's own. While for both Burton and Speke the tantalizing, fleeting opportunity to map East Africa ended the day Speke died, for Bombay, the work of mapping his own continent continued unabated. He would spend the rest of his life exploring the home from which he had been stolen as a child and which he had reclaimed through quiet courage. In the ensuing years, he added to his already astonishing achievements not only by helping Stanley to find Livingstone but, with the British explorer Verney Lovett Cameron, becoming the first to cross the entire continent from east to west, sea to sea. In the end, Bombay would become not only one of the most accomplished guides in the history of

African exploration but likely the most widely traveled man in Africa, estimated to have covered some six thousand miles of grasslands, forests, deserts, and mountains, most of it by foot.

The undeniable contributions made by men like Bombay forced European explorers to begin to acknowledge their reliance on native porters, translators, and guides and to recognize, however reluctantly, the essential role that they played in exploration on every continent. In a speech to the Royal Geographical Society in 1871, its then president, Sir Henry Creswicke Rawlinson, admitted that if they did not "place some reliance upon native explorers... [and] accept the information so obtained, there would be a perfect blank in our maps of many regions." That same year, the Society awarded Livingstone's aides, James Chuma, Abdullah Susi, and Jacob Wainwright, silver medals after they carried the missionary-explorer's body nearly a thousand miles to the coast, a journey of nine months, so that it could be buried at Westminster Abbey. Bombay, although he was never invited to England to receive the awards he had earned over many decades of exploration, was given a silver medal and a lifetime pension. The following year, a gold medal was awarded to Nain Singh, an Indian explorer who helped to map much of Central Asia and Tibet, surveying the Brahmaputra River and determining the location and altitude of the Tibetan city of Lhasa.

Outside of the smallest of scientific circles, however, the names of non-European explorers remained largely unknown. More than three quarters of a century after Bombay traveled with Cameron across equatorial Africa, the Tibetan mountaineer Tenzing Norgay made the first ascent of the world's highest mountain, Sagarmatha, now widely known as Mount Everest, with Edmund Hillary in an expedition sponsored by the Royal Geographical Society. Norgay received both the British George

Medal—for gallantry "not in the face of the enemy"—and the Star of Nepal, but while Hillary's has long been a household name, Norgay's has only recently come to the attention of a wider audience.

In 2009, the Royal Geographical Society took a serious step toward trying to change the misguided perception that European explorers alone mapped the world. A major exhibition titled Hidden Histories of Exploration, researched in the Society's archives and written by Professor Felix Driver and Dr. Lowri Jones, was featured at its headquarters in London. "The history of exploration has often invited celebration.... But what, and whom, shall we celebrate?" the exhibition asked. In answer, it highlighted men whose work had been essential to some of the most famous expeditions in history, among them Sidi Mubarak Bombay.

In the nineteenth and twentieth centuries, the result of African exploration was not only mapping the continent but seizing it, region by region. By the time of Burton's death, it was clear to every European nation not only where Africa's lakes and rivers, mountains and forests lay but that it held vast, enviable natural resources, from diamonds and gold to iron, uranium, and petroleum. In what quickly became known as the "scramble for Africa," the continent was invaded, occupied, and colonized. By the early 1900s, seven European countries would control more than 90 percent of Africa, leaving only scattered pockets of independence—the Empire of Ethiopia in the east and Liberia in the west—on a continent of more than eleven million square miles. It was not until the late twentieth century that Africa was finally able to free itself from European colonization. Along the way, in 1964, a hundred years after Speke's death, the region of Tanganyika and the island of Zanzibar were united, in name as well as nationhood, to form the sovereign state of Tanzania.

Individual freedom was an even harder battle to win than national independence. Britain had passed the Slave Trade Act in 1807 and the Slavery Abolition Act in 1833—thirty-two years before the United States passed the Thirteenth Amendment—but in East Africa slavery would not be formally abolished until the early twentieth century. Even then, it continued largely unabated. In the end, it would take not pressure from Europe, which had continued to profit from slavery in other parts of the world, but regional factors, including the collapse of Arab markets that relied on slave labor, to finally shut down the East African slave trade.

Enslaved people themselves also took decisive and effective action to end slavery and to offer support to those who had regained their freedom. Hundreds of thousands escaped from slavery, facing extraordinarily dangerous and uncertain conditions. Others used the abolition laws of the colonial powers that had seized so much of Africa to put pressure on the men who owned them. Among the most powerful and lasting efforts to end slavery were those steps taken by "Bombay Africans," people who had been kidnapped as children, rescued from slave ships in the Indian Ocean, and raised in orphanages in Bombay (now Mumbai). After being recruited by Europeans to help in exploring Africa, many of these men and women, including James Chuma and Abdullah Susi, David Livingstone's famous aides, mounted anti-slavery campaigns. They also helped to found settlements in East Africa, such as Freretown and Rabai, which became places of safety and opportunity for those who had once been enslaved.

Although Bombay did not live long enough to witness the end of the slave trade, he did see the market where he had been sold for cloth closed for good. In 1873, the British consul John Kirk put pressure on the sultan of Zanzibar Barghash ibn Said to sign a treaty forbidding the export of slaves from the mainland and, three years later, shutting down the infamous slave market of Zanzibar. Three years after that, in 1879, Christ Church Cathedral was built on the site, and in 2014 the World Monuments Fund gave a nearly million-dollar grant to protect it and to build a museum that tells the tragic and shameful history of the East African slave trade.

In 1885, Sidi Mubarak Bombay died at the age of sixty-five. No memorial was built for him after his death, nor any biographies written about him in subsequent years. His name is rarely seen in the annals of exploration, but it could be argued that he accomplished more than any single explorer ever to enter the continent of his birth. More than that, he had lived and died in Africa a free man.

•

Richard Burton's life would last longer than either Speke's or Bombay's, but its final years bore little resemblance to the twilight of a national hero. Moving from consulate to consulate, he was ignored by the British government, the Royal Geographical Society, and the wider public, despised by Speke's family and friends, and relegated to near poverty. Early in 1886, he was surprised by a cable informing him that the queen had approved for him a knighthood. By then, however, he had become so angry and resentful that Isabel worried he would not accept it. "You know I suppose that they have K.C.M.G[d] me," he wrote to his friend the novelist Maria Louise Ramé, known by the pen name Ouida, "and I'm ungrateful enough to comment 'Half gives who late gives.'"

In the end, all that Burton had left was what he had begun with—literature and languages. His controversial translations of ancient Arabic texts became, in many ways, his salvation. Not only did they bring in sorely needed funds, but they filled his days and engaged his mind. They also gave him one aspect of public life that he had missed the most: a good fight. "I don't care a button about being prosecuted," he told Isabel with relish as he worked on his translation of *The Arabian Nights*. "If the matter comes to a fight, I will walk into court with my Bible and my Shakespeare and my Rabelais under my arm, and prove to them that, before they condemn me, they must cut half of *them* out."

Isabel fretted over Burton's translations of erotic texts, not just because of how they would be received or the danger of his violating the obscenity laws, but because she feared for his immortal soul. She was quick to refute any suggestion that his interest was other than academic. "Do not let any one suppose for a moment that Richard Burton ever wrote a thing from the impure point of view," she wrote. "He dissected a passion from every point of view, as a doctor may dissect a body, showing its source, its origin, its evil, and its good, and its proper uses, as designed by Providence and Nature." Her husband, famous not just for his languages, writings, and travels, but for his outrageous stories and unblushing interest in the sexual proclivities of every culture, was, she insisted, personally irreproachable in thought and action. "In private life he was the most pure, the most refined and modest man that ever lived," she declared. "He was so guilt-less himself that he could never be brought to believe that other men said or used these things from any other standpoint."

Although Isabel could not stop Burton from translating any text that caught his eye and appetite, by the final years of his life the balance of power between them had slowly begun to shift. Burton had long bragged of being able to control his wife through hypnosis, taking command of her mind at any time and from any distance. After he had a major heart attack in 1887, however, accompanied by long and violent seizures, she took control of him. Her husband, who had traveled to some of the most remote corners of the world, usually without her, would from that moment on, she decided, "always require *great care and watching.*" As he recovered, lying in bed or being pushed in a wheelchair through the quiet streets of Trieste, she happily fussed over him, and he let her.

At the same time, however, Burton began a new translation, this time of *The Scented Garden*. A medieval Arabic text, its sexual explicitness would, Burton knew, shock and outrage the British people, and sell out immediately. Isabel did not object because, she later admitted, his doctors had told her that "it was so fortunate, with his partial loss of health, that he could find something to interest and occupy his days." Burton believed that this book would be both one of his most important works and, he promised Isabel, his final translation of erotic writing. It was, he believed, a life insurance policy for his wife. He knew that it would "make a great row in England," but it was her "jointure," he told her, "and the proceeds are to be set apart for an annuity for you."

On October 19, 1890, a day that Isabel would later recall as "the last happy day of my life," she came home from church to find Richard working on the translation. As she kissed him in greeting, he showed her half a page of the manuscript in the original Arabic. "To-morrow I shall have finished this, and I promise you that I will never write another book on this subject," he told her. "I will take to our biography." Thrilled and relieved, Isabel replied, "What a happiness that will be." Burton, however, would never write his promised biography, nor finish *The Scented Garden*. By 7:00 the next morning, his heart and hands had stopped for good.

•

For forty years, Isabel's life had revolved around Richard Burton. All that was left of who she had been before she met him, and the life she might have lived if she had not, was her religion, and she clung to it now more tightly than ever before. To go on without Richard seemed unimaginable, impossible. Her greatest hope was that she would quickly follow him to the grave. "I wish to go into a convent for a spiritual retreat for fifteen days," she wrote to her sister-in-law, Maria Stisted. "After that I should like to live very quietly in a retired way in London till God shows me what I am to do, or, *as I hope, will take me also.*"

While Isabel felt that her life was over, however, her work was not. Her mission now, she believed, was not only to protect her husband's legacy but to save his soul. In Burton's final hours, knowing that the end was near, she had sent for the young priest who led the church she attended in Trieste. When he arrived an hour before Burton was declared dead, she begged him to administer extreme unction, the sacrament given to Catholics as they lay dying. Knowing that Burton was not only not Catholic but an open agnostic, the priest had hesitated. So urgent were Isabel's pleas, however, and so insistent was she that her husband had years earlier "abjured his heresy and professed himself as belonging to the church," he had finally relented. Burton's adoring niece, Georgiana Stisted, would later write bitterly that "Rome took formal possession of Richard Burton's corpse, and pretended, moreover, with insufferable insolence, to take under her protection his soul."

To the astonishment of Burton's friends and the disgust of his family, Isabel insisted on a Catholic funeral for her agnostic husband. She arranged to have his body embalmed so that it might be shipped back to England, where he would be buried in a tomb of her own design, carved to look like the tent they had made for their travels to Syria. In Trieste, every flag was low-

ered to half-staff, and it seemed as though the entire town came
out to view the flag-draped coffin and to follow the mournful
procession of carriages, overflowing with flowers, as they made
their way toward St. Mary's Church. Inside, children from a local
orphanage sang the Gregorian chant *Dies irae, dies illa.* Day of
wrath, O day of mourning. "Sobs were heard all around," Isabel
wrote. "I alone was tearless; I felt turned to stone."

After her husband's funeral, Isabel entered the home she
had shared with Burton for nineteen years and locked herself
in his rooms, alone with his manuscripts. Picking up the nearly
complete translation of *The Scented Garden,* she began to read. "I
remained for three days in a state of perfect torture," she wrote,
"as to what I ought to do about it." The manuscript she held in
her hands, Isabel knew, was not only her husband's final gift to
her, it was the embodiment of his genius and passion. "It was his
magnum opus," she wrote, "his last work that he was so proud of,
that was to have been finished on the awful morrow—that never
came." It was also, she believed, a sin. "My head told me that sin
is the only rolling stone that gathers moss," she wrote, "that what
a gentleman, a scholar, a man of the world may write when living, he would see very differently to what the poor soul would
see standing naked before its God, with its good or evil deeds
alone to answer for, and their consequences visible to it for the
first moment, rolling on to the end of time."

As darkness fell, Isabel sat on the floor in front of the hearth,
the two volumes of *The Scented Garden* laid out before her, the fire
casting flickering shadows on its pale pages. She had been offered
thousands of pounds for the manuscript, money that would help
to pay for the elaborate tomb she had planned for her husband,
and for her own final, lonely days. Shattered and sickened, she
struggled with what for her was the most painful choice she had
ever forced herself to make. "My heart said, 'You can have six

thousand guineas,'" she wrote. "'Your husband worked for you, kept you in a happy home with honour and respect for thirty years. How are you going to reward him?'" What she owed Burton, she believed, was not to use the work as he had intended, but to sacrifice it to save his soul. "That your wretched body may be fed and clothed and warmed for a few miserable months or years, will you let that soul, which is part of your soul, be left out in cold and darkness till the end of time," she asked herself. Her answer came quickly. "Not only not for six thousand guineas, but not for six million guineas will I risk it."

Picking up the first sheet of the manuscript, Isabel stretched her quivering hand toward the fire. "Sorrowfully, reverently, and in fear and trembling," she wrote, "I burnt sheet after sheet, until the whole of the volumes were consumed." She expected to be judged harshly, even hated, by the thousands of people who admired her husband and worshipped his work, and she was right, but she cared only for the judgment of one man. "Will he rise up in his grave and curse me or bless me?" she asked herself as she watched Richard Burton's final work turn to ashes in the flames. "The thought will haunt me to death."

ACKNOWLEDGMENTS

One of the first lessons I learned while working at *National Geographic* was that no writer tells a story alone. For this book, as with every book I have written, I have had the benefit of extraordinarily knowledgeable and generous advisers, people who have volunteered their time and expertise to guide me through a multitude of complicated subjects. After working on this book for five years, I have more people to thank than I could hope to include in these pages, but I will do my best.

Among the many experts I consulted for this book, no one has left a more lasting mark than Donald Young. A highly respected authority on Richard Burton, Don is the author of the exhaustively researched master's thesis "The Selected Correspondence of Sir Richard Burton" as well as the fascinating and beautifully bound book *The Search for the Source of the Nile,* both of which were indispensable sources for me as I began my research. Having lived in East Africa for the great majority of his life, Don also has an immense knowledge of and respect for the region's land, its people, and its history. He helped me to plan and carry out a research trip that began in Kenya, his adopted home, and continued to Zanzibar, mainland Tanzania, and Uganda, making it possible for me to follow the path that Burton, Speke, and Bombay had taken more than 150 years earlier. Even after I returned to the United States, Don continued to help me at every turn, connecting me with historians and archivists in East Africa, answering questions, and reading my manuscript. He has become not only an admired and valued adviser but a lifelong friend.

I am also deeply indebted to one of the world's greatest paleo-anthropologists, Donald Johanson, who introduced me to Don Young. I first met Donald more than twenty years ago in Addis Ababa, Ethiopia, while on a research trip for *National Geographic*. He had just completed another dig, working near the site where years earlier he had discovered Lucy, one of the most complete skeletons of *Australopithecus afarensis*. It was a day I will never forget, both because I was meeting a legendary scientist, and because it was the beginning of a long and cherished friendship.

When I returned to East Africa to research this book in the spring of 2020, I had the great good fortune to meet a number of exceptionally knowledgeable experts on the region and its history. In Zanzibar, I worked with Said Suleiman Mohammed, a local historian who gave me a detailed historical tour of the island, from the building that once housed the British consulate, where Richard Burton and John Hanning Speke sought help from Hamerton and Rigby; to the ruins of the sultan's once majestic palace; to the wrenching museum built on the grounds of the market where Sidi Mubarak Bombay and countless others were sold into slavery. I am also grateful for the help of Professor K. S. Khamis, head of the Zanzibar National Archives and author of *A Brief History of Zanzibar*, whose work helped me to understand the many changes that took place over hundreds of years on this singular archipelago.

In mainland Tanzania, I met Kelvin Ngowi, conservator of antiquities for the Ministry of Natural Resources and Tourism at the Dr. Livingstone Memorial Museum in Ujiji Kigoma. Ngowi recounted for me the story of David Livingstone and Henry Morton Stanley's famous meeting on the banks of Lake Tanganyika, a meeting that Sidi Mubarak Bombay not only witnessed but helped make possible. Ngowi also took me to the path, lined with stately mango trees, that for hundreds of years led thousands of enslaved people out of Ujiji on their desperate, forced journey to the coast.

In Uganda, nearly as awe-inspiring as watching the Nile as it rushes from the Nyanza was visiting the kingdom of Buganda, which held on to much of its autonomy even after Uganda won its independence. While there, I met with Nalinnya Carol, the executive director of the Buganda Heritage & Tourism Board, and Bugandan guides Herbert Ssewajje and Ndawla Fred. They explained the kingdom's current accomplishments and challenges as well as its rich history and took me to see the palace of King Mutesa I, who met Speke and Bombay. While in Buganda, I also benefited from spending time with Taga Nuwagaba, author and illustrator of *Totems of Uganda*. Taga spent years tracking down the totems of each cultural group in Uganda, of which there are fifty-two in Buganda alone, meticulously researching his subjects, explaining the animals themselves and telling their stories, and drawing breathtaking illustrations of each totem, from the gray-crowned crane to the drop-tail ant.

In Kampala, I met with the distinguished professor of politics and anthropology Dr. Mahmood Mamdani, who is the Herbert Lehman Professor of Government at the School of International and Public Affairs, Columbia University, and was then also director of the Makerere Institute of Social Research. Dr. Mamdani, an expert on the study of African history and politics and the intersection of politics and culture, is the author of a number of brilliant and thought-provoking books, including *When Victims Become Killers: Colonialism, Nativism, and Genocide in Rwanda* and, most recently, *Neither Settler nor Native: The Making and Unmaking of Per-*

manent Minorities. He was kind enough to invite me to his office to discuss his work and the lives of Sidis who are still living in India. For introducing us, I would like to thank our mutual friend, the biographer Deborah Baker. I am also grateful to Dr. Mamdani for introducing me to the extraordinary work of the poet Ranjit Hoskote. Ranjit's poem "Sidi Mubarak Bombay," which he generously allowed me to excerpt for the epigraph of this book, is everything I hoped to say about Bombay and more, set in only a few wrenching, breathtakingly beautiful lines. The poem is part of Ranjit's gorgeous new book, *Hunchprose*.

Early in my research, I also made several trips to the United Kingdom to work in some of the world's finest archives. My first stop was the National Library of Scotland in Edinburgh, home to a treasure trove of letters, journals, notes, and sketchbooks, especially those of Speke and his later travel companion, James Grant. In the library's Archives & Manuscript Collections, I would like to thank curators Alison Metcalfe and Kirsty McHugh as well as special collections assistant Jamie McIntosh. I am also grateful for the help of Claire Wotherspoon on the Manuscripts Reference Team at the vaunted British Library in London; Jonathan Smith, archivist and modern manuscript cataloguer at Trinity College Library, Cambridge; Nancy Charley, archivist for the Royal Asiatic Society; Chris Day at the National Archives of the United Kingdom; Judith Coles at the Bath Medical Museum; and Jane Sparrow-Niang, author of *Bath and the Nile Explorers* and volunteer at the Bath Royal Literary & Scientific Institution.

Among the most valuable and fascinating of the archives I visited while in England was the library at the Royal Geographical Society, without whose extensive and carefully curated collection I could not have written this book. I am grateful to everyone who protects this archive and makes it accessible to researchers, but in particular I would like to thank Julie Carrington and Jan Turner, who answered my many queries and requests not just while I was in their library but for years before and after, as I wrote to them from thousands of miles away. I am also very thankful to Professor Felix Driver of the department of geography at the Royal Holloway University of London. Professor Driver, along with Dr. Lowri Jones, is the author of the Hidden Histories of Exploration exhibit at the Royal Geographical Society, a groundbreaking and important study of the porters and guides who made possible so many of the famed expeditions that the Society sponsored. Professor Driver also generously sent me a copy of his book about the exhibit.

While on a later research trip to England, I was also extremely fortunate to visit Neston Park, where John Hanning Speke lost his life. Alison Kippen, who runs Neston Park's Estate Office, was incredibly fast and helpful in her replies to my emails and facilitated my meeting with James Fuller, the great-great-grandson of George Fuller, who was hunting with his cousin John Hanning Speke on that fateful day. James gave me a tour of his breathtakingly beautiful estate, which is now home to an organic farm—complete with a joinery, an ice creamery, and a state-of-the-art dairy—has been the setting for BBC films, and is part of the Countryside Stewardship Scheme, which protects wildlife corridors. James took me and my overawed daughter not just to the field in which Speke and Fuller were hunting on September 15, 1864, but to the low stone wall from which Speke fell after his gun went off. He even gave us one of the chipped and weathered flagstones from the wall, which now sits in pride of place in my office.

I would like to thank my friend, the esteemed biographer, journalist, and professor, Dr. Pamela Newkirk, who generously gave her time and talent to read the manuscript for this book and offer invaluable advice. I am grateful to Amicia Demoubray, who introduced me by email to several members of the Speke family; Dr. Steve Hindle, the W. M. Keck Foundation Director of Research, and Anne Blecksmith, Head of Reader Services, at the Huntington Library in San Marino, California; the historian Dr. Sylviane Anna Diouf, visiting scholar at the Center for the Study of Slavery and Justice at Brown University and author of several critically acclaimed books on the African diaspora, including *Africans in India: From Slaves to Generals and Rulers;* Dr. Julius Lejju of the Mbarara University of Science & Technology in Mbarara-Uganda; Drs. Joost Fontein and Freda Nikirote of the British Institute in Eastern Africa; Catriona Foote, Senior Library Assistant, Special Collections at the University of St. Andrews; Dr. Edward Alpers, research professor in the department of history at the University of California Los Angeles; Naresh Fernandes, author of *City Adrift: A Short Biography of Bombay,* who generously pointed me in the direction of several important sources; and the editors at Burtoniana.org, who have gathered an enormous amount of information about Burton's life and works, as well as compiling a four-volume book of his letters and memoirs.

On a personal note, I am grateful to my dear friends Denis and Susie Tinsley, who, once again, invited me to stay in their incredibly beautiful and welcoming home (which was blessedly warm even in February) while I did research in London; Dr. Ajay Singh, a family friend and highly skilled ophthalmologist and surgeon who explained to me the eye diseases that members of the expedition contracted while in East Africa and introduced me to the work of Sir William Bowman; Jennifer Fox, who so carefully and thoughtfully fact checked my manuscript; and Riya Raj, my hardworking young intern, who is always willing to jump into a new project, no matter how strange.

Few authors have had the opportunity to work with the same team from one book to the next. Over the past twenty years I have been exceedingly fortunate not only to work with the same people but with three of the very best in the industry. My editor, Bill Thomas; agent, Suzanne Gluck; and publicist, Todd Doughty, have guided, advised, supported, and encouraged me through four books—and will, I hope, be willing to stick with me for many years to come. I am deeply grateful for their wisdom, talent, and friendship.

As always, I owe my most profound thanks to my family: my parents, Larry and Connie Millard; my sisters, Kelly Sandvig, Anna Shaffer, and Nichole Millard; and my children, Emery, Petra, and Conrad Uhlig, who never fail to astonish me with their kindness, strength, and intelligence. Finally, and forever, I am grateful beyond measure to my incomparable and irreplaceable husband, Mark Adams Uhlig.

NOTES

MANUSCRIPT SOURCES

British Library, BL
Houghton Papers, Trinity College, HPTC
Huntington Library, HL
Morgan Library, ML
National Library of Scotland, NLS
Royal Asiatic Society, RAS
Royal Geographical Society, RGS

TITLE ABBREVIATIONS

The Book of the Thousand Nights and a Night: The Arabian Nights
First Footsteps in East Africa: First Footsteps
General Rigby, Zanzibar and the Slave Trade: Rigby
Journal of the Discovery of the Source of the Nile: Journal of the Discovery
The Lake Regions of Central Africa: Lake Regions
The Life of Captain Sir Richard F. Burton: The Life
Personal Narrative of a Pilgrimage to Al-Madinah & Meccah: Personal Narrative
Travels in Central Africa, and Explorations of the Western Nile Tributaries: Travels in Central Africa
What Led to the Discovery of the Source of the Nile: What Led

PROLOGUE

2   "at the center of a flaming core of reason": Bob Brier, "Napoleon in Egypt," *Archaeology* (May/June 1999), 46.

6   "I do not wish well": Driver, "The Active Life," 2005.

CHAPTER ONE: A BLAZE OF LIGHT

11   "looked at my clothes, overhauled my medicine chest": Richard Burton, *Personal Narrative,* vol. 1, 166.

12   "This," he later wrote, "was a mistake": Richard Burton, *Personal Narrative,* vol. 1, 166–67.

12   "to pass through the Moslem's Holy Land": Richard Burton, *Personal Narrative,* vol. 1, 23.

12   Although "neither the Koran nor the Sultan": John Hayman, ed., *Sir Richard Burton's Travels in Arabia and Africa: Four Lectures from a Huntington Library Manuscript,* "The Visitation at El Medinah," 20.

12   "A blunder, a hasty action, a misjudged word": Isabel Burton, *The Life,* vol. 1, 178.

13   a "huge white blot": Richard Burton, *Personal Narrative,* vol. 1, 1.

13   He "honored me," Burton wrote: Richard Burton, *Personal Narrative,* vol. 1, 1.

13   Burton was "singularly well-qualified": Letter Book, RGS Archives, Murchison to J. C. Melvill, in Jon R. Godsall, "Fact and Fiction in Richard Burton's Personal Narrative of a Pilgrimage to El-Medinah and Meccah," *Journal of the Royal Asiatic Society* 3, no. 3 (November 1993): 341.

13   Over the next eighteen years: John Hayman, ed., *Sir Richard Burton's Travels in Arabia and Africa: Four Lectures from a Huntington Library Manuscript,* "The Visitation at El Medinah," 3.

14   "In consequence of being brought up abroad": *The Life,* vol. 1, 32.

14   "The man riveted my attention": Bram Stoker, *Personal Reminiscences of Henry Irving,* volume 1, xl.

14   "the jaw of a devil and the brow of a god": Algernon Charles Swinburne, quoted in Arthur Symons, "A Neglected and Mysterious Genius," *The Forum,* vol. 67 (1922), 240.

15   "the 'Blacking-shop' of Charles Dickens": *The Life,* vol. 1, 31, 28–29.

15   "We shrieked, we whooped, we danced for joy": *The Life,* vol. 1, 31–32.

15   Burton's father taught him chess: *The Life,* vol. 1, 46.

15   "that unwise saying of the wise man": *The Life,* vol. 1, 46.

15   "nerves without flesh, hung on wires": *The Life,* vol. 1, 38.

15   "We soon learned not to neglect the mask": *The Life,* vol. 1, 34.

16   Burton earned the coveted French title: Theodore A. Cook, preface to Richard F. Burton, *The Sentiment of the Sword,* https://ejmas.com/jnc/jncart_burtonsentimentsword01_0200.htm.

16   "was the great solace of my life": *The Life,* vol. 1, 56.

16   "innocence of the word not of the thought": Richard Burton, *The Arabian Nights,* xxxv.

17   "a man who could learn a language running": *The Life,* vol. 1, 101.

17   "I was intended for that wretched being": *The Life,* vol. 1, 81.

17   "I never worked more than a quarter of an hour": *The Life,* vol. 1, 101.

17   Realizing that one of the fastest ways: *The Life,* vol. 1, 89.

17   Over the following years: N. M. Penzer, "The Centenary of Sir Richard Francis Burton," RAS. Years later, after being accosted by a stranger who had tried to learn Persian by book and was shocked and insulted when "the celebrated Oriental scholar and linguist, Richard Burton" had no idea what he was saying, Burton replied dryly, "Oh, was it Persian you were speaking?...I only know the language as it is spoken and written in Persia by Persians."

18   "Were it not that the author is so proud of his knowledge": "Falconry in the East," *Notices of New Books,* RAS.

18   "For many years I have been employed": Burton, *Remarks on a Critique of the "Falconry of the Indus,"* E.I.U. Service Club, 14, St. James's Square.

18   "The task may appear a formidable one": Burton, letter to *Bombay Times,* February 1848.

18   "linguists are a dangerous race": Richard Burton, *Lake Regions,* 103.

19   When Rigby sat for his examination: J. W. Heldring, *The Killing of Dr. Albrecht Roscher,* 101.

19   "my native tongue": Frank Harris, *Contemporary Portraits,* 194.

19   "It may be said without immodesty": Richard Burton, "The Biography of the Book and Its Reviewers Reviewed," *The Book of the Thousand Nights and a Night,* Supplemental Six (Benares, 1888), 416.

20   He had even undergone: Frank McLynn, *Snow Upon the Desert,* 74.

20   "If they find a certain amount": Richard Burton, *Personal Narrative,* vol. 1, 127.

20   In the weeks since Burton had first met: Richard Burton, *Personal Narrative,* vol. 1, 165–66.

21   "a roll of canvas, carefully soiled": Richard Burton, *Personal Narrative*, vol. 1, 24–25.

21   Anything that might have raised suspicion: Richard Burton, *Personal Narrative*, vol. 1, 167.

21   "Eloquent in abuse": Richard Burton, *Personal Narrative*, vol. 1, 62.

21   What he had gotten was a quick-witted: Richard Burton, *Personal Narrative*, vol. 1, 6.

22   "suspected me from the first": Richard Burton, *Personal Narrative*, vol. 1, 151–52.

22   "The would-be Haji": Richard Burton, *Personal Narrative*, vol. 1, 167.

22   "Determining with a sigh to leave it behind": Richard Burton, *Personal Narrative*, vol. 1, 167–68.

23   "What nation, either in the West or in the East": Richard Burton, *Personal Narrative*, vol. 2, 237.

23   "the true hero of Paradise Lost": Richard Burton, *The Arabian Nights*, ix, 135n.

23   "The more I study religion": Richard Burton, "Terminal Essay," *The Arabian Nights*.

24   "I may truly say that": Richard Burton, *Personal Narrative*, vol. 2, 160–61.

24   "I thought, 'Now something is going to happen to me'": *The Life*, vol. 1, 177.

24   "nothing could preserve him from the ready knives": Richard Burton, *Personal Narrative*, vol. 2, 207, note 2.

24   "I will not deny that, looking at the windowless walls": Richard Burton, *Personal Narrative*, vol. 2, 207–8.

25   Finally, as he pretended to pray: Richard Burton, *Personal Narrative*, vol. 2, 207–8.

25   "began to long to leave Mecca": *The Life*, vol. 1, 178.

25   He was, he wrote, "worn out with fatigue": Richard Burton, *Personal Narrative*, vol. 2, 276.

25   "equally observed in the Calvinist": Richard Burton, *Personal Narrative*, vol. 2, 259.

26   "It is a great thing to be welcomed home": *The Life*, vol. 1, 32.

CHAPTER TWO: SHADOWS

27   Growing in grandeur over the years: Edwin de Leon, *Thirty Years of My Life on Three Continents*, vol. 1, 158, in Jon R. Godsall, *The Tangled Web*, 107.

27   From its balconied windows: Burton to Shaw, November 16, 1853, RGS.

28   "Well, damn it, Hawkins": *The Life*, vol. 1, 182.

28   "I won't say it was aggravated": Burton to Shaw, November 16, 1853, RGS.

28   "How melancholy a thing is success": Richard Burton, *First Footsteps*, 159–60.

29   Two years later: Rebmann then made an extraordinary claim: He had seen snow, he said, on top of Mount Kilimanjaro. To the minds of the supremely confident armchair geographers in England, the idea that snow could be found anywhere near the equator, even on a mountain peak, was not only highly unlikely but utterly laughable. Rebmann had been openly ridiculed by the revered British geographer William Cooley, who had never stepped foot in Africa, a fact that had not prevented him from considering himself an expert on the continent and writing widely about it. "The constant effort of Mr. Rebmann, to prove the existence of snow on Kilíma Njaro by inference from phenomena generally insignificant or ill understood, naturally gives rise to the presumption that he did not actually see snow," Cooley sneered in his book *Inner Africa Laid Open*. "He fixes his eyes on abstractions, and closes them against realities." Cooley dismissed as "a fireside tale" the reports by people who lived at the base of Kilimanjaro that there was indeed snow on its summit, and even when, ten years later, a German explorer and a British geologist climbed to the top and stood in a snowfall, he refused to admit that he had been wrong. Neither Cooley's reputation nor his confidence was diminished by the episode.

29   Although Burton had little time: R. Coupland, *East Africa and Its Invaders*, 400.

29   Burton himself had heard similar stories: Donald Young and Quentin Keynes, *The Search for the Source of the Nile*, 10.

30   "I have not seen him but don't intend to miss": Burton to Shaw, November 16, 1853, RGS.

31   "An average rise [of the Nile]": Toby Wilkinson, *The Nile*, 6.

31   Fears about the Nile's floods and efforts: B. W. Langlands, "Concepts of the Nile," 2–4.

32   As anyone who sought to understand it: B. W. Langlands, "Concepts of the Nile," 16.

32   Not until the nineteenth century, when the Turkish officer: B. W. Langlands, "Concepts of the Nile," 18–19.

33   "At one and the same moment": Jon R. Godsall, *The Tangled Web*, 147.

33   whoever found "the true sources of the White Nile": Adrian S. Wisnicki, "Cartographical Quandaries: The Limits of Knowledge Production in Burton's and Speke's Search for the Source of the Nile."

33   it would take "some gallant heart": *The Journal of the Royal Geographical Society of London*, vol. 33, p. 101.

34   "I hear that the Geographical has been": Burton to Shaw, October 1853, RGS.

34   "To me there was a double dullness": Burton, *Personal Narrative*, vol. 1, 31.

34   It was, he wrote, "the possibility of bringing my compass to bear": Jon R. Godsall, "Richard Burton's Somali Expedition," *Journal of the Royal Asiatic Society*, Series 3 (2001), 163.

35   All he needed was "a few good men": Burton to Shaw, Nov. 16, 1853, RGS.

35   "only my John the Baptist": Burton to Shaw, December 15, 1853, RGS.

CHAPTER THREE: BOND FOR OUR BLOOD

37   "he goes as a private traveller": Burton, *First Footsteps*, 3.

37   After being shuttled around India: Lionel James Trotter, *The Bayard of India*, 169.

37   "The countries opposite to Aden were so dangerous": Jon R. Godsall, "Richard Burton's Somali Expedition," *Journal of the Royal Asiatic Society*, Series 3 (2001), 168.

38   "not relish the chance of losing his cod": Burton to Shaw, November 16, 1853, RGS.

38   "fulfil the primary and great object": Richard Burton, *First Footsteps*, 4.

38   "In his younger days, thirsting for distinction": *The Life*, vol. 1, 118.

39   "basing his views on the oldest and most experienced": Jon R. Godsall, "Richard Burton's Somali Expedition," 138–39.

39   "abound[s] in poetry and eloquence": Burton, *First Footsteps*, p. 115.

39   "accustomed to daguerreotype": Jon R. Godsall, "Richard Burton's Somali Expedition," 164.

40   A member of the Indian navy, Stroyan: Richard Burton, *First Footsteps*, 7.

40 "It was not without difficulty": Burton, *First Footsteps,* 7.

40 He had been named Conservator of Forests: "Obituary, Dr. Stocks, F.L.S.," *Gentleman's Magazine,* vol. 42, July–December 1854.

40 "So great was his knowledge": "Obituary, Dr. Stocks, F.L.S.," *Gentleman's Magazine.*

40 "amiable, cheerful, and engaging disposition": "Obituary, Dr. Stocks, F.L.S.," *Gentleman's Magazine.*

41 "The fellow writes well but is modest": Burton to Shaw, November 16, 1853, RGS.

41 "Stocks, J. Ellerton, Bombay medical": *Allen's Indian Mail,* September 19, 1854.

42 "The Commander-in-Chief...observing to what": John Hanning Speke, *What Led,* 1.

43 "Every year...I obtained leave": John Hanning Speke, *What Led,* 1.

43 "He had acquired a curious taste": Richard Burton, *Zanzibar,* vol. 2, 378.

43 "While on the subject of superstition": John Hanning Speke, "Captain Speke's Discovery of the Victoria Nyanza, the Supposed Source of the Nile—Part II," *Blackwood's Edinburgh Magazine,* November 1859, 575–76.

43 "A sedentary life": Alexander Maitland, *Speke,* 15.

44 "In shooting," he had explained: Speke to Grant, March 1854, NLS.

44 An ensign with the 13th Bengal Native Infantry: Karl A. Meyer, *Tournament of Shadows: The Great Game and the Race for Empire in Central Asia,* 210.

44 Finally he decided that, instead of: Speke to Shaw, October 26, 1859, RGS.

44 "To my utter astonishment and discomfiture": John Hanning Speke, *What Led,* 2.

45 "He eminently possessed the power of asking": Richard Burton, *Zanzibar,* vol. 2, 376.

45 he believed "the scheme to be quite unfeasible": John Hanning Speke, *What Led,* 2.

45 "A man of lithe, spare form": Richard Burton, *Zanzibar,* vol. 2, 373–74.

46 "He had no qualifications": *The Life,* vol. 1, 315.

46 "the hardships of African exploration": Richard Burton, *First Footsteps,* 7.

46 "Since I have managed to square myself": Speke to Grant, October 12, 1854, NLS.

46   "assuming the fullest responsibility": Richard Burton, *Zanzibar*, vol. 2, 381.

47   "I saw that he was going to lose": *The Life*, vol. 1, 315.

CHAPTER FOUR: THE ABBAN

48   "hot-bed of scurry and ulcer": Richard Burton, *First Footsteps*, 186.

48   "the ancient metropolis of a once mighty race": Richard Burton, *First Footsteps*, 8–9.

49   "Thus everybody had a duty to perform": John Hanning Speke, *What Led*, 6.

49   "specimens of natural history in all its branches": John Hanning Speke, *What Led*, 6.

49   Herne even helped him build: John Hanning Speke, *What Led*, 7.

49   Burton, who felt more comfortable: Richard Burton, "Narrative of a Trip to Harar," 138.

50   "Lowering ourselves in this manner": John Hanning Speke, *What Led*, 7.

50   "It was anything but pleasant to the feel": John Hanning Speke, *What Led*, 7.

50   "The Abban acts at once as broker": Richard Burton, *First Footsteps*, 54.

51   "ranked highly in his country": John Hanning Speke, *What Led*, 7.

51   "Arabs, when traveling under their protection": John Hanning Speke, *What Led*, 7.

51   "being trifled with": John Hanning Speke, *What Led*, 40.

51   Taking 20 rupees: John Hanning Speke, *What Led*, 13.

52   "I strove with every effort in my power": John Hanning Speke, *What Led*, 13–14.

52   "The Abban was detained": John Hanning Speke, *What Led*, 15.

52   "at liberty to do whatever he pleased": John Hanning Speke, *What Led*, 15.

52   "A wicked feeling was almost": John Hanning Speke, *What Led*, 27.

53   "three and a half months' persecution": John Hanning Speke, *What Led*, 33–34.

53   "My success at Harrar has emboldened me": Burton to Shaw, February 25, 1855, RGS.

53   "All we can do is resign ourselves": Burton to Sarah, November 14, 1848, in Thomas Wright, *The Life of Sir Richard F. Burton,* vol. 1, 83.

54   Alone in Aden, Burton was left: Georgiana Stisted, *The True Life of Capt. Sir Richard F. Burton,* 164, 412.

54   "Speke has been plundered": Burton to William M. Coghlan, February 21, 1855, Russell E. Train Africana collection, Smithsonian.

54   "Against my inclination": John Hanning Speke, *What Led,* 34.

54   As well as being fined 200 rupees: John Hanning Speke, *What Led,* 34.

55   "This perhaps was scarcely the right time": John Hanning Speke, *What Led,* 34.

55   "During thirty years, not an Englishman": Richard Burton, *First Footsteps,* postscript.

55   "the true key of the Red Sea": Jon R. Godsall, "Richard Burton's Somali Expedition," *Journal of the Royal Asiatic Society,* Series 3 (2001), 136.

56   "by this means alone should we have men on whom we could depend": John Hanning Speke, *What Led,* 34.

56   "They were all raw recruits": John Hanning Speke, *What Led,* 34.

56   he "aspired to something better": Richard Burton, *Zanzibar,* vol. 2, 382.

CHAPTER FIVE: THE ENEMY IS UPON US

57   its "guns roar[ing] forth a parting salute": Richard Burton, *First Footsteps,* 189.

57   "During the height of the fair": C. J. Cruttenden, "Memoir on the Western or Edoor Tribes, Inhabiting the Somali Coast of N.E. Africa," *The Journal of the Royal Geographical Society of London,* vol. 19, 1849, 49–76; Richard Burton, *First Footsteps,* 176.

58   A sentry kept guard: John Hanning Speke, *What Led,* 34–35; Richard Burton, *First Footsteps,* postscript.

58   "The Somali would never be": John Hanning Speke, *What Led,* 39.

59   Most nights, Burton: John Hanning Speke, *What Led,* 39.

59   Speke stored his guns and sword: John Hanning Speke, *What Led,* 39.

59   "were undecided what to do": John Hanning Speke, *What Led,* 39.

60   Quickly reclaiming the region: Richard Burton, *First Footsteps,* 177.

60   "We were now alone": John Hanning Speke, *What Led,* 39.

60   "It was hard to refuse": John Hanning Speke, *What Led*, 39.

61   "My anger knew no bounds": John Hanning Speke, *What Led*, 39–40.

61   "Our visitors swore by the divorce-oath": Richard Burton, *First Footsteps*, postscript.

61   Soon after, everyone in the expedition: Richard Burton, *First Footsteps*, postscript.

62   "There suddenly arose": John Hanning Speke, *What Led*, 40.

62   Jumping up and racing: Speke to Burton, April 1855, BL.

62   They were under attack: Richard Burton, *First Footsteps*, postscript, footnote.

62   "The enemy swarmed like hornets": Richard Burton, *First Footsteps*, postscript.

64   "The well-known voice": Richard Burton, *First Footsteps*, postscript.

64   "I spent the interval before dawn": Richard Burton, *First Footsteps*, postscript.

65   Hearing Herne's story: Richard Burton, *First Footsteps*, postscript.

65   After lunging back out of the tent: John Hanning Speke, *What Led*, 40.

66   "The way the scoundrel handled me": John Hanning Speke, *What Led*, 41.

66   "I was now becoming very weak": John Hanning Speke, *What Led*, 41.

66   "Were I a good Mohammedan": John Hanning Speke, *What Led*, 41.

67   dropping dates into their curling palms: Richard Burton, *First Footsteps*, postscript, footnote.

67   Not long after his original guard: John Hanning Speke, *What Led*, 42.

67   The man who had been left: John Hanning Speke, *What Led*, 42–43.

68   Speke suddenly realized: John Hanning Speke, *What Led*, 43.

69   "What a gloomy prospect was now before me": John Hanning Speke, *What Led*, 43.

70   "This was," he wrote, "the severest affliction": Richard Burton, *First Footsteps*, postscript.

CHAPTER SIX: INTO THE MOUTH OF HELL

73   Burton called the war "an unmitigated evil": *The Life*, vol. 1, 225.

73   "opportunity of recovering my spirits": *The Life*, vol. 1, 226.

74   After dismissing Burton as "a clever man": Jon R. Godsall, "Rich-

ard Burton's Somali Expedition," *Journal of the Royal Asiatic Society,* Series 3 (2001), 138–39.

74 "It may seem harsh to criticize": Gordon Waterfield, "Burton Attacked in Official Reports," in *First Footsteps,* 263.

75 "The attack which occurred was an accident": Herne to Burton, April 1855, BL.

75 "If all the guards had been on sentry": Speke to Playfair, October 24, 1859, in *First Footsteps,* 1966, 284.

75 It was not a shortage of guards: Speke to Playfair, October 24, 1859, in *First Footsteps,* 1966, 284.

75 "Burton's defying danger and bragging": Speke to Playfair, in *First Footsteps,* 1966, 284.

75 "He said that *he* was the Head of the Expedition": Isabel Burton's annotation in Isabel Burton, *Life,* vol. 1, 223.

76 "Burton and Herne had run away": John Hanning Speke, *What Led,* 43.

76 To Speke, who had planned: Speke to Burton, July 22, 1859, BL.

77 "I venture to submit a few remarks": Richard Burton, *First Footsteps,* 215.

77 "Nothing," he wrote, "vexes the mind so much": John Hanning Speke, *What Led,* 12–13.

77 "a miserable-looking cripple": John Hanning Speke, *What Led,* 44.

77 "A touching lesson": *Life,* vol. 1, 137.

78 "They literally closed as wounds do": John Hanning Speke, *What Led,* 45.

78 Finding the "summons for war": John Hanning Speke, *What Led,* 45.

78 "I was more of a sportsman and traveller": John Hanning Speke, *What Led,* 46.

78 Laurence now lived: Ann Taylor, *Laurence Oliphant,* 36.

79 "Of course he is dying to go back": Margaret Oliphant, *Memoir of the Life of Laurence Oliphant and of Alice Oliphant, His Wife,* 96.

79 "stalwart, erect, sound in wind and limb": Georgiana Stisted, *The True Life of Capt. Sir Richard F. Burton,* 163.

80 The trials he had endured: Georgiana Stisted, "Reminiscences of Sir Richard Burton," 337.

80 "Lieutenant Burton," Speke later wrote: John Hanning Speke, *What Led,* 114.

80 "the traffic in slaves through the [Somali] territories": John Hanning Speke, *What Led,* 147.

80 "England, at once the most unmilitary": *The Life,* vol. 1, 225.

80   Two years into the war, Burton believed: *The Life,* vol. 1, 225.

81   By the time Burton arrived in Crimea: *The Life,* vol. 1, 229.

82   Raglan died in his tent: Burton to Shaw, August 18, 1855, RGS.

82   "The unfortunate Lord Raglan": *The Life,* vol. 1, 228.

82   "It did not occur to the Government": Winston S. Churchill, *A History of the English Speaking Peoples,* 1956, 58.

82   "I could never return to England": Joseph Cummins, *The War Chronicles,* 108.

83   "You cannot conceive of the miserable apathy": Burton to Shaw, August 18, 1855, RGS.

83   After doing what he could to improve: *The Life,* vol. 1, 244.

83   "infallibly set me down for a spy": *Life,* vol. 1, 244.

83   Still feeling ownership over the ideas: Ann Taylor, *Laurence Oliphant,* 39.

84   "The tragedy again and again": Frank Harris, *Contemporary Portraits,* 193.

CHAPTER SEVEN: WHAT A CURSE IS A HEART

85   "one of the oldest and proudest houses": Isabel Burton, *The Romance of Isabel Lady Burton,* 3.

86   "a country gentleman pure and simple": Isabel Burton, *The Romance of Isabel Lady Burton,* 15.

86   "Great attention was paid to our health": Isabel Burton, *The Romance of Isabel Lady Burton,* 16.

87   "Creepers covered the walls": Isabel Burton, *The Romance of Isabel Lady Burton,* 17–18.

87   "pretty honeysuckle and jessamine porch": Isabel Burton, *The Romance of Isabel Lady Burton,* 18.

87   "As far as books were concerned": Raymond Blathwayt, "The Reader," *The Bookman,* May 1896.

87   "I used to think out": Isabel Burton, *The Romance of Isabel Lady Burton,* 19.

87   "I was enthusiastic about gypsies": Isabel Burton, *The Romance of Isabel Lady Burton,* 21.

88   "You will cross the sea": Isabel Burton, *The Romance of Isabel Lady Burton,* 22.

88   "You will bear the name of our tribe": Isabel Burton, *The Romance of Isabel Lady Burton,* 21–22.

89   "never felt so patriotic": Isabel Burton, *The Romance of Isabel Lady Burton*, 40.

89   "He had very dark hair": Isabel Burton, *The Romance of Isabel Lady Burton*, 52.

90   "As God took a rib out of Adam": Isabel Burton, *The Romance of Isabel Lady Burton*, 37–38.

90   "myth of my girlhood": Isabel Burton, *The Romance of Isabel Lady Burton*, 52.

91   she had raised Isabel to marry: Raymond Blathwayt, "The Reader."

91   When Isabel turned "red and pale": Isabel Burton, *The Romance of Isabel Lady Burton*, 54.

91   "He waltzed with me once": Isabel Burton, *The Romance of Isabel Lady Burton*, 61.

92   "Richard has just come back": Isabel Burton, *The Romance of Isabel Lady Burton*, 72.

92   "And now Richard has gone": Isabel Burton, *The Romance of Isabel Lady Burton*, 73.

92   "I should love Richard's wild": Isabel Burton, *The Romance of Isabel Lady Burton*, 69.

92   "brought me up like a boy": Raymond Blathwayt, "The Reader."

93   "I wish I were a man": Isabel Burton, *The Romance of Isabel Lady Burton*, 91.

93   "pretty or handsome": Georgiana Stisted, "Reminiscences of Sir Richard Burton."

93   "the ugliest stage of my life": Isabel Burton, *The Romance of Isabel Lady Burton*, 23.

93   "What a curse is a heart!" Isabel Burton, *The Romance of Isabel Lady Burton*, 65.

93   "How I envy the women": Isabel Burton, *The Romance of Isabel Lady Burton*, 76.

94   "My plan was to be": Isabel Burton, *The Romance of Isabel Lady Burton*, 77–78.

94   "Would to God I were!" Isabel Burton, *The Romance of Isabel Lady Burton*, 81.

94   Two months later, as she was walking: *The Life*, Isabel's comments, vol. 1, 249.

95   When Isabel returned to the gardens: *The Life*, Isabel's comments, vol. 1, 249.

95   So overcome with emotion: *The Life*, Isabel's comments, vol. 1, 250.

96   "turn his attention to the 'Unveiling of Isis'": *The Life,* Isabel's comments, vol. 1, 249.

96   One afternoon in October: *The Life,* Isabel's comments, vol. 1, 254–55.

96   That night Isabel could not sleep: Isabel Burton, *The Romance of Isabel Lady Burton,* 88.

97   The next morning, Isabel: Isabel Burton, *The Romance of Isabel Lady Burton,* 88–89.

CHAPTER EIGHT: *HORROR VACUI*

98   The Society had yet to find a permanent home: Madeleine Jones Lowri, "Local Knowledge and Indigenous Agency in the History of Exploration" (thesis, University of London, 2010).

99   "daily visited by intelligent strangers": G. R. Crone and E. E. T. Day, "The Map Room of the Royal Geographical Society," *The Geographical Journal* 126 (March 1960): 12.

99   Before the eighteenth century, most European mapmakers: B. W. Langlands, "Concepts of the Nile," 14; Greg Miller, "Why Ancient Mapmakers Were Terrified of Blank Spaces, *National Geographic,* November 20, 2017.

100   "More than five-sixths of the region": https://library.princeton.edu/visual_materials/maps/websites/africa/maps-continent/continent.html.

101   A simple sketch of East Africa: Richard Burton, *Lake Regions,* 366.

101   Not only was the body of water enormous: Richard Burton, *Lake Regions,* 366.

101   "In this section-map": John Hanning Speke, *What Led,* 46.

102   "still stood upon his 'Single Sea'": Richard Burton, *Zanzibar,* vol. 1, 65.

102   "In these days every explorer": Richard Burton, *Lake Regions,* 23.

102   "the range of mountains marked upon our maps": R. C. Bridges, "Sir John Speke and the Royal Geographical Society," 29.

103   "had suffered with me in purse and person": Richard Burton, *Zanzibar,* vol. 1, 8.

103   "This settled the matter": John Hanning Speke, *What Led,* 46.

103   "Here was revealed to me": John Hanning Speke, *What Led,* 46.

104   The East India Company had at first: R. C. Bridges, "Sir John Speke and the Royal Geographical Society," 29.

104   "was highly injurious to future travelers": Richard Burton, *Lake Regions*, 23.

104   "a great loser by reputation": Speke to Playfair, October 24, 1859, NLS.

105   "Captain Burton... knew nothing of": John Hanning Speke, *What Led*, 47.

105   "Of the gladdest moments": Richard Burton, *Zanzibar*, vol. 1, 16–17.

105   "full, complete, unvarnished, uncastrated": Richard Burton, *The Arabian Nights*.

106   "The order, coolness, and cleanliness": Richard Burton, *Lake Regions*, 35.

107   "Truly prepossessing was our first view": Richard Burton, *Zanzibar*, vol. 1, 18.

107   As it grew dark, the beach sparkled: Richard Burton, *Zanzibar*, vol. 1, 27–28.

107   "had made a howling desert": Richard Burton, *Lake Regions*, 124.

107   "Zanzibar is a peculiar place": Burton to Monckton Milnes, April 27, 1857, HPTC.

108   "claret-chest, which lay on its side": Richard Burton, *Zanzibar*, vol. 1, 34.

108   "fair and ruddy": Richard Burton, *Zanzibar*, vol. 1, 35.

108   "The worst symptom in his case": Richard Burton, *Zanzibar*, vol. 1, 35.

109   "when everything," Speke wrote, "would be deluged": John Hanning Speke, *What Led*, 48.

109   why Rebmann had not acknowledged "in any way": Burton to Shaw, January 5, 1857, BL.

109   The Royal Geographical Society had also encouraged: John Hanning Speke, *What Led*, 49.

109   "I am resolved not to take": Burton to Back, April 9, 1857, RGS.

110   "was indeed sadly given to breaking": Richard Burton, *Zanzibar*, vol. 1, 489.

110   "being no sportsman": John Hanning Speke, *What Led*, 50.

110   "I thought it would be much more agreeable": John Hanning Speke, *What Led*, 50.

110   Finally, on January 17, they reached Mombasa: John Hanning Speke, *What Led*, 49.

111   Rebmann's "presence would give a Missionary semblance": Burton to Shaw, April 22, 1857, BL.

111 Speke, annoyed that they had "frittered away": John Hanning Speke, *What Led*, 49–51.

112 "I could not but perceive": Richard Burton, *Zanzibar*, vol. 2, 388.

112 "His presence," Burton wrote: Burton letter, to unknown recipient, April 1857, BL.

112 Although Elphinstone had agreed: Richard Burton, *Lake Regions*, 36.

112 "with me a companion and not a friend": Richard Burton, *Lake Regions*, 36.

112 "I have now had ample analogous proof": Speke to Georgina Speke, May 1857, BL.

113 "unfair appropriation of *my* remarks": Speke to Burton, June 20, 1860, NLS.

113 "Much of the change he explained to me": Richard Burton, *Zanzibar*, vol. 2, 388.

113 "habit of secreting thoughts": Richard Burton, *Zanzibar*, vol. 2, 385.

114 "He ever held, not only": Richard Burton, *Zanzibar*, vol. 2, 382.

114 "The river was extremely tortuous": John Hanning Speke, *What Led*, 52.

114 "terrified by the splash of oars": *The Life*, vol. 1, 264.

114 "All around reigned the eternal": *The Life*, vol. 1, 264.

CHAPTER NINE: BOMBAY

115 the expedition stopped in Chogué: There are several spellings for this station. Burton spelled it Chogway. Speke, in a paper for the Royal Geographical Society, spelled it Chongwe.

115 "Five men were readily enlisted": John Hanning Speke, *What Led*, 52.

116 "the gem of the party": *The Life*, vol. 1, 266.

116 "A large body of Wasuahili merchants": John Hanning Speke, *What Led*, 63.

117 "As all the residents had at different times": John Hanning Speke, "Journal of a Cruise on the Tanganyika Lake, Central Africa," *Blackwood's Edinburgh Magazine*, September 1859, 345.

119 "At the head of this file": Alan Moorehead, *The White Nile*, 17–18.

119 On Zanzibar in the mid-1800s: Alan Moorehead, *The White Nile*, 19.

120 Ambar had begun his steady climb: Habshi Amarat, *African Elites in India*, 46–47.

121 "I served with this master for several years": John Hanning Speke, "Journal of a Cruise on the Tanganyika Lake, Central Africa," 345.

121 "in half-starved inactivity": John Hanning Speke, "Journal of a Cruise on the Tanganyika Lake, Central Africa," 345.

123 "His good conduct and honesty of purpose": John Hanning Speke, "Journal of a Cruise on the Tanganyika Lake, Central Africa," 344.

123 "We thought...so highly of his qualifications": *The Life*, vol. 1, 266–67.

123 "an occasional loin-cloth covering": John Hanning Speke, "Captain Speke's Discovery of the Victoria Nyanza, the Supposed Source of the Nile—Part II," *Blackwood's Edinburgh Magazine*, October 1859, 397.

123 The dollars Burton carried on the expedition: Richard Burton, *Lake Regions*, Appendix I, 528.

123 "He works on principle": *The Life*, vol. 1, 266.

123 "I do not...feel so much pleasure in solitude": Speke to Blackwood, September 2, 1859, NLS.

124 "revel on a feast of milk and flesh": John Hanning Speke, *What Led*, 53.

124 "I called on volunteers": John Hanning Speke, *What Led*, 53.

124 "Cheerily did we trip along": John Hanning Speke, *What Led*, 53.

124 "become much attached to Bombay": John Hanning Speke, *What Led*, 56.

CHAPTER TEN: DEATH WAS WRITTEN

126 "violent bilious fever": John Hanning Speke, *What Led*, 56.

126 "Jack Speke & I look like ghosts enjaundiced": Burton to Milnes, April 27, 1857, HPTC.

127 "hot, heavy, and painful": *The Life*, vol. 1, 276–77.

127 "physicking ourselves": John Hanning Speke, *What Led*, 56.

127 "lived only in the evening": Richard Burton, *Lake Regions*, 22, 64.

127 "The Consul had also warned me": Richard Burton, *Zanzibar*, vol. 1, 472.

127 "cautioned him to no purpose": Richard Burton, *Lake Regions*, 67.

128 "heavily ironed to a gun": Richard Burton, *Lake Regions*, 70.

128 "Rather than return to Bombay": Richard Burton, *Zanzibar*, vol. 1, 37.

128 "in the condition of a bed-ridden old woman": Burton to Shaw, April 22, 1857, BL.

128 "of the shock his nerves had received": John Hanning Speke, *What Led*, 115.

129   "The atmospheric air's being so surcharged": John Hanning Speke, *What Led, 56.*

129   "For this to subside": John Hanning Speke, *What Led, 56.*

129   "should . . . be avoided, the dye soon turns dark": Richard Burton, *Lake Regions,* 408.

129   "blackmail, so much dreaded by travelers": Richard Burton, *Lake Regions,* 181.

130   "when cheap, for 12 dollars": Richard Burton, *Lake Regions,* Appendix I, 531.

130   "all manner of cheap and useless chow-chow": Richard Burton, *Zanzibar,* vol. 2, 379.

130   "In some regions," he wrote: Richard Burton, *Lake Regions,* Appendix I, 529.

130   The most varying and complicated: Richard Burton, *Lake Regions,* Appendix I, 529.

130   "Any neglect in choosing beads": Richard Burton, *Lake Regions,* Appendix I, 529; Karlis Karklins, "Identifying Beads Used in the 19th-Century Central East Africa Trade."

131   "in his pay and under his command": Richard Burton, *Lake Regions,* Appendix II, 552.

131   The head clerk of the Zanzibar customs house: Richard Burton, *Lake Regions,* 33.

131   Burton agreed to pay: John Hanning Speke, "Journal of a Cruise on the Tanganyika Lake, Central Africa," *Blackwood's Edinburgh Magazine,* September 1859, 340.

131   He promised the same amount: Richard Burton, *Lake Regions,* Appendix II, 550.

131   The British consul "offered to defray": Richard Burton, *Lake Regions,* 26, 551.

131   "purely conditional": Richard Burton, *Lake Regions,* Appendix II, 552.

132   "Though almost lethargic from the effects": Richard Burton, *Lake Regions,* 22.

132   Burton, who expected to be gone: Richard Burton, *Lake Regions,* 27.

132   As well as tents, mosquito nets: Richard Burton, *Lake Regions,* 14.

133   "The ivory of these animals": John Hanning Speke, "Captain Speke's Discovery of the Victoria Nyanza, the Supposed Source of the Nile—Part III," *Blackwood's Edinburgh Magazine,* November 1859, 569.

133   Speke liked to shoot at their ears: John Hanning Speke, "Captain

Speke's Discovery of the Victoria Nyanza, the Supposed Source of the Nile—Part III."

133 On another occasion, a female came up: John Hanning Speke, "Captain Speke's Discovery of the Victoria Nyanza, the Supposed Source of the Nile—Part III."

133 "used for display to amuse the Arabs": John Hanning Speke, *What Led*, 116.

133 "have made it their sport, to murder elephants": Richard Burton, *The Nile Basin*, 166.

134 "He was ever remarkable for the caution": Richard Burton, *Zanzibar*, vol. 2, 398.

134 Burton had hoped to hire 170 porters: Richard Burton, *Lake Regions*, 26–27.

134 "hearing that their employer was a muzungu": Richard Burton, *Lake Regions*, 26.

134 "Thirty animals, good, bad, and indifferent": Richard Burton, *Lake Regions*, 27.

134 "allowed by our law to do so": *The Life*, vol. 1, 281.

134 "He was the slave of an Arab Shaykh": Richard Burton, *Lake Regions*, 104.

134 "was warmly attached" to him: John Hanning Speke, "Captain Speke's Discovery of the Victoria Nyanza, the Supposed Source of the Nile—Part II," *Blackwood's Edinburgh Magazine*, October 1859, 397.

136 "With brow severe and official manner": Richard Burton, *Lake Regions*, 33.

136 "minute doses of morphine": Richard Burton, *Lake Regions*, 22.

136 The apothecary argued that: Burton to new British consul at Zanzibar, October 1857, BL.

136 "He looked forward to death": Richard Burton, *Lake Regions*, 34.

137 "He strongly advised them": Richard Burton, *Lake Regions*, 32.

137 "he assumed me to be profoundly ignorant": Richard Burton, *Lake Regions*, 35.

137 "The loud wail of death": Richard Burton, *Lake Regions*, 35.

138 "In the solitude and the silence": Richard Burton, *Lake Regions*, 35.

CHAPTER ELEVEN: AN OLD ENEMY

139 Following a blood-red flag: Richard Burton, *Lake Regions*, 48, 239–40.

139 In Swahili, Burton would later write: Richard Burton, *Lake Regions*, 236.

140 "The world is a great book": Richard Burton, *Lake Regions*, 235.

140 "The excitement of finding myself": Richard Burton, *Lake Regions*, 49.

140 "mostly lads, lank and light": Richard Burton, *Lake Regions*, 112, 241.

141 "purer and bluer": Burton, *Lake Regions*, 148.

141 "like a monstrous land-serpent": Richard Burton, *Lake Regions*, 241.

141 "Their example is followed": Richard Burton, *Lake Regions*, 243.

141 The agreed-upon signal: Richard Burton, *Lake Regions*, 54.

142 Using everything from broken pots: Richard Burton, *Lake Regions*, 234.

142 "Here and there a little facetiousness": Richard Burton, *Lake Regions*, 241.

142 "The demon of Slavery reigns": *The Life*, vol. 1, 285.

142 "to their hearths and homes": Richard Burton, *Lake Regions*, 77.

144 After passing through a muddy swamp: Richard Burton, *Lake Regions*, 49.

144 "Emma my seeress": Frederick Hockley, *Psychic Facts*, ed. W. H. Harrison, 1880.

145 "contain a 'good spirit'": Burton to Milnes, July 2, 1861, BL.

145 "suspect treachery everywhere": Richard Burton, *Scinde; or, The Unhappy Valley*, 1851, 263.

145 "I once tried in vain": Richard Burton, *First Footsteps*, 31.

145 "When fully primed by the spirit": Richard Burton, *Lake Regions*, 50.

146 "fully trusted in the truth of the report": Richard Burton, *Lake Regions*, 63.

146 "that Lieut. Colonel Hamerton's decease": Richard Burton, *Lake Regions*, 132.

146 "During our eighteen months": Richard Burton, *Lake Regions*, 16.

146 an "irreparable loss": Richard Burton, *Lake Regions*, 178–79, 100–103.

147 "usually better to let these quarrels": Richard Burton, *Lake Regions*, 158.

147 "an altercation took place": John Hanning Speke, *What Led*, 59.

147 He had quickly become a favorite: Richard Burton, *Lake Regions*, 431.

147 "He toiled like a char-woman": Richard Burton, *Lake Regions*, 431.

147 "He would do no wrong": John Hanning Speke, "Captain Speke's Discovery of the Victoria Nyanza, the Supposed Source of the Nile—Part II," *Blackwood's Edinburgh Magazine*, October 1859, 397.

148   "I saw with pleasure the kindly face": Richard Burton, *Lake Regions*, 197.

148   One night, as they made preparations: Richard Burton, *Lake Regions*, 201–2.

148   "The red-faced, apoplectic chanticleer": Richard Burton, *Lake Regions*, 239.

149   On a good day, the expedition would leave: Richard Burton, *Lake Regions*, 239.

149   "We were wretched": Richard Burton, *Lake Regions*, 75.

149   "formed by nature": Richard Burton, *Lake Regions*, 107–9.

150   "Kicking and plunging, rearing and pawing": Richard Burton, *Lake Regions*, 49.

150   "The asses shy, stumble, rear": Richard Burton, *Lake Regions*, vol. 1, 281.

150   A notoriously vicious donkey: Richard Burton, *Lake Regions*, vol. 1, 201.

150   "cast adrift in the wilderness": Richard Burton, *Lake Regions*, 153.

150   One night, the men were woken: Richard Burton, *Lake Regions*, 57, 59, 62.

151   "The tall stiff trees groaned": Richard Burton, *Lake Regions*, 65.

151   "The earth . . . emits the odor": Richard Burton, *Lake Regions*, 78.

151   "The humidity of the atmosphere": Richard Burton, *Lake Regions*, 80.

151   Wood mildewed, match heads shrank: Richard Burton, *Lake Regions*, 80.

151   "Night after night, at the end": Richard Burton, *Zanzibar*, vol. 2, 388.

152   "led the hardest of lives": Richard Burton, *Zanzibar*, vol. 2, 377.

152   "No apology is offered": Richard Burton, *Lake Regions*, 87–88.

152   "My first occupation was to map the country": Adrian Wisnicki, "Cartographical Quandaries: The Limits of Knowledge Production in Burton's and Speke's Search for the Source of the Nile," 471.

153   "large blue-bells upon the trees": Richard Burton, *Lake Regions*, 72.

153   They passed herds of quietly grazing zebra: Isabel Burton, *Life*, vol. 1, 285.

153   "the porters regard with a wholesome awe": Richard Burton, *Lake Regions*, 72.

153   Even elephants seemed to prefer: Richard Burton, *Lake Regions*, 210.

154   "bulldog head and powerful mandibles": *The Life*, vol. 1, 285.

154 attacking "man and beast ferociously": Richard Burton, *Lake Regions*, 72.

154 "This peculiarity," he argued, "being confined": Richard Burton, *Lake Regions*, 210.

155 When Livingstone was a young man: David Livingstone, *Missionary Travels and Researches in South Africa*, 1858, 11–12.

156 "Burton has always been ill": Speke to Shaw, July 2, 1858, RGS.

156 "When lying in bed, my toes": John Hanning Speke, "Captain Speke's Discovery of the Victoria Nyanza, the Supposed Source of the Nile—Part III," *Blackwood's Edinburgh Magazine*, November 1859, 572; John Hanning Speke, *What Led*, 104.

156 "Unaccustomed to sickness": Richard Burton, *Zanzibar*, vol. 2, 388.

156 "I had during the fever-fit": Richard Burton, *Lake Regions*, 74.

157 "A single large body": Richard Burton, *Lake Regions*, 128.

157 "Trembling with ague": Richard Burton, *Lake Regions*, 156.

158 "He … advanced mechanically": Richard Burton, *Lake Regions*, 156.

158 "Death," he wrote, "appeared stamped": Richard Burton, *Lake Regions*, 157.

158 "For the first time since many days": Richard Burton, *Lake Regions*, 159–60.

158 "We were saddened by the sight": Richard Burton, *Lake Regions*, 128.

158 "The land is stony and rugged": Richard Burton, *Lake Regions*, 128.

159 "Said bin Salim, to whom": Richard Burton, *Lake Regions*, 77.

159 Whenever an easily edible animal: Richard Burton, *Lake Regions*, 243.

159 "Man revenges himself": Richard Burton, *Lake Regions*, 149.

159 "I calculated our rate of expenditure": John Hanning Speke, *What Led*, 59.

160 "We are still suffering": Burton to Hamerton, September 6, 1857, BL.

160 "with swimming head and trembling hands": Richard Burton, *Lake Regions*, 77.

160 "Sir, I have taken the liberty": Burton to British consul at Zanzibar, October, 1857, BL.

CHAPTER TWELVE: TANGANYIKA

162 "Snay had travelled as much as": John Hanning Speke, "Captain Speke's Discovery of the Victoria Nyanza, the Supposed Source of the Nile—Part II," *Blackwood's Edinburgh Magazine*, October 1859, 394.

163   "The missionaries had run three lakes": John Hanning Speke, *What Led,* 59–60.

163   "journeying westward to the smaller waters": John Hanning Speke, "Captain Speke's Discovery of the Victoria Nyanza, the Supposed Source of the Nile—Part II," 394.

163   he "saw at once that the existence": Richard Burton, *Lake Regions,* 389.

164   A week after they arrived in Kazeh: Richard Burton, *Lake Regions,* 260.

164   who was "laid up by a shaking ague": Richard Burton, *Lake Regions,* 260.

164   "I thought Captain Burton would die": John Hanning Speke, *What Led,* 60.

164   Although he would remain in Kazeh: Richard Burton, *Lake Regions,* 418.

164   "in truth, more dead than alive": Richard Burton, *Lake Regions,* 263.

165   "Doubtlessly impressed with the belief": Richard Burton, *Lake Regions,* 266.

165   "The attack had reached its height": *The Life,* vol. 1, 295.

165   "the principal labor of the expedition": *The Life,* vol. 1, 295.

165   "with the resolve to do or die": *The Life,* vol. 1, 295.

166   "The few books—Shakespeare": Richard Burton, *Zanzibar,* vol. 2, 388–89.

166   "If one of us was lost": *The Life,* vol. 1, 295.

166   "My companion, whose blood": Richard Burton, *Lake Regions,* 275–76.

166   an "inky blot" on his eyes: Richard Burton, *Lake Regions,* 276.

166   "inflammation of the iris": Letter from Speke's eye doctor, Sir William Bowman, in John Hanning Speke, "Journal of a Cruise on the Tanganyika Lake, Central Africa," *Blackwood's Edinburgh Magazine,* September 1859, 342.

167   "rendered reading a painful task": Richard Burton, *Zanzibar,* vol. 2, 373.

167   "In the case of ophthalmia": Robert Wilson, *History of the British Expedition to Egypt,* 310–11.

167   "purple-black with nimbus": Richard Burton, *Lake Regions,* 306.

168   "webs of flitting muscae": Richard Burton, *Lake Regions,* 276.

168   "I gazed in dismay": *The Life,* vol. 1, 298.

168   "A narrow strip of emerald green": Richard Burton, *Lake Regions,* 307.

169   "Forgetting toils, dangers": *The Life,* vol. 1, 298–99.

169   "one of the most beautiful inland seas": John Hanning Speke, "Journal of a Cruise on the Tanganyika Lake, Central Africa," 342.

169   "You may picture to yourself": John Hanning Speke, "Journal of a Cruise on the Tanganyika Lake, Central Africa," 342; John Hanning Speke, *What Led,* 61.

169   Carefully making their way down: Richard Burton, *Lake Regions,* 319.

170   After reaching Ujiji: Richard Burton, *Lake Regions,* 347.

170   As most of their candles: Richard Burton, *Lake Regions,* 262, 335.

170   "almost amphibious": Richard Burton, *Lake Regions,* 821.

171   "little cockle-shell canoes": John Hanning Speke, "Journal of a Cruise on the Tanganyika Lake, Central Africa," 343.

171   "The first aspect of these canoes": Richard Burton, *Lake Regions,* 338.

171   "I lay for a fortnight upon the earth": Richard Burton, *Lake Regions,* 333.

171   "First a crew had to be collected": John Hanning Speke, "Journal of a Cruise on the Tanganyika Lake, Central Africa," 342.

172   "curious distortion of face": Richard Burton, *Lake Regions,* 333.

172   With the help of Bombay: John Hanning Speke, "Journal of a Cruise on the Tanganyika Lake, Central Africa," 342.

172   By early March, Speke was ready: John Hanning Speke, "Journal of a Cruise on the Tanganyika Lake, Central Africa," 344.

172   "I litter down amidships": John Hanning Speke, "Journal of a Cruise on the Tanganyika Lake, Central Africa," 346.

173   "an ocean-tempest in miniature": John Hanning Speke, "Journal of a Cruise on the Tanganyika Lake, Central Africa," 348.

173   Should their canoe sink: Richard Burton, *Lake Regions,* 345.

173   "The traditions of Tanganyika hold": John Hanning Speke, "Journal of a Cruise on the Tanganyika Lake, Central Africa," 346.

174   "He went his course, struggling up": John Hanning Speke, *What Led,* 67–68.

175   The infection left behind by the beetle: John Hanning Speke, *What Led,* 67–68.

175   "It was not altogether an unmixed evil": John Hanning Speke, "Journal of a Cruise on the Tanganyika Lake, Central Africa," 350.

175   The beetle itself, dead: John Hanning Speke, *What Led,* 67–68.

175   "The dhow I had come for": John Hanning Speke, "Journal of a Cruise on the Tanganyika Lake, Central Africa," 352.

175   "She looked very graceful": John Hanning Speke, "Journal of a
       Cruise on the Tanganyika Lake, Central Africa," 355.

176   "Feeling now satisfied": John Hanning Speke, "Journal of a Cruise
       on the Tanganyika Lake, Central Africa," 355–56.

177   "His paraphernalia were in a similar state": Richard Burton, *Lake
       Regions*, 336.

177   "Although I did not venture on it": John Hanning Speke, "Journal
       of a Cruise on the Tanganyika Lake, Central Africa," 352.

177   "When we compared statements": Richard Burton, *Lake Regions*,
       336–37.

177   "We had no other resource": John Hanning Speke, "Captain
       Speke's Discovery of the Victoria Nyanza, the Supposed Source of
       the Nile—Part II," 391.

178   The son of a local sultan visited the men: Richard Burton, *Lake
       Regions*, 353.

178   After asking Bombay about Speke's conversation: Richard Burton,
       Lake Regions, 353.

178   While on the journey to the Rusizi: Richard Burton, *Lake Regions*,
       354.

179   After living on nothing but milk: *The Life*, vol. 1, 303.

179   "I naturally inquired": Richard Burton, *Lake Regions*, 358.

179   "Old Want began to stare at us": Richard Burton, *Lake Regions*,
       360–61.

179   "Had this timely supply not reached us": John Hanning Speke,
       "Captain Speke's Discovery of the Victoria Nyanza, the Supposed
       Source of the Nile—Part II," 393.

180   "They were the first received": Richard Burton, *Lake Regions*, 361.

180   Burton had warned of the simmering resentment: Richard Bur-
       ton, *Personal Narrative*, 38.

180   "He was a loss to his country": Richard Burton, *Lake Regions*, 65.

180   "The consul's death," he wrote: Richard Burton, *Lake Regions*, 65.

180   "Such tidings are severely felt": Richard Burton, *Lake Regions*, 387.

181   "was fated to resemble a flight": Richard Burton, *Lake Regions*,
       378.

CHAPTER THIRTEEN: TO THE END OF THE WORLD

182   "You can employ the time": John Hanning Speke, *What Led*, 75.

182   "the charm of the scenery": Richard Burton, *Lake Regions*, 381.

183   "Almost every one had lost": Richard Burton, *Lake Regions*, 387.

183   "Stronger than any physical relief": Richard Burton, *Lake Regions,*
        389.

184   "This is a shocking country for sport": Speke to Shaw, July 2, 1858,
        RGS.

184   "Up to the present time": Speke to Shaw, July 2, 1858, RGS.

184   "a little sour": *The Life,* vol. 1, 290.

185   "I should proceed alone": John Hanning Speke, "Captain Speke's
        Discovery of the Victoria Nyanza, the Supposed Source of the
        Nile—Part II," *Blackwood's Edinburgh Magazine,* October 1859, 393.

185   "This man called the river Kivira": John Hanning Speke, "Captain
        Speke's Discovery of the Victoria Nyanza, the Supposed Source of
        the Nile—Part II," 395.

185   "My companion, who had recovered": Richard Burton, writing
        from Unyanyembe, July 2, 1858, published in the *Proceedings of the
        Royal Geographical Society,* January 24, 1859.

186   "The difficulty was exaggerated": Richard Burton, *Lake Regions,*
        390.

186   "The Arabs at Unyanyembé": John Hanning Speke, *What Led,* 95.

186   "What knowledge of Asiatic customs": Richard Burton, *Lake
        Regions,* 411.

186   "I begged for leave to take": John Hanning Speke, *What Led,* 75.

186   "that it was as much his duty": John Hanning Speke, "Captain
        Speke's Discovery of the Victoria Nyanza, the Supposed Source of
        the Nile—Part II," 396.

187   "positively forbade his going": John Hanning Speke, *What Led,* 116;
        Richard Burton, *Lake Regions,* 390.

187   Soon after word got out: Speke, "Captain Speke's Discovery of the
        Victoria Nyanza, the Supposed Source of the Nile—Part II," 396.

187   "It was for this youth": John Hanning Speke, "Captain Speke's Dis-
        covery of the Victoria Nyanza, the Supposed Source of the Nile—
        Part II," 397.

187   Told that it would take him roughly: John Hanning Speke, *What
        Led,* 80.

188   To help carry their provisions: Speke, "Captain Speke's Discov-
        ery of the Victoria Nyanza, the Supposed Source of the Nile—
        Part II," 408.

188   "The white beads which I have brought": John Hanning Speke,
        "Captain Speke's Discovery of the Victoria Nyanza, the Supposed
        Source of the Nile—Part II," 400.

188   "begged that I would cast his horoscope": John Hanning Speke,

"Captain Speke's Discovery of the Victoria Nyanza, the Supposed Source of the Nile—Part II," 403.

188   To protect them from the searing sun: John Hanning Speke, "Captain Speke's Discovery of the Victoria Nyanza, the Supposed Source of the Nile—Part II," 410–11.

189   "The vast expanse of the pale-blue waters": John Hanning Speke, *What Led*, 92.

189   "If any way of going round": John Hanning Speke, *What Led*, 96.

189   Another man, who had traveled extensively: John Hanning Speke, *What Led*, 94.

190   "I no longer felt any doubt": John Hanning Speke, "Captain Speke's Discovery of the Victoria Nyanza, the Supposed Source of the Nile—Part II," 412.

190   "This is a far more extensive lake": John Hanning Speke, "Captain Speke's Discovery of the Victoria Nyanza, the Supposed Source of the Nile—Part II," 412.

190   "I felt as much tantalised": John Hanning Speke, *What Led*, 98.

191   Using Indian cotton-tape: Richard Burton, *Lake Regions*, 407–9.

191   I "expressed my regret": John Hanning Speke, *What Led*, 111.

192   "It was an inspiration perhaps": Richard Burton, *Lake Regions*, 410–11.

192   "Jack, wholly ignorant of Arabic": *The Life*, vol. 1, 314.

192   "By a tacit agreement it was": Richard Burton, *Lake Regions*, 412.

192   "We will go home": *The Life*, vol. 2, 424.

193   "resigned myself to my fate": *Journal of the Royal Geographical Society of London*, NLS, in Maitland, *Speke*, 143.

CHAPTER FOURTEEN: THE KNIVES ARE SHEATHED

197   He had begun to show signs: Richard Burton, *Lake Regions*, 429.

198   "full of vermin": Richard Burton, *Lake Regions*, 429.

198   "half stupefied by pain": Richard Burton, *Lake Regions*, 429.

198   "thus relieving the excruciating and torturing twinges": Richard Burton, *Lake Regions*, 429.

198   "He was once more haunted": Richard Burton, *Lake Regions*, 430.

199   "He was awfully grieved": *The Life*, vol. 1, 322.

199   "Fearing that increased weakness": Richard Burton, *Lake Regions*, 430.

199   "The knives," he said, "are sheathed": *The Life*, vol. 1, 322.

200   "Said bin Salim had long forfeited": *The Life*, vol. 1, 323.

200   "after receiving and returning news": Richard Burton, *Lake Regions,* 437.

201   "Jack and I caught sight of the sea": *The Life,* vol. 1, 326.

201   "We lost nearly all our crew": Richard Burton, *Lake Regions,* 528.

201   "The dead are buried amongst the living": Christopher Rigby, *Rigby,* 79.

202   "Sick and way-worn": Richard Burton, *Lake Regions,* 523.

202   In March of the previous year: Christopher Rigby, *Rigby,* 71.

203   "The consulate was no longer": *The Life,* vol. 1, 327.

203   It did not help that Burton openly: J. W. Heldring, *The Killing of Dr. Albrecht Roscher,* 189.

203   "Contrast Rigby's scruples as a host": Christopher Rigby, *Rigby,* 247, footnote.

203   "Arrived at Zanzibar, he fell into bad hands": Richard Burton, *Zanzibar,* vol. 2, 389.

203   "Had I not been with him": Speke to Rigby, October 6, 1860, in Rigby, *Rigby.*

203   "When I had reason to ask him": Speke to Rigby, October 6, 1860.

204   "Speke is a right good, jolly": Rigby to Miles, March 26, 1859, in Rigby, *Rigby.*

204   Even before he had learned: Burton to Shaw, June 24, 1858, RGS.

205   "As it appeared to me that Colonel Hamerton": Rigby to H. L. Anderson, Secretary to Government, Bombay, in Rigby, *Rigby,* 246.

205   "Our followers were to receive": *The Life,* vol. 1, 310.

206   "Jack agreed with me thoroughly": Richard Burton, *Lake Regions,* Appendix II, 553.

206   "desire to see me depart": Richard Burton, *Zanzibar,* vol. 2, 389.

206   "I was unwilling to leave": Richard Burton, *Lake Regions,* 525.

207   Rigby's "place . . . was well filled up": Richard Burton, *Lake Regions,* 526.

207   "the fever . . . clung to me like the shirt of Nessus": Richard Burton, *Lake Regions,* 526. In Greek mythology, the Shirt of Nessus was a poisoned tunic that killed Heracles.

207   Steinhaüser "repeatedly warned me": Richard Burton, *Zanzibar,* vol. 2, 389.

207   After leaving China, Oliphant had woken: Ann Taylor, *Laurence Oliphant,* 63–64.

208   "did not take leave of his host": Richard Burton, *Zanzibar,* vol. 2, 390.

208   "I shall hurry up, Jack": *The Life,* vol. 1, 327.

209 "Capt. Speke...will lay before you": Burton to RGS, April 19, 1859, BL.

209 "He was persuaded to act": Richard Burton, *Zanzibar*, vol. 2, 390.

209 "Burton was a jealous man": As Isabel Burton recalled Speke telling her, related in Isabel's annotations in *The Life*, vol. 1, 424–25.

CHAPTER FIFTEEN: 'TWAS ME HE SHOT

210 "I may have told you before": Speke to Shaw, May 8, 1859, RGS.

210 "We talked the whole matter over": Clements Markham, *The Fifty Years' Work of the Royal Geographical Society*.

211 "Sir Roderick," Markham noted, "at once took him up": Clements Markham, *The Fifty Years' Work of the Royal Geographical Society*.

212 During his second term, Murchison: S. H. Beaver, "Geography in the British Association for the Advancement of Science," *The Geographical Journal* 148, no. 2 (July 1982): 173–81.

212 "second in popularity and utility to no other": R. C. Bridges, "Sir John Speke and the Royal Geographical Society," 27.

212 "These were the days when": Richard Burton, *Zanzibar*, vol. 2, 390–91.

213 "Many of us are well acquainted": Extracts from "Reports by Captains Burton and Speke, of the East African Expedition, on Their Discovery of Lake Ujiji &c., in Central Africa," *Proceedings of the Royal Geographical Society of London* 3, no. 3 (1858–1859).

213 "Sir Roderick, I need only say": John Hanning Speke, *Journal of the Discovery*, 31.

214 "Speke," he said, "we must send you there again": John Hanning Speke, *Journal of the Discovery*, 31.

214 "the hero of the hour": *The Life*, vol. 1, 330.

214 "much against my own inclination": *The Life*, vol. 1, 328.

214 "My companion now stood forth": Richard Burton, *Zanzibar*, vol. 2, 391.

214 "no man can better appreciate": Richard Burton, *Nile Basin*, 6.

214 "Jack is one of the bravest fellows": *The Life*, vol. 1, 331.

215 "You have alluded, Sir": John Hanning Speke, *The Journal of the Royal Geographical Society of London*, vol. 29, 1859.

215 "dwell upon the discovery": John Hanning Speke, *The Journal of the Royal Geographical Society of London*, v. 29, 1859.

216 "We shall confine our notice": "The Geographical Society," *The Examiner*, June 18, 1859.

216   An explorer and mathematician, Galton: Dorothy Middleton, "The Search for the Nile Sources," *The Geographical Journal* 238 (June 1972): 211.

217   "Burton was a man of eccentric genius": Francis Galton, *Memories of My Life*, 199.

217   "I do not recollect of any passage": Blackwood to Eliot, in Roland F. Anderson, "George Eliot Provoked," *Modern Philology* 71 (August 1973).

218   "Not a man killed nor a fellow tortured": Burton to Milnes, May 31, 1863, HPTC.

218   "He took great delight": *The Bookman*, October 1891.

219   "He said it was so funny": *The Life*, vol. 1, 397.

219   "His usual conversation in those days": Francis Galton, *Memories of My Life*, 202.

219   "Since I came home I have had": Speke to Rigby, September 3, 1859, NLS.

220   "On proposing to go to the Lakes": Speke to Rigby, September 3, 1859, NLS.

221   "We have had a very interesting visitor": Blackwood to Eliot, August 15, 1859, NLS.

221   "As a great number of friends": John Hanning Speke, "Journal of a Cruise on the Tanganyika Lake, Central Africa," *Blackwood's Edinburgh Magazine*, September 1859.

222   Burton "tells me that he has written": Speke to Shaw, October 28, 1859, RGS.

222   "his regret that the gold medal": Speke to Rigby, January 19, 1860, in Rigby, *Rigby*; Speke to Shaw, January 17, 1860, in Rigby, *Rigby*.

223   "I am sure everybody at Zanzibar": Speke to Rigby, October 6, 1860, in Rigby, *Rigby*.

223   "I consider it positively iniquitous": Speke to Rigby, April 6, 1859, in Rigby, *Rigby*.

223   "Captain Speke since his departure": Rigby to H. L. Anderson, Secretary to Government, Bombay, July 15, 1859, in *Lake Regions,* Appendix II, 551.

224   "I must express my extreme surprise": Burton to Bombay Government, November 11, 1859, in *Lake Regions,* Appendix II, 553–54.

225   "Sir,—I have been indebted": Burton to Rigby, January 16, 1860, in *The Life,* vol. 2, 575–76.

226   "achieved results of such importance": RGS, Minutes Books of the

Expedition Committee Meeting, December 2, 1859, and January 10, 1860.

226 "in the opinion of the Committee": RGS, Minutes Books of the Expedition Committee Meeting, December 2, 1859, and January 10, 1860.

226 "Having taken into consideration": J. Cosmo Melville to Burton, January 14, 1860, in *Lake Regions*, Appendix II, 555.

226 "I represented the whole question to Captain Rigby": Burton to Melville, in *Lake Regions*, Appendix II, 555.

227 "Of all the painful things": Speke to Rigby, December 2, 1859, NLS.

227 "weak legs and rotten gut": Speke to Rigby, October 17, 1859, NLS; Speke to Rigby, November 25, 1859, NLS.

227 "Burton I believe will require": Speke to Rigby, December 2, 1859, NLS.

227 "He had doubtless been taught": Richard Burton, *Zanzibar*, vol. 2, 392.

227 "I taught him archery by day": Richard Burton, *Zanzibar*, vol. 2, 389.

CHAPTER SIXTEEN: AN EXILE'S DREAM

228 She had written to him faithfully: Isabel Burton, *The Romance of Isabel Lady Burton*, 150.

229 "How curious it would have been": Isabel Burton, *The Romance of Isabel Lady Burton*, 109.

229 "That brow which rose": Isabel Burton, "We Try to Effect a Reconciliation," *The Life*, vol. 1, 329.

230 "I feel strange": Isabel Burton, *The Romance of Isabel Lady Burton*, 149.

230 "I felt quite stunned": Isabel Burton, *The Romance of Isabel Lady Burton*, 150.

230 "He had had twenty-one attacks": Isabel Burton, *The Romance of Isabel Lady Burton*, 150.

231 "He was still...my earthly god and king": Isabel Burton, *The Romance of Isabel Lady Burton*, 151.

231 "When I came home to you": Isabel Burton, "My Appeal to My Mother," *The Life*, vol. 1, 333.

232 Georgiana Stisted, Burton's niece: Georgiana Stisted, "Reminiscences of Sir Richard Burton."

232 "I begin to believe": Burton to Luke Burke, June 9, 1861(?), HL.

233 "Now Mezzofanti is dead": Giuseppe Caspar Mezzofanti was an Italian cardinal who spoke thirty-eight languages.

233 "He leads a good life": Isabel Burton, "My Appeal to My Mother," *The Life,* vol. 1, 332–37.

234 "The only answer to this letter": Isabel Burton, "My Appeal to My Mother," *The Life,* vol. 1, 337.

234 The only option left them: Isabel Burton, "My Appeal to My Mother," *The Life,* vol. 1, 332.

235 "His mind slowly gave way": Georgiana Stisted, *The True Life of Capt. Sir Richard F. Burton,* 163–64.

235 He had not spoken: Georgiana Stisted, *The True Life of Capt. Sir Richard F. Burton,* 163–64.

235 "I was driven out of town by an intense longing": Burton to Milnes, Dover, [no date] 1859.

236 "Everybody remarked he looked ill": Georgiana Stisted, *The True Life of Capt. Sir Richard F. Burton,* 252.

236 "All that summer he seemed": Georgiana Stisted, "Reminiscences of Sir Richard Burton," 406.

CHAPTER SEVENTEEN: HARD AS BRICKS

237 "Tell Bombay I was swelling": Speke to Rigby, August 3, 1859, NLS.

238 "a chap who won't go to the devil": Alexander Maitland, *Speke,* 111.

238 "The queerest, coolest fish in Rugby": Thomas Hughes, *Tom Brown's School Days,* London, Macmillan, 1857, 119.

239 "I hear Smyth is feverishly inclined": Speke to Shaw, October 26, 1857, RGS.

239 In the end, the perfect companion: "I volunteered to accompany him; my offer was at once accepted," Grant, quoted in "Nile Basins and Nile Explorers," *Blackwood's Edinburgh Magazine* 97 (January–June 1865): 102.

239 "Mother thinks no end of our friend": Speke to Shaw, April 15, 1860, RGS.

239 "I feel I never shall be robbed": Speke to Rigby, August 3, 1859, NLS.

240 "a most valuable production": Speke to John Blackwood, Sunday, no date, 1859, NLS.

241 "It was far from my thoughts": John Petherick, *Travels in Central Africa,* 78.

241 "The interest...is much more intense": Speke to Petherick, October 1859, in John Petherick, *Travels in Central Africa,* 9.

241 "I have asked Petherick to come here": Speke to Shaw, October 1859, RGS.

241 "like a rampant hippopotamus": Speke to Blackwood, April 11, 1860, NLS.

241 "Petherick much to the amusement of the girls": Speke to Blackwood, April 18, 1860, NLS.

242 "The expense of such an expedition": John Petherick, *Travels in Central Africa,* 89–90.

242 The Royal Geographical Society attempted only: R. C. Bridges, "Sir John Speke and the Royal Geographical Society," 34.

243 "I may say," he later wrote, "that the attachment": Francis Galton, *Memories of My Life,* 200–201.

243 "I hereby agree to accompany": James Grant Papers, NLS.

244 "He used to snub me so unpleasantly": Speke to Shaw, October 28, 1859, RGS.

244 "Burton and I met at the R.G. Society today": Speke to Rigby, November 25, 1859, NLS.

244 he did not "wish to have any further": Burton to Shaw, November 1859, RGS.

244 "I cannot leave England addressing you": Speke to Burton, April 16, 1860, BL.

245 "Sir, I have received your note": Burton to Speke, April 18, 1860, BL.

CHAPTER EIGHTEEN: THE PRINCE

249 "He was delighted to see us": John Hanning Speke, *Journal of the Discovery,* 8.

250 "Colonel Rigby now gave me": John Hanning Speke, *Journal of the Discovery,* 13.

250 "All our previous information": John Hanning Speke, *Journal of the Discovery,* 264.

250 "I christened the Lake after the Queen": Quoted in Mary S. Lovell, *A Rage to Live,* 324.

251 "My views...about retaining native": Richard Burton, *Zanzibar,* vol. 2, 393.

252 "The payment of these men's wages": John Hanning Speke, *Journal of the Discovery,* 13–14.

252   "He is a very dear friend": Speke to Rigby, December 12, 1860, NLS.

252   "not a shade of jealousy or distrust": Grant quoted in Oliphant, "Nile Basins and Nile Explorers," *Blackwood's Edinburgh Magazine* 97 (January–June 1865): 102.

252   "Notice. If I die": James Grant Papers, NLS.

252   As he patiently awaited: James Grant, *A Walk Across Africa*, 18–19.

253   He "set out on the march": John Hanning Speke, *Journal of the Discovery*, 245.

253   "The Sultan's men slip away": Speke to Rigby, no month, day 3rd, 1860, NLS.

254   "Should they desert": John Hanning Speke, *Journal of the Discovery*, 28.

254   "We had to trust to chance": James Grant, *A Walk Across Africa*, 31.

254   While the others hunched dejectedly: James Grant, *A Walk Across Africa*, 31–32.

255   "The symptoms, altogether": John Hanning Speke, *Journal of the Discovery*, 144–45.

255   "Thinking then how I could best": John Hanning Speke, *Journal of the Discovery*, 150.

255   Grant suffered from frequent fevers: James Grant, *A Walk Across Africa*, 152.

256   "I have heard today from Rigby": Speke to Blackwood, October 1, 1860, NLS.

256   "We have been so strongly recommended": Georgina Speke to John Blackwood, September 25, 1861, NLS.

256   "All right & ready to fight": Speke to Blackwood, February 1, 1861, BL.

257   "If the Society only knew": Speke to Rigby, October 22, 1860, NLS.

257   By now only two kingdoms: In Karagwe, while Speke impatiently waited to be allowed to continue his journey, he convinced one of the king's sisters-in-law and her daughter to let him take their measurements. Both of the women, prized for their beauty, had been forced to gain so much weight they could barely stand. The girl, who was only sixteen, sat "sucking at a milk-pot, on which the father kept her at work by holding a rod in his hand, for as fattening is the first duty of fashionable female life, it must be duly enforced by the rod if necessary," Speke wrote. "Her features were lovely, but her body was as round as a ball."

257   "I struck out on my claim": John Hanning Speke, *Journal of the Discovery*, 284.

258   "I had made up my mind": John Hanning Speke, *Journal of the Discovery*, 288.

258   "I could neither sit in the sun": John Hanning Speke, *Journal of the Discovery*, 310–11.

258   As heavily as he relied on Bombay: John Hanning Speke, *Journal of the Discovery*, 231–32.

259   "How can we go?" John Hanning Speke, *Journal of the Discovery*, 270–71.

259   "It was the first and last time": John Hanning Speke, *Journal of the Discovery*, 271–72.

260   The trader, he believed: "Considering your promise to keep two or three boats two or three years for me," Speke later wrote to Petherick, "I sacrifice everything to fulfil the engagement." Speke to Petherick, March 28, 1862, in John Petherick, *Travels in Central Africa*, 117.

260   "The new year was ushered in": John Hanning Speke, *Journal of the Discovery*, 242.

260   "You will have to drop your dignity": Speke to Petherick, March 28, 1862, in John Petherick, *Travels in Central Africa*, 116–17.

261   "One thing only now embarrassed me": John Hanning Speke, *Journal of the Discovery*, 244–45.

261   "At the time I was positively unable": James Grant, *A Walk Across Africa*, 246–47.

262   "Here at last I stood on the brink": John Hanning Speke, *Journal of the Discovery*, 459.

262   "shave their heads and bathe": John Hanning Speke, *Journal of the Discovery*, 461.

262   "What a place, I thought to myself": John Hanning Speke, *Journal of the Discovery*, 479.

262   "We could no more throw off": John Hanning Speke, *Journal of the Discovery*, 433.

262   "The expedition had now performed": John Hanning Speke, *Journal of the Discovery*, 467.

263   "as if I only wanted a wife and family": John Hanning Speke, *Journal of the Discovery*, 470.

264   "a mysterious silence": John Hanning Speke, *Journal of the Discovery*, 601.

264   "I had a wild hope": Dorothy Middleton, "The Search for the Nile Sources," *The Geographical Journal* 238 (June 1972): 216.

265   After Baker had shared with Speke: John Hanning Speke, *Journal of the Discovery*, 603.

265   "I naturally felt much annoyed": John Hanning Speke, *Journal of the Discovery*, 607.

265   As his expedition was severely depleted: John Hanning Speke, *Journal of the Discovery*, 606.

265   Four days later, Petherick and his wife: John Petherick, *Travels in Central Africa*, 119, 126, 131.

266   Before he even stepped out of his boat: John Petherick, *Travels in Central Africa*, 127–28.

266   That night, Speke agreed to dine: John Petherick, *Travels in Central Africa*, 20.

CHAPTER NINETEEN: DAMN THEIR SOULS

268   "a blaze of light, without a focus": Isabel Burton, *The Life*, 32.

268   "He was one of the very few": Richard Burton, *Zanzibar*, vol. 1, 14–15.

269   "I'll tell you what it is": Burton journal, British Museum.

270   Fascinated by scalping: Richard Burton, *The City of the Saints*, 112.

270   "I do not believe that an Indian": Richard Burton, *The City of the Saints*, 115.

270   "to instruct him is the surest way": John Hanning Speke, *What Led*, 111.

270   "Priests may be good servants": Richard Burton, *Two Trips to Gorilla Land and the Cataracts of the Congo*, 1876, chapter 16.

271   "The first impression left upon my mind": Richard Burton, *The City of the Saints*, 245.

271   "all those who have many wives": John Hanning Speke, "Captain Speke's Discovery of the Victoria Nyanza, the Supposed Source of the Nile—Part II," *Blackwood's Edinburgh Magazine*, October 1859, 409.

271   "The literalism with which the Mormons": Richard Burton, *The City of Saints*, 430.

272   "I was walking out with two friends": *The Life*, vol. 1, 337.

272   "If I had not the courage to risk it": *The Life*, vol. 1, 338.

272   She was "going to marry": *The Life*, vol. 1, 337.

273   "live like a vegetable": Isabel Burton, *The Romance of Isabel Lady Burton*, 66.

273   Finally beginning to feel physically prepared: Isabel Burton, *The Romance of Isabel Lady Burton*, 162–65.

274   "I consent with all my heart": *The Life*, vol. 1, 340–41.

274   Wearing a white bonnet: *The Life*, vol. 1, 342.

274   "a very large sign of the Cross": Isabel Burton, *The Romance of Isabel Lady Burton*, 106.

275   "Now, Burton, tell me": Isabel Burton, *The Romance of Isabel Lady Burton*, 166.

275   Not long after his wedding: *The Life*, vol. 1, 345.

275   "Needless to say I have gratefully": Burton to Milnes, March 20, 1861, HPTC.

276   "They'd never send him": Frank Harris, *Contemporary Portraits*, vol. 1, 192.

276   "At the age of forty": *The Life*, vol. 1, 345–46.

276   "Under normal circumstances": Richard Burton, *Zanzibar*, vol. 1, 183.

277   "To be first in such matters": Richard Burton, *A Mission to Gelele, King of Dahome*, 1864, 241.

277   "You are a good man": Richard Burton, "Narrative of a Trip to Harar," *The Journal of the Royal Geographical Society of London*, vol. 25, 1855.

277   "I must keep my hand in": Burton to Blackwood, January 9, 1861, quoted in Mary Blackwood Porter, *Annals of a Publishing House: William Blackwood and His Sons*, vol. 3., Edinburgh: W. Blackwood and Sons, 1897.

277   "uncommonly suicidal": Richard Burton, *Wanderings in West Africa from Liverpool to Fernando Po*, vol. 1, 66.

277   "confirm by inductive science": Robert Kenny, "From the Curse of Ham to the Curse of Nature," *The British Journal for the History of Science* 40, no. 3 (September 2007): 369.

278   "condemned to be the slave": John Hanning Speke, "Captain Speke's Discovery of the Victoria Nyanza, the Supposed Source of the Nile—Part III," *Blackwood's Edinburgh Magazine*, November 1859, 570.

278   "I cannot but congratulate ourselves": Richard Burton, *Memoirs Read Before the Anthropological Society of London*, vol. 1.

279   "Hardly had we begun": Richard Burton, *Wanderings in West Africa from Liverpool to Fernando Po*, vol. 1, 66.

CHAPTER TWENTY: NESTON PARK

281   Accustomed to a small: Richard Burton, *The Nile Basin*, 21.

281   Inside, dignitaries from the Count of Paris: "The Source of the Nile," *Oxford University Herald*, June 27, 1863.

281   Others would be disappointed altogether: "The Nile Discoveries," *The Caledonian Mercury*, June 24, 1863.

282   "To have solved the problem of ages": *Newcastle Chronicle*, August 29, 1863.

282   "my faithful children": John Hanning Speke, *Journal of the Discovery*, 611.

282   "I had promised to give them all": John Hanning Speke, *Journal of the Discovery*, 388.

282   Those who had deserted: Bridges, "Sir John Speke and the Royal Geographical Society," 37.

283   "he was sure the impatient": "The Nile Discoveries," *The Caledonian Mercury*, June 24, 1863.

283   "In the year 1858, when I discovered": *The Illustrated London News*, Supplement 43 (July 4, 1863): 17.

284   "The Council," he confided to Grant, "are displeased with him": Murchison to Grant, May 1864, RGS.

284   "very brief and imperfect character": James Casada, "James A. Grant and the Royal Geographical Society," 247.

284   "The council regret": "The Upper Basin of the Nile, from Inspection and Information," *Journal of the Royal Geographical Society of London*, vol. 33, 1863.

284   The Society also added footnotes: R. C. Bridges, "Sir John Speke and the Royal Geographical Society," 40.

285   "discredit the whole book": David Finkelstein, "Unraveling Speke: The Unknown Revision of an African Exploration Classic," 122.

285   he would "consent to have certain alterations made": Grant to Blackwood, 1863.

285   "Don't fear critics": Speke to Blackwood, March 30, 1863.

285   "He writes in such an abominable": David Finkelstein, "Unraveling Speke: The Unknown Revision of an African Exploration Classic," 122.

285   "Then ordering the return home": David Finkelstein, "Unraveling Speke: The Unknown Revision of an African Exploration Classic," 122.

286   "There is not a doubt of its being": David Finkelstein, "Unraveling Speke: The Unknown Revision of an African Exploration Classic," 122.

286   "Burton is a thorough good fellow": David Finkelstein, "Unraveling Speke: The Unknown Revision of an African Exploration Classic," 122.

286   "like an endless thread [that] required no end of breaking": Quoted in Finkelstein, "Unraveling Speke: The Unknown Revision of an African Exploration Classic," *History in Africa*, vol. 30, 2003, 122.

287   "Speke tells far too much": Rigby to Grant, July 30, 1864, NLS.

287   "Should you feel inclined": Speke to Petherick, in Burton, *The Nile Basin*, 170–71.

288   Speke had "met and dined with him": Blackwood to Speke, November 21, 1863.

288   Speke had given in: John Petherick, *Travels in Central Africa*, 139.

288   "The blow," he wrote, "was as hard": John Petherick, *Travels in Central Africa*, 140.

288   "Is it possible that Speke": John Petherick, *Travels in Central Africa*, 19.

288   "I wish to God I had never seen the beast": Speke to Blackwood, 1863.

289   "most unjustly brought against": R. C. Bridges, "Sir John Speke and the Royal Geographical Society," 38; Murchison to Grant, May 1864.

289   "thrown overboard without pity": Richard Burton, *The Nile Basin*, Part I, 192.

289   he was fortunate to be "clear of": Murchison to Grant, May 1864.

289   "I shall never travel": Speke to Blackwood, July 6, 1864, NLS.

290   "As I saw that some people": Murchison to Layard, July 1, 1864, BL.

291   "I understand from Murchison": Russell to Layard, June 1, 1864.

291   Instead, Murchison had placed his trust: R. C. Bridges, "The Sponsorship and Financing of Livingstone's Last Journey," *African Historical Studies*, 1968.

291   "A cold shiver comes over me": W. Garden Blaikie, *The Personal Life of David Livingstone*, 343.

291   "He had both a fine imaginative power": Bram Stoker, *Personal Reminiscences of Henry Irving*, xl.

292   "I am so sorry," she said he told her: *The Life*, vol. 1, 216.

292   "Such a breach once made": Richard Burton, *Zanzibar*, vol. 2, 393.

293   "if Burton appeared on the platform": *The Life*, vol. 1, 389.

293   "He worked upon Speke": *The Life*, vol. 1, 425.

293   "Forgive me," he said simply: *The Life*, vol. 1, 425, note.

294   "I shall never forget his face": *The Life*, vol. 1, 389.

295   "I could not but remark": Richard Burton, *Zanzibar*, vol. 2, 397–98.

295   After a long moment, someone called: *The Life*, vol. 1, 389.

296   "I was apprehensive of an accident": Fuller memorandum, February 1914.

296   The three men had been shooting: Davis deposition, London *Times*, September 17, 1864.

297   "Don't move me": London *Times*, September 24, 1864.

297   "Such a wound": Snow deposition, London *Times*, September 17, 1864.

CHAPTER TWENTY-ONE: THE WEARY HEART GROWS COLD

298   "crowded to suffocation": *The Life*, vol. 1, 405.

298   giving vent "to its impatience": *Bath Chronicle*, September 17, 1864.

299   After reading the note himself: Francis Galton, *Memories of My Life*, 202.

299   "All the great people were": *The Life*, vol. 1, 405.

299   he "sank into a chair": *The Life*, vol. 1, 389.

299   "I have to apologize": *Bath Chronicle*, September 17, 1864.

300   "that their most heartfelt condolence": *Bath Chronicle*, September 17, 1864.

300   Later that day, Clements Markham: *Bath Chronicle*, September 17, 1864.

301   Eleven days later: *Tiverton Gazette*, September 27, 1864.

301   "The bones of the traveller rest": *Tiverton Gazette*, September 27, 1864.

301   "Had I gone thither": James Grant, *A Walk Across Africa*, 347.

301   Now, clutching a wreath: Livingstone's journal, September 23, 1864.

302   "were audible over the whole": *Tiverton Gazette*, September 27, 1864.

302   "The deceased," they determined, "died from": London *Times*, September 17, 1864.

302   "Speke was the last man": London *Times*, September 19, 1864.

303   "By God," he was said: Jeremy Paxman, "Richard Burton, Victorian Explorer," *FT Magazine*, May 1, 2015.

303   "He wept long and bitterly": *The Life*, vol. 1, 426.

303   Speke "was not easily forgotten": Georgiana Stisted, *The True Life of Capt. Sir Richard F. Burton*, 252.

303   "Nothing will ever be known": Burton to Frank Wilson, December 21, 1864, ML.

303   "Had we met at Bath": Richard Burton, *The Nile Basin*, Part I, 24.

304   "Physically," a young foreign officer: Fawn Brodie, *The Devil Drives*, 244.

304   "Dismissal ignominious": Isabel Burton, *The Romance of Isabel Lady Burton*, 501.

304   "I am glad to say": *The Life*, vol. 1, 259.

304   "at the distance of many hundreds": Wilfrid Scawen Blunt, *My Diaries*, vol. 2, 128.

305   She was "very much amused": Isabel Burton, *The Inner Life of Syria, Palestine, and the Holy Land*, 224.

305   "Never had we known him": Georgiana Stisted, *The True Life of Capt. Sir Richard F. Burton*, 363.

306   "I could not have believed": Richard Burton, *Zanzibar*, vol. 1, 1–2.

306   "Captain Speke and Captain Burton can no longer": London *Times*, September 19, 1864.

306   "Why should 'the very controversy' ": Richard Burton, *The Athenaeum*, January 14, 1865.

307   "rather *infra dig* to discover a miss": Burton to Henry Walter Bates, January 18, 1872, RGS.

307   Bombay had been grief-stricken: Henry Morton Stanley, *How I Found Livingstone in Central Africa*, 271.

307   "The famous Bombay": Henry Morton Stanley, *How I Found Livingstone in Central Africa*, 27.

307   There, Stanley found Livingstone: Henry Morton Stanley, *How I Found Livingstone in Central Africa*, 331.

308   "I detest & shrink from": Henry Morton Stanley, diary, August 11, 1872, in Jeal, *The Impossible Life of Africa's Greatest Explorer*, 2008, 133.

308   "My success," Stanley wrote: Stanley to Rev. Horace Waller, July 29, 1872.

308   "has confirmed the discoveries": James Augustus Grant, "On Mr. H. M. Stanley's Exploration of the Victoria Nyanza," *Proceedings of the Royal Geographical Society*, November 29, 1875.

309   He and his old friend: "When a British Official Dodged Victorian Prudery to Publish the Kamasutra in English," *Quartz India*, June 27, 2019.

310   "Probably no European": Robert Irwin, *The Arabian Nights: A Companion*, 36.

310   "I have struggled for forty-seven years": *The Life*, vol. 1, 442.

310   "shown themselves fully equal": Richard Burton, *To the Gold Coast for Gold*, vol. 2, 1.

310   "Those who noticed the article": Richard Burton, "A Trip Up the Congo or Zaire River," *The Geographical Magazine*, July 1, 1875.

311   "Lies are one-legged": Richard Burton, "Terminal Essay," *The Arabian Nights*.

311   One night not long after: George Smalley, "Mr. Smalley on Capt. Burton," *New York Tribune*, no. 358, RAS.

311   Hearing a voice: George Smalley, "Mr. Smalley on Capt. Burton."

312   "I looked at him with that": George Smalley, "Sir Richard Burton: Some Personal Recollections of an Extraordinary Man," *New York Tribune*, November 2, 1890.

312   "You will find plenty": George Smalley, "Mr. Smalley on Capt. Burton."

313   "If a thousand buy it": Isabel Burton, editor's preface, *The Lusiads*.

313   "If a concurrence of adverse": Isabel Burton, editor's preface, *The Lusiads*, xvi. "Malebouche" is an Anglo-Norman noun meaning a "bad-mouth," or a person who is slander personified. Burton's motto comes from the epic poem *Gerusalemme liberata* by the sixteenth-century Italian poet Torquato Tasso, to whom he gives credit at the beginning of the book. Tasso's quote is: *"Brama assai, poco spera e nulla chiede."*

EPILOGUE: ASHES

316   A few months after Speke's funeral: Isabel Burton, "Who Last Wins," *Fraser's Magazine for Town and Country*, vol. 79, January–June 1869.

316   "I only took the cast after death": Isabel Burton, "Who Last Wins," *Fraser's Magazine for Town and Country*, vol. 79, January–June 1869.

317   "A Moulded mask at my feet": Isabel Burton, "Who Last Wins." Zingian was the ancient term for much of the coast of East Africa, referring to the Indian Ocean.

317   "the history of Noah": John Hanning Speke, "Captain Speke's Discovery of the Victoria Nyanza, the Supposed Source of the Nile—Part III," *Blackwood's Edinburgh Magazine*, November 1859, 570.

317   "the origin of Seedis, his caste": John Hanning Speke, "Captain Speke's Discovery of the Victoria Nyanza, the Supposed Source of the Nile—Part III, *Blackwood's Edinburgh Magazine*, November 1859, 570.

318   Speke's argument that the Hutu: John Hanning Speke, *Journal of the Discovery*, 203.

319   In a speech to the Royal Geographical Society: Adrian Wisnicki, "Cartographical Quandaries," 465.

320   "The history of exploration has often invited": The Hidden Histories Exhibition.

321   "Bombay Africans": The Royal Geographical Society presented an exhibit about Bombay Africans in 2008, as part of its Crossing Continents: Connecting Communities project.

322   "You know I suppose": Burton to Ouida (Maria Louise Ramé), April 2, 1886, BL.

323   "I don't care a button": *The Life*, vol. 1, 284.

323   "Do not let any one suppose": Isabel Burton, *The Romance of Isabel Lady Burton*, 723.

324   "always require *great care and watching*": Isabel Burton to Alice Bird, April 10, 1887.

324   "it was so fortunate": Burton had already published the book once—under the title *The Perfumed Garden*—but had never been happy with either the translation or the title.

324   "make a great row in England": Isabel Burton, *The Romance of Isabel Lady Burton*, 723–24.

324   as "the last happy day of my life": Burton, Isabel, *Life*, 529.

324   "To-morrow I shall have finished this": Isabel Burton, *The Romance of Isabel Lady Burton*, 723.

324   "What a happiness that will be": *The Life*, vol. 1, 410.

325   "I wish to go into a convent": Isabel Burton to Maria Stisted, quoted in an early biography of Burton: Thomas Wright, *The Life of Sir Richard Burton*, 246–47.

325   "abjured his heresy": Mary Lovell, *A Rage to Live*, 732.

325   "Rome took formal possession": Georgiana Stisted, *The True Life of Capt. Sir Richard F. Burton*, 414.

326   "Sobs were heard all around": *The Life,* vol. 1, 417.

326   "I remained for three days": Isabel Burton, *The Romance of Isabel Lady Burton,* 724.

326   "It was his *magnum opus*": Isabel Burton, *The Romance of Isabel Lady Burton,* 725.

326   As darkness fell, Isabel sat: Isabel Burton, *The Romance of Isabel Lady Burton,* 726.

327   "Sorrowfully, reverently": Isabel Burton, *The Romance of Isabel Lady Burton,* 726.

SELECT BIBLIOGRAPHY

Aga, Selim. *Incidents Connected with the Life of Selim Aga, a Native of Central Africa*. Aberdeen: W. Bennett, 1846.

Alpers, Edward A. *East Africa and the Indian Ocean*. Princeton: Markus Wiener Publishers, 2009.

———. *Ivory & Slaves in East Central Africa*. Berkeley: University of California Press, 1975.

Amarat, Habshi. *African Elites in India*. Ahmedabad: Mapin Publishing, 2006.

Baker, J. N. L. "John Hanning Speke." *The Geographical Journal* 128, no. 4 (December 1962): 385–88.

Banaji, D. R. *Bombay and the Sidis*. London: Macmillan, 1932.

Bassett, Thomas J. "Indigenous Mapmaking in Intertropical Africa." *History of Cartography*, vol. 2, book 3. Chicago: University of Chicago Press, 1987.

Blunt, Wilfrid Scawen. *My Diaries: Being a Personal Narrative of Events, 1888–1914*. New York: Alfred A. Knopf, 1923.

Bridges, R. C. "Europeans and East Africans in the Age of Exploration." *The Geographical Journal* 139, no. 2 (June 1973): 220–32.

———. "Sir John Speke and the Royal Geographical Society." *The Uganda Journal* 26, no. 1 (March 1962): 23–43.

Brodie, Fawn M. *The Devil Drives: A Life of Sir Richard Burton*. New York: W. W. Norton, 1967.

Burton, Isabel. *The Inner Life of Syria, Palestine, and the Holy Land: From My Private Journal*. London: Henry S. King & Co., 1876.

————. *The Life of Captain Sir Richard F. Burton,* volumes 1 and 2. London: Chapman & Hall, LD, 1893.

Burton, Isabel, and W. H. Wilkins. *The Romance of Isabel Lady Burton: The Story of Her Life.* New York: Dodd Mead & Company, 1897.

Burton, Richard F. *The Book of the Thousand Nights and a Night, A Plain and Literal Translation of the Arabian Nights' Entertainments, with Introduction Explanatory Notes on the Manners and Customs of Moslem Men and a Terminal Essay upon the History of the Nights.* Printed by the Burton Club for Private Subscribers Only, 1885.

————. *The City of the Saints "and Across the Rocky Mountains to California."* London: Longmans, 1861.

————. *First Footsteps in East Africa; or, An Exploration of Harar.* London: Tylston & Edwards, 1894.

————. *The Lake Regions of Central Africa.* New York: Harper & Brothers, 1860.

————, trans., Isabel Burton, ed. *The Lusiads.* London: Bernard Quaritch, 1880.

————. "Narrative of a Trip to Harar." *The Journal of the Royal Geographical Society of London,* vol. 25. London: John Murray, Albemarle Street, 1855, 136–50.

————. *The Nile Basin.* London: Tinsley Brothers, 1864.

————. *Personal Narrative of a Pilgrimage to Al-Madinah & Meccah,* vols. 1 and 2. New York: Dover, 1964.

————. *Wit and Wisdom from West Africa; or, a Book of Proverbial Philosophy, Idioms, Enigmas, and Laconisms.* London: Tinsley Brothers, 1865.

————. *Zanzibar: City, Island and Coast,* vols. 1 and 2. Honolulu: University Press of the Pacific, 2003.

Burton, Richard F., and Verney Lovett Cameron. *To the Gold Coast for Gold.* Charleston: BiblioBazaar, 2006.

Carnochan, W. B. *The Sad Story of Burton, Speke, and the Nile; or, Was John Hanning Speke a Cad?: Looking at the Evidence.* Stanford: Stanford General Books, 2006.

Casada, James A. "James A. Grant and the Royal Geographical Society." *The Geographical Journal* 140, no. 2 (June 1974): 245–53.

Casey, Bart. *The Double Life of Laurence Oliphant: Victorian Pilgrim and Prophet.* New York: Post Hill Press, 2015.

Cassanelli, Lee V. *The Shaping of Somali Society: Reconstructing the History of a Pastoral People, 1600-1900.* Philadelphia: University of Pennsylvania Press, 1982.

Clarke, Edward Daniel. *Travels in Various Countries of Europe, Asia and Africa,*

Part the Second: Greece Egypt and the Holy Land. London: T. Cadell and W. Davies Strand, 1814.

Collins, Robert O. *The Nile.* New Haven: Yale University Press, 2002.

Coupland, R. *East Africa and Its Invaders: From the Earliest Times to the Death of Seyyid Said in 1856.* Oxford: Clarendon Press, 1938.

Cummins, Joseph. *The War Chronicles: From Flintlocks to Machine Guns.* Beverly: Fair Winds Press, 2009.

De Silva Jayasuriya, Shihan, and Jean-Pierre Angenot. *Uncovering the History of Africans in Asia.* Leiden: Brill, 2008.

De Silva Jayasuriya, Shihan, and Richard Pankhurst, eds. *The African Diaspora in the Indian Ocean.* Asmara: Africa World Press/Brill, 2003.

Downs, Jonathan. *Discovery at Rosetta: The Ancient Stone That Unlocked the Mysteries of Ancient Egypt.* New York: Skyhorse, 2008.

Driver, Felix. "The Active Life: The Explorer as Biographical Subject." *Oxford Dictionary of National Biography,* 2005.

Dugard, Martin. *Into Africa: The Epic Adventures of Stanley & Livingstone.* New York: Broadway Books, 2003.

Fabian, Johannes. *Out of Our Minds: Reason and Madness in the Exploration of Central Africa.* Berkeley: University of California Press, 2000.

Finkelstein, David. "Unraveling Speke: The Unknown Revision of an African Exploration Classic." *History of Africa* 3 (2003): 117–32.

Galton, Francis. *The Art of Travel; or, Shifts and Contrivances Available in Wild Countries.* London: Phoenix Press, 1872.

———. *Memories of My Life.* London: Methuen & Co., 1908.

Geikie, Archibald. *Life of Sir Roderick I. Murchison.* London: John Murray, 1875.

Gilson Miller, Susan, trans. and ed. *Disorienting Encounters: Travels of a Moroccan Scholar in France in 1845–1846.* London: University of California Press, 1992.

Godsall, Jon R. *The Tangled Web: A Life of Sir Richard Burton.* Leicester: Matador, 2008.

Goldsmid, Sir Frederic John. *James Outram: A Biography,* vols. 1 and 2. London: Smith, Elder, & Co., 1880.

Grant, James Augustus. *A Walk Across Africa; or, Domestic Scenes from My Nile Journal.* London: William Blackwood & Sons, 1864.

Harris, Frank. *Contemporary Portraits.* New York: Mitchell Kennerley, 1915.

Hayman, John, ed. *Sir Richard Burton's Travels in Arabia and Africa: Four Lectures from a Huntington Library Manuscript.* San Marino: Huntington Library, 1990.

Heldring, J. W. *The Killing of Dr. Albrecht Roscher.* Bloomington: Xlibris, 2011.

Henderson, Philip. *The Life of Laurence Oliphant: Traveller, Diplomat and Mystic*. London: Robert Hale, 1956.

Hitchman, Francis. *Richard F. Burton, K.C.M.G., His Early Private and Public Life*, vols. 1 and 2. London: Sampson Low, Marston, Searle & Rivington, 1887.

Hopper, Mathew S. "East Africa and the End of the Indian Ocean Slave Trade." *Journal of African Development* 13, no. 1–2 (Spring–Fall 2011): 39–66.

Hoskote, Ranjit. *Hunchprose*. New Delhi: Penguin/Hamish Hamilton, 2021.

Humphries, John. *Search for the Nile's Source: The Ruined Reputation of John Petherick, Nineteenth-Century Welsh Explorer*. Cardiff: University of Wales Press, 2013.

Irwin, Robert. *The Arabian Nights: A Companion*. London: Allen Lane/Penguin, 1994.

Jeal, Tim. *Explorers of the Nile: The Triumph and Tragedy of a Great Victorian Adventure*. New Haven: Yale University Press, 2011.

Johnston, Harry Hamilton. *The Nile Quest: A Record of the Exploration of the Nile and Its Basin*. London: Lawrence & Bullen, 1903.

Jutzi, Alan, ed. *In Search of Sir Richard Burton: Papers from a Huntington Library Symposium*. San Marino: Huntington Library, 1993.

Karklins, Karlis. "Identifying Beads Used in the 19th-Century Central East Africa Trade." *BEADS: Journal of the Society of Bead Researchers*, vol. 4, 1992.

Kennedy, Dane. *The Highly Civilized Man: Richard Burton and the Victorian World*. Cambridge: Harvard University Press, 2005.

———. *The Last Blank Spaces: Exploring Africa and Australia*. Cambridge: Harvard University Press, 2013.

Khamis, K. S., and H. H. Omar. *Historia Fupi Ya Zanzibar*. Zanzibar: Idara ya Nyaraka, Makumbusho na Mambo ya Kale, 1994.

Krapf, J. L. *Travels, Researches, and Missionary Labors During an Eighteen Years' Residence in Eastern Africa*. Boston: Ticknor & Fields, 1860.

Langlands, B. W. "Concepts of the Nile." *The Uganda Journal* 26, no. 1 (March 1962): 1–22.

Lawrance, Benjamin N., Emily Lynn Osborn, and Richard L. Roberts. *Intermediaries, Interpreters, and Clerks: African Employees in the Making of Colonial Africa*. Madison: University of Wisconsin Press, 2006.

Livingstone, David. *The Last Journals of David Livingstone, in Central Africa, from 1865 to His Death*, vol. 1. London: John Murray, 1874.

———. *The Last Journals of David Livingstone, in Central Africa, from 1865 to His Death*, vol. 2. New York: Dossier Press, 2015.

Lovell, Mary S. *A Rage to Live: A Biography of Richard and Isabel Burton*. New York: W. W. Norton, 1998.

Ludwig, Emil. *The Nile: The Life-Story of a River*. New York: Viking, 1937.

MacKenzie, John. *David Livingstone and the Victorian Encounter with Africa*. London: National Portrait Gallery, 1996.

Maitland, Alexander. *Speke*. Newton Abbot: Victorian Book Club, 1973.

Markham, Clements R. *The Fifty Years' Work of the Royal Geographical Society*. London: John Murray, 1881.

McCarthy, James. *Selim Aga: A Slave's Odyssey*. Edinburgh: Luath Press, 2006.

McLynn, Frank. *Burton: Snow Upon the Desert*. London: John Murray, 1990.

———. *Hearts of Darkness: The European Exploration of Africa*. New York: Carroll & Graf, 1992.

Meyer, Karl A. *Tournament of Shadows: The Great Game and the Race for Empire in Central Asia*. New York: Basic Books, 1999.

Midant-Reynes, Beatrix. *The Prehistory of Egypt: From the First Egyptians to the First Pharaohs*. Oxford: Blackwell, 1992.

Moorehead, Alan. *The White Nile*. New York: Dell Publishing, 1960.

Morris, Jan. *Heaven's Command: An Imperial Progress*. London: Harvest, 1973.

Newman, James L. *Paths Without Glory: Richard Francis Burton in Africa*. Washington: Potomac Books, 2010.

Oliphant, Margaret. *Memoir of the Life of Laurence Oliphant and of Alice Oliphant, His Wife*. London: William Blackwood & Sons, 1892.

Oliver, Caroline. *Western Women in Colonial Africa*. London: Greenwood, 1982.

Ondaatje, Christopher. *Journey to the Source of the Nile*. Buffalo: Firefly Books, 1999.

———. *Sindh Revisited: A Journey in the Footsteps of Captain Sir Richard Francis Burton, 1842–1849: The Indian Years*. Toronto: HarperCollins, 1996.

Paas, Steven. *Johannes Rebmann: A Servant of God in Africa Before the Rise of Western Colonialism*. Eugene: Wipf & Stock, 2018.

Pallaver, Karin. "Nyamwezi Participation in Nineteenth-Century East African Long-Distance Trade." *Africa* 41, no. 3–4 (2006): 513–31.

Penzer, Norman M. *An Annotated Bibliography of Sir Richard Francis Burton*. Mansfield Centre: Martino Publishing.

Petherick, John, and Katherine Harriet Edlman Petherick. *Travels in Central Africa, and Explorations of the Western Nile Tributaries*, vols. 1 and 2. London: FB & Ltd. Dalton House, 2017.

Playfair, Robert Lambert. *An Account of Aden. Reprinted from "A History of Arabia Felix."* Aden: The Jail Press, 1859.

Porter, Andrew. *The Oxford History of the British Empire: The Nineteenth Century*. Oxford: Oxford University Press, 1999.

Ralli, Augustus. *Christians in Mecca*. London: Kennikat Press, 1909.

Ray, John. *The Rosetta Stone and the Rebirth of Ancient Egypt*. Cambridge: Harvard University Press, 2007.

Reid, Richard J. *A History of Modern Uganda*. Cambridge: Cambridge University Press, 2017.

Rice, Edward. *Captain Sir Richard Francis Burton*. Cambridge: Da Capo, 2001.

Richards, Alfred Bates, Andrew Wilson, and Clair Baddeley. *A Sketch of the Career of Richard F. Burton*. London: Waterlow & Sons Limited, 1886.

Rigby, Christopher Palmer, Mrs. Charles E. B. Russell, ed. *General Rigby, Zanzibar and the Slave Trade*. New York: Negro Universities Press, 1970.

Rotberg, Robert I. *Africa and Its Explorers: Motives, Methods, and Impact*. Cambridge: Harvard University Press, 1970.

Saad, Elias N. *Social History of Timbuktu*. Cambridge: Cambridge University Press, 1983.

Sattin, Anthony. *The Gates of Africa: Death, Discovery, and the Search for Timbuktu*. New York: St. Martin's Press, 2003.

Schaffer, Simon, Lissa Robers, Kapil Raj, and James Delbourgo, eds. *The Brokered World: Go-Betweens and Global Intelligence, 1770–1820*. Sagamore Beach: Watson Publishing International, 2009.

Schwartz, Stuart B. *Implicit Understandings: Observing, Reporting, and Reflecting on the Encounters Between Europeans and Other Peoples in the Early Modern Era*. Cambridge: Press Syndicate of the University of Cambridge, 1994.

Sheth, Ketaki. *A Certain Grace: The Sidi: Indians of African Descent*. New Delhi: Photoink, 2013.

Simpson, Donald. *Dark Companions: The African Contribution to the European Exploration of East Africa*. London: Paul Elck, 1975.

Sinema, Kyrsten. *Who Must Die in Rwanda's Genocide: The State of Exception Realized*. London: Lexington Books, 2015.

Speke, John Hanning. *Journal of the Discovery of the Source of the Nile*. London: J. M. Dent & Co., 1863.

———. *What Led to the Discovery of the Source of the Nile*. Edinburgh: William Blackwood & Sons, 1864.

Speke, John Hanning, James Augustus Grant, and George Carless Swayne. *Lake Victoria; a Narrative of Explorations in Search of the Source of the Nile. Compiled from the Memoirs of Captains Speke and Grant*. London: British Library, 1868.

Stafford, Robert A. *Scientist of Empire*. Cambridge: Cambridge University Press, 1989.

Stanley, Henry M. *How I Found Livingstone in Central Africa*. London: Sampson Low, Marston & Company, 1895.

Stilwell, Sean. *Slavery and Slaving in African History*. Cambridge: Cambridge University Press, 2014.

Stisted, Georgiana M. *The True Life of Capt. Sir Richard F. Burton*. New York: Cosimo Classics, 2004.

———. "Reminiscences of Sir Richard Burton." *Temple Bar*, July 1891.

Stoker, Bram. *Personal Reminiscences of Henry Irving*, vols. 1 and 2. London: William Heinemann, 1906.

Sutton, J. E. G. "The Antecedents of the Interlacustrine Kingdoms." *Journal of African History* 34 (1993): 33–64.

Taylor, Ann. *Laurence Oliphant, 1829–1888*. Oxford: Oxford University Press, 1982.

Temple-Raston, Dina. *Justice on the Grass: Three Rwandan Journalists, Their Trial for War Crimes, and a Nation's Quest for Redemption*. New York: Free Press, 2005.

Trotter, Lionel James. *The Bayard of India: A Life of General Sir James Outram, Bart. G.C.B., etc*. London: William Blackwood and Sons, 1923.

Troutt Powell, Eve M. *A Different Shade of Colonialism: Egypt, Great Britain, and the Mastery of the Sudan*. Berkeley: University of California Press, 2003.

Wilkinson, Toby. *The Nile: Downstream Through Egypt's Past and Present*. London: Bloomsbury, 2014.

———. *The Rise and Fall of Ancient Egypt*. New York: Random House, 2010.

Wilson, Robert T. *History of the British Expedition to Egypt*. Philadelphia: Conrad & Co., 1803.

Wisnicki, Adrian. "Cartographical Quandaries: The Limits of Knowledge Production in Burton's and Speke's Search for the Source of the Nile." *History in Africa* 35 (2008): 455–79.

———. "Charting the Frontier: Indigenous Geography, Arab-Nyamwezi Caravans, and the East African Expedition of 1856–59." *Victorian Studies* 51, no. 1 (Autumn 2008): 103–37.

———. *Fieldwork of Empire, 1840–1900: Intercultural Dynamics in the Production of British Expeditionary Literature*. New York: Routledge, 2019.

Wright, Thomas. *The Life of Sir Richard Burton*, vols. 1 and 2. London: Everett & Co., 1906.

Young, Donald. "The Selected Correspondence of Sir Richard Burton, 1848–1890." Thesis, University of Nebraska, 1979.

Young, Donald, and Quentin Keynes. *The Search for the Source of the Nile: Correspondence Between Captain Richard Burton, Captain John Speke and Others, from Burton's Unpublished East African Letter Book; Together with Other Related Letters and Papers in the Collection of Quentin Keynes.* London: The Roxburghe Club, 1999.

INDEX

Abban, abbanship, 50–51, 54
Adam Bede (Eliot), 217
Adams, Henry, 235
Aden, 5, 19, 37, 104
  Burton and Speke in, following
    East African Expedition, 207,
    208–9
  Somaliland Expedition starting in,
    36–38, 40, 42, 53, 55
  Speke and, 44–47, 130
  Steinhaüser and, 207–8
Africa
  Burton's explorations of West
    Africa, 276–77
  cholera epidemic in, 201
  cotton of Gujarat as trade goods,
    119
  European colonization, "scramble
    for Africa," 320
  Hamitic Myth and, 278, 317–18
  languages of, 250
  mapmaking, early and ephemeral,
    100–101
  maps, blank sections on, 99–100
  maps, oldest known 99
  missionaries in, 101, 143, 270
  two highest mountains, 29, 341n29

  uncharted regions, 99–100
  See also East Africa; Somaliland
    and the Somalis; *specific countries*
    and kingdoms
Aga, Selim, 310–11
Aga Khan, 27
Albert, Prince Consort, 265
Alexander, Sir James, 299
Alexander the Great, 31
Alexandria, Egypt, 1–4
  Speke in, 282, 283
Alice's Adventures in Wonderland
  (Carroll), 278
Ambar, Malik, 120
Andrade, Gaetano, 105, 148, 149, 156,
  164, 172–73, 187
Anthropological Society of London,
  278–79
ants and insects, 154
  ant types, 154
  beetle enters Speke's ear, 174–75,
    293
  disease and, 156
Aquascutum, 82
Arabian Nights, The (trans. Burton), 310
  reviews, 310
  "Terminal Essay," 311

Arbuthnot, Foster Fitzgerald, 309–10
Arctic expedition, 102
Artémise (warship), 132, 136, 180
    guns of, sound heard by Burton,
        146
Art of Travel, The (Galton), 216
Arundell, Blanche, 94, 97
Arundell, Elizabeth Gerard, 86, 91,
        231–34, 272, 274
Arundell, Henry, 86, 274
Arundell, Sir Thomas, 86
Arundell family
    ancestral lineage of, 85
    Catholicism and, 85
    Furze Hall, 87, 88
    old song about, 86
Ascot Racecourse, Berkshire, 94
Athenaeum, The, 309

Back, Admiral Sir George, 102, 110
Badger, George Percy, 19
Badr, Sidi, 120
Baker, Florence, 264
Baker, Samuel, 264–65, 266
Balaklava, Battle of, 81
Bantu people, 143
Baudelaire
    censorship and, 217
    Les Fleurs du mal, 217
Beatson, W. F., 83
    Beatson's Horse cavalry unit, 83
Bechuanaland (Botswana), 155
Bimbashi, Selim, 32
Bioko (Fernando Po), 275–77, 290
    Burton's consular appointment,
        275, 277
    Burton's literary output and,
        276–77
Bird, George, 274–75
Blackwood, John, 220–21
    authors published by, 221
    ghostwriter hired for Speke, 286

Oliphant and, 221
    Speke and, 221–23, 241, 289
    Speke's anger at Burton and, 256
    Speke's *Journal of the Discovery of
        the Source of the Nile* and, 284,
        287–88
    summer home in Scotland, Fife,
        221
Blackwood, William, 285, 286
Blackwood's Magazine, 220–21
    Speke's journals and, 206, 221–22,
        241
Blaeu, Willem Janszoon, 100
Blyth, Edward, 76–77
Bombay, India, 34, 105
    accusations against Burton sent
        to the British government in,
        223, 226
Bombay, Sidi Mubarak, 116–25, 132
    Burton's East African Expedition
        and, 116–25, 132, 135, 147–48, 164,
        168, 172, 178, 187–90, 200, 206
    death of, 322
    dysentery and, 164
    enslavement of, 116–20, 201, 321
    exploration by, miles traveled in
        Africa, 319
    farewell to Burton, 207
    freedom of, and return to Africa,
        121
    guiding Cameron, 318
    guiding Stanley and finding
        Livingstone, 307–9, 318
    Lake Tanganyika reached by, 168
    languages spoken by, 122, 123
    name acquired by, 121
    nicknames for, 147
    silver medal and monetary reward
        for, 282, 319–20
    slave of, Mabruki, 135, 147, 187, 252
    Speke and, 123–25, 147, 198, 237–38,
        249, 258–60, 318
    Speke's death and, 307

Speke's first journey to Lake
Nyanza and, 187–90
Speke's journey to Kasengé and,
172–73, 178
Speke's Lake Nyanza Expedition
of 1860 and, 237, 249, 251, 254,
258–60, 262
talents and qualities, 122–23,
147–48, 200, 237
Book of the Sword, The (Burton), 16
Botanical Gardens, London, 94
Boulogne, France, 15, 79, 89–90, 92, 93,
95, 96, 235, 269
Bowman, Sir William, 166
Britain. *See* Great Britain
British Association for the
Advancement of Science, 212–13,
221, 291–92
annual meeting in Bath, 291, 295,
298
Burton speaking on Dahomey,
291, 303
Burton-Speke "great Nile debate,"
291–95, 298–99
news of Speke's death and, 299–301
British Museum, 4
Buganda, Kingdom of, 143, 257, 285
King Mutesa I, 143, 260
Lake Nyanza Expedition reaches,
260
modern-day Kampala and, 257
Buist, George, 74
Bunyoro, Kingdom of, 261
Burton, Edward, 14, 15, 47, 79, 180,
234–35
Burton, Hagar, 88, 94
Burton, Isabel Arundell, 85–97
adventure sought by, 89–90, 92–93,
273
on Burton, 219
Burton and, early encounters,
89–90, 92, 94–96, 235
Burton as destiny, 88, 91–93, 95, 97

Burton defends Speke and, 214–15
Burton opposed by her mother,
228–34, 272, 274
Burton proposes, 95
Burton's American journey and,
272–73
Burton's apparition appears to, 96
Burton's consular appointments
and, 276, 304
Burton's consular appointment to
Trieste and, 305, 322–27
Burton's death and, 324–26,
379n324
Burton's help with Speke's bust
and, 316
Burton's ill health and appearance,
230–31
Burton's letter/poem from
Zanzibar, 229
Burton's London reunion with,
230–31
Burton's *Lusiads* translation and,
312
Burton's name carved into the
Leaning Tower of Pisa and,
229
Burton-Speke "great Nile debate"
and, 294
Burton-Speke rift and, 292–93
Burton's ultimatum, 272–73
Catholicism and, 85, 96, 232, 325
character of, 87, 92, 94, 96
childhood, 86–88
European travels, 229
family and heritage, 85–86
fencing lessons, 273, 274
friendship with a Romani woman,
87, 94
horoscope prediction for, 88–89
*The Inner Life of Syria, Palestine, and
the Holy Land,* 305
nicknamed "Daisy," 88, 94
picture of Burton kept by, 230

Burton, Isabel Arundell *(continued)*
  prepares to become Burton's wife,
    273–74
  protecting Burton's legacy, 332,
    325–27
  religious conversion of Burton
    and, 232, 233–34, 270, 274, 325
  "Rules for my Guidance as a
    Wife," 273
  The Scented Garden burned by,
    326–27
  Speke's death and, 300
  Stella Club founded by, 94
  thirty-year marriage to Burton,
    304–5
  weds Burton, 274
  "Who Last Wins," 316–17,
    378n316–19
Burton, John Hill, 286
Burton, Joseph Netterville, 11, 79, 183
Burton, Maria, 11, 79
Burton, Richard Francis
  adage on journeys and, 140
  agents, Grindlay brothers, 275
  alter ego, El Haj Abdullah, 11, 20,
    22, 26, 28, 49
  anger and depression following
    the East African Expedition,
    202, 228, 268, 277
  Anthropological Society of
    London founding member,
    278
  anthropology and, 269
  appearance, 14, 89, 230–31, 235–36
  Arabic couplet about betrayal, 227
  background and childhood,
    12–15, 86
  on big game hunting, 133–34
  blame for Stroyan's death and, 70
  British Association for the
    Advancement of Science
    annual meeting in Bath and, 291,
    294–95, 298–301, 303
  in Cairo, 27–29, 34
  Cannibal Club and, 277–80, 310
  character of, 39, 56, 84, 113, 217–18,
    312, 313
  consular appointment to Bioko,
    275, 277, 290
  consular appointment to
    Damascus, 304
  consular appointment to Santos,
    Brazil, 304
  consular appointment to Trieste,
    305, 322–27
  as controversial figure, 217, 231–32
  Crimean War and, 73, 80–84
  death of, 322–27
  defense of Selim Aga, 310–11
  depression always following
    completed expeditions, 202, 228
  dislike of England, 15
  East India Company service, 13,
    17, 34
  Erhardt's and Rebmann's inland
    sea and, 101–2
  eyes of, 14
  family and, 53–54
  family losses and, 234–35
  father's death, 183
  fencing ability, 15
  final years, 322–27
  first time on the Nile, 34
  friendships of, 217–18
  Galton's assessment of, 217
  Grant's reprimand and response,
    308–9
  hallucinogenic drugs and, 145
  Hamerton described by, 180–81
  health of, 126–27, 156, 164–66, 177,
    178, 191, 202, 208, 216, 219, 230–31,
    236
  health of, broken, 304, 305
  heart attack (1887), 323–24
  hypnosis and, 114, 323
  interest in the supernatural, 144

knighthood and, 322

"linguists are a dangerous race" assertion, 18, 19

literary ability of, 285

Lord Lytton on, 276

monsoon's affecting of, 128–29

Mormons and, 269, 271

mother's death, 53–54

motto *poco spero, nulla chiedo,* 313, 378n313

mystery of the Nile's source and, 96, 306–7, 308

nadir of his life (1859), 234–35

Oliphant and, 83–84, 208, 209, 214, 292

ophthalmia and, 167, 168

on polygamy, 272

polygenism and, 278, 310

as a polyglot and linguist, 12, 17–18, 137, 184, 269, 339n17

position on retaining native nomenclature for geographical features, 251

possessions lost in a fire, 275

preference for Arab dress, 49

as public speaker, 291

racial views, 310–11

relationship and marriage to Isabel Arundell, 85–97, 228–34, 273–75, 322–27

religion and, 23, 232, 233–34, 270–71, 274

Rigby and, 19, 161, 201, 202–4

Rigby's accusations and response, 223–27

Royal Geographical Society and, 28, 212, 214, 215 (*see also* Royal Geographical Society)

sexual encounters and interest in sexual practices, 16

siblings of, 14, 15

slavery and, 135, 142

Smalley's meeting with, 311–12

Somali attack on, javelin injury, and lifelong scar, 64, 69, 79–80

Speke and "the great Nile debate," 291–95, 298–99, 303–4

Speke as rival, 214, 216, 220, 222–23

Speke defended by, 214–15

Speke described by, 45–46

Speke in the East African Expedition as second in command, 98, 103–6, 124–25, 132–34, 138, 147, 151–58, 163, 164, 169, 171–76, 179, 182–93, 197–201, 206, 222 (*see also* East African Expedition)

Speke in the Somaliland Expedition and wounding, 46–47, 56, 60–79, 77–78 (*see also* Somaliland Expedition)

Speke remembered by, 315–16

Speke's accusations against Petherick and, 288–89

Speke's betrayals of, 208–9, 223–27, 228, 244

Speke's communication with ended, 244–45

Speke's death and, 299, 300–1, 303

Speke's death and Burton's letter to *The Times,* 303–4

Speke seen as ignorant by, 186

Speke sent to the Wady Nogal by, 49, 76

Speke's genuine concern for, 165–66

Speke's grievances and jealousy, 75–77, 112–13, 125, 138, 192, 199, 203, 204, 209, 210, 222, 227, 244, 289

Speke's hunting and, 133

Steinhaüser and, 105, 112, 125, 138, 207, 268–72

"an unlucky Burton," 236

warning of Indian rebellion, 180

West African exploration, 277, 291

Zanzibar and, 107–10

Burton, Richard Francis: expeditions
    American journey, 268–72
    East African Expedition of 1857,
        102–3, 123–42, 162–85, 191–93,
        197–209
    expedition to the Lake Regions of
        East Africa proposed by, 102–3
    Harar expedition, 48, 53, 74, 79, 92
    Mecca expedition, 11–13, 19–26, 92,
        144–45
    Somaliland Expedition of 1854, 6,
        33–34, 48, 56, 57–70, 73–76
Burton, Richard Francis: writings
    The Arabian Nights (translation),
        310–11
    The Book of the Sword, 16
    The City of the Saints, 270
    *A Complete System of Bayonet
        Exercise,* 16
    erotica translations, 309–10,
        322–27
    ethnological writings, 16
    Falconry in the Valley of the Indus, 18
    fictional publishing house of, 309
    First Footsteps in East Africa, 76
    Kama Sutra (translation), 309–10
    The Kasidah (best known epic
        poem), 276
    The Lake Regions of Central Africa,
        255–56
    lost manuscript on Zanzibar
        reappears, 305–6
    The Lusiads (translation), 312, 313,
        378n313
    pseudonym for, Francis Baker, 276
    Royal Geographical Society
        Journal account of the East
        African Expedition, 222–23, 284
    The Scented Garden (unfinished
        translation, destroyed), 324,
        326–27
    Wit and Wisdom from West Africa,
        277

Cairo, Egypt
    Burton in, 26, 27, 29
    Shepheard Hotel, 25, 27, 29
Cameron, Verney Lovett, 318
Camões, Luís de, 312
Cannibal Club, 278–80, 310
    members of, 278–79
    pornography and, 279
    Swinburne and the Cannibal
        Catechism, 279–80
Cardigan, James Brudenell, 7th Earl
    of, 81
    sweater named after, 82
Carter, Henry, 38
Cary, John, 100
Ceylon (Sri Lanka), 78
Champollion, Jean-François, 4
"Charge of the Light Brigade, The"
    (Tennyson), 81
cholera, 201
Chuma, James, 319, 321
Churchill, Winston, 27, 82
Church Missionary Society, 101
    message for Rebmann and, 109–10
Chwezi people, 143
City of the Saints, The (Burton), 270
Cochet, Ladislas, 203
Coghlan, William, 74, 80
coins: Maria Theresa thaler or
    "dollars," 123
Complete System of Bayonet Exercise, A
    (Burton), 16
Conrad, Joseph, *Heart of Darkness,* 221
Cooley, William, 102
    Inner Africa Laid Open, 341n29
Creswicke Rawlinson, Sir Henry, 319
Crimean War, 73, 78
    Arundell's Stella Club and, 94
    Battle of Balaklava, 81
    Battle of Sebastopol, 79
    Burton and, 73, 80–84
    "The Charge of the Light
        Brigade," 81

Oliphant and, 78–79, 83–84
    siege of Kars and, 79, 83–84
    Speke and, 78, 79, 98
    Treaty of Paris, 85
crocodiles, 114, 173, 263

da Gama, Vasco, 106, 312
Dahomey, Kingdom of, 277
    Burton's talk on, 291, 303
Darwin, Charles, 7, 212, 216
    On the Origin of Species, 212, 278
Davis, Daniel, 296–97
de Bono, Amabile Musa, 263–64
Disraeli, Benjamin, *Tancred*, 87, 95
divorce-oath, 61
Dodgson, Charles (Lewis Carroll), 278
    Alice's Adventures in Wonderland, 278
Dormer, Kitty, 292
Dracula (Stoker), 14
Dragon of Salem (British ship), 207
Driver, Felix, 320

East Africa
    Arab traders in, 143
    Bantu populations, 143
    beauty of, 140, 142
    Burton on missionaries in, 270–71
    caravans of, 132, 141–42, 156
    Chwezi people, 143
    evil spirits as white, 271
    exploration by Krapf, Rebmann, and Erhardt, 29–30, 341n29
    freed slave settlements in, 321
    Hima people, 143
    kingdoms of, 143
    Krapf's stories of huge inland lakes, 29
    Lake Nyanza, 163, 168, 182, 185
    Lake Nyasa, 163
    Lake Regions of East Africa, 96, 102
    Lake Tanganyika, 102, 134, 137–38, 139, 168–83
    map by Erhardt and Rebmann, 101–2, 103
    Mountains of the Moon, 27, 31, 34, 100, 221, 282
    Nyamwezi people, 143–44
    Rubeho Mountains, 157
    slavery abolished, 321
    slave trade in, 107, 116
    smallpox epidemics, 156
    trade networks of, 143
    Unyanyembe people, 144
    Vili people, 143
    Wakaranga, Wavinza, and Wajiji people, 170
    Western Rift Valley, 168
    Yao people of, 116–17
East African Expedition of 1857, 6–7, 102–3, 105–14, 122–42, 146
    Aden stopover, 105
    animal encounters, attacks, 153–56
    Back's support for, 102
    boat needed for, 137, 170–72, 175–76
    Bombay, a Yao, and, 115–25, 132, 135, 147–48, 164, 168, 200, 206
    Burton describes Lake Tanganyika, 168–69, 182–83
    Burton describes the Pangani River, 114
    Burton describes Speke's return from Kasengé, 176–77
    Burton describes the Wajiji people, 170
    Burton satisfied by the expedition's findings, 184
    Burton's and Speke's personal funds used for, 205, 206, 226
    Burton's health and, 152, 156, 164–66, 171, 177, 178, 182, 183, 184, 191, 202
    Burton's instructions for, 102
    Burton's opinion of members, 149

East African Expedition of 1857
(*continued*)
Burton's reaction to Speke's claim
of discovering the White Nile's
source, 192–93
Burton's search for Rebmann,
109–11
at Chogué military station, 115, 124,
131, 352n115
clothing chosen for, 129
coastal excursion from Zanzibar,
110–14
consulate contacted for help, 159–61
daily routine of, 148–49
dangers of, 137, 159
desertions from, 146
disappointments, mishaps, and
tragedies of, 138, 146–47, 148
disease and fevers, 126–27, 152,
155–57, 158, 164, 167, 168, 172, 201
donkeys for, 134, 149, 206
ending of, 206–7
equipping and hiring for, 109, 115,
129–30, 131, 132, 135, 144, 149, 160,
162, 164
essential members of, 149
exhaustion of food supplies and
starvation, 158–59, 179
expected duration of, 132
first stop, Kuingani, 141, 144–46
flag for, 139, 140
following slave trade routes, 142
funding, 104, 131, 204–6, 219, 226
Goanese cooks, 105, 126, 148, 149,
156, 164
Hamerton's advice, 136–37
Hamerton's death and lost
support, 146
Hamerton's help with, 131, 160
iron lifeboat, *Louisa*, 110, 134, 137, 171
items carried on Burton's person,
129
Kazeh reached, 162–64

Kazeh return, 181–85, 190
kirangozi, or guide, 140
kuhonga carried with, 129–31, 132,
159, 176
Lake Tanganyika and, 102, 134–35,
137, 139, 160, 162, 168–81, 182
medical help unavailable to, 165
messages left along the route, 141
Mombasa reached, 110–11
ophthalmia and, 167, 168
order of members on the march,
140
pace of, 148, 162
pagazi or porter, 140
"Pass Terrible" reached, 157
payment for members of, 131,
205–6
portmanteau lost, 146
Ramji joins, with guards and
porters, 131, 132, 134, 164
Ramji's payment and, 223
route advice, 111, 163
Said as *ras kafilah*, or caravan
guide for, 131, 134, 148, 159, 179,
186–87, 200
scientific instruments, 105–6, 129,
152–53
setting off from Wale Point and
Kaole, 132, 134, 136, 139
signal for danger, 141
size of, 132, 149
slaves in, 135, 147, 164
"slug" map and, 163
soldiers for, 149
Speke argues for detour to the
Nyanza, 185
Speke as second in command, 98,
103–6, 110–14, 124–25, 132–34, 138,
147–48, 151–58, 163, 169, 171–76,
180, 182–93, 197–201, 206, 222–23
Speke-Burton relationship
during, 112, 152, 165–67, 184–85,
197–99

Speke gets a beetle in his ear,
174–75, 293
Speke's discontent, 110, 111, 112, 125,
138, 184–85, 253
Speke sets out on the Tanganyika
for Kasengé, 172–75
Speke's expedition to Lake
Nyanza and, 182, 185–93
Speke's illness called "little irons,"
197–99
Steinhaüser and, 105–6, 112
terrain covered by, 153
in Ujiji, 169–72, 176–77, 179–81
in Ujiji, caravan arrives, bringing
supplies and evil tidings, 180–81
weather and damage caused by,
149–150
Zanzibar and, 105–10, 129, 132
Zanzibar returned to (1859), 201–2
in Zimbili, 164
East India Company, 13, 17, 40
Bombay Examination
Committee, 19
Burton as an interpreter, 17
Burton on leave from, 34, 53
Burton's East African Expedition
and, 104
Burton's search for Nile source
and, 36
language examination process in, 18
Rigby in, 18–19
Egypt
British victory over France in, 1, 2
European obsession with, 3–5
French scholars in, 2
Napoleon's invasion, 1, 27
Nile floodplain and population
density, 30
Rosetta Stone and, 1, 2–4
elephants, 117, 133, 137, 153, 184
tusks harvested from, 118
Elgin, 8th Earl of, 207
Elgin Marbles, 207

Eliot, George (Mary Ann Evans)
Adam Bede, 217
Blackwood and, 221
Elphinstone (sloop-of-war), 105–6, 107
Elphinstone, Lord, governor of
Bombay, 105, 112, 222
England. See Great Britain
Erhardt, Jakob, 29, 33
belief in an inland African sea, 101
funding for, 104
"slug" map drawn by, 101–2, 103,
163
Ethiopia, 320
Ahmar Mountains, 48
Harar, 48, 53, 120
Ethnological Society of London, 277
monogenism vs. polygenism and,
278
Everest, George, 226
Everest, Mount (Sagarmartha), 226
Hillary expedition and guide
Tenzing Norgay, 319
explorers, 5
acknowledging native guides,
319–20
The Art of Travel and, 216
da Gama in Zanzibar, 106
discoveries leading to conquest
and colonization, 5–6, 320
French explorer Maizan's murder
in Africa, 127–28
hiring men in Zanzibar, "native
testimony," 121–22
Krapf, Rebmann, and Erhardt in
East Africa, 29–30
Livingstone as Britain's most
famous, 7, 154–55
McGrigor's first full ascent of the
Nile, from sea to source, 317
murder of Albrecht Roscher, 253
nineteenth century, filling in maps
and solving mysteries, 30
penetration of the Sudd by, 32

explorers *(continued)*
Petherick and the Nile's tributaries, 240
renaming geographical features, 251, 263
source of the Nile as Holy Grail of, 30
Speke in Tibet, 43–44
See also Burton, Richard Francis; Livingstone, David; Speke, John Hanning; Stanley, Henry Morton

Falconry in the Valley of the Indus (Burton), 18
Findlay, Alexander George, 299
First Footsteps in East Africa (Burton), 76
Flaubert, Gustave
censorship and, 217
Madame Bovary, 217
Forster, E. M., 220
Franklin, John, 102
Frost, Mr. (apothecary), 132, 136, 180
Fuller, George, 296–97, 302
Fuller, John Bird, 295

Galle, Ceylon, 208
Galton, Francis, 216–17, 219, 242–43, 299
The Art of Travel, 216
eugenics and, 216
"nature versus nurture" coined by, 216
summing up Burton and Speke, 217
Gondokoro (German mission), South Sudan, 240, 242
Baker meets Speke in, 264–65
de Bono and Speke, 263–64
Lake Nyanza Expedition reaches, 263–64
Speke's plan to meet Petherick in, 260–61, 263–64
Speke's speech and, 288
Grant, James Augustus, 239, 255
account of the Lake Nyanza Expedition, 289
executions witnessed by, 253
fevers and illnesses of, 255, 261
lands in Zanzibar, 249
reprimanding Burton, 308
return to London (1863), 282
Royal Geographical Society presentation about the source of the Nile, 281, 282–83
second in command, Lake Nyanza Expedition of 1860, 239, 243, 249, 252–53, 254, 255, 368n239
Speke and, 243, 251–52, 256, 288, 294
Speke's death and, 301–2
Stanley's expedition and, 308
Great Britain, 5
Abolition of the Slave Trade Act, 107
censorship and puritanism in, 217
colonization by, 6
corrupt military command and, 81
Hamitic Myth and, 318
Industrial Revolution, 81–82
Obscene Publications Act, 217
occultist Hockley in, 144–55
Rosetta Stone and, 2–4
Second Industrial Revolution, 81–82
siege of Alexandria and, 3
Slavery Abolition Act, 321
Slave Trade Act, 321
strategy to find the source of the Nile and, 4
Victorians and the supernatural, 144
Victorian "wideawake" hat, 188
Gujarat, India, 119

hallucinogenic drugs, 145
Hamed bin Sulayyim, Shaykh,
　175–76, 178
Hamerton, Atkins, 108–9, 203
　accompanying the expedition
　　leaving Zanzibar, 132, 135
　advice to Burton, 136
　death of, 146, 160, 181, 183, 202, 206
　death on the face of, 136, 137
　funding for the East African
　　Expedition and, 130–31, 204–5,
　　224, 227, 252
　helping Burton and Speke, 127
　warning Burton about dangers for
　　his expedition, 127–28
　warning French explorer Maizan,
　　127–28
Hamilton, William Richard, 1
　motto for the Royal Geographical
　　Society and, 5
　retrieving the Parthenon
　　sculptures, 4
　search for the Rosetta Stone and,
　　1, 2, 3
Hamitic Myth, 278, 317–18
　Rwandan genocide and, 318
Hankey, Frederick, 218, 235
Harar, Ethiopia, 48, 53, 120
Harar expedition, 48–49, 53, 74, 79, 92
　Burton in Arab dress and, 48, 49
Harris, Frank, 276
Heart of Darkness (Conrad), 221
Herne, G. E., 39, 48, 49, 58–9
　Somali attack and, 62–66, 69, 74
Herodotus, 4, 31
Hillary, Sir Edmund, 319
Hima people, 143
hippopotamuses, 110, 114, 118, 133–34,
　138, 252, 263
　ivory from, 118
History of the British Expedition to Egypt
　(Wilson), 167
HMS *Furious*, 207–9, 210

HMS *Terror*, 102
Hockley, Frederick, 144
Hoskote, Ranjit, "Sidi Mubarak
　Bombay" (poem), ix
Hughes, Thomas, 238
　Tom Brown's School Days, 238
Hume, David, 286
Hunt, James, 278
hypnosis, 144

ibn Said, Barghash, 321
India
　African slaves in, 120–21
　Bengal, 120
　cotton of Gujarat, 119
　Deccan, 120
　First War of Independence, 180
　rulers as former slaves, 120
　slavery in, 120
　Speke's brother killed in, 180
　13th Bengal Native Infantry, 238
　titles for slaves in, Habshi or Sidi,
　　120–21
Inner Africa Laid Open (Cooley),
　341n29
*Inner Life of Syria, Palestine, and the
　Holy Land, The* (Isabel Burton),
　305

Johnson, Samuel, 6
Jones, Lowri, 320
*Journal of the Discovery of the Source of
　the Nile* (Speke), 287–90
　critics and, 287
　Hindu map revealed as a fraud,
　　287
　Rigby's criticism, 287
　Speke's attack on the men who
　　helped him, 287–88
*Journal of the Royal Asiatic Society of
　Bengal*, 76

Journal of the Royal Geographical Society of London, 33, 221
  edition featuring Burton's East African Expedition, 222, 284
  Speke's disappointing article in, 284

Kagera River, 317
Kama Sutra (trans. Burton and Arbuthnot), 309
Karagwe, Kingdom of, 143, 257, 370n257
  King Rumanika, 143
Kazeh, East Africa, 162, 181, 182–83
  East African Expedition reaches, 162–64
  East African Expedition returns, 182–85
  Lake Nyanza Expedition reaches, 253–54
Kenya, Mount, 29
Khartoum, Sudan, 31, 240, 242, 287
  Petherick as British vice-consul, 240–41, 267, 288
khat, 145
Kilimanjaro, Mount, 29, 111, 341n29
Kilwa Island, 117, 118, 201
kirangozi, or guide, 140–41
Kirk, John, 321
Krapf, Johann, 27, 29
  African exploration by, 29–30
  in East Africa, 29
  language study of, 29
  loss of his wife and children, 29
  Nile expedition, 33
kuhonga, or gifts, 129–30, 131, 159, 176
  East African Expedition and, 129–30, 131, 159, 172, 176
  Lake Nyanza Expedition and, 258
  masango or brass wires as, 130
  ushanga or beads as, 130

Kuingani village, East Africa, 141, 144–46
  medicine man's prophecy, 145–46

Ladha Damha, Zanzibar's collector of customs, 134, 137–38
  Kutchi dialect and, 137
Lake Nyanza (Lake Victoria), 163
  Burton's response to renaming, 250–51
  fish of, 189
  multiple names for, 163, 251
  rivers flowing from, 185
  size and depth, 189–90
  Speke claims as source of the White Nile, 190, 208–9, 210–11, 216, 261–62, 308, 309
  Speke describes, 189–90
  Speke names for the Queen, 251
  Speke's first expedition to, 169, 182, 185–90, 215
  Speke's map to, 211
  Stanley's circumnavigation of, 308
  waterfalls of, Speke names Ripon Falls, 263
Lake Nyanza Expedition of 1860, 208–9, 210–14, 216, 219, 237–45, 249–67, 282
  Baker sent to Gondokoro to meet Speke, 265, 266–67
  Baraka and Speke, 258, 260
  big game hunting and, 252
  Bombay as member of, 237, 249, 251–52, 254, 262, 282
  crossing Karagwe and Buganda, 257, 260, 370n257
  desertions from, 253–54
  funding for, 219, 242
  Gondokoro reached by, 263
  from Gondokoro to Alexandria by boat, 282

Grant as second in command for, 239, 243, 249, 252–53, 254, 282, 368n239
Grant sent ahead to Bunyoro, 261, 263
Grant's fevers and leg inflammation, 255, 261
hiring members and equipping, 237–45, 255
illness, disease, and, 255
Khartoum, Sudan as final destination, 240
kuhonga, or gifts carried with, 258
leaves Kazeh and stalled in Uzinza, 254
leaves Zanzibar for Kazeh, 253
low provisions and, 254
members receive medals and monetary rewards, 282
news relayed to in Gondokoro, 265
Petherick and, 240–42, 260–61, 265–67, 371n260
plans to follow the White Nile to Gondokoro, 240
return to Zanzibar, 282
Rigby and, 252, 254
route for, 240
Said bin Salim hired for, 251
size of, 253
source of the White Nile found, 262–63
Speke's Christianity and, 262
Speke's claim of royalty and, 257–58, 260–61
Speke's decisions and, 239–40
Speke's fury and attack on Bombay, 259–60
Speke's illness and treatment, 255
Speke's treatment of Petherick and enmity earned, 266–67
Stanley's expedition to, 308
Zanzibar as start of, 240, 249–53

Lake Nyasa, 163
Lake Regions of Central Africa, The (Burton), 255–56
Speke depicted in, 255–56
Lake Tanganyika (Sea of Ujiji), 102, 134, 137, 139, 160, 162–81
Arab presence at, 170
black beetles and Speke's ordeal, 174–75
Burton and Speke, first Europeans to reach, 170
Burton chooses as the source of the Nile, 306, 307, 309
Burton describes, 168–69, 182–83
crocodiles in, 173
East African Expedition reaches, lacks boat, 168, 170–71
as the longest and second deepest freshwater lake, 168, 189
peoples living along, 170
rumor of a river flowing from the north of, 171, 178, 308
Speke renames features as "Speke Channel" and "Burton Point," 251
Speke's journey to and from Kasengé, 172–77
Uvira, northernmost trading center, 178
Lawrence, T. E., 27
Layard, Austen Henry, 290
Leaves of Grass (Whitman), 217
Les Fleurs du mal (Baudelaire), 217
Liberia, 320
lions, 154–55
Livingstone, David, 7, 154–55, 212–13, 215, 291
body carried out of Africa by native guides, 319
burial in Westminster Abbey, 319
death of, 308
disappearance of, 307

Livingstone, David (continued)
  expedition to circumnavigate the
    Nyanza, 291, 307
  lion attack on, 154–55
  medals for his guides, 319
  Stanley finds him in Africa, 307, 308
Loango, Kingdom of, 143
London
  Bavarian Catholic Church,
    Burton-Arundell wedding in,
    274
  Belgrave Square, 211, 213
  Burton returns (1859), 214
  Hatchett's Hotel, Piccadilly, 210
  Speke precedes Burton in
    returning to (1859), 210
London's Great Exhibition, 100
Luo people, 143, 250–51
Lusiads, The (trans. Burton), 313
  Burton's preface, 313, 378n313
Lytton, Lord, viceroy of India, 276
  on Burton, 276

Maasai tribe, 111
Mabruki (slave), 135, 147, 164, 187, 188,
  251–52
Macqueen, James, 251
Madame Bovary (Flaubert), 217
Maharaja of Jodhpur, 27
Maizan, Eugène, 38, 127–28
Majid, Sayyid, Sultan of Zanzibar,
  109, 132, 201
malaria, 127
  dangers of quinine, 127
maps, mapmakers
  blank sections, Africa and, 99–100
  early African mapmaking, 100
  of East Africa, drawn by Erhardt
    and Rebmann, 101, 163
  ephemeral maps, 100
  exhibited at London's Great
    Exhibition, 100

horror vacui and, 99
oldest known maps of Africa, 99
Petherick's, of the upper Nile, 240
Rigby's Hindu map, 250, 287
Royal Geographical Society
  collection, 98–99
Speke mapping East Africa, 152
Speke's sketch of Nyanza travels,
  211
Markham, Clements, 210, 301
Martin, R. Montgomery, 100
Mary Ann (English brig), 38
McGrigor, Neil, 317
Mecca, 11–12
Mecca expedition, 19–26, 92
  Burton's belongings and, 20
  Burton's preparation and disguise,
    19–20
  Burton's sextant and, 11–12, 20, 22
  Burton visits the Kaaba, 22–23,
    24–25
  occultist Hockley and, 144–45
  servant Mohammed's suspicions,
    21–22
Mezzofanti, Giuseppe Caspar,
  368n233
Milnes, Richard Monckton, 218, 235,
  275
  Cannibal Club and, 279
  country manor, Fryston Hall, 235
  erotica collection, 218, 235
Mombasa
  Burton and Speke arrive in, 110
  Rebmann and the Kisuludini
    mission house, 110
Mormons, 269, 271
  polygamy and, 271–72
Mountains of the Moon, 27, 31, 34,
  100, 221, 282
Murchison, Sir Roderick Impey, 12,
  33, 104
  Burton and, 215
  defense of Petherick by, 289

distances himself from Speke,
  289–91, 294
family and heritage, 211
as geologist, 211
hunting and, 211
news of Speke's death and, 299,
  300–1
as Royal Geographical Society
  president, 211, 215
Speke's ingratitude and, 284–85
Speke's memory and, 315
as Speke's mentor, 211–13, 215–16,
  220, 221, 240, 242, 282–83, 284
Speke's telegram from Alexandria,
  "the Nile is settled," 282
Tarradale House, 211

Napoleon Bonaparte, 1, 2, 27
Napoleonic Wars, 80
  *History of the British Expedition to
    Egypt* (Wilson), 167
Napoleon III and Princess Eugénie,
  290
Nightingale, Florence, 80
Nile River, 2
  annual flooding, 30
  Baker's search for the source of
    the White Nile, 264
  branches of, Blue and White, 31
  British strategy to find the
    source, 5
  in Cairo, 27
  facts about, 31
  failed expeditions to the source, 5
  fascination with, 30
  hippopotamuses and crocodiles
    in, 263
  Kagera River as most remote
    headstream, 317
  Krapf, Rebmann, and Erhardt
    expedition, 33
  Krapf's search for the source, 27, 29

McGrigor's first full ascent, from
    sea to source, 317
  Nile perch, 263
  obstacles to exploration of, 32
  Petherick exploring the tributaries
    of, 240
  Roman attempts to explore the
    White Nile, 32
  search for the source of the White
    Nile (Bahr-el-Abyad), 101, 102,
    171
  Speke reaches the White Nile at
    Urondogani, 262–63
  Speke's discovery of the White
    Nile's source, 190, 239, 262, 282,
    308, 317
  Stanley's discovery of the White
    Nile's source, 308–9
  the Sudd and, 32
  theories about the source, 4, 27,
    31–32
  See also East African Expedition of
    1857; Lake Nyanza Expedition
    of 1860
Norgay, Tenzing, 319
Nyamwezi people, 143–44
  Burton hires guides and porters
    from, 144

Obscene Publications Act, 217
Ogaden caravan, 59
Oliphant, Sir Anthony, 78–79
Oliphant, Laurence, 78–79, 83–84,
  207–8
  Blackwood and, 221
  Burton and, 83–84, 208, 209
  Burton-Speke rift and, 209, 214, 292
  The Coming Campaign (pamphlet),
    79, 83
  religious conversion of, 293
  Royal Geographical Society and,
    216

Oliphant, Laurence *(continued)*
    Speke and, 208, 214, 221–22, 290,
        292–93
On the Origin of Species (Darwin), 212,
        278
ophthalmia, 167, 168
"orientalism," 4
*Outline of the Somali Language and
    Vocabulary, An* (Rigby), 19
Outram, James, 37–38, 39, 45, 46, 48,
        49–50, 59, 74, 75

pagazi or porter, 140
Pangani River, Tanzania, 114
    Chogué military station on, 115, 123,
        126, 131, 353n123
Papworth, Edgar George, 316
Pemba, 106, 201
Peninsular and Oriental Steam
        Navigation Company
        (P&O), 42
Petherick, John, 240–42
    appearance, 241
    boats and provisions left for Speke
        by, 265
    funding for, 242–43, 265
    hardships in reaching in
        Gondokoro, 265–66, 287
    map drawn by, 240
    Murchison's and Burton's defense
        of, 288–89
    route for, Khartoum to
        Gondokoro, 242
    rumors of his death, 265
    Speke given false information
        about, 265
    Speke recruits for Lake Nyanza
        Expedition, 240–42
    Speke's disdain and, 266
    Speke's false accusations about,
        287
    Speke's family at Jordans and, 241
    Speke's plan to meet in
        Gondokoro, 260, 371n260
Petherick, Katherine, 265, 266,
        288
Phipps, Constantine, 6
Playfair, Robert, 75, 104
Pliny the Elder, 31
Ptolemy, 31
    theory about the Nile's source, 31

Raglan, FitzRoy Somerset,
        1st Baron, 82
    command mistakes, 82
    Crimean War and, 82
    sleeve named for, 82
Ramé, Maria Louise (Ouida), 322
Ramji, head clerk of the Zanzibar
        customs house, 131, 132, 134, 137,
        164, 223
Rebmann, Johannes, 29–30, 33,
        341n29
    belief in an inland African sea, 101
    Burton's search for, 109–10
    in Mombasa, meeting with Burton
        and Speke, 110–11
    "slug" map drawn by, 101, 103, 109,
        163
Reeve, Henry, 310
Rigby, Christopher Palmer, 18–19
    attack on Zanzibar and, 202
    as British consul in Zanzibar, 161,
        201–6, 223–24
    as Burton's enemy, 19, 161, 201,
        202–4, 224
    carriage accident of, 202
    cholera epidemic in Zanzibar
        and, 201
    Hindu map and, 245, 249–50
    Lake Nyanza Expedition of 1860
        and, 251–52, 254
    *An Outline of the Somali Language
        and Vocabulary*, 19

refusal to bid farewell to Burton, 206

refusal to honor funding promise to Burton, 205–7

Speke and, 203–4, 214, 219–20, 222–23, 244, 253–54

Speke returns to Zanzibar and, 249

Speke's book criticized by, 287

Speke's complaints about Burton and, 256–57

Speke urges to make accusations against Burton, 223, 226–27

Ripon, Lord, 215, 263

Rodriguez, Valentine, 105, 148, 149, 156, 164, 166

Roosevelt, Theodore, 27

Roscher, Albrecht, 253

Rosetta Stone, 1, 2–4

Royal Geographical Society, 5

acknowledging native guides, 319

Baker sent to Gondokoro to meet Speke, 265

British Association for the Advancement of Science and Section E, 212, 291, 300

Burlington House as home to, 281, 283

Burton awarded the Founder's Medal, 215

Burton's correspondence with, 28, 29, 34–35, 41, 53, 83

Burton's East African Expedition of 1857 and, 102, 204, 225–26

Burton's Harar expedition and, 53, 79

Burton's Mecca expedition and, 13, 28

Burton's personal funding not reimbursed, 226

Burton's reports from East Africa, 152

Burton's Somaliland Expedition of 1854, 33–77

Burton writes about Nyanza as Nile's source, 208–9

encourages Burton to meet with Rebmann, 109

Erhardt and Rebmann's "slug map" at, 101–2, 163

Expedition Sub-Committee, 216, 219, 225–26, 242–43

exploration as focus of, 212, 213

exploration of interior Africa and, 37–38

failed Carter expedition to Somaliland, 38

famous members, 7

founding aims of, 98

geography vs. geology and, 212

government funding for, 99

Hidden Histories of Exploration exhibition (2009), 320

Hillary's Everest expedition and, 319

"hungry forties," 211

Livingstone offered a Nyanza expedition by, 291

location of, 98

map room and map collection, 98–99

Markham as president, 210

medals and monetary reward for native guides, 282, 319

motto, 5

Murchison as president, 13, 33, 211–13, 215

number of members, 212

scientists and, 212

search for Dr. Livingstone, 307

search for the source of the Nile and, 33, 34, 102

Speke and, 219–20

Speke awarded the Founder's Medal, 283

Royal Geographical Society
(continued)
   Speke claims credit for
      discovering the White Nile's
      source, 192, 211, 282
   Speke cut off by, 291
   Speke instigates list of accusations
      against Burton, 223–24
   Speke precedes Burton in
      returning to England, 208–9
   Speke's and Grant's presentation
      about the source of the Nile,
      281, 282–83
   Speke's desire for a new Nile
      expedition, 209, 216
   Speke's expedition to Lake
      Nyanza approved and funded,
      219–20, 240, 242
   Speke's ingratitude and his
      account of the Nyanza
      expedition, 284
   Speke's papers and, 221
   Speke undercuts Burton, 214
   Stanley awarded the Patron's
      Medal, 308
   Wady Nogal and, 49
Rub' al-Khali or "Empty Quarter," 13
Rubeho Mountains, 157
Rufiji River, 201
Rusizi River, 178, 308
Russell, Lord John, 291

Sade, Marquis de, 218
"safari," 139
Said bin Salim, 131, 132, 146, 148, 156,
      159, 179
   firing of, 200
   refuses to travel with Speke, 186–87
Saunders, Trelawney, 99
"savants," 2
Scented Garden, The (lost work,
      Burton), 324, 326–27

Schamyl (Muslim leader), 79, 83
Shaw, Norton, 210
   correspondence with Burton, 28,
      34–35, 41, 53, 83, 204–5
   correspondence with Speke, 156,
      184, 204, 210, 222, 239, 241
   news of Speke's death and, 299
   Speke instigates list of accusations
      against Burton and, 223–24
"Sidi Mubarak Bombay"
      (Hoskote), ix
Simpson, Sir James, 82
Singh, Nain, 319
slavery, 6, 107, 116
   abolished in East Africa, 321
   abolished in Great Britain, 321
   anti-slavery campaigns, 321
   average prices for human
      enslavement, 119
   Bombay, a Yao, captured and sold,
      116–17
   Burton frees five kidnapped
      people, 142
   Burton writing about, 142
   description by Smee, 118–19
   in India, path to freedom and,
      120–21
   Kilwa island and, 117, 118
   Lincoln issues the Emancipation
      Proclamation, 278
   Livingstone's fight against, 212
   trade routes for, 142
   Ujiji province and, 170
   in the United States, 119, 321
   Zanzibar and, 118–19, 131, 170, 201
Smalley, George Washburn, 311–13
smallpox, 156–57
Smee, Thomas, 118–19
Smith, Joseph, 271
Smyth, Edmund, 44, 103, 238–39
   adventures of, 238
   fictional character "Crab Jones"
      based on, 238

Snay bin Amir, Shaykh, 162–63, 164, 179, 185, 198
Snow, Thomas Fitzherbert, 297
Somaliland and the Somalis, 36, 37
    annual monsoon, 59
    Berbera (city), 48, 55, 57–60, 80
    Berbera Fair, 39, 48, 57, 60
    Burton angering the Somalis, 55
    Speke and, 44
    trade network of, 37
    violence against Europeans by, 38
    the Warsangali of, 50–51
Somaliland Expedition of 1854, 6, 33–77
    Berbera and, 57–60
    Burton and blame for Stroyan's death, 70
    Burton criticized for, 74
    Burton injured and scarred, 64
    Burton learns Somali, 39
    Burton recruits members for, 39–40
    Burton's acceptance of risk, 37, 38
    Burton's command of, 7, 34
    Burton's plan for, 35, 39
    camels and equipment, 60
    departure from Aden, 56
    East India Company's conditions for, 36
    ending of, 70
    First Footsteps in East Africa and, 76
    guards hired and armed, 56
    Herne and, 39, 48, 58, 62–65, 69
    Krapf consulted, 35
    Ogaden caravan and, 59
    Outram's obstacles to, 37–38
    preparations for, 48–49
    route for, 36, 55
    security for, 58
    size of, 58
    Somali attack on, 61–66
    Somali women join in Berbera, 60–61
    Speke and, 44–47, 55–56, 58–59, 60–63, 65–69, 75–76
    Stroyan and, 39–40, 48, 58, 62
    Stroyan killed, 70
    waiting for a supply ship from Aden, 59
    weaponry for, 59
Speke, Edward, 180, 234, 296
Speke, Georgina, 113, 256
Speke, John Hanning, 42–47, 74, 237–45, 249–67, 281–91
    Abban named Sumunter and, 50–53, 54–55
    in Aden, 44–47, 130, 207
    ambition of, 203
    ancestral home of, Jordans, 237, 239
    appearance and temperament, 42, 45–46, 47, 50
    Arab dress and, 49–50, 186
    awards and medals, 283
    big game hunting and, 43–44, 110, 114, 133–34, 184, 252
    Blackwood describes, 221
    brother, Edward, killed, 180, 234, 297
    burial at Jordans, 301
    Burton and, 98
    Burton and journal of, 76, 77
    Burton betrayed by, 208–9, 223–27, 228, 244
    Burton contrasted with, 42
    Burton describes, 45–46
    Burton ends communication, 244–45
    Burton reconciliation attempted, 244–45
    Burton resented by, 75–77, 112–13, 125, 138, 192, 199, 203, 204, 208, 210, 222, 227, 244, 289–90
    Burton's depiction of in *The Lake Regions of Central Africa*, 255–56
    Burton's remembrance of, 316

Speke, John Hanning (*continued*)
Burton undercut by, 214, 216, 283
bust of, by Papworth, 316
calls himself "hard as bricks," 239
character of, 52–53, 56, 113–14, 186,
286, 287
Christianity and, 270
congratulations from Queen
Victoria, 283
Crimean War and, 78, 98
deafness from a beetle in his ear,
174–75, 293
death in fatal shooting accident,
295–97, 301–2
desire to command new
expedition to East Africa, 211
*Diary and Observations made by
Lieutenant Speke, when Attempting
to Reach the Wady Nogal*
published by Burton, 77
on Erhardt and Rebmann's inland
sea, 101
Erhardt and Rebmann's slug map
and, 103
as forgotten by history, 315, 317
in France with Oliphant, 290, 292
Galton's assessment of, 217
Grant and, 239, 243, 252–53, 256,
368n239
"the great Nile debate," 291–95,
298–99
Hamerton and, claims about,
203–4
hired gun carrier, Bombay, and,
122–23, 124–25, 147–48, 187, 198,
237–38, 249, 307, 318
India trip with Burton to secure
leave, 105
*Journal of the Discovery of the Source
of the Nile*, 286–90
Kensington Gardens memorial,
315

Lake Nyanza renamed Lake
Victoria, 251
letter to Playfair in Aden, 104–5
maps and, 287
military career, 42, 44, 78
monogenism and, 278
obituary in *The Times*, 302, 306
Oliphant and, 78, 208, 209, 214, 221,
292–93
ophthalmia and temporary
blindness, 167, 169, 175, 188
perseverance, 42
Petherick and, 240–41, 265–67
Petherick falsely accused by,
287–90
on polygamy, 271
public opinion turns against,
288–90
as public speaker, 294–95
publisher John Blackwood and,
220–23, 256, 284, 285, 287, 289
racial views, Hamitic Myth and,
231, 278, 317–18
recovery of wounds, 77–78
renaming geographical features,
251, 263
return to England (1859), 208–10
Rigby and, 203–4, 214–15, 219–20,
222–23, 227, 244, 256–57, 287
Royal Geographical Society
presentation about the source
of the Nile, 281, 282–83
Royal Geographical Society
president Murchison and,
213–14, 215–16, 220, 221, 240, 242,
282–83, 284, 290–91, 294
at Royal Geographical Society's
map room, 98
search for the source of the Nile
and, 79
shortcomings for African
exploration, 46

Smyth and, 44, 103, 238–39
speeches given by, 221
sunglasses for, "French grey
    spectacles," 189
White Nile's source discovered by,
    190, 192–93, 210–11, 216, 239, 308,
    315, 316
"wideawake" hat, 188
writing ability lacking, 284–86
Speke, John Hanning: expeditions
East African Expedition as second
    in command, 98, 103–6, 110–14,
    124, 132–34, 138, 147–48, 151, 152,
    156–58, 163, 164, 169, 172–77, 179,
    182–93, 197–201, 206, 222–23
East African Expedition, canoe
    trip on Lake Tanganyika, 171–76
East African Expedition, diseases
    and maladies during, 155–58,
    164–67, 171, 197–99
East African Expedition, Lake
    Nyanza side trip and, 182,
    185–90, 215–16
East African Expedition, Lake
    Tanganyika reached, not seen,
    169
exploration of Tibet, 43
Lake Nyanza Expedition of 1860,
    209, 210–13, 216, 219, 237–45,
    249–67, 282
Somaliland Expedition and
    wounding, 42, 44–47, 54–55,
    62–63, 65–69, 74
Somaliland expedition rewritten
    by, 75
Wady Nogal expedition and
    failure of, 49–52, 77, 176
Speke, William, 302
Stanley, Henry Morton, 293, 307–8
Bombay and, 307
fame and, 308
finds Dr. Livingstone, 307, 308
finds the source of the Nile,
    308
Patron's Medal award, 308
Steinhaüser, John, 105–6, 112, 125, 138,
    207–8
North American journey with
    Burton, 269–72
Stisted, Georgiana, 79, 232, 235–36,
    325
Stisted, Maria, 325
Stocks, John Ellerton, 40–41
shocking death of, 41, 42, 70
Stoker, Bram, 292
    Dracula, 14
encounter with Burton, 14
Stratford de Redcliffe, Lord, 83
Stroyan, William, 39–40, 48–49, 58
Burton's demand for retribution
    for, 80
murder of, 62–63, 70, 73, 80
Suez, Egypt, 11
supernatural
Burton's apparition appears to
    Isabel Arundel, 96
Burton's interest in, 144
medicine man of Kuingani and,
    144–45
occultist Hockley and, 144–45
Oliphant's dream, 207–8
scrying, 144
Victorian interest in, 144
Surrey County Lunatic Asylum,
    235
Susi, Abdullah, 319, 321
Swinburne, Algernon Charles, 14,
    279–80
Sykes, William, 33

Tancred (Disraeli), 87, 95
Tanzania, 320
Tasso, Torquato, 378n313

Tennyson, Alfred Lord, 235, 278
  "The Charge of the Light
    Brigade," 81
Tennyson, Leo, 278
Thuwaini bin Said, 108, 201–2
typhoid fever, 126–27
Tibet
  Lake Manasarovar, 44
  Singh and finding city of Lhasa,
    319
  Speke exploration, 43–44
Times of London
  Burton's letter on Schamyl, 83
  Burton's letter on Speke, 303–4
  Speke's obituary, 302–3, 306
Tom Brown's School Days (Hughes), 238
Trollope, Anthony, 220
typhoid fever, 126–27

Ujiji, East Africa, 163
  caravan arrival in, bringing Burton
    supplies and evil tidings, 179–81
  East African Expedition and,
    163–72, 176–77, 179–82
  as ivory and slave depot, 170
  tembe (circular hut) for Burton, 170,
    171, 176, 179
Unguja, 106
United States
  American Civil War, 265, 269,
    311
  Burton and Steinhaüser visit,
    269–72
  Burton descriptions of Native
    Americans, 269–70
  The City of the Saints (Burton) and,
    270
  Lincoln issues the Emancipation
    Proclamation, 278
  Mormons in, 269, 271
Unyanyembe people, 144
  chief, Fundikira, 144

Urondogani, on the White Nile, 262,
    263
Uzinza, Kingdom of, 254

Victoria, Queen, 283
Vili people, 143
Virgil, 31

Wady Nogal (the Happy Valley), 49
  Speke expedition journal, 76
  Speke's failed expedition, 49–52,
    77, 176
Wainwright, Jacob, 319
Wajiji people, 170
Wakaranga people, 170
Wavinza people, 170
Wazira, Muinyi, 149
Whitman, Walt
  censorship and, 217
  Leaves of Grass, 217
"Who Last Wins" (Isabel Burton),
    316, 378n316
"wideawake" hat, 188
William Blackwood and Sons,
    220–21
Wilson, Robert, History of the
    British Expedition to Egypt,
    167
Wit and Wisdom from West Africa
    (Burton), 277

Yao people of Tanzania and
    Mozambique, 116–17
Young, Brigham, 271

Zanzibar, 5, 34, 55, 104, 126–28
  British consulate building in, 202
  British consul Hamerton in,
    108–9, 127–28

British consul Rigby in, 161, 179,
    202–5, 249–50
Burton's plea for help and, 161
cholera epidemic in, 201–2
as East African Expedition base,
    106–10, 181
East African Expedition returns
    to, 201
European explorers hiring men to
    lead their caravan, 122
French consul Cochet in, 203
geography and history of,
    106–7

monsoon (the Masika) holds up
    Burton's expedition, 109, 128–29
as part of Tanzania, 320
slave market museum, 322
slavery and, 118–19, 131, 170, 201
slavery ended in, 321–22
Speke's expedition to Lake
    Nyanza beginning in, 240
Speke's expedition to Lake
    Nyanza ending in, 282
sultanate of, dispute over, 108,
    201–2
sultan of, 108, 132

ILLUSTRATION CREDITS

Page 1: (*top*) Alamy; (*bottom*) By permission of the London Borough
of Richmond upon Thames Borough Art Collection, Orleans
House Gallery

Pages 2–3: The Royal Geographical Society

Page 4: The Royal Geographical Society

Page 5: (*top* and *bottom*) Alamy

Page 6: The Royal Geographical Society

Page 7: (*top*) Alamy; (*bottom*) The National Portrait Gallery, London

Page 8: (*top*) Look and Learn; (*bottom*) Alamy

Page 9: (*bottom*) Look and Learn

Page 10: (*top* and *bottom*) Alamy

Page 11: (*top* and *bottom*) Bath in Time

Page 12: By permission of the London Borough of Richmond upon
Thames Borough Art Collection, Orleans House Gallery

Page 13: (*top left* and *bottom*) By permission of the London Borough of
Richmond upon Thames Borough Art Collection, Orleans
House Gallery; (*top right*) Alamy

Page 14: (*top*) Alamy; (*bottom*) Bath in Time

Page 15: The Royal Geographical Society

Page 16: The Royal Geographical Society